Norbert Pohlmann | Helmut Reimer | Wolfgang Schneider (Eds.)

ISSE 2011 Securing Electronic Business Processes

IT

By the author:

Future of Trust in Computing
by D. Grawrock, H. Reimer, A.-R. Sadeghi and C. Vishik

Autonomous Land Vehicles
by K. Berns and E. v. Puttkamer

Microsoft Dynamics NAV
by P. M. Diffenderfer and S. El-Assal

Using Microsoft Dynamics AX 2009
by A. Luszczak

From Enterprise Architecture to IT Governance
by K. D. Nieman

www.viewegteubner.de

Norbert Pohlmann | Helmut Reimer |
Wolfgang Schneider (Eds.)

ISSE 2011
Securing Electronic
Business Processes

Highlights of the Information Security Solutions
Europe 2011 Conference

With 103 Figures

**VIEWEG+
TEUBNER**

Bibliographic information published by the Deutsche Nationalbibliothek
The Deutsche Nationalbibliothek lists this publication in the Deutsche Nationalbibliografie;
detailed bibliographic data are available in the Internet at http://dnb.d-nb.de.

1st Edition 2012

Editorial Office: Dr. Christel Roß | Andrea Broßler

Vieweg+Teubner Verlag is a brand of Springer Fachmedien.
Springer Fachmedien is part of Springer Science+Business Media.
www.viewegteubner.de

Cover design: KünkelLopka Medienentwicklung, Heidelberg
Typesetting: Oliver Reimer, Jena
Printing company: AZ Druck und Datentechnik, Berlin
Printed on acid-free paper

ISBN 978-3-8348-1911-6

Contents

About this Book

The Information Security Solutions Europe Conference (ISSE) was started in 1999 by eema and TeleTrusT with the support of the European Commission and the German Federal Ministry of Technology and Economics. Today the annual conference is a fixed event in every IT security professional's calendar.

The integration of security in IT applications was initially driven only by the actual security issues considered important by experts in the field; currently, however, the economic aspects of the corresponding solutions are the most important factor in deciding their success. ISSE offers a suitable podium for the discussion of the relationship between these considerations and for the presentation of the practical implementation of concepts with their technical, organisational and economic parameters.

From the beginning ISSE has been carefully prepared. The organisers succeeded in giving the conference a profile that combines a scientifically sophisticated and interdisciplinary discussion of IT security solutions while presenting pragmatic approaches for overcoming current IT security problems.

An enduring documentation of the presentations given at the conference which is available to every interested person thus became important. This year sees the publication of the nineth ISSE book – another mark of the event's success – and with about 30 carefully edited papers it bears witness to the quality of the conference.

An international programme committee is responsible for the selection of the conference contributions and the composition of the programme:
- **Ammar Alkassar**, Sirrix AG (Germany)
- **Ronny Bjones**, Microsoft (Belgium)
- **Pavel Čeleda**, Masaryk University (Czech Republic)
- **Roger Dean**, eema (United Kingdom)
- **Jan De Clercq**, HP (Belgium)
- **Marijke De Soete**, Security4Biz (Belgium)
- **Jos Dumortier**, K.U. Leuven (Belgium)
- **Walter Fumy**, Bundesdruckerei (Germany)
- **Riccardo Genghini**, S.N.G. (Italy)
- **Michael Hartmann**, SAP (Germany)
- **John Hermans**, KPMG (The Netherlands)

- **Jeremy Hilton**, Cardiff University (United Kingdom)
- **Francisco Jordan**, Safelayer (Spain)
- **Frank Jorissen**, tygris (Belgium)
- **Marc Kleff**, Siemens Enterprise Communications (Germany)
- **Hasse Kristiansen**, Ernst & Young (Norway)
- **Jaap Kuipers**, DigiNotar (The Netherlands)
- **Matt Landrock**, Cryptomathic (Denmark)
- **Norbert Pohlmann (chairman)**, University of Applied Sciences Gelsenkirchen (Germany)
- **Bart Preneel**, K.U. Leuven (Belgium)
- **Steve Purser**, ENISA
- **Helmut Reimer**, TeleTrusT (Germany)
- **Wolfgang Schneider**, Fraunhofer Institute SIT (Germany)
- **Jon Shamah**, EJ Consultants (United Kingdom)
- **Robert Temple**, BT (United Kingdom)

The editors have endeavoured to allocate the contributions in these proceedings – which differ from the structure of the conference programme – to topic areas which cover the interests of the readers.

Norbert Pohlmann   *Helmut Reimer*   *Wolfgang Schneider*

TeleTrusT Deutschland e.V. (TeleTrusT Germany)

The IT security association TeleTrusT Germany was founded in 1989 to provide a reliable framework for deployment of trustworthy information and communication technology.

Today, TeleTrusT is a widespread competence network for IT security currently representing more than 110 members from industry, science and public institutions, with associated member organizations in Germany and other countries.

In various TeleTrusT working groups IT security experts, users and interested parties meet each other in frequent workshops, round-tables and expert talks. The activities focus on reliable and trustworthy solutions complying with international standards, laws and statutory requirements.

TeleTrusT is keen to promote the acceptance of solutions supporting identification, authentification and signature schemes in electronic business and its processes. TeleTrusT facilitates information and knowledge exchange between vendors, users and authorities. TeleTrusT aims on standard compliant solutions in interoperable schemes.

TeleTrusT comments on political and legal issues related to IT security, organizes events and participates in conferences. TeleTrusT is carrier of the "European Bridge CA" (provision of public key certificates for secure e-mail communication) and runs the expert certification programme "TeleTrusT Information Security Professional (T.I.S.P.).

Keeping in mind the raising importance of the European security market, TeleTrusT seeks co-operation with European and international organisations and authorities with similar objectives. Thus, this year's European Security Conference ISSE is being organized in collaboration with eema, ENISA and the Czech Chamber of Commerce.

Contact: TeleTrusT
Dr. Holger Muehlbauer, Managing Director
Chausseestrasse 17, 10115 Berlin, GERMANY
Tel.: + 49 30 / 4005 4310
holger.muehlbauer@teletrust.de
www.teletrust.de

eema

For 24 years, EEMA has been Europe's leading independent, not-for-profit e-Identity & Security association, working with its European members, governmental bodies, standards organisations and interoperability initiatives throughout Europe to further e-Business and legislation.

EEMA's remit is to educate and inform over 1,500 Member contacts on the latest developments and technologies, at the same time enabling Members of the association to compare views and ideas. The work produced by the association with its Members (projects, papers, seminars, tutorials and reports etc) is funded by both membership subscriptions and revenue generated through fee-paying events. All of the information generated by EEMA and its members is available to other members free of charge.

Examples of recent EEMA events include The European e-ID interoperability conference in Brussels (Featuring STORK, PEPPOL, SPOCS & epSOS) and The European e-Identity Management Conference in Tallin.

EEMA and its members are also involved in many European funded projects including STORK, ICEcom and ETICA

Any organisation involved in e-Identity or Security (usually of a global or European nature) can become a member of EEMA, and any employee of that organisation is then able to participate in EEMA activities. Examples of organisations taking advantage of EEMA membership are *Volvo, Hoffman la Roche, KPMG, Deloitte, ING, Novartis, Metropolitan Police, TOTAL, PGP, McAfee, Adobe, Magyar Telecom Rt, BBS, National Communications Authority, Hungary, Microsoft, HP,* and the *Norwegian Government Administration Services* to name but a few.

Visit www.eema.org for more information or contact the association on +44 1386 793028 or at info@eema.org

The new German ID Card:
An Innovative System Gains Acceptance

Ulrich Hamann

Bundesdruckerei GmbH
Oranienstrasse 91, 10969 Berlin, Germany
info@bdr.de

Abstract

Introduction of the new ID card in Germany on 1 November 2010 also marked the start of one of the world's largest IT projects. In the meantime, around 6 million of these state-of-the-art multifunction cards are in circulation, and the infrastructures created for the new online ID function are rapidly becoming established on the market.

1 A sovereign document – the key to greater identification security

Introduction of the new ID card and its background systems is making electronic identity the key issue for reliable and trustworthy internet activities. For the first time ever, people can authenticate themselves just as well in the "virtual" world as in the "real" world, while at the same time being able to verify the identity of their vis-à-vis on the internet. Many individual processes were needed to engrain this new quality of trustworthy mutual reciprocity in the awareness of the general public and in the everyday activities of official authorities and commercial enterprises. In the meantime, the German ID card system has stood the test, and its introduction represents an important milestone on the way to greater ID security in the digital world – both on a national and an international scale.

2 Trust must be mutual

In order to guarantee safe exchange of confidential data, the new ID card system was developed according to the *mutual authentication* principle. The sovereign document, with its reliable identity data, supports the mutual transfer of information using so-called authorisation certificates, which certify institutions and companies as being trustworthy service partners.

In this way, business sectors that depend on their customers providing reliable information about identity or age for online transactions can be sure of obtaining reliable data without additional authentication procedures. Vice versa, the internet user obtains precise information about registered eGovernment and eBusiness services. Furthermore, the new ID card's so-called *pseudonym function* allows the user to log in anonymously to selected websites. This is of particular advantage in online social networks, since it allows the user to make use of all the provided functions without leaving an unwanted personal data trail.

Fig. 1: The new ID card contains a security chip. This is used to store the digital
photo and personal data of the card holder.

The technological core of the new eID management concept is a contactless security chip. This is embedded inside the new polycarbonate card and supports three added electronic functions:
- the online ID function,
- the qualified electronic signature (QES) and
- the sovereign biometrics function.

3   Secure authentication in the internet

The primary new function is so-called *online ID function* (or in short: eID function) which can be activated at any time, as the card holder wishes. Users can for example take advantage of the online ID function to sign an Internet petition without having to change over to another medium[1]. In local urban and rural administrations, German citizens can call up selected services on their home PC, for example ordering copies of birth, marriage and death certificates, registering their dog at the tax office, library services or enquiries to the land survey register. Other information (for example on child allowances or traffic offences) can also be called up safely using the online ID function of the respective authority.

At the same time, an increasing number of companies are showing interest in the new online authentication processes. Apart from simplifying log-in and registration procedures – customer data such as name and address no longer have to be captured manually – what is important for them is the certainty that the person or company on the other side of the virtual "shop counter" really does exist and that they are dealing with a business partner whose data security credentials have already been checked. One of the first companies to use mutual authentication processes was the "Gothaer Allgemeine" insurance company, which has been offering its customers a variety of eID functions ever since November 2010. The German pensions authority "Deutsche Rentenversicherung" has also been working along similar lines. With their new ID cards, insured persons and retirees can now review their pensions account or call up the current status of their future pension online.

---

1   www.openPetition.de

4 Legally valid electronic signature

In addition to online authentication, every German citizen is offered the option of a *qualified electronic signature* (QES). This can be used for example to sign contracts, issue powers of attorney or make legally binding applications online. At this year's Cebit the regional government of Hessen, together with Bundesdruckerei and SAP, demonstrated how a so-called *ad-hoc QES* can be transferred to the new ID card within a matter of minutes. Processes such as these, which ensure modern, user-friendly eID management procedures meeting statutory data privacy requirements, can bring considerably higher flexibility and efficiency to a lot of official and commercial business processes.

5 Travelling safely

To ensure that it can still be used as a safe ID and travel document, the new German ID card – similar to the e-passport – has been equipped with additional biometric security features which only state authorities can access. In order to provide this so-called *biometrics function,* all the visible identity data on the front and back of the ID card are stored in the security chip, along with a digitized photograph of the card holder. Optionally, at the holder's request, two fingerprints can be stored as well. All the biometric data are protected by the use of additional security protocols and are on no account available for private applications such as the online ID function.

6 High-performance technology in credit-card format

Apart from its innovative features, the new ID card is different in appearance from its predecessor in several ways, the most noticeable being its new credit-card format (ID1). Other new visible features are the postal code in the address field, a space for entering a religious name or pseudonym, and a six-digit number on the front of the card. This Card Access Number (CAN) gives state authorities access to the data stored on the security chip – for example during police checks or at border controls.

Fig 2: Front and back of the new ID card

7 Modules to protect electronic identity

All the data on the new ID card are classified as being similarly sensitive and are appropriately protected from unauthorised access. This is ensured by the Chip Authentication and Terminal Authentication security protocols organized using *Extended Access Control* (EAC). The information stored on the security chip is transferred from the ID card to the data recipient using end-to-end encryption (E2EE), which means that data can only be transferred when a reading device used privately or by an official authority is able to identify itself to the security chip as having "read permission". To do this, the card holder enters a PIN to activate background transfer of various security protocols. Once the PIN has been entered, the card holder, and no-one else, then decides what data are to be transferred and to whom.

Security protocol	Abbreviation	
Password Authenticated Connection Establishment	PACE	Access control. PACE protects the security chip from unauthorised reading from a distance
Extended Access Control	EAC	Extended access control consists of two sub-protocols:
	CA Chip Authentication	Establishment of a safe connection and detection of "cloned" security chips
	TA Terminal Authentication	Authentication of the reading device
Passive Authentication	PA	Checks the authenticity and integrity of the data stored on the chip

Fig. 3: Interlocking security protocols to protect sensitive data

This protection mechanism, used for the first time in the new German ID card, is guaranteed by the new security protocol PACE (*Password Authenticated Connection Establishment*), which also checks the authenticity and integrity of the data stored on the chip (*Passive Authentication*, PA). By means of a specific digital manufacturer's signature, used by Bundesdruckerei to complete the personalisation process of an electronic document, it is possible to track and verify, at any time, that the stored information has been integrated into the chip by the lawfully authorised ID card manufacturer, and by no-one else.

8 Overview of the entire process chain

On 18 June 2009, German parliament passed the "Law on identification cards and electronic proof of identity". The first documents were to be delivered and all systems were to be operational a mere 29 months later. Not much time for a highly ambitious project that had to be coordinated with a considerable number of competent partners!

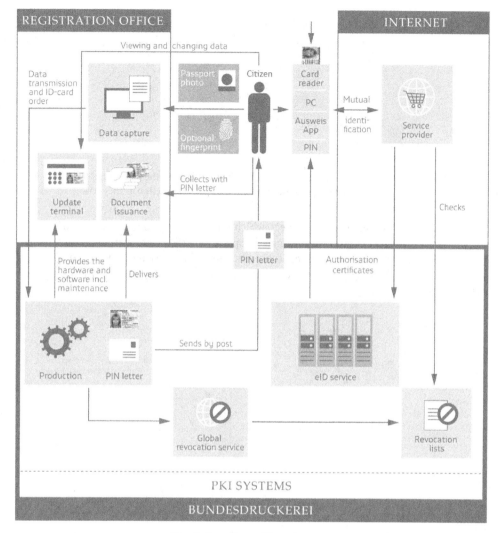

Fig. 4: Overall new ID card system

Bundesdruckerei in Berlin has played an important role in this process, both in preparing the project and by ensuring operation during the first few months. Bundesdruckerei is not only responsible for producing the documents, but also for providing secure Public Key Infrastructures (PKI) and supplying the hardware and software components required by the approx. 5,500 passport and ID card issuing authorities. These include not only high-performance fingerprint scanners, but around 20,000 totally new update terminals as well.

Fig. 5: With the aid of the update terminal, applicants can view the data stored on their new ID card and activate and deactivate the online ID function as they wish.

In order to successfully implement this project, which is quite rightly considered to be one of the most extensive worldwide, centrally coordinated application trials were started as early as autumn 2009. Almost 300 companies and institutions had joined in these trials by November 2011. Bundesdruckerei and D-TRUST, its own trust center, provided several services including the new *eID Service* for this purpose.

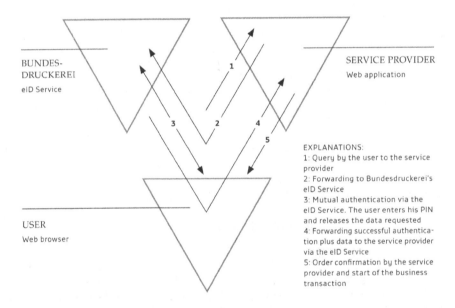

Fig. 6: Mutual data exchange via Bundesdruckerei's eID Service inter

As a trusted communications interface, the eID Service handles management and verification of authorisation certificates and revocation lists and guarantees high-security data exchange to every authorised user of the online ID function.

Since the entire process involves considerable effort in terms of security technology, a lot of German companies have decided not to create their own eID system architecture but to conclude a service contract with highly specialised eID service providers instead. The main advantage here is that providers such as Bundesdruckerei can deliver full-service packages containing all the required system modules – from application for and provision of authorisation certificates, right up to efficient operation of an eID server. At the same time, companies benefit from the comprehensive system know-how and valuable experience Bundesdruckerei was able to gain from the German ePassport project and which now helps it in adapting existing IT infrastructures. As a result, Bundesdruckerei was able to offer all online ID function applications quickly and at a reasonable price.

9 A complex overall system for more than 60 million users

By introducing innovative procedures and technology modules, Germany has opened up new possibilities for the protection and use of electronic identities and – after successful introduction of the electronic passport – has achieved a pioneering role on the international high-security market. As opposed to travel documents that only have to be valid for international travel, the new ID card is not "simply" about data transfer within limited communication structures (e.g. verification of identity at international borders or during domestic police checks), but about a potentially open network for the "man on the street". Today, the online ID function can be just as easily used for checking, releasing and transporting confidential information from eGovernment or eBusiness applications as for specific business processes, something only known in sovereign identification processes up to now. In this way, all citizens and service providers can make use of their right to informational self-determination and protect themselves from identity misuse and online crime using a new set of instruments meeting cutting-edge security standards.

Fig. 7 and 8: Colour and laser-engraving personalisation of the new ID cards at Bundesdruckerei

10 Cutting-edge technology made in Germany

In order to successfully implement this step, a wide range of new developments was needed – also and particularly in terms of technology. For instance, Bundesdruckerei set up a completely new production line, including special machinery, which can produce as many as 8 million new ID cards annually. In addition, countless innovations have found their way into the ID card production project, one of the most striking being *Innosec˚ Fusion* colour personalisation technology based on a digital printing method and used for integrating the ID photo. In this process, Bundesdruckerei's proprietary special inks combine with the card material so that the image data and actual card body are inseparably merged after lamination, giving the cards extremely high protection against manipulation.

11 The new system is becoming established

The new ID card has the potential of promoting the secure use of modern IT infrastructures, both on a national and an international scale. This especially applies to the rapidly growing online market: users of the new eID functions are better protected against identity theft and phishing, and service providers benefit by having reliable customer data at their disposal. This is a win-win situation which has made German eGovernment und eBusiness applications considerably more secure and efficient and which forward-looking companies are becoming increasingly aware of. In the past few months, the demand for valid authorisation certificates has been growing continually. Citizens can obtain information about new applications and the many existing applications using the online ID card portal www.ccepa.de/onlineanwendungen.

Nevertheless, the first year of life with the ID card has also taught stakeholders in Germany that migration to or entry into a system of this complexity cannot be achieved without generously planned lead times. The online business community has to develop innovative applications, infrastructures have to be modified and new IT architectures have to be integrated. Germany is forging ahead with these processes, since there is obviously an increased market demand for secure identities, also on an international scale.

12 The new ID card – just a national solution?

The challenge facing us now is to be prepared for such developments by providing sustainable technologies and user-friendly applications as well as electronic identification documents and eID systems that can be used internationally. A number of EU member states already have their own eID concepts. At the same time, calls to coordinate national solutions more efficiently and make them available for cross-border electronic services are becoming ever louder. In order to allow the uniform exchange of information throughout Europe, despite the many different eID card systems in circulation, initiatives such as the European *STORK* (*Secure Identity across Borders linked)* project have been born in an endeavour to achieve widespread harmonisation of national eID solutions.

13 Conclusion

With the introduction of the new ID card, Germany has produced a timely and consistent response to the progressive merging of the offline and online worlds. The politically encouraged mutual authentication process, which is already reflected in existing infrastructures, is an important milestone in this process. In the years to come, the number of competitive online offerings based on new eID management systems will multiply. Buzz concepts such as informational self-determination, sparing use of data and cutting down red tape, paired with the increased need for security in the modern online community, are constantly creating new impulses which help to step up developments in the field of *secure identities*. There will be a large number of players taking part in this process – politicians, science and research experts and participants from the international high-security branch. The issue of "Secure ID" presents a global challenge that affects all sections of society. Anyone who is involved in this market and contributes to finding new solutions will be able to make an active contribution to moulding the media future of generations to come.

Proof, not Promises:
Creating the Trusted Cloud

Arthur W. Coviello, Jr.[1] · Howard D. Elias[2] · Pat Gelsinger[3] ·
Richard McAniff[4]

[1]EMC Corporation, Executive Vice President, RSA, Executive Chairman
[2]EMC Corporation, Information Infrastructure and Cloud Services
[3]EMC Corporation, EMC Information Infrastructure Products
[4]VMware, Inc., Chief Development Officer

Abstract

Clouds and virtualization offer powerful new ways to manage and use digital information, but they also create new complexities for organizations in meeting the fundamental challenge of getting the right information to the right people over an infrastructure that they can trust. Why? Because clouds and virtualization irrevocably change the nature of control and visibility. Infrastructure becomes virtual, not physical. People access infrastructure from devices that are outside of IT's direct control. Information moves with incredible speed across networks and the cloud, making it hard to know where sensitive information resides. And with an IT infrastructure that is virtual and shared via the cloud, organizations must learn new ways to achieve visibility into risks, threats, and compliance performance. The good news is forward-thinking businesses can clear these hurdles today.

The formula for building trust in the cloud is to achieve control over and visibility into the cloud's infrastructure, identities, and information. The technologies needed to establish this level of cloud control and visibility already exist. Organizations are applying these technologies in creative ways to build trusted clouds that can meet the most rigorous security and compliance requirements while delivering the flexibility, fluidity, and massive scale that hold such business promise for organizations worldwide.

1 The Challenge

Over the decades, IT architecture and platform strategies have evolved from mainframe to client-server to the Web. Still, one of the fundamental goals of IT organizations endures: that is, getting the right information to the right people over a trusted infrastructure so information can be leveraged for business advantage.

Realizing this goal has become exponentially harder and more difficult to verify as:
- Digital information rises in value and becomes pervasive in every business process
- Bandwidth grows and access points proliferate
- Business risks multiply, particularly as employees increasingly use consumer devices to access enterprise IT services
- Infrastructure evolves to the new world of virtualization technology and cloud computing

N. Pohlmann, H. Reimer, W. Schneider (Editors): Securing Electronic Business Processes, Vieweg (2011), 9-20

As a result, a dangerous trust void has opened up, standing squarely between organizations and their ability to reap the cloud's well-documented business benefits in efficiency, agility, and cost savings.

Management teams, auditors, and regulators need proof that today's organizations are adhering to security and compliance requirements, while still ensuring that digital information can flow more rapidly and freely than ever.

However, proving security and compliance in virtualized and, ultimately, cloud environments requires a fundamental rethinking of long-standing security beliefs and practices. This is because of two pivotal shifts, both of which center on control and visibility.

1. Virtualization forever changes how organizations achieve control and visibility over core elements of their IT environment.
   - Infrastructure becomes logical not physical, rendering static, perimeter-based approaches to security and policy enforcement fruitless. Logical, dynamic boundaries pose new challenges (and opportunities) for cloud control and visibility.
   - Identities (the people, devices, and systems accessing IT-based services) become harder to confirm, simply because there are more of them. Interactions between machine identities outnumber interactions between human ones, and the cloud accelerates exposure to threats from mobile devices and social media tools, which IT organizations typically don't control and can't fully secure. Furthermore, strong authentication becomes essential as organizations increasingly add external cloud services to the IT mix.
   - Information can replicate and relocate at instantaneous speed in the cloud, making it hard to safeguard sensitive workloads and prove that information is managed according to policy.
2. Organizations increasingly surrender control and visibility to external providers in the cloud service-delivery chain. This applies whether it's IaaS for private and hybrid cloud hosting, PaaS for application development, or SaaS for applications such as Salesforce. com. In contrast to having complete ownership, management, and inspectability over all IT service components in traditional data centers, organizations must now rely on outside providers to implement controls and ensure compliance.

The reality is organizations don't yet know how to compensate for these fundamental shifts in control and visibility, nor do they understand how to take advantage of the opportunities these shifts represent.

This should not be. *The vision, expertise, experience, and technology to architect a foundation for trusted clouds are available now.*

2 Solving the Trust Equation: Control + Visibility = Trust

There is no denying trust in the cloud hinges on control and visibility.

Establishing trust first requires control and second a level of internal visibility that can be stepped up or expanded for external service providers. However, if control plus visibility is the formula for trust, how do we go about solving for it?

Solving for trust in internal (private) clouds is less challenging than in public and hybrid clouds because organizations control all IT assets, as well as the geographic location of their data. Control and visibility in internal clouds is about adapting existing processes to the virtual environment while capitalizing on the new advantages of virtualization.

When it comes to public and hybrid clouds, most organizations have begun cautiously moving forward, migrating low-risk (tier 2) functions and bestowing trust based on contractual assurances, strong vendor relationships, and brand reputations.

However, while performance promises and contractual penalties may provide an adequate standard of trust for some applications, a much higher standard of trust is needed for mission-critical (tier-1) functions.

Mission-critical functions require control and visibility into the cloud's performance. They also require additional precautions to ensure that information in the cloud is protected against loss or system unavailability, as well as from external threats and privacy breaches. Only this heightened level of control and visibility can deliver the critical proof (evidence) that leads to trust:
- Proof that cloud infrastructure meets security specifications and that information is managed in accordance with policies
- Proof that authorized users are who they say they are
- Proof of performance and compliance to satisfy internal management as well as auditors and regulators

Essential to proof is the ability to inspect and monitor actual conditions first-hand and not just rely on outside attestations, especially for applications handling regulated information or sensitive workloads. Organizations need transparency into service providers' environments to ensure compliance with policies and SLAs. They need an integrated view of their IT environments, both internal and external, to correlate risks, spot threats, and coordinate the implementation of countermeasures.

Today, organizations struggle to have control and visibility in their physical IT environments. This struggle need not be exacerbated in the cloud. The good news is virtualization technology creates the right conditions for organizations to improve control and visibility beyond what's available in today's physical environments.

3 Virtualization: the Cornerstone of Visibility and Control

Security and compliance reshape what's possible in the cloud just as much as the cloud reshapes what's possible in security and compliance.

While trusted clouds are attainable using today's technologies, innovations are coming to market that enable clouds to actually become safer and more trustworthy than conventional, non-virtualized IT environments. Given the low state of trust in the cloud today for mission-critical applications, this assertion may seem surprising. What makes this future possible? Virtualization.

Virtualization is a Catalyst for Trust

Virtualization fuels the cloud's ability to surpass the level of control and visibility that physical IT delivers. By consolidating multiple systems on a single platform, organizations gain a centralized control point for managing and monitoring every virtual infrastructure component.

Virtualization's unparalleled visibility and consolidated control over the entire virtual environment transforms IT into a vital resource for improving security and compliance in three striking ways.

1. Logical and information-centric
    In clouds, the strongest security results when organizations protect information, not infrastructure. That's because in virtualized environments, static, physical perimeters give way to dynamic, logical boundaries. Logical boundaries form the new perimeters for trust, and virtual machines adapt security to their particular workloads, carrying their policies and privileges with them as they travel across the cloud.

2. Built-in and automated
    In clouds, where information, VMs, and entire virtualized networks can relocate in the blink of an eye, security measures must be just as dynamic as the virtual assets they protect. Achieving this means building security into virtualized components and, by extension, distributing security throughout the cloud. In addition, automation will be absolutely essential to enabling security and compliance to work at the speed and scale of the cloud. Policies, regulations, and best practices will increasingly be codified into security-management systems and implemented automatically, reducing the need for intervention by IT staff.

3. Risk-based and adaptive
    Static security approaches based on rules and signatures can't address advanced external threats or insider threats. Instead, organizations are developing capabilities to assess risks instantly and to initiate countermeasures. In the near future, trusted clouds will employ predictive analytics based on their understanding of normal states, user behaviors, and transaction patterns to spot high-risk events and enable organizations to proactively adapt defenses.

These three principles fundamentally change how security is applied and how compliance is proven in virtualized and cloud environments. Solutions based on these principles are transforming the cloud from an IT environment fit only for lowrisk functions to an IT environment fit for an organization's most important business processes.

4 The EMC and VMware Difference: Proof Not Promises

Stronger security (control) proven through direct monitoring (visibility) is the highest standard for trust in the cloud. This proof-driven standard of trust is the difference that EMC and VMware are delivering today.

We believe in the transformative power of virtualization—so much so that we're focusing our cloud-security strategy, solutions portfolio, and development initiatives on making security and compliance in the cloud 1) logical and information-centric, 2) built-in and automated, and 3) risk-based and adaptive.

Our adherence to these three principles enables us to provide organizations with cloud solutions that are adaptable to any type of workload—even mission-critical ones. This means organizations can deploy trusted clouds that meet the security and compliance requirements of any business process currently running in their conventional data centers. It also means organizations can gain the ability to directly inspect and monitor conditions in virtual environments, enabling them to base their trust on first-hand observations, not just outside attestations. Finally, it means organizations can leverage shared virtualization platforms to consolidate control over their clouds.

For years, EMC, its security division RSA, and VMware have worked to embed security, management, and compliance controls into the virtualization platform. We're also leveraging virtualization to improve security, management, and compliance in the cloud. Our cloud solutions are engineered to take full advantage of the powerful introspection and control capabilities inherent in VMware's industry leading virtualization platform, which runs 84 percent of virtualized applications today.

5 Delivering Control and Visibility for Trusted Clouds

EMC's vision for trusted cloud computing, described in "Proof, not Promises: Creating the Trusted Cloud," asserts that trust in the cloud hinges on having control and visibility over both internal (private) clouds and cloud services delivered through external providers.

For years, EMC, its security division RSA, and VMware have leveraged our experience and expertise in information management, security, and virtualization to deliver extraordinary control and visibility in the cloud. Our solutions are closely integrated within VMware's virtualization platform to take full advantage of the virtual layer's unique control and visibility capabilities.

Today, we each offer products and services addressing the biggest challenges surrounding trust in the cloud:

- Information: How can organizations discover and control sensitive information to ensure compliance with policies and regulations? Can organizations ensure the availability and recoverability of mission-critical data in cloud environments?
- Infrastructure: How can organizations ensure their cloud infrastructure conforms to security specifications and has not been tampered with? How can organizations sharing cloud resources achieve secure multitenancy? How do they accelerate deployment of trusted clouds in a standardized manner?
- Identity: How can organizations be confident users are who they say they are to prevent fraud and unauthorized access to sensitive information? How can they ensure that only authorized devices and virtual machines have access to appropriate information and resources?

5.1 Control and Visibility over Information

Information is becoming the currency of business and is among the most valuable and sought-after assets in clouds.

Protecting digital information is a requirement of doing business. It is tantamount to protecting business advantage. Gaining control over information in the cloud and preserving full visibility into where and how it's handled for security and compliance reporting is arguably the most significant challenge facing organizations.

Like all computing models, clouds have historically been "information blind," meaning they can't distinguish credit card data from the corporate cafeteria menu. Sensitive information must be handled with great care—it must be encrypted, mapped to hardware clusters with specific security profiles and/or geographic attributes, and closely monitored for compliance and auditing. In addition, multinational corporations now regard the geographic location (or "geolocation") of their data as a hot compliance issue, as countries have enacted laws forbidding certain kinds of information about their citizens from leaving their jurisdictional boundaries.

Control and visibility over information in the cloud is challenging primarily because information can move instantly. Often, information moves for perfectly legitimate reasons such as load balancing, data backup, and disaster recovery. While information mobility is great for resource utilization and service availability, it can be a nightmare for information compliance.

5.2 Discovering and Controlling Sensitive Information

The intelligence to identify high-risk, high-value information and govern how it's treated is a challenge that EMC has worked to address since the earliest days of the cloud. Several of the solutions described below integrate with the RSA® Data Loss Prevention (DLP) Suite, which is designed to discover where sensitive or regulated information resides or is moving and alerts organizations of high-risk events or activities that may violate governance policies. DLP is also engineered to automate first-line remediation functions, such as blocking the transmission of sensitive data or quarantining, deleting, archiving, or applying rights management to files that contain private data.

VMware is also helping to create information awareness in clouds with its VMware® vShield™ suite of security products, which provides control and visibility at the hypervisor level to enable security and compliance for dynamic virtual environments. The VMware vShield security suite includes virtual firewalls, logical zoning, and edge network security. Supplemental capabilities are being integrated to enhance information security for customers.

For example, RSA and VMware are integrating policy modules from RSA DLP into the VMware vShield solution to discover sensitive or regulated data and create information-centric zones of secure IT resources. Designed to comply with the most exacting security and compliance standards, VMware vShield with DLP will be a ready-made solution engineered to accelerate organizations' deployment of virtualized environments and clouds with the embedded intelligence to manage and monitor the most heavily regulated data types, including personally identifiable information, payment card information, and patient health information. By using the solution's secure zones to automate the control and monitoring of sensitive, valuable information, organizations can move mission-critical business processes that formerly consumed a lot of IT resources to a far more efficient and scalable cloud delivery model.

RSA DLP's data-intelligence functions are also available with EMC's cloud solutions to help ensure information is managed in compliance with policies and regulations. For example, EMC demonstrated that RSA DLP capabilities can be integrated into the EMC Atmos® cloud storage service to make it content-aware. The EMC Atmos distributed cloud storage platform can combine its metadata-tagging system with RSA DLP to automate the distribution and placement of information in compliance with business policies. Atmos solutions are engineered to combine massive scalability—petabytes of storage across hundreds of nodes—with intelligent, automated controls for data management. Cloud services such as the Atmos platform give organizations the flexibility of on-demand storage, while preserving content-aware controls, to help ensure geolocation in compliance with jurisdictional privacy laws.

5.3 Ensuring Availability and Recoverability of Mission-Critical Information

Trusting tier-1 applications to the cloud means ensuring the availability and recoverability of critical information. EMC's Data Domain® systems are designed to reduce the footprint for virtual-machine backups by as much as 40 to 60 times. Backups are easier to manage and store, and the unique deduplicated data is small enough to replicate over existing networks for highly efficient disaster recovery, without the risks and costs of tape-based backups. When using Data Domain storage with well-understood best practices for backup and VMware system snapshots, a deployment can simplify management of consistent images. Once stored, the images are ready to restore locally or, with network-efficient replication, at a remote disaster-recovery site. This enables cost-efficient protection of even massive volumes of information in virtual environments.

6 Control and Visibility over Infrastructure

Proving that the physical and virtual infrastructure of the cloud can be trusted can be prohibitively difficult, particularly when it comes to cloud services from external service providers.

Verifying secure conditions in the foundations of the cloud is important for one simple reason: If organizations can't trust the safety of their computing infrastructure, the security of all the information, applications, and services running on top of that infrastructure falls into doubt.

6.1 Inspecting the Cloud's Foundations

EMC is collaborating with Intel to make the cloud's foundational infrastructure as open to inspection, analysis, and reporting for compliance as the cloud's application- services layer. By combining the VMware vSphere™ platform and the RSA Solution for Cloud Security and Compliance with Intel Trusted Execution Technology (TXT), EMC will enable cloud service providers and organizations to validate launch-time security for every physical and virtual component in the entire computing stack. This security data can be streamed into the RSA Archer™ eGRC console to furnish proof to tenants, auditors, and regulators that the cloud infrastructure stack is secure. Clouds implementing an integrated solution stack built on Intel's hardware root of trust will enable organizations and IaaS tenants to self-inspect, validate, and prove the integrity of their cloud infrastructure, from processor through the virtualization layer. For organizations running sensitive workloads in clouds, the visibility provided through this integrated solution promises to greatly simplify and streamline compliance reporting and audits.

Solutions based on a hardware root of trust can verify a secure infrastructure, but when that infrastructure is shared, even between different groups within the same organization, how can organizations ensure virtual partitions stay intact?

6.2 Laying the Infrastructure for Secure Multitenancy

To achieve secure partitions and multitenancy, virtual environments and clouds based on the industry-leading VMware vSphere platform can leverage built-in security features within the VMware vShield product family. The hypervisor-level firewall in the VMware vShield platform is engineered to enforce proper segmentation and trust zones for applications. In private clouds, this means organizations can set up virtual firewalls so that applications with different security requirements—for example, production and testing, finance, and sales—can be hosted in the same virtual data center. In a service-provider environment, VMware vShield solutions enable different tenants to share IT resources safely by creating logical security boundaries that provide complete port-group isolation.

To ensure secure storage in public clouds, the EMC Symmetrix® VMAX™ platform is the industry's first cloud storage solution capable of secure multitenancy. The platform embeds RSA Data Protection Manager to safeguard cloud-based information through hardware-based encryption and key management. The VMAX platform's hardened data security features ensure sensitive information can be encrypted and rendered unusable to outside parties, all without slowing down the performance of the system. EMC Symmetrix VMAX systems scale to two petabytes and are designed for mission-critical virtual data centers.

6.3 Accelerating Deployment of Trusted Clouds

Ensuring service levels for availability, scalability, and recoverability requires trusted platforms. That's what EMC, VMware, Cisco, and Intel have delivered through the Virtual Computing Environment coalition. The VCE coalition's Vblock™ platform is engineered to provide a standardized, complete virtual infrastructure, from storage and networks to management, security, and compliance—all integrated and tested to ensure performance and scalability. Vblock systems greatly simplify and accelerate the deployment of enterprise-class clouds, giving organizations and service providers the ability to meet high service levels for performance, availability, and scalability.

7 Control and Visibility over Identity

While protecting against unauthorized or fraudulent users is a challenge in any IT environment—virtualized or not—clouds heighten the risk of intrusion simply because they increase potential points of exposure and because the number of identities, most of which are machines, becomes more plentiful and ephemeral in clouds. Furthermore, clouds heighten the organization's exposure to mobile devices and social-media platforms, which IT organizations typically don't own, control, or secure.

The best way to deal with mounting risks of unauthorized access to private clouds is to be more discerning about who's trying to get in and to detect high-risk activities once they're inside.

7.1 Verifying Users in Heigh-risk Transactions

Essential to this is risk-based authentication, which detects abnormal conditions, such as a user signing in from an unknown device at an IP address in the Ukraine when earlier in the day that same user logged in from a corporate office in Dallas, Texas. RSA Adaptive Authentication is designed to conduct instantaneous, behind-the-scenes risk assessments of users attempting to log into enterprise services. When it detects suspicious conditions, the system automatically takes secondary steps to verify the user's identity by posing additional authentication challenges using information that only the genuine user would know (e.g., "Enter the ZIP code for your home address"). RSA Adaptive Authentication is engineered to evaluate more than 100 risk indicators, correlating factors such as the type of access device being used, the user's past behavioral patterns, and external threat intelligence from RSA eFraudNetwork™ feeds. A unique risk score is assigned to each activity, and users are only interrupted when high-risk conditions are identified and/or organizational policies could be violated.

7.2 Detecting Fraudulent Users Inside Clouds

It's inevitable that some enterprise access credentials will be compromised with the thousands of malware variants out there stealing passwords. RSA® Transaction Monitoring can help identify and mitigate damage from fraudulent users after they've gained access to an organization's cloud. RSA's fraud-detection platform leverages the same risk assessment engine used by more than 8,000 financial institutions to protect their 250 million online users worldwide. It layers on top of any authentication system to recognize deviant and potentially malicious activity in real time. When it spots high-risk events, RSA Transaction Monitoring is engineered to interrupt user activities by presenting additional authentication challenges, including out-of-band verification techniques, such as requiring a suspicious user to enter randomly generated passwords sent to the genuine user's mobile phone.

8 The Value of Unified Control and Visibility

Designed for static, physical computing systems, conventional security-management systems are too slow and rigid to handle inherently dynamic, virtualized environments and clouds. Traditional security management relies disproportionately on manual processes and human intervention to manage dependencies and configure policies—an unreliable, unscalable process that won't work in clouds, where entire virtual networks can move at the blink of an eye.

As the rate of change accelerates and users' expectations grow, IT teams need to streamline management processes so they can more rapidly and efficiently control, monitor, and report performance across their IT environments, physical and virtual, internally operated and externally hosted. Addressing these challenges will require IT management tools that leverage automation.

8.1 Automating Security and Compliance Management

Automation can deliver the efficiency, control, and scale needed for cloud environments while minimizing costs and ensuring security and compliance. VMware virtualization and cloud-management solutions replace inefficient, manual processes for change control and configuration with policy-based controls and built-in automation. Designed into each layer of the virtualized technology stack, VMware virtualization and cloud management solutions offer policy-driven processes and "set and forget" administration for change management and configuration. This enables organizations to dynamically map application dependencies across their data centers, monitor application performance, and help ensure compliance.

The RSA Archer eGRC Platform is designed to provide a highly flexible, well-integrated framework for managing, monitoring, and reporting on governance, risk, and compliance conditions across the IT environment. The platform integrates with an organization's other IT systems to automate data exchange without requiring IT teams to touch a single line of code. It merges hundreds of disparate data streams from different IT systems to create holistic models of key business processes, which can be analyzed and managed from within a single console. These integrated models give organizations point-and-click controls for configuring policies, automating processes, governing workflows, and setting user privileges simultaneously across multiple environments. More importantly, they also enable organizations to report on governance, risk, and compliance at a business level, not at an individual application level. This business-level visibility, combined with the Archer eGRC Platform's ability to set controls for multiple IT environments simultaneously, establishes a unified operating system for critical business processes and greatly simplifies governance, risk, and compliance.

9 Building the Expertise to Building the Cloud

As cloud technology rapidly matures, public and private cloud offerings have ballooned in popularity, with hybrid clouds beginning to pick up traction as well. The next question organizations must answer is how to tie together business requirements for trust with their cloud policies, controls, and governance models. This process begins with examining applications or workloads to define their optimal placement in relation to cloud models or an organization's legacy computing environment. It then makes a comprehensive evaluation and transformation of the governance of information to ensure the proper stewardship, ownership, and classification of assets.

9.1 Optimizing Cloud Strategies

EMC Consulting has developed an adaptable methodology to provide customized workload analysis through three filters: economic, trust, and functional. EMC Consulting helps customers optimize their cloud infrastructure, including significantly lowering risk by adhering to a set of secure and compliant trust requirements.

Balancing the need for transparency and compliance with private, public, and hybrid cloud options based on economics, feasibility, and trust, EMC Consulting has created the EMC Cloud Advisory Service with Cloud Optimizer. This innovative service is designed to establish benchmarks to measure information assets in accordance with industry and organization-centric trust, delivering potential savings of up to 25 percent of IT budgets. EMC Consulting works with customers to set strategy, develop the business case, define the architecture, and build governance models to achieve cloud operational excellence.

EMC Consulting's Cloud Optimization approach starts by identifying workloads that are candidates for movement to the cloud based on usage, the asset's origination and destination points, and the sensitivity of the information. This is followed by an economic-impact analysis to judge how an asset's value will change once the workload shifts to the cloud. However, before trust filter analysis can be applied, organizations must understand the characteristics and requirements of a trustworthy computing environment. These six non-mutually exclusive requirements as defined by EMC Consulting include:

Control
- **Availability:** Ensure access to resources and recovery following interruption or failure
- **Integrity:** Guarantee only authorized persons can use specific information and applications
- **Confidentiality/Privacy:** Protect how information and personal data is obtained and used

Visibility
- **Compliance:** Meet specific legal requirements and industry standards and rules
- **Governance:** Enforce policies, procedures, and controls and establish usage rights
- **Risk Management:** Manage threats to business interruption or derived exposures

After an organization understands the different trust profiles of the potential destinations for workloads (public, private, and hybrid clouds, and in-house legacy environments) and how their own infrastructure satisfies the six trust requirements, a trust filter analysis will help determine what cloud options are best suited for their specific industry and architecture needs. A functional evaluation is applied to specify which workloads can be moved to which cloud model without loss of functionality. Once economic, trust, and functional filters are successfully applied, the preferred cloud-deployment destination for each workload will emerge, providing a purposeful and built-in secure framework for trust enablement within clouds.

10 Control and Visibility for the Cloud, Delivered by the Cloud

As organizations move IT-based services to the public or hybrid cloud, they traditionally lose both control and visibility over the information, infrastructure, and identities in those clouds. The loss of control and visibility is compounded when organizations deploy cloud services from multiple providers.

The Cloud Trust Authority will address this problem. It will provide a unified platform for managing security controls and gaining visibility to prove compliance across multiple cloud providers. Incorporating technologies from RSA and VMware, the Cloud Trust Authority will deliver a core set of functions required across a wide variety of clouds, including identity management, data security, and security and compliance reporting. Customers will be able to manage all these services via the Cloud Trust Authority console, making it simple and easy to configure and deploy the capabilities needed to enable trusted, compliant use of cloud service providers.

Among the highlights of the Cloud Trust Authority's inaugural set of capabilities will be its Identity Service. The Identity Service federates access privileges and identity management across multiple clouds to enable secure and federated single sign-on and directory synchronization with options for strong authentication.

Beyond its Identity Service, the Cloud Trust Authority will also enable organizations to compare the trust profiles of various cloud providers against the standards and best practices developed by the Cloud Security Alliance, among other security frameworks. By developing a linked community of private and public clouds with similar trust profiles, RSA will make it easier for enterprises to rapidly add capabilities and on-board new cloud providers, dramatically lowering the barriers to trusted cloud computing.

11 Summary

Before organizations can take advantage of the cloud's agility, efficiency, and cost benefits for a wide range of IT services, they need to first ensure the cloud can be trusted. EMC believes trust in the cloud can be achieved by establishing control and visibility in two vital ways:

- Providing organizations sufficient control over cloud security and compliance to adapt to any type of workload, even mission-critical ones
- Giving IT teams the ability to directly inspect and monitor conditions in both internal and hybrid clouds, thus enabling organizations to base their trust on first-hand observations, not just outside attestations

EMC's technology partnerships with IT industry leaders have resulted in a variety of innovative solutions that deliver superb control and visibility into virtualized and cloud environments. To help organizations accelerate their deployment of trusted clouds, EMC Consulting provides strategic guidance and technology expertise for pervasive virtualization, application migration to virtual infrastructure, and risk/ readiness assessments for moving applications and business processes to the cloud.

Cloud Computing & Enterprise Security Services

How Cloud Security Strongly Depends on Process Maturity, Automation and Scale

Eberhard von Faber [1(+2)] · Michael Pauly [1]

[1] T-Systems
{Eberhard.Faber | Michael.Pauly}@t-systems.com

[2] Brandenburg University of Applied Science
Eberhard.vonFaber@fh-brandenburg.de

Abstract

Security is the most discussed topic in cloud computing. Therefore, the (enterprise) users ask their provider about antivirus protection, firewalls and access control. But only a few of them know the processes inside a data centre needed to produce scalable, dynamic and flexible ICT-services on large scale. The essential elements here are centralization and consequent re-use, virtualization on all levels of the ICT stack, as well as interoperability and standardization to ensure that this will work. By considering principles of modern ICT production, it is shown that process maturity, automation and large scale are essential to achieve an adequate level of security.

1 Introduction

Cloud computing is - from a provider's point of view - characterized by resource pooling and rapid elasticity, in order to realize scalable, flexible and dynamic IT services. ICT service provisioning from a cloud require the ICT service provider to use modern technology and industrial ways of production. The essential elements are (i) centralization and consequent re-use, (ii) virtualization on all levels of the ICT stack, and (iii) interoperability and standardization to ensure that this will work. Of course, all systems are interconnected as a prerequisite.

This paper takes a look behind the curtain of the production of cloud services. By considering principles of modern ICT production, it is shown that process maturity, automation and large scale are essential to achieve an adequate level of security.

Cloud computing obviously also require the application of standard ICT security solutions such as firewalls, intrusion prevention, anti-malware, monitoring, and access control. The management of these security solutions is subject to and common to all types of service provisioning and not specific to cloud computing. However, delivering secure cloud computing requires more than such standard technology. It is necessary to use specific technology for ICT service provisioning which in turn gives rise to additional challenges. This becomes apparent when considering the specific methods of modern ICT production.

N. Pohlmann, H. Reimer, W. Schneider (Editors): Securing Electronic Business Processes, Vieweg (2011), 23-33

In chapter 2 the production of cloud services is described from a provider's perspective. Chapter 3 focused on the central role of interconnection of all ICT resources for cloud service provisioning. Chapter 4 describes challenges of dynamic resource allocation and sharing. Standardised software images are used here. Chapter 5 addresses the security issues related to software engineering and provisioning.

Database and storage services are fundamental for cloud computing. Some of the security issues of the database and storage management are depicted in chapter 6. A precise assignment of responsibilities and tasks as well as an identity and access management system is essential to ensure that security requirements are met. This is the focus of chapter 7. Cloud computing has consequences in terms of security. There are advantages as well as critical issues for user organisations. The make or buy decision is discussed in chapter 8. A summary is given in chapter 9.

2 ICT Production and Cloud from a Provider's View

With cloud computing in its pure form the whole infrastructure moves from the customer site into a provider operated data centre. The provider is in charge of the hardware and software as well as the whole production process. The customers only use a – thin or fat – client workplace to work with or use the IT service needed for business.

The ICT service provider delivers this kind of services to a variety of customers often on a global basis. This is required since economies of scale and other benefits from the division of labour are the central motivation for users for "ICT outsourcing" of any kind. Consequently, ICT must be produced in an industrial way with a one-to-many business model. The data centre typically provides an area for ICT equipment which is as large as a football / soccer pitch.

Fig. 1: Modern Data Centre for industrialised ICT Production

The whole design of the data centre is in the authority of the provider (Fig. 1). He is the only who is responsible for the provision process, the automation as well as the hard- and software he use for the realization. The difference between conventional outsourcing and cloud computing is, that using cloud services the producing ICT fabric is a black box or a non-transparent obscure cloud. Refer for instance to [EvFMiP10] for more detail.

The black box approach gives the provider the degrees of freedom he needs to realize the economies of scale [vFab2011]. That means he has to select the sort of resources on the one hand and to choose the sharing model of the resources on the other hand. The common base for the most cloud resources is a x86 infrastructure in combination with a scalable storage system. For the virtualization of the server layer hypervisor based software is used.

Sharing resources between different user organisations efficiently include two points: "doing the right thing" and "doing the things right". "Doing the right things" means, from the provider perspective, to select the "right" hardware and software in order to build up large scalable environments, which can be operated using a high level of automation. Note that this selection is a first important issue in terms of ICT security. "Doing the things right" means to choose the right automation and to optimize the processes. The utilization has also to be precisely predicted to avoid oversubscription or vacancy of resources.

3 System Interconnection as a Basis

Economies of scale result from sharing resources between user organisations. In order to distribute costs of acquisition (and operation) over user organisations, they have to share hardware and software. A cloud being reserved for one single organisation (wrongly called "private" by NIST, refer to [NIST2011]) may scale, but the one user organisation must carry all costs themselves. Where are the economies of scale expected to come from?

The sharing of hardware and software has the other advantage that the production is made flexible and resource allocation can easily follow demands. In case of a large number of users and voluminous resources, the continuous reorganization of server resources is required – also for maintenance. But how does this work? Virtualisation allows sharing resources between different user organisations.

Building up a large and flexible infrastructure, it is necessary to use virtualization techniques at every layer: network, compute and storage. We start with the security issues in network virtualisation.

Sharing a computing infrastructure and storage requires that every user must potentially have the ability to get connected to every system. Consequently, all systems must be interconnected. This seems to directly contradict to basic security requirements such as confidentiality and integrity of data. But actually, on the Internet, for example, this is common practise. So, there are solutions for most security issues, e.g. the use of Virtual Private Networks (VPN) to share the existing network.

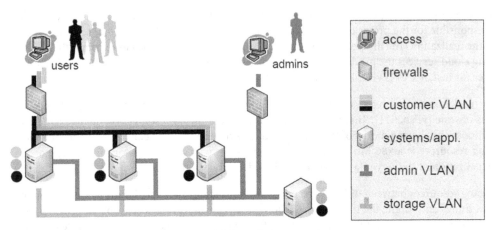

Fig. 2: VLAN Network Segmentation

Networking in data centres is complex. Fig. 2 shows a typical shared data centre environment. There are three types of networks: the customers' (allowing users to access their systems), the one for storage (which connects the computer systems with central storage) and the network for the administrative personnel. Data of different user organisation and services are separated by using VLAN (Virtual Local Area Network) technology. Moreover, the total network consists of several physical segments so that the configuration and management of that complex matter is a real security issue.

Additionally, there are central management areas were all user access from the WAN (Wide Area Network) such as Internet is connected to the internal structure. In this service area the VPN tunnels are terminated; and firewalls and other security solutions control the communication. The data centre backbone, providing connections to other data centres for example, is similarly protected. Both interconnection areas are mostly shared by different user organisations and services. Their protection is critical and complex in nature. Note that the administrative access from remote requires its own highly secured infrastructure.

4 Dynamic Resource Allocation and Sharing

Fig. 3 shows two typical situations for dynamic allocation of computing resources which has to be handled automatically. A hypervisor or Virtual Machine Monitor (VMM) allows running different software packages (called Virtual Machines, VM) on one physical machine where each VM is deemed to have its own full-size computer system. A VM cannot interfere with another one. The virtualization software allocates CPU time and memory resources which are shared by several VM.

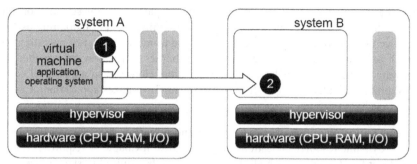

1 increasing dynamically resources inside the same system

2 moving a VM to another system (with free resources)

Fig. 3: Dynamic Resource Allocation

The second case is more interesting. If a VM requires more resources but resources run out on the physical machine, the administrator must move the VM to another physical machine. This move while all software is running is a security critical issue. Actually the VM is duplicated and changes are reproduced on the new instance till the original system can be switched off. The exchange of data between the user and the application is maintained during the move which requires stepwise re-configuration of networks. User data integrity is also obligatory. But where do all the settings come from?

5 Software Engineering and Provisioning

Moving virtual machines to another physical server (within or to outside the network segment) require a high level of automation. Therefore, images are used containing the operating system, the application, middleware as well as all the configuration information needed. These software packages (called Virtual Machines, VM) are not installed on a computer but copied to it. Activities such as copying, starting, moving, stopping of VM are mostly performed by a team of administrators located outside the data centre.

Hence, the next security critical issue is the engineering of the images. When being executed the software must interact with its computer periphery including central storage (see below) and other required network communication. The software must allow dynamic configuration of all parameters which might differ if the software package runs on another physical system with a different environment. These parameters must be set when the image is started as original instance or as a duplicate during a move. Most settings become security critical since failure would not only affect availability but confidentiality and integrity. These settings and the automation of their management is a severe security issue.

Software may contain vulnerabilities which are mitigated by applying patches. Hence, patches are to be applied both on running systems (hypervisors or VMM) and on archived software images. This is not an easy task since there are thousands of patches, images and systems, there is a great deal of combinations for which testing is required and an extra archive, server and management infrastructure is needed. Operations have to cope with a trade-off: Industrial production prefer systems that are stable and identical. Security wants systems to be updated immediately and adapted to meet specific requirements.

More critical than the balance between stability and timely patching is the selection of software and the pre-configuration of software systems called hardening. System hardening usually expects all nonessential software components to be removed from a computer or operating system. This is way all software components may have vulnerabilities which may be exploited. If that piece of software is removed, the related risk vanishes too. However, in a cloud, all computer systems must provide an identical operating environment. This makes application or customer specific hardening hard to attain.

The engineering part is one thing, the management and provisioning of the images (and VM) is another. The dynamic resource allocation being described in Chapter 4 requires images to be archived and be at hand together with all the software scripts required to start, move and stop a VM. This infrastructure is complex in nature and very security critical because resources are assigned to user organisations or services in their correct networking environment as described in Chapter 3. Note that this part and its security implications are sometimes neglected when considering VM technology and virtualisation of computing resources in general.

6 Database and Storage Management

The computers of modern dynamic computing environments are, of course, not equipped with hard disks. This would reduce the economies of scale and is not compatible with the dynamic resource allocation described in Chapter 4. Consequently, all storage is centralized and shared. When a VM is moved, the link to physical and logical units of the central storage is carried along.

ICT continuity services, backup and disaster recovery facilities are part of that central storage service. Even this aspect of availability could fill volumes. In this paper, however, we concentrate on confidentiality and integrity. A holistic concept of management is required to ensure that confidentiality and separation of data is guaranteed throughout the whole process, also in emergency.

A central storage system must be separated into physical and logical units in order to keep data of different user organisations and services apart. File systems and database management systems are the entities accessing these storage areas. Fig. 4 visualises the infrastructure which uses a Storage Area Network (SAN); other technologies are also used. The data being stored belong to an application which in turn is accessed and utilised by the end-user.

The concept of rights management is denoted in the right hand side of Fig. 4. Easy to imagine that managing digital identities, roles and rights as well as credentials and keys is a specific area of work being very security critical.

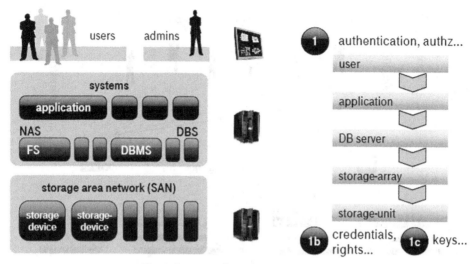

Fig. 4: Storage and Database Management

Note that a variety of technologies is involved here. Digital identities with roles and rights are defined and used on the network and storage level, they are used and administered for the database and file access, and finally access is controlled at the application level. Each level may use its own values as well as specific protocols to securely transfer and store security critical data including passwords. Nevertheless, the hierarchy must built an integrated whole. Hence, an identity and access management system is required which ensures that. Co-operation of different production teams and central services must also be guaranteed. In reality, there is a difference between the operational levels (below application) and the upper level (application). Large corporations hesitate to use shared identity management systems and often it is not possibility to standardise the identity management accordingly since the business processes, the applications, and internal organisation and related workflows are too different.

7 Privileged User Management

A particular type of access which requires specific attention is those allowing the performance of administrational tasks. The latter are manifold and cover provisioning of devices, configuration of networks and storage, operations management including dynamic resource allocation as well as central management activities such as service management, operations control and monitoring including log and event management.

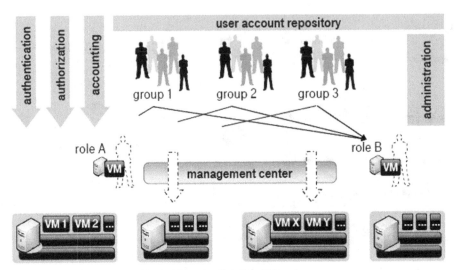

Fig. 5: Managing Privileged User Access

Hence a precise assignment of responsibilities and tasks as well as an identity and access management system is essential to ensure that security requirements are met. Note that this crucial part consists of managing the provider's personnel, the organisation of business and processes related to ICT production and the management of IT accounts with all the data being required. Fig. 5 visualises some principles of Identity and Access Management (IAM) on the one hand and business and process organisation on the other. The management of privileged user access goes far beyond having an identity and access management system. Moreover, it comprises many activities related to Human Resources, is influenced by and integrated into the internal organisation of the whole corporation and ICT production in particular, and it covers cooperation aspects organised in a variety of business processes of the ICT service provider.

8 Make or Buy?

One major issue being considered by ICT security professionals is the sharing of resources. This is seen critical since "users are not alone". It is worth mentioning that this situation is typical for long ago. In "ancient times" there were monolithic stand-alone systems which were protected as an isolated fortress (see left in Fig. 6). Since many years sharing of resources is very common. User organisations naturally use the Internet or any dedicated networks that are shared in use with other users (see right in Fig. 6). Starting with "housing", infrastructure services were shared including critical ones such as power supply, disaster recovery, internal networking and LAN-WAN security. Organisations do use common applications and related infrastructures for communication and for collaboration. That means that they do also share the risks resulting from using the same software of the same vendor and of using services from some providers as those transferring the whole stuff through the Internet from A to B. The cloud is new but maybe a continuation of a long term development of industrialisation of ICT and its delivery.

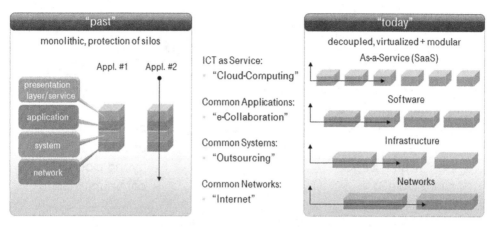

Fig. 6: Sharing of Resources ("ancient times" and today)

But this should only provide a background. Real business is more complex. Actually there is a trend of buying instead of doing things alone.

Even big user organisations hesitate to manage all the above tasks themselves. The main reason may be economical (avoid huge investments) but there are more obstacles for doing things themselves. The comprehensive management of the processes allocates too much resource, especially experts, and the set-up of such an environment allocates time and capital. Moreover, it is a challenge to have all the security expertise at hand required to manage daily operations, set-up of new services, maintenance and emergency and other critical situations. The principle of economies of scale and the advantages of division of labour also count in terms of providing security services. A large ICT service provider has simply more size to compensate peak demands and effectively use expert resources in better times. He also has the ability to accumulate very specific expert expertise rarely required by an IT department.

However, cloud computing has some consequences in terms of security. Most important, users put all eggs into one basket. And the ICT service provider does it too. All the advantages of centralisation (and sharing) resources, of standardisation and industrialised production with high-quality and reliability have their price. First, security requirements and measures need to be standardised too. That means "best-fit" instead of "full custom" in terms of security. Secondly, any flaw or error most probably affects many user organisations and services. Thirdly, the technology being used is developed and complex and may cause security problems which may not exist in proven legacy systems. Fourth, the risk exposure may be different. The attack surface, the potential targets for an attack and the motivation for an attack increase with the number of customers using shared resources over distributed networks, compute and storage systems. The probability to be attacked would be smaller in case of a one company, high-expense and isolated ICT environment.

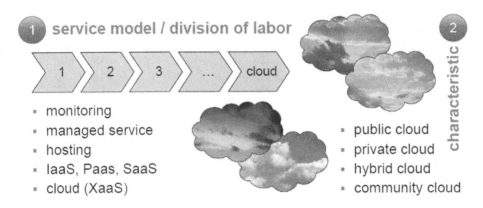

Fig. 7: Selection of the delivery model

So, user organisations shall carefully consider the services being purchased from third party and evaluate the provider (refer to [EvFMiP10]). There are different service models (see Number 1 in Fig. 7) with different division of labour and therefore different service provider related risks. Note that the benefits are different as well. But also third parties provide cloud services with different characteristics and different risk profiles (see Number 2 in Fig. 7). A "private" and a "public" cloud have, for instance, a different attack surface and risk exposure.

User organisations should not solely consider technology being promised to be used. This paper has demonstrated with a variety of examples that process maturity, automation and scale are equally important to provide an adequate level of security.

9 Conclusion

The influence of automation, standardization and large scale production on security aspects is immanent. The above examples show that this non-technology part is very important. A high level of security and assurance necessitates that the processes are adequately mastered by the ICT service provider. Process maturity turns out to be the essential parameter for the provisioning of secure ICT services.

A cloud provider has to automate its production and produce ICT services in a standardized and industrialized way. This means that user organisations get best-fit instead of full-custom solutions. Economies of scale, mainly a reduction of costs, can only be achieved if systems and services are standardised and shared between different user organisations.

This modern ICT production leads to the consequence, that a failure in technology or processes has an impact on many (maybe all) user organisations and services. But systematic failure may also occur in a single purpose home-grown operating environment. Outsourcing provides an advantage. A cloud provider has a vital self-interest to master all the ICT security issues. He also has to control, streamline and improve all the necessary administration and management processes. It is also the provider's business to automate them in order to avoid error, to increase quality and to reduce costs of service delivery. Note that all errors and corrective action result in costs for the ICT service provider and affects its competitive ability and viability.

The necessary investments will only pay if the ICT service provider (internal or external) produces ICT services on a large scale. But it is also the other way around. Large scale production provides other benefits of scale, also in terms of security. They are predominantly being produced by the high degree of division of labour necessary for modern industrialized production. This leads to a situation of having security specialists for all topics with excellent expertise. Resource management and allocation can also be much better. There are many facts apart from using the right technology and controls that are verifiably required to achieve an adequate level of security. Process maturity, automation and large scale are fundamental for reliable security.

All figures are illustrative.

References

[EvFMiP10] Eberhard von Faber and Michael Pauly: User Risk Management Strategies and Models – Adaption for Cloud Computing; in: Securing Electronic Business Processes, Proceedings of the Information Security Solutions Europe, ISSE 2010, Vieweg+Teubner, Wiesbaden, 2010, ISBN 978-3-8348-1438-8, p. 80-90

[vFab2011] Eberhard von Faber: Blackbox Cloud-Computing; <kes> Die Zeitschrift für Informations-Sicherheit, Special März 2011, S. 40-42

[NIST2011] Peter Mell and Timothy Grance: The NIST Definition of of Cloud Computing (Draft); Special Publication 800-145, NIST, January 2011

Market Overview of Security as a Service Systems

Christian Senk · Andreas Holzapfel

University of Regensburg
Universitätsstraße 31, 93053 Regensburg, Germany
{christian.senk | andreas.holzapfel}@wiwi.uni-regensburg.de

Abstract

Companies are facing increasing threats regarding the security and safety of their IT systems. Whereas the Cloud computing paradigm itself induces certain security-related risks, it is also discussed as a possible solution to obtain IT security services in a flexible way. The outsourcing of IT security according to Cloud computing principles is referred to as Security as a Service. Such systems are the next step of the evolution of traditional managed security services.

In the present work we provide an overview and evaluation of today's Security as a Service market. Therefore, we conducted a web-based survey, identifying and classifying Security as a Service solutions. In addition, we evaluated each product based on three Cloud-specific criteria.

The survey included 65 products of 16 providers. We surveyed that the market's focus is currently on content and endpoint security applications. However, only few of the reviewed products fulfill of the specified criteria. Thus, the expected core benefit of cost-flexibility cannot be achieved. We thus expect substantial developments in the Security as a Service market within the next few years.

1 Introduction

In order to explain the relevance of the topic we introductorily emphasize the potential of Security as a Service technologies as an innovative way for IT security outsourcing. Based on an existing research gap the research objective and the applied methodology are specified.

1.1 Motivation for Security as a Service Systems

Companies are facing increasing threats regarding the security and safety of their IT systems. Reasons include the opening of security domains for web-based access in the course of current developments in the fields of identity federation [Homm07] and Cloud computing [BrGo10, Smit10, RiRa10]. Whereas the Cloud computing paradigm itself induces certain security-related risks, it is also discussed as a possible solution to obtain IT security services in a flexible way. At this, Cloud computing opens up new opportunities to integrate flexible and economically innovative security solutions in order to cope effectively with these rising security demands [Gart08]. The outsourcing of IT security according to Cloud computing principles is referred to as Security as a Service [HaMB09, RiRa10]. Such systems are considered to be the next step of the evolution of traditional managed security services [RiRa10]. According to the assessment of Gartner Research the market for Security as a Service will grow significantly and correspondent technologies will be widely accepted within the next four years [Smit10].

1.2 Research Objective and Methodology

Cloud computing is currently a highly discussed topic in research and practice. Meanwhile, many security software products are labeled as Cloud solution. Though, early research indicated that this is often done mistakenly referring to an imprecise understanding of Cloud computing and according system design principles.

In the present work we provide an overview and evaluation of today's Security as a Service market. Therefore, we conducted a web-based survey, using a search engine and a set of specific key words. However, the investigation raises no claim to completeness. Search results were categorized according to a modified security application classification system. In addition, we evaluated each product based on three Cloud-specific criteria.

2 Preliminary Work

The discussion of the present research's results requires a common conceptual understanding of Security as a Service and a clear delimitation from related approaches. Therefore a definition of both Cloud computing technologies in general and Security as a Service solutions in particular is provided.

2.1 Definition and Characteristics of Cloud Computing

The National Institute of Standards and Technology (NIST) defines Cloud computing as "a model for enabling convenient, on-demand network access to a shared pool of configurable computing resources (e.g., networks, servers, storage, applications, and services) that can be rapidly provisioned and released with minimal management effort or service provider interaction" [MeGr09]. These resources are referred to as Cloud services and can logically be assigned to the infrastructure, (Infrastructure as a Service, IaaS), platform (Platform as a Service, PaaS), or application layer (Software as a Service, SaaS) [Furt10, HöKa11, RiRa10, PiCh09]. Other forms which appear in the literature can usually be traced back to these three layers [HöKa11].

Cloud computing solutions promise adopters several benefits induced by the flexibility of the underlying sourcing model. To realize this potential, such services must comply with certain Cloud-specific design principles. According to a conducted literature review, we identified three primary characteristics for Cloud services:
- **Multi-tenancy and on-demand service provisioning:** The service provider runs a single instance of the Cloud system serving multiple clients (tenants) [Furt10, HöKa11, MaKu09, StWH10]. Thus, there is no need to set up separate service instances for different client organizations. Different tenants use (and customize) dedicated virtual partitions of the same system [Furt10, StWH10]. This offers advantages for both the service provider and the client. As the resources are not dedicated to single tenants service clients are able to use services on demand with a guaranteed quality of service level and only for the amount of time they are needed [Furt10, HöKa11]. On the service provider's site virtualized parti-

tions for clients are enforcing economies of scale as only one underlying infrastructure has to be managed.

- **Service virtualization:** Service use must be possible without the deployment of dedicated hardware and software resources at the client organization's infrastructure [RiRa10]. The client must not get in touch with the service provider's underlying infrastructure [HöKa11, MaKu09]. What the client needs has to be offered as an abstracted service accessible by any device from all over the Internet [Furt10, HöKa11]. On the service provider's site a scalable and flexible infrastructure has to be provided as basis for service provisioning and continuity [HöKa11].
- **Pay-per-use model:** The Cloud service provides mechanisms for adapting service usage to the client's needs [Furt10]. At this, pricing conforms with the actual demand and not on fixed-term licenses [Furt10, HöKa11, AFGJ09]. Furthermore, service pricing has to be transparent to the customer even before any usage or purchase intention [AFGJ09]. This increases both flexibility in service usage and provider selection [RiRa10]. Service clients can consume as much resources as needed without any up-front commitment necessary [HöKa11].

2.2 Security as a Service

Security as a Service (SECaaS[1]) is a service-oriented approach to IT Security architecture and thus a consequent and necessary evolution of traditional security architectures [HaMB09, Pete09]. It is defined as "the delivery of security functionality over infrastructure components in a service-oriented manner" in accordance with the SaaS model [HaMB09]. At this, increasing demands for security, transparency and flexibility drive the service-oriented encapsulation of application- and domain spanning, reusable security controls and thus the obtainment of such services from external providers [BMOS10, HaMB09].

As for Cloud services in general the identified design criteria apply for SECaaS solutions as well. Depending on the degree of fulfillment of these criteria existing security services can be delimited from "real" SECaaS services (Fig. 1):

- **On-premises security services:** The security system is deployed, operated and maintained on the client's side. This requires dedicated IT and human resource capacities. Service costs do not scale with its degree of capacity utilization. None of the identified Cloud principles apply.
- **Traditional Managed Security Services:** A dedicated security service instance is set up for a client organization by an external service provider. The provider is responsible for the operation and maintenance of the system [KeWW09]. Such security services do not provide for multi-tenancy. Hence, the instant use of such service is not feasible. Additionally, service usage may involve the deployment of dedicated software and hardware components and due to the required initial effort clients are often bound to providers by fixed-term licenses [Hube02]. Traditional Managed Security Service thus follows the Application Service Providing model.
- **Cloud-based security services (Security as a Service):** Only by fulfilling all of the identified characteristics a security service can be referred to as SECaaS. The service is fully operated and maintained by the service provider with no dedicated client-sided hardware

---

1　In literature Security as a Service is often abbreviated to SaaS (e.g. [HaMB09; RiRa10]. Because of the collision with the correspondent Software as a Service abbreviation we use SECaaS instead.

or software necessary. Full virtualization of the security service ensures the highest degree of capacity utilization. This makes the service usage highly cost-effective to the customer and enables fine-grained pay-per-use models. A virtualized multi-tenancy architecture not only enables the instant start of service use but also leverages inherent data aggregation benefits for service providers. Further, the potential operational and organizational flexibility is maximized.

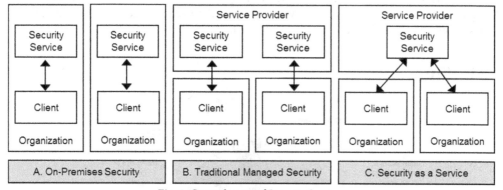

Fig. 1: General types of Security Services

Based on the taxonomy of [Kark10] we classify Security as a Service using the following security application domains:

- **Application Security:** Services for secure (and safe) operation of software applications. This includes application firewalls, services for network intrusion detection as well as application-based vulnerability and source code analyzer.
- **Compliance Management:** Services supporting the client organization's compliance management including services for benchmarking, validation of compliance with internal and external specifications, and third party evaluations.
- **Content Safety:** Services addressing the safety of data including backup and email archiving.
- **Content Security:** Services protecting content data from intended attacks. This includes email encryption as well as filtering and monitoring of emails and internet traffic.
- **Endpoint Security:** This domain covers security services for hosts in the clients' network including malware protection, data encryption, host-based intrusion detection and the management of configuration items.
- **Identity and Access Management:** Services providing user and rights management, authorization verification, management of identity federations, single sign-on systems or strong respectively multi-factor authentication.
- **Managed Devices:** Services for the management of client-sided security systems. This includes hosted application firewalls, services for network intrusion detection and prevention and holistic Security Information and Event Management (SIEM) systems.
- **Security Information and Event Management:** Services implementing certain SIEM functions, e. g. archiving of log-data, continuity management, detection of attacks and system failures, reporting, incident response, forensic analysis, and the collection and analysis of log data.

- **Vulnerability and Threat Management:** Services addressing threat detection and vulnerability analysis, patch and change management, as well as notifications on current attacks, vulnerabilities and worm breakouts.

Content Safety was split into Content Safety and Content Security to bear the consequences of safety concerning protection against unforeseen events and security concerning protection against threats and tangible attacks [Gatt04, PiCh09]. Furthermore, we merged Vulnerability Management and Threat Management to Vulnerability and Threat Management as threats affect existing vulnerabilities and products show to address them both [MaKu09].

3 Findings

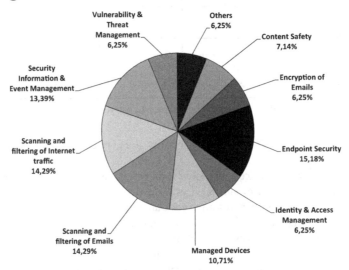

Fig. 2: Distribution of products (Content Security itemized)

Altogether our survey encountered 67 products from 16 providers. As shown in Fig. 2, according to the identified security application domains, these products are covering the domains as follows: Application Security (1.77%), Compliance Management (4.42%), Content Safety (7.08%), Content Security (34.51%), Endpoint Security (15.93%), Identity and Access Management (6.19%), Managed Devices (10.62%), Security Information and Event Management (13.27%), Vulnerability and Threat Management (6.19%). Representing the largest domain, Content Security is split up into its types of service Email Encryption (6.25%), Scanning and Filtering of Internet Traffic (14.29%) and Scanning and Filtering of Emails (14.29%).

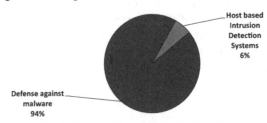

Fig. 3: Composition of Endpoint Security

As illustrated in Fig. 3, Endpoint Security is split into Defense against Malware (94%) and Host-based Intrusion Detection Systems (6%). Services for pure Data Encryption and Surveillance of configuration items could not be identified.

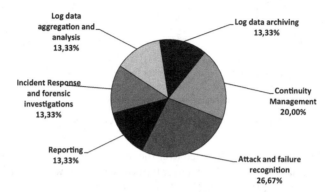

Fig. 4: Composition of Security Information and Event Management

Security Information and Event Management is composed of Attack and Failure Recognition (26.67%), Continuity Management (20%), Incident Response and Forensic Investigations (13.33%), Log Data Archiving (13.33%), Log Data Aggregation and Analysis (13.33%), Log Data Archiving (13.33%) and Reporting (13.33%) (Fig. 4).

Managed Devices contains Managed/Hosted (Application) Firewall (33.33%), Managed/Hosted Network Intrusion Detection and Prevention with DDoS Protection (50%) and Managed/Hosted SIEM (16.67%). Identity and Access Management is split into User Administration and Rights Management (28.57%), Federation (14.29%), Cross-Company/Cross-Website Single Sign On (14.29%), and Strong Authentication/Multi-Factor-Authentication (42.48%). Vulnerability and Threat Management is composed of Threat Detection (28.57%), Notification on Attacks and Vulnerabilities (42.68%) and Vulnerability Analysis (28.57%).

The market's focus is currently on content and endpoint security applications. This is supported by the results of an online survey we conducted in the same period researching the acceptance of SECaaS systems[2]. Of 177 participants, 42.94% confirmed the current use or use intent of endpoint security services. For content security services, this is 50.85%. Concerning the other application domains, the use or use intent is lower.

As the focus of services becomes measurable through service granularity, we analyzed how many domains and types of services the products cover. This shows the possible service use as differentiated or comprehensive solutions.

---

2   Complete results of the study will be published separately.

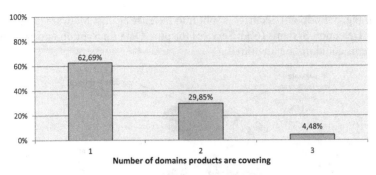

Fig. 5: Distribution of products over domains

As shown in Fig. 5 the products are distributed over the security application domains as follows: 62.69% focus on one domain whereas 29.85% cover types of service of two domains. The remaining 2.98% spread over four (1.49%) and six (1.49%) domains.

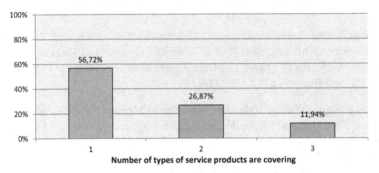

Fig. 6: Distribution of products over types of service

The distribution over domains notwithstanding, we also analyzed how products distribute over all types of service (Fig. 6): 56.72% match one type, 26.87% match two types and 11.94% match three types of service. The remaining 4.48% of all products cover four (2.99%) and six (1.49%) types of service.

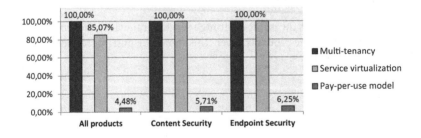

Fig. 7: Products fulfilling defined criteria (complete sample)

Only few of the reviewed products fulfill all of the specified criteria (Fig. 7). Whereas all analyzed services implement multi-tenancy, complete virtualization of the resource is just provided by 85.07%. A sophisticated pay-per-use model is only implemented in 4.48% of the considered offerings. Thus, the expected core benefit of cost-flexibility cannot be achieved.

Regarding the Endpoint and Content Security products on which the market is currently focusing all products fulfill the demand of multi-tenancy and on-demand service provisioning and service virtualization. Furthermore, 5.71% of all Content Security products and 6.25% of all Endpoint Security products offer a sophisticated pay-per-use model.

4 Related Work

Only few related work exists and there is no clear definition of SECaaS in scientific literature. In 2009 Forrester Research conducted a market survey for managed security services without differentiating conventional managed security services and Cloud services [Kark10].

5 Conclusions

At present the market for Cloud-based IT security products is focused on solutions for content and endpoint security. A possible explanation is the higher ease of implementation and integration of such services. The application domains of compliance and application security might provide horizontal niches for security service providers. Furthermore, services focus on fine-grained purposes. However, most surveyed security services do not fulfill the identified Cloud characteristics. In particular, most products do not offer a sophisticated pay-per-use model with transparent pricing. Thus, they do not provide for the full theoretical potential of SECaaS. In this respect, we expect substantial developments in the SECaaS market within the next few years.

References

[AFGJ09] Armbrust, M., Fox, A., Griffith, R., Joseph A. D., Katz, R. H., Konwinski A., Lee, G., Patterson D. A., Rabkin, A., Stoica I., and Zaharia, M.: Above the Clouds: A Berkeley View of Cloud Computing. EECS Department, University of California, 2009.

[BMOS10] Bertino, E., Martino, L., Paci, F., and Squicciarrini, A.: Security for Web Services and Service-Oriented Architectures. Springer, Heidelberg, 2010.

[BrGo10] Brock, M. and Goscinski, A.: Toward a Framework for Cloud Security. In: Algorithms and Architectures for Parallel Processing. C.-H. Hsu, L. Yang, J. Park and S.-S. Yeo: Lecture Notes in Computer Science. Springer Berlin / Heidelberg, 2010, p. 254-263.

[Furt10] Furht, B.: Cloud Computing Fundamentals. In: Handbook of Cloud Computing. B. Furht and A. Escalante: Springer US, Boston, MA, 2010, p. 3-20.

[Gart08] Gartner: Gartner Says Security Delivered as a Cloud-Based Service Will More Than Triple in Many Segments by 2013, www.gartner.com/it/page.jsp?id=722307, 2008, Accessed 24 July 2010.

[Gatt04] Gattiker, U. E.: The Information Security Dictionary: Defining The Terms That Define Security For E-business, Internet, Information And Wireless Technology. Kluwer Academic Publishers, Norwell, MA, USA, 2004.

[HaMB09] Hafner, M., Mukhtiar, M., and Breu, R.: SeAAS - A Reference Architecture for Security Services in SOA. In: UCS 15, 2009, p. 2916-2936.

[HöKa11] Höfer, C. and Karagiannis, G.: Cloud computing services: taxonomy and comparison. In: Journal of Internet Services and Applications, 2011, p. 1-14.

[Homm07] Hommel, W.: Architektur- und Werkzeugkonzepte für föderiertes Identitäts-Management. Dr. Hut, München, 2007.

[Hube02] Huber, M.: IT-security in global corporate networks. Center for Digital Technology and Management, München, 2002.

[Kark10] Kark, K.: Market Overview: Managed Security Services. http://www.verizonbusiness.com/resources/analystreports/ar_forrester_managed_security_services2010_en_xg.pdf, 2010, Accessed 16 March 2011.

[KeWW09] Keuper, F., Wagner, B., and Wysuwa, H.: Managed Services: IT-Sourcing der nächsten Generation. Gabler, 2009.

[MaKu09] Mather, T., Kumaraswamy, S., and Latif, S.: Cloud Security and Privacy: An Enterprise Perspective on Risks and Compliance. O'Reilly Media, Inc., 2009.

[MeGr09] Mell, P. and Grance, T.: The NIST Definition of Cloud Computing. In: National Institute of Standards and Technology 53, 6, 50, 2009.

[Pete09] Peterson, G.: Service-Oriented Security Indications for Use. In: Computing in Science and Engineering 7, 2009, p. 91-93.

[PiCh09] Pietre-Cambacedes, L. and Chaudet, C., Disentangling the relations between safety and security. In: Proceedings of the 9th WSEAS international conference on Applied informatics and communications. World Scientific and Engineering Academy and Society (WSEAS), Stevens Point, Wisconsin, USA, 2009, p. 156-161.

[RiRa10] Rittinghouse, J. and Ransome, J.: Cloud Computing: Implementation, Management, and Security. CRC, Boca Raton, 2010.

[Smit10] Smith, D. M.: Hype Cycle for Cloud Computing, 2010. http://www.gartner.com/DisplayDocument?doc_cd=201557, 2010, Accessed 13 July 2011.

[StWH10] Stanoevska-Slabeva, K., Wozniak, T., and Hoyer, V.: Practical Guidelines for Evolving IT Infrastructure towards Grids and Clouds. In: Grid and Cloud Computing: A Business Perspective on Technology and Applications, K. Stanoevska-Slabeva, T. Wozniak and S. Ristol: Springer, Berlin, 2010, p. 225-243.

[VRCL08] Vaquero, L. M., Rodero-Merino, L., Caceres, J., and Lindner, M.: A break in the Clouds. In: SIGCOMM Comput. Commun. Rev 39, 1, 50, 2008.

[Will10] William Y Chang, H. A.-A. J. F. S.: Transforming Enterprise Cloud Services. Springer-Verlag New York Inc., 2010.

[ZhCB10] Zhang, Q., Cheng, L., and Boutaba, R.: Cloud computing: state-of-the-art and research challenges. In: Journal of Internet Services and Applications 1, 1, 2010, p. 7-18.

New Digital Security Model

Morten Jørsum

National IT and Telecom Agency
Holsteinsgade 63, 2100 København Ø, Denmark
mojo@itst.dk

Abstract

Due to the fact that the traditional security perimeter is challenged and that there is an increasing demand to enhance privacy and to secure cloud computing it is necessary to develop a new way of designing security. In this paper it is described how a new security model can meet these challenges by adopting the following principles:
1) Provide security for all parties in a transaction (including users).
2) De-couple user data from users' physical identity.
3) Utilize attribute-based credentials and transaction isolation.
4) Move from an identification-oriented paradigm towards a validation-orientated paradigm.

1 Introduction

Due to the extensive digitalisation of the public sector, as well as the private sector, the challenge of providing security and protecting privacy in IT solutions is increasing.

One challenge is that companies no longer can protect their systems by using a strong perimeter because the perimeter can be opened, when for instance the employees exchange documents in Google Docs instead of using the companies' internal systems.

Another challenge is to secure the users' privacy in the digital world. More and more data about the users is created - data such as Google searches, and who, when, and where the last login on a government services took place. The users constantly leave digital fingerprints on the Internet. Often, they are not even aware of it and to an even lesser degree do they realise who use this information and for what purpose.

In addition, the traditional perception that security is equal to physical control over data is challenged by cloud computing where data no longer is located within the organisation or in the data centre of a classic outsourcing company. Therefore, to realize the potential of cloud computing new security models are needed.

To comply with the challenges it is necessary to supplement the existing security models with new ones. The requirements for the new security models are based on the desire for a balanced security with strong privacy protection, flexible processes that can adapt to new demands as well as the possibility of moving data into the cloud.

Many traditional security models are based on the fundamental assumption, that the users must be identified. Addressing the challenges, the National IT and Telecom agency in Denmark

(NITA) has published a paper discussing a new model for security where the opposite is the case: A model that includes less user identification and a higher degree of privacy; a model that lets the users maintains a certain degree of anonymity and pseudonymity.

This new perception of security requires that security and privacy are integrated into the design of the solution (preventive action) as opposed to adding it (curative action) to the developed solution.

These requirements can be met by the concept of Privacy-by-Design.

In the following, NITA will present the objectives for the new security model, give an introduction to the concept of Privacy-by-Design and Security-by-Design, describe the new security model and illustrate how it can be applied in practice.

If you want additional information about the new security models, NITA has launched a discussion paper on New Digital Security Models. You find the paper here: http://digitaliser.dk/resource/896495.

2 Objectives for the New Security Model

NITA has developed the new security model based on a series of principles and requirements. The objectives for the new security model are listed below:

1. There must be security for all parties of a transaction - the owners of the solution as well as the users.

2. The users must have the possibility to control which data is provided to the solutions and further be able to control whether their data in different solutions can be interconnected.

3. Stored information about the users is not to be ascribed directly to their physical identity unless it is strictly necessary and negotiated. Therefore, virtual identities rather than identified keys (such as social security numbers) are to be used.

4. The users' data is not to be linkable. Thus, external parties can't work together on extracting more information than the user explicitly has approved.

5. The service providers must be guaranteed that they only receive valid user information and that the information relates to the user providing it.

6. It must be possible to establish mechanisms which ensure the users' responsibility. An example is the "proof of liability" that makes it possible to identify a user who does not follow the rules e.g. by committing crime. The responsibility mechanisms must not lead to a compromise of safety for all transactions where there have not been irregularities.

7. A security model must wherever possible be arranged so that the consequences of security breech in one system or for one user are limited to the local context. Thus, the security breech does not scale to other systems or other users.

8. Generally, all transactions shall be isolated and it shall be secured that the control is not just outside the cloud but that the control is client-sided.

9. The design should when possible follow the notion that many different stakeholders might have different knowledge about a transaction (fine grained) and use different technologies (semantic interoperability) while keeping the control client-sided.

3 Privacy-by-Design

As mentioned in the introduction the objectives for the security model are compliant with the concept of Privacy-by-Design (PbD).

The general notion of PbD is that business processes, IT systems, and infrastructure from the beginning must be designed to prevent breach of privacy.

Further, privacy must be attained without users doing anything explicitly. Therefore, privacy must be incorporated in the systems from the beginning - before any information is collected.

Privacy is not to be seen as an opposition to security (for the owner of the solution). On the contrary, the essential point is that the two properties can be attained at the same time.

PbD is user-centric in the sense that the users can have control of their data.

Based on the concept of PbD it is possible to develop a security model, which enables:
- That only the necessary information about the users is disclosed.
- That disclosure is done under the users' control.
- That the users can perform transactions using a virtual identity without being identified unless strictly necessary.

4 Security-by-Design

There have been a number of challenges by the concept of PbD. One challenge is the focus on risk from one stakeholder's point of view - typically the users'. Therefore, the concept Security-by-Design (SbD) has been developed as an improvement and operationalisation of PbD.

The central element in SbD is to move away from identification-based security by eliminating identification as much as possible in some use cases and skip directly to those aspects or properties that need to be validated.

SbD prevent a variety of security issues by using new cryptographic mechanisms and conscious system design.

5 The Current Security Model

Traditional credentials have a number of strong security features, but they do also present a number of potential challenges:
- The explicit connection to the user's physical identity forces the user to be identified by the service provider.
- Certificates contain unique keys allowing the user's actions across services to be coupled.
- Even when assertions only contain pseudonyms and only are used once (transient pseudonyms), the issuer has knowledge about the coupling between the user's identity and his pseudonyms.
- Security breaches may affect many stakeholders at the same time.
- When users are identified and data is easily interconnected without the involvement of the user, pressure for using and combining data in new ways may appear.

These challenges are traditionally dealt with by setting high security-demands for development and operation of IT systems containing sensitive data, which prevents misconduct by third parties (e.g. hacker attacks). These high demands may lead to significant cost increases for development, operation and system administration as well as hinder usage of cloud computing.

6 The New Security Model

The new security model consists of several building blocks or concepts that can be used in different designs and for different purposes. In the following, these building blocks and concepts are presented.

6.1 From Identification to Identity

Addressing the challenges, it is recommended to move from a simple one-dimensional perception of identity (all is packed into a single digital key or credential) to a flexible and nuanced identity model where different security-considerations are dealt with by specific mechanisms.

This can be done by breaking identity down into logically separate components each of which can be made:
- Interoperable (compared and substituted - e.g. upgraded algorithms).
- Concrete (semantically compared to operationally formulated policies or requirements, which thereby becomes supervisory as an alternative to plug-on security).
- Limited (non-invasive and purpose-specific, so that security does not amount to a choice between evils).

6.2 Attribute-based Credentials

A central element in the new security model is the so-called "attribute-based credentials". An attributed-based credential is a credential that does not identify the user but instead comprises a virtual identity (pseudonym). For this reason they are sometimes called Anonymous Credentials. The attribute is not traceable to the issuing process and the user has direct controls of which attributes from the credential that are released.

Attribute-based credentials have a number of similarities to traditional security credentials:
- They contain a collection of attributes with information about the holder (user) of the credential.
- The credentials cannot be forged or changed as they are protected by the issuer's digital signature, which is validated by the recipient and they are, as traditional credentials, based on cryptography.
- They may be blocked (revoked) and have an expiry date.
- They may only be used with a private (secret) key, which alone is known to the holder.

But the attribute-based credentials separate themselves from traditional credentials by also containing the following features:
- They do not contain any information that directly reveals the holder's identity - e.g. they do not contain social security numbers etc. Instead, the attribute-based credential will be used together with a virtual identity (pseudonym), which is detached from the physical person.

- Attribute-based credentials presented at a service provider can not be traced back to the issuing process. Even the issuer of the credentials cannot, after the issuing process on the individual credential, tell to whom it has been issued even though the holder was known at the time when it was issued.

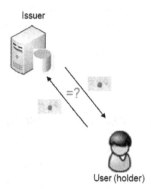

Fig. 1: A credential is not traceable even to the issuer

- A holder may use different attribute-based credentials at different service providers without the possibility to determine that it was the same user.

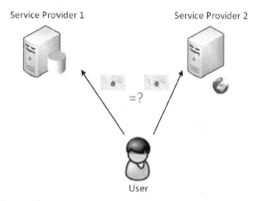

Fig. 2: The user cannot be traced across service providers

- An attribute-based credential is technically not sent to the service provider, but is presented via a protocol, where the user proves it to contain certain attributes with certain values.
- The user has in the dialogue with the service provider complete control over which attributes from the credential he will reveal (so-called selective disclosure).

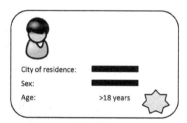

Fig. 3: Selective disclosure of attributes from credential

- They can have a build-in mechanism ensuring that attribute-based credentials are only used a certain number of times.
- It is possible to sign data with the private key belonging to an attribute-based credential and thereby attain the same properties as by a traditional digital signature.
- It is possible for a user to send encrypted data to a service provider and subsequently prove properties about them without revealing the content (so-called verifiable encryption).

Note, when attribute-based credentials are used, the issuer and service provider do not exchange user-data directly. The exchange is done via the user and is subject to the user's control. Practically, the user must possess an agent/client facilitating the usage of attribute-based credentials.

6.3 Virtual Identities and Transaction Isolation

As mentioned above, by introducing the new security model a switch from an identification-based paradigm to a validation-oriented paradigm takes place. This means that instead of all applications identifying the users and coupling local data to the identity (e.g. social security number) data is coupled to virtual identities (pseudonyms), which are subject to validation (i.e. the user can prove that he represents a pseudonym via a secret key).

The user can accumulate completely isolated islands of profile-information attached to different virtual identities by different service providers.

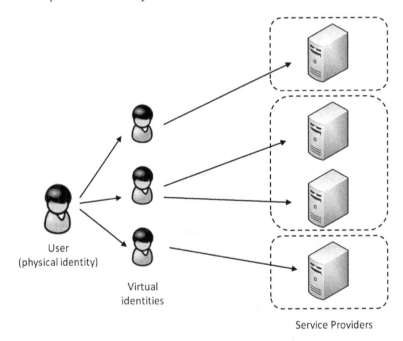

User
(physical identity)

Virtual
identities

Service Providers

Fig. 4: Use of virtual identities for separating user-data at the service providers

However, responsibility-mechanisms can be implemented so it will be possible to reveal the physical person behind a virtual identity under pre-defined circumstances (e.g. identity escrow).

7 Data in the Cloud

Traditional security models, based on the paradigm of perimeter-security, are not always adequate for moving personal data (or personally identifiable information) to the cloud due to the increased risks and loss of control.

By designing applications in a new way including usage of attribute-based credentials, user data attached to the virtual identities, and transaction isolations, the risk-barriers can be broken.

If the application and its data are compromised, they will not be linkable to physical persons, but only to virtual identities and data will be confined to local transactions and may not be linked to other data restricting the consequences to the local context. Thus, the need to protect data and the relating costs may be reduced dramatically. Note that these advantages are attained without having to trust or be dependent on the cloud supplier.

8 Cases

For the purpose of exemplifying the new security model, NITA has developed two cases. The cases are fictitious examples illustrating realistic situations where security can be achieved through employment of the new security model. Case B will also show how to avoid using personally identifiable data in the cloud. The cases are further developed in the discussion paper referred to in the introduction.

8.1 Case A

The first case describes how it can be ensured, that the reporting of data to tax authorities (SKAT) can be done without providing SKAT knowledge on the source of the income (e.g. sperm donation).

One solution is that SKAT has to establish an IT system where citizens can report taxable income via their social security number and then receive a non-identifying ticket that can be used once (an attribute-based credential with a virtual identity), wherein the reported income appears.

The solution solves some of the problems related to keeping the sperm donors' identity secret from SKAT. But the solution also has unsolved challenges:
- SKAT's income report application cannot be hosted in the cloud because income-data is linked to social security numbers in the current model.
- If a person loses his NemID (digital signature) others may commit identity-theft and report taxes on his social security number.

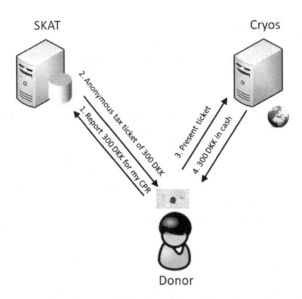

Fig. 5: Report of tax data without identification

In order to meet these challenges, the first, simple solution design may be changed by SKAT, so that reporting tax is not linked to social security numbers but to virtual identities instead. Each citizen, thereby, has a virtual tax-account, to which he may report tax-income to SKAT if he proves ownership of a secret key attached to the virtual identity and only possessed by the citizen. SKAT will then potentially be able to move their tax report application and data into the cloud because the data no longer is personally identifiable. The issuing of attribute-based credentials, after reporting of data to tax authorities, is unchanged from the simple solution.

8.2 Case B

The other case deals with how security can be designed in a situation where an electronic job portal is hosted in the cloud. Through the job portal a user can make an electronic application for a job as teacher.

The solution is based on the idea that a number of institutions establish IT systems, which can issue authoritative documents (e.g. diplomas) as attribute-based credentials, containing only a virtual identity. Each of these issued document types could be based on the user being authenticated e.g. by a digital signature to ensure that proofs were only issued for the right person or, more ideally, they could be based on having virtual identities attached to secret keys, which then could be used for authentication.

Then a potential applicant would be able to create an application in a job portal, without being identified, and upload the electronic credentials documenting the required information.

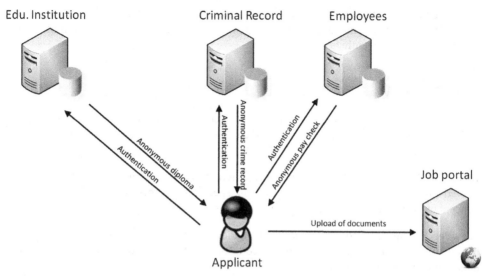

Fig. 6: Non-identifying application

9 Interaction with the Users

The proposed security model makes it possible to design applications giving the users control over their data. This requires, however, that the users actively participate and that the user-interaction is effective, intelligible, and user-friendly to the group of intended users. Imaginable, in a number of situations a part of the users do not want - or have enough knowledge - to participate actively in orchestration of credentials and identities. In such case it is relevant to design the application so it allows the user to choose. Some users may fundamentally trust public and private companies (e.g. banks) to treat their data securely and are, therefore, not interested in being given the choice.

Thus, the new security model does not necessarily force the users to do anything different from the way they currently use the solutions. The essence is that the new security paradigm, in contrast to the traditional security model, provides the user with liberty of choice in relation to when to become actively involved in the orchestration of identities and credentials.

10 Relation to Existing (Danish) Solutions

Implementation of the new security model does not require an abandonment of the current solutions. The new security model can be a natural further development of existing standards, architectures and solutions within the Danish public sector for user identity, single sign-on and access management.

The new security model is fundamentally a federated model where users are given access to services by presenting credentials (security tokens) issued by a third party. The primary difference is the new kind of credential, which allows the user not to be identified.

Another resemblance is that the user often has to be authenticated before a credential can be issued. In such case, the national Danish digital signature called NemID may be used in the same way as the solution is currently being used.

11 Summary

Due to the fact that the traditional security perimeter is challenged and that there is an increasing demand to enhanced privacy and to secure cloud computing it is necessary to develop a new way of designing security.

Therefore, NITA has published a paper discussing a new model for security that utilizes attribute-based credentials, transaction isolation and purpose specific keys. This model is able to support the concept of Privacy-by-Design in the design of IT systems.

This new security model introduces a move from an identification-oriented paradigm towards a validation-orientated paradigm. Hereby, data is coupled to virtual identities, which are subject to validation, instead of the users.

By implementing the new security model it will in many cases be possible to use cloud computing with less risk, even though sensitive data are involved. If the application and its data are compromised they will not be linkable to physical persons but only to virtual identities. Data will only have meaning for local transactions and can, therefore, not be connected to other data. Thereby the consequences of compromising data are confined to the local context.

Subsequently a number of practical cases have been described. The cases illustrate how the objectives for the new security model can be used when designing specific applications.

12 Further Work

The discussion paper on New Digital Security Models released by NITA in January 2011 has been well received and there has been a positive dialogue on the subject.

NITA is now searching for potential pilot projects where the new security model can be tested in practice.

Connect to the Cloud - New Challenges for Enterprise Single Sign-on and Identity Provisioning

Martin Raepple

SAP AG
Dietmar-Hopp-Allee 16
69190 Walldorf, Germany
martin.raepple@sap.com

Abstract

Integration between applications deployed on-premise and in the (Internet) Cloud becomes a strategic topic for many organisations using the new software delivery model in which software and its associated data are hosted outside the corporate firewall (also known as on-demand software or Software-as-a-Service, SaaS). In particular, this applies to integrating existing Security and Identity Management infrastructure to provide users seamless access to the new applications which requires account provisioning and Single Sign-on (SSO). While some SaaS vendors started by offering proprietary mechanisms, there is considerable momentum behind predominant standards and protocols like SAML, OAuth and OpenID. This paper provides an overview of the most relevant security and identity management standards that currently co-exist for on-premise and on-demand in this context, and discusses current approaches taken by the industry to integrate these partly overlapping technologies.

1 Identity Camps

Security and identity management standards have always been a fast evolving area. Standard bodies like the Organization for the Advancement of Structured Information (OASIS) or the Kantara Initiative (formerly known as the Liberty Alliance Project) are the place for the IT industry to formally specify these technologies which led to important standards such as the Security Assertion Markup Language (SAML), Web Services Security (WS-Security), or the Service Provisioning Markup Language (SPML). Focusing on Enterprise scenarios, these standards primarily enable secure integration of systems and applications in heterogeneous landscapes deployed on-premise. Many traditional IT vendors support these mature on-premise technologies in their security software packages or technology platforms.

With the rise of Cloud Computing and the accelerated proliferation of applications operated and hosted by external providers (Software-as-a-Service, SaaS), secure integration across systems and administrative domains has gained in importance. Although the technologies specified by the above mentioned standard bodies already cover a broad spectrum of security requirements, major SaaS providers have been actively working on developing a new set of security standards such as OAuth and OpenID that meet requirements unique to application characteristics in the Cloud, which includes support for web services based on a Representational State Transfer (REST) style architecture [Fiel00]. RESTful web service APIs expose URIs (e.g. `http://example.com/customers/4711`) to access the server-side resources using the HTTP protocol and define a CRUD[1]-like set of operations based on the HTTP verbs (e.g. POST, GET, PUT and DELETE). According to a current snapshot of protocols used by about 3300 public Cloud APIs listed in the web services directory of ProgrammableWeb.com (see figure 1), nearly three-quarters can be consumed by RESTful clients, and only 17% expose a SOAP-based interface.

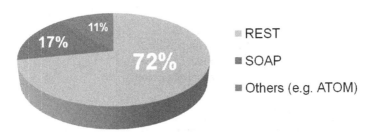

Fig. 1: Cloud APIs by Protocol / Style

Today, enterprises adopting SaaS to reduce the time to productive use of new applications, are facing a number of security and integration challenges. Given the large number of existing systems leveraging on-premise identity technologies, it seems unlikely that the new standards developed for Cloud applications will replace them any time soon. Thus, a key question for businesses is how to bridge the gap between these two "identity camps" to protect investments made in existing on-premise security infrastructures and to enable seamless access between on-premise and on-demand applications.

2 Integration Scenarios

Figure 2 illustrates a typical integration scenario for SaaS applications access in the Enterprise. The employee logs on to the central corporate authentication service with his username and password from a workstation located in the intranet (step 1). The authentication service confirms a successful login by issuing a "token" which can be used to logon to other applications on the intranet without re-entering the username and password again. Kerberos is a widely used technology for this sort of internal SSO mechanism with the Kerberos Ticket being the token issued from the Kerberos Ticket Granting Server. Other examples include short-lived X.509 certificates generated by an internal Certification Authority (CA) or digitally signed browser cookies issued by an intranet portal.

---

1 Create, Read, Update and Delete

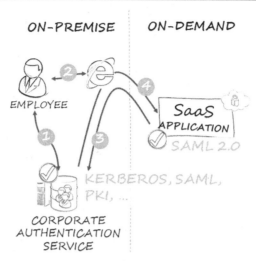

Fig. 2: Web Browser-based SSO to SaaS applications ("Front-channel SSO")

Many SaaS applications can be accessed over the Internet by using a Web Browser. When the employee launches the Web Browser on his local workstation (step 2), the issued SSO token from the previous step should be used to authenticate the user. This usually requires a transformation of the internal SSO token into a format that is transferable across administrative and network domains and consumable by the external SaaS application.

The SAML protocol has been developed to solve this problem of cross-domain Web Browser SSO. The SaaS application acts as the SAML service provider (SP) in this scenario. When the employee attempts to access the SaaS application with the Web Browser, it sends a HTTP redirect in step 3 to the employee's Web Browser, including a generated SAML Authentication Request message that should be submitted to the corporate SAML Identity Provider (IdP). A corporate authentication service or identity management system usually acts as the SAML IdP which authenticates the employee based on the previously issued SSO token. For Kerberos, the Simple and Protected GSSAPI Negotiation Mechanism (SPNEGO) is used by the Web Browser to seamlessly authenticate the employee with the IdP. After successful logon and decoding the SAML Authentication Request, the IdP generates a SAML Response which contains the cross-domain token, a SAML Assertion. A SAML Assertion contains an XML-defined statement that is digitally signed by the IdP and asserts to the SaaS application that the employee successfully authenticated with the IdP at a particular time using a particular method of authentication. The SAML Response is sent to the employee's Web Browser which again forwards it to the SaaS application. If the response is successfully verified, the employee is logged on at the SaaS application and the Web Browser is redirected to the initially requested URL. Since all communication between the SAML IdP and SP is transmitted via the Web Browser, this scenario is also referred to as "Front-channel SSO".

Although the SAML protocol is a well-established approach for Web Browser-based access to SaaS applications such as Google Apps [Googl11] or Salesforce.com [Sale11], SSO for RESTful APIs is out of scope of the supported use cases in the SAML specification [Saml05]. Figure 3 shows this type of integration scenario:

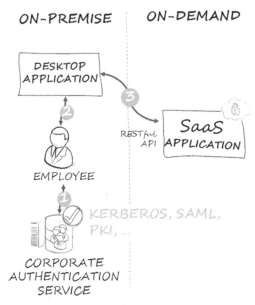

Fig. 3: API-based SSO to SaaS applications ("Back-channel SSO")

After successful logon at the corporate authentication service using the preferred mechanism for intranet SSO (step 1), the employee launches a desktop application (step 2). In this scenario, the employee does not access the Web user interface (UI) of the SaaS application. Instead, the desktop application calls the SaaS application's RESTful APIs on behalf of the user to send and retrieve data (step 3). To authenticate the API calls, the desktop application should avoid storing any secret cloud credentials of the user. It should ideally reuse the SSO token issued by the corporate authentication service to obtain a new token that can be used to make authorized API calls to the Cloud. Unlike the previous scenario, the messages are exchanged directly between the systems, which is also referred to as "Back-channel SSO".

For SOAP-based web services, the OASIS Web Services Security SAML Token Profile [WSSS06] defines a binding of a SAML Assertion to a SOAP message. No such standard currently exists for HTTP/RESTful services. However, OAuth and in particular the upcoming version 2.0 of the specification will address this issue as described in the following section.

3 OAuth to the rescue?

Many cloud applications, especially those managing social networks, offer services to integrate with other web sites to fetch and post social data about friends and activities. Sharing the secret credentials, typically username and password, with the cloud application to provide access to this private user data stored on the other web sites would be a bad idea.

Therefore, a group of SaaS providers started in 2006 to specify OAuth. OAuth is a RESTful protocol that allows granting access to private resources on one web site (the service provider) to another web site, desktop or mobile application (the consumer) without sharing any secret credentials of the user. OAuth basically replaces username and password with a token that is unique to the user, the consumer and the service provider. Although this sounds similar to protocols like SAML or Kerberos, OAuth is not designed for SSO. The typical flow of obtaining such a token for secure API authorization with OAuth 1.0 [Hamm10] is shown in figure 4:

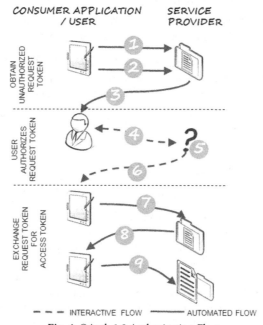

Fig. 4: OAuth 1.0 Authorization Flow

1. The consumer application must be first registered which allows the service provider to identify it based on a unique consumer key (id). As a result of this registration step, both sides also share the so-called consumer secret which is used to sign requests sent by the consumer application.

2. The consumer application requests an OAuth Request Token from the service provider.

3. If the signature of the request is verified successfully, the service provider grants a request token to the consumer application.

4. The consumer application directs the user to the service provider

5. The service provider presents an authorization page asking the user to give permission to the consumer application to access his data. This can include a request to approve or reject a set of fine-grained permissions specific to the respective consumer application. It is important to understand that OAuth does not specify how the service provider authenticates the user in this step.

6. Upon successful authentication and authorization, the service provider generates a verification code (OAuth Verifier) which is tied to the Request Token and presented to the user.

7. After entering the verification code, the consumer application will send a request for an OAuth Access Token to the service provider. This call contains the Request Token obtained in step 3 which has been authorized by the user in step 5 and must be signed with the consumer secret.

8. The service provider verifies that the Request Token has been authorized by the user and will return an OAuth Access Token providing access to protected resources accessible through the service provider's RESTful web service APIs. Along with the Access Token, the service provider returns an associated Token Secret which is used by the consumer application to prove ownership of the token.

9. The consumer application can now make authorized calls to the service provider's APIs using the OAuth Access Token and Token Secret instead of the user´s secret Cloud credentials.

Compared to SSO tokens like Kerberos Tickets or SAML Assertions, the OAuth Access Token is just an opaque string that represents an access permission granted to the consumer application and authorized by the user. By default, OAuth access tokens do not expire after a certain lifetime, nor do they provide any semantics to support advanced identity federation scenarios like a SAML 2.0 Assertion.

4 Combining OAuth and SAML

Integration with existing SSO technologies like SAML has been identified as an important requirement for the upcoming version 2.0 of OAuth, which is still work in progress [HaRH11] as of August 2010. In OAuth 2.0, the Request Token has been replaced by the Authorization Code and represents only one possible way to obtain an Access Token from the OAuth service provider. Other mechanisms representing the user's authorization to access his protected resources, called Authorization Grants in general, are either defined in the core specification itself, or in separate specification documents, called Profiles. Profile documents make use of an extension mechanism in OAuth 2 for additional Authorization Grant Types. As one of the first Authorization Grant profiles, the SAML 2.0 Bearer Assertion Profile [CaMo11] specifies how to bind a SAML Assertion to the HTTP request of the consumer for an OAuth Access Token. This profile document defines HTTP parameters for transporting the Assertion during interactions with the service provider token endpoint, which is conceptually similar to what the Web Services Security SAML Token Profile specifies for SOAP. An example request [CaMo11] for an Access Token using a SAML Assertion previously issued by a trusted IdP to the consumer application is shown in figure 5.

```
POST /token.oauth2 HTTP/1.1

Host: authz.example.net

Content-Type: application/x-www-form-urlencoded

grant_type=urn%3Aietf%3Aparams%3Aoauth%3Agrant-type%3Asaml2-bearer

assertion=PEFzc2VydGlvbiBJc[...omitted for brevity...]
```
Fig. 5: Example OAuth 2 Access Token Request using the SAML Bearer Assertion Profile

The process by which the consumer obtains the assertion prior to sending it with Access Token request to the service provider is out of scope for OAuth and the SAML Bearer Assertion Profile. One option for a rich desktop application acting as the OAuth consumer is to use the WS-Trust protocol [WSTr07] to request a SAML Bearer Assertion from a corporate Security Token Service (STS). Figure 6 illustrates this complete end-to-end SSO scenario based on the following prerequisites:

- The desktop application has been successfully registered as an OAuth consumer with the SaaS application's OAuth service provider (see step 1 in figure 4).
- The SaaS application has established a trust relationship with the corporate authentication service, i.e. it trusts SAML Assertions issued by the authentication service SAML 2.0 STS. This typically requires an out-of-band exchange of the X.509 certificate used by the STS to sign the Assertions.

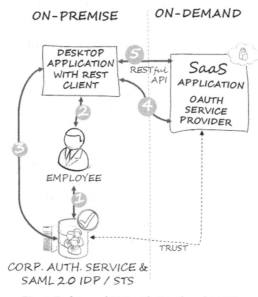

Fig. 6: End-to-end SSO with OAuth and SAML

1. The employee logs on with the workstation to the corporate authentication service and obtains a corporate SSO Token (e.g. Kerberos Ticket).

2. The employee launches a desktop application that integrates with the SaaS application in the Cloud by calling its RESTful APIs. These APIs require a valid OAuth Access Token.

3. To avoid any interactive user approval at the OAuth service provider (step 5 in figure 4) and provide a true end-to-end SSO user experience, the desktop application needs a valid SAML Assertion to request and authorize the Access Token. Therefore it sends a WS-Trust RequestSecurityToken (RST) message to the corporate authentication service's STS. This message is authenticated with the corporate SSO token obtained in step 1. The Request-SecurityTokenResponse (RSTR) message from the STS contains a SAML Assertion that asserts the employee's identity and successful authentication.

4. The desktop application requests an Access Token from the SaaS application's service provider token endpoint. This message contains the previously obtained SAML Assertion which represents the user's approval to authorize the request. If the SAML Assertion and request signature is verified successfully, the OAuth service provider will send a response with the OAuth Access Token and Token Secret values.

5. The desktop application is now able to make authorized API calls with the OAuth Access Token.

All of the steps above do not require any user interaction and provide a standards-based solution for true end-to-end SSO for on-premise applications making RESTful API calls to the Cloud. With the use of OAuth, the user is in full control of the desktop application's authorization when it accesses protected data on his behalf. Being able to manage permissions for this type of cross-domain access becomes even more important when the API calls are made in the opposite direction, i.e. when the SaaS application makes inbound calls to an on-premise backend system on behalf of externally authenticated users in the Cloud. Corporate security policies usually require restricted permissions for these calls which can be managed securely using OAuth.

However, the use of OAuth in this scenario comes at a certain administrative cost:
- The desktop application must be capable of securely storing the consumer secret and Access Token secret.
- The SaaS application's OAuth service provider must manage a potentially large number of Access Tokens depending on the number of employees and desktop application deployments in the enterprise.

One method to mitigate this overhead is to replace the OAuth Access Token with a regular, short-lived session identifier (ID) that can only be used for making API calls and that expires after a preset time of inactivity or when the employee terminates the desktop application. To obtain a new API session silently without any user interaction, the desktop application should be able to bind the SAML Assertions to the HTTP message in the same way it is defined for the Access Token request by the SAML Bearer Assertion Profile. However, this SAML binding is currently only defined within the scope of OAuth 2, and not as a generally valid binding for HTTP/REST. Section 6 outlines the approach taken by SAP's on-demand solution for collaborative decision-making, SAP StreamWork, to obtain a REST API session from a SAML Assertion.

5 Federated Identity Provisioning in the Cloud

All integration scenarios discussed so far require the existence of a user account for the employee in the Cloud for the employee. To reduce the administration effort for managing the lifecycle of digital identities in a distributed system landscape, organisations are deploying Identity Management (IdM) systems to automate the processes of creating (provisioning), changing and revoking (de-provisioning) user accounts and to provide a central view of the identities across all systems, directories and applications in the enterprise.

Integration of SaaS applications requires identity provisioning across administrative domains, which is referred to as federated identity provisioning. Although this is not a new discipline, SaaS applications still lack a standards-based provisioning interface. Even within the on-premise landscape, the adoption of the only existing standard in this space, the OASIS Service Provisioning Markup Language (SPML) [Spml06], is still very low. Although most IdM system vendors provide an SPML connector for their on-premise suites, most applications and platforms in the enterprise do not expose the corresponding interface to process this standard provisioning protocol. For many SaaS vendors, SPML is not an option due to its complexity and tight coupling with SOAP.

Efforts to define a new identity provisioning standard for the Cloud based on a RESTful interface are carried out again in parallel by the two identity camps: The SaaS vendors around Google and Ping Identity are working on a specification for a "Simple Cloud Identity Management (SCIM)"

[DrMA11] protocol, while the members of the OASIS Provisioning Services Technical Committee have proposed a simplified RESTful binding for SPML under the working title "RESTPML" [Rest11]. It remains to be seen which one will convince both the SaaS application providers as well as the IdM system vendors. As long as there is no broad consensus, enterprises have to deal with different and proprietary service interfaces from each SaaS provider.

6 SAP StreamWork REST APIs for SAML-based SSO

SAP StreamWork (http://www.streamwork.com) is a collaborative decision-making solution which is being provided as a SaaS offering. The collaboration space in SAP StreamWork, an "Activity", is shared by a group of people which is called participants. Any participant can extend an activity with business tools that use proven methodologies to solve problems. This might include a pro/con table, polls for collecting feedback, SWOT analyses, cost/benefit analyses, etc.

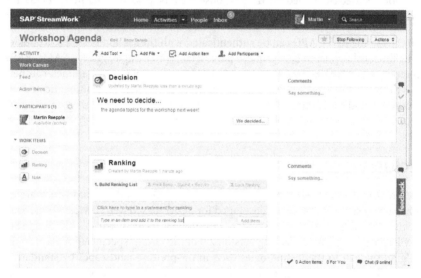

Fig. 7: SAP StreamWork Web Browser interface

SAP StreamWork supports standards-based SSO with SAML 2.0 for Web Browser-based access. It also exposes a rich set of RESTful APIs that are used for embedding SAP StreamWork into other on-demand or on-premise applications. SAP StreamWork implements an OAuth service provider based on version 1.0a [Hamm10] of the specification. Authorization of all API calls requires the use of a valid OAuth Access Token or REST API session. Both can be obtained from a SAML Assertion to support integration with corporate security infrastructure as described below.

6.1 OAuth Access Token from a SAML Assertion

SAP StreamWork enhances OAuth 1.0a with a proprietary extension to request an OAuth Access Token on a user's behalf by supplying a SAML Assertion. This binding is similar in semantics (but not form since OAuth 2.0 is not backwards compatible with OAuth 1.0a) to the SAML Bearer Assertion Profile in the proposed OAuth 2.0 specification. Along with the regular parameters for the

OAuth Access Token request, an additional parameter `SAMLResponse` can be passed to the OAuth service provider token endpoint at `https://streamwork.com/oauth/access_token`. The value of this parameter is the base64-encoded SAML Response as defined in the SAML 2.0 specification [Saml05]. The resulting Access Token that the consumer application obtains can be used to make subsequent REST API calls, as with a regular OAuth Access Token.

6.2 REST API session from a SAML Assertion

A SAML REST API session is a session created by a POST request to `https://streamwork.com/v1/session` from a SAML assertion, and can be considered as a binding of SAML to HTTP/REST. For a new REST API session, the consumer application's request must set the standard HTTP Authorization header (which is also used by other HTTP authentication schemes) to `Authorization: SAML:2.0:Assertion`. Similar to the OAuth Access Token request from a SAML Assertion, a base64-encoded SAML Response must be passed either in the POST body or the Authorization header of the request.

Subsequent calls to the REST APIs can be authenticated with the session passed as a cookie, or, if supported by the local application, as a query parameter. For example, given a SAML REST API session value of `594e6630bcb9171f9488d83901f01b7`, a sample query parameter authenticated REST call to retrieve all StreamWork activities of the user who has been authenticated with the SAML Response would be `https://streamwork.com/v1/activities?_cstar_session =594e6630bcb9171f9488d83901f01b7`.

7 Conclusion

REST is the predominant architecture style for application APIs in the Cloud which are incompatible with existing security standards developed for SOAP-based web services. Thus, SaaS providers have developed their own set of standards to support security features like Single Sign-on and Identity Provisioning. The upcoming version 2.0 of the OAuth specification plays an integral role in bridging the gap to the technologies used in on-premise landscapes by standardizing a binding for SAML within the context of the protocol. However, Cloud standards still lack a generally valid SAML binding for HTTP/REST to support other tokens like session IDs as well. With SAP StreamWork, such a general binding is available by using a specific HTTP Authentication Scheme identifier and passing a SAML Response. For identity provisioning, the situation is similar: Adoption of the SPML standard among SaaS providers is very low, and two different solutions for a RESTful provisioning interface are currently proposed: SCIM by the SaaS camp and RESTPML by the enterprise camp.

References

[Fiel00]   Fielding, Roy Thomas: Architectural Styles and the Design of Network-based Software Architectures, http://www.ics.uci.edu/~fielding/pubs/dissertation/top.htm, 2000

[Googl11] Google: SAML Single Sign-On (SSO) Service for Google Apps, http://code.google.com/google-apps/domain/sso/saml_reference_implementation.html, 2011.

[Sale11]   Salesforce.com: Configuring SAML Settings for Single Sign-On, https://login.salesforce.com/help/doc/en/sso_saml.htm, 2011.

[Saml05]   Assertions and Protocols for the OASIS Security Assertion Markup Language (SAML) V2.0, http://docs.oasis-open.org/security/saml/v2.0/saml-core-2.0-os.pdf, OASIS Standard, March 15, 2005

[WSSS06]   Web Services Security: SAML Token Profile 1.1, http://docs.oasis-open.org/wss/v1.1/wss-v1.1-spec-os-SAMLTokenProfile.pdf, OASIS Standard, February 1, 2006

[Hamm10] Hammer-Lahav, E. (Ed.): The OAuth 1.0 Protocol, IETF RFC 5849, April 2010

[HaRH11]   Hammer-Lahav, E. (Ed.), Recordon, D., Hardt D.: The OAuth 2.0 Authorization Protocol draft-ietf-oauth-v2-20, July 25, 2011

[CaMo11]   Campbell B., Mortimore C.: SAML 2.0 Bearer Assertion Profiles for OAuth 2.0 draft-ietf-oauth-saml2-bearer-05, August 2011

[WSTr07]   WS-Trust 1.3, http://docs.oasis-open.org/ws-sx/ws-trust/200512/ws-trust-1.3-os.html, OASIS Standard, March 19, 2007

[Spml06]   OASIS Service Provisioning Markup Language (SPML) Version 2, http://www.oasis-open.org/committees/download.php/17708/pstc-spml-2.0-os.zip, OASIS Provisioning Services Technical Committee, April 1, 2006

[Rest11]   RESTPML: A RESTful binding for SPML, http://wiki.oasis-open.org/provision/restpml, OASIS Provisioning Services Technical Committee, 2011

[DrMA11] Drake T., Mortimore C., Ansari M.: SCIM Protocol, http://www.simplecloud.info/specs/draft-scim-rest-api-01.html, May 2011

From Trusted Cloud Infrastructures to Trustworthy Cloud Services

Michael Gröne · Norbert Schirmer

Sirrix AG security technologies
Im Stadtwald, Geb. D3.2, 66123 Saarbrücken, Germany
{m.groene | n.schirmer}@sirrix.com

Abstract

Trustworthy Cloud services may only be built upon a strong basis of a Trusted Cloud. Such trusted infrastructures are also needed to reach IT security compliance in enterprises. The cloud model of "Infrastructure as a Service" (IaaS), combined with the trusted components proposed in this paper and researched in actual EU and Germany-wide cloud computing projects is a big chance for higher security in enterprises, especially for SMEs.

We describe two current projects that reflect these topics and the associated security work packages to develop mechanisms and technologies for future-oriented isolation of security domains and information flow control. These are Trustworthy Clouds (TClouds) at EU level and Emergent in Germany as part of the Software-Cluster project. The overall solution resulting from research and development done in both projects is one that establishes security guarantees on the data stored by enterprise platforms on infrastructure clouds and cloud services without affecting the enterprise workflows. An innovative use case in the home healthcare sector demonstrates how future cloud infrastructures and services may look like.

1 Cloud Computing, Security and Trust

Over the past years there has been much written and told about Cloud Computing, a applicable definition was given by NIST in 2011 [DrMe11]. Cloud services promise the needs-based distribution of IT infrastructures, platforms and services through standardized interfaces on the web. A pay-per-use model is given and the resources scale to the needs of their users, both to save IT costs. Fixed investments for an in-house IT are replaced by variable costs, a rigid in-house IT infrastructure gives way to flexible and dynamic services. Even if these characteristics fit perfectly into today's fast moving and flexible business processes, there are a number of problems that hinder wide adoption of public Cloud Computing in enterprise environments, in particular that are IT security concerns.

On the other side requirements for cost savings and flexibility, especially in small and medium-sized enterprises (SMEs), are the factors driving forward the overall use of public cloud services. From an IT security perspective the main requirement is to reach at least the same security level as it should be in a local infrastructure combined with new security requirements resulting from the new risks of outsourcing the infrastructure to cloud providers.

N. Pohlmann, H. Reimer, W. Schneider (Editors): Securing Electronic Business Processes, Vieweg (2011), 64-76

1.1 Cloud as a Chance for Higher Security in SMEs

Our thesis is that Cloud Computing is a distinctive chance for improving IT security in SMEs. When looking at today's SMEs with 200-1,000 employees, IT security is in fact an infrastructure topic, not a business driven one. For this reason, compliance is nearly absent. In today's IT infrastructures there are strong needs for information flow control rather than traditional access control policies. Current examples of hacking attacks on the NATO or the German federal police and reports of massive attacks worldwide such as "Operation Shady RAT" [Alpe11] show that. If infrastructure security is part of the cloud service an SME definitely may reach higher security and reach compliance with existing enterprise security policies. Moreover, this helps SME with collaboration with partners, e.g. when working together on confidential data.

A significant increase of IT security compliance, driven by Cloud Computing, is foreseeable, especially in SMEs. There are projects which contribute to reach that goal.

1.2 New technology; new risks

Privacy and security concerns pose a significant risk towards the new technology used for Cloud Computing. The attacker model of public cloud computing has significantly changed compared to the one in an enterprise domain (usually protected by firewalls, gateways, etc.). Cloud administrators may access customer data; everyone may access services available to the public Internet. Therefore, confidential information must be protected against cloud insiders as well as other customers. Simple authentication mechanisms of cloud users only by username and password are too weak to protect against brute force attacks, which could be issued by literally anybody, and attacks as mentioned above, such as stealing of password-databases.

One essential type of service supported by public clouds is "Infrastructure as a Service" (IaaS), which allows providing virtual infrastructures, such as virtual machines, network, or storage. However, holistic security policies and the enforcement of those policies on these resources are often unclear. In the "Software as a Service" (SaaS) model of cloud computing, due to the functionality and characteristics of the applications used, data is processed in plain text (regardless if it is stored encrypted or not). Without further means cloud service providers or their subcontractors may easily use customer information for their own purposes. Security guarantees expected by business-critical and privacy-sensitive applications and infrastructures are often missing, leaving IT security experts and lawyers to advice that confidential information or critical data should not be stored on a public cloud. In particular, initially the users have to gain trust in an equally secure and legally compliant processing of sensitive user data by the cloud vendors.

Several security-related reports such as ENISA's „Cloud Computing - Benefits, risks and recommendations for information security" [CaHo09] were published to address those concerns.

At the same time Cloud Computing services offer tremendous opportunities for progress in IT security towards trustworthy IT and compliance. Now, Cloud Computing is reality and first experiences from the currently largest EU and Germany-wide Cloud Computing projects with major activities focussing on security and trust are introduced in this paper.

1.3 The Projects TClouds and Emergent

The project "Trustworthy Clouds (TClouds) - Privacy and Resilience for Internet-scale Critical Infrastructure" [TClo11] started in October 2010 and has a running time of over three years. It is funded by the European Commission. With 7.5 million euros in funding, TClouds is targeting the development of a secure, highly reliable and privacy-compliant cloud infrastructure. The well-balanced Consortium consists of 14 partners from seven different countries, including IBM, Philips, EDP and Sirrix AG.

Launched in July 2010, "Emergent", a sub-project of the "Software-Cluster" [Soft11], is funded by the German Federal Ministry of Education and Research, with 39 companies, including SAP, Software AG, Sirrix AG, John Deere, academic institutions and other actors in a region, a running time of over five years and up to 40 million euros in funding. The participants are targeting research and development of fundamentals for emergent software to build up future business software by using trustworthy cloud services and secure information flows between federated domains.

We share our experiences in trustworthy Cloud Computing and innovative research results out of both projects focused on our topics and the components we are involved in as part of the projects security work packages. Below we
- illustrate an example cloud scenario and identify the requirements of Trusted Cloud Computing,
- show integration of internal IT infrastructures into a trusted cloud infrastructure and our topics in the projects,
- present an example use case out of the TClouds project,
- give an outlook onto future work and
- a conclusion which completes our paper.

2 Cloud Scenario, Requirements and Mechanisms

The common Cloud Computing scenario means outsourcing of IT infrastructures, such as servers and storage. Those systems are running in datacenters off-premise. Due to outsourcing the risk of a malicious insider at the cloud provider, e.g. a cloud admin, is a core threat to be tackled. In Cloud Computing the basic model is IaaS, which involves virtual infrastructures that are owned by cloud providers. Virtual infrastructures consist of virtual machines (VMs), virtual networks and virtual storage. Users of the IaaS cloud type could benefit in the way of scalability, availability and resilience, increased connectivity and pervasive reachability and cost reduction. Customers require isolation from other customers, which may be competitors. They need strict isolation of servers and data. This is traditionally ensured by physical isolation of virtual infrastructures. Datacenter providers, such as IBM, HP and other providers encapsulate every virtual infrastructure on physical isolated server clusters, storage and network infrastructures (cf. **Fig. 1**).

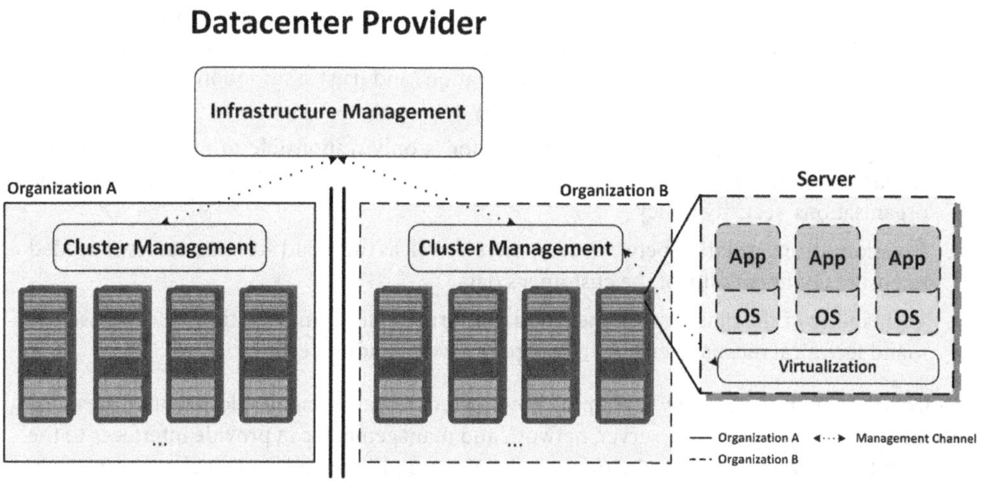

Datacenter Provider

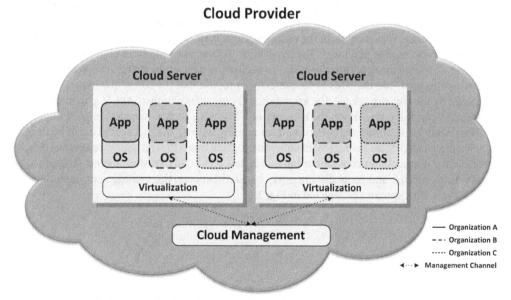

Fig. 1: Physically isolated virtual environments in a datacenter

Today, such usage of datacenters is also referred to as private Cloud Computing. Since resources are dedicated to customers and cannot be transparently scaled on users' demands private Cloud Computing is not as far as effective and scalable as public Cloud Computing is. As a matter of fact physical isolated virtual infrastructures are often too expensive for SME customers.

Public cloud IaaS is used as a more efficient and therefore much cheaper solution to fulfil customer needs for outsourcing of IT infrastructures. Here all customers share the same resources.

Fig. 2: Classical public cloud provider – Infrastructure as a Service (IaaS)

This scenario and its challenges result in an increasing need to devise effective approaches taking advantage of cloud infrastructures to reach effectiveness and scalability of a public cloud without compromising security requirements (especially isolation) and trust assumptions like in a private cloud. The central security requirements for security are:

1. Segregation of duties: the Cloud administrator is only responsible to manage the cloud resources whereas the organization administrator (of the customer) is responsible for the organisations' security policy

2. Isolation: strong isolation between customers as well as the cloud administrators is needed to ensure confidentiality of the customer's data.

3. Verifiability of the platform: as the cloud platform is off-premise of the customer we demand technical means to ensure its integrity beyond audits, certification or SLAs.

We address those requirements by explaining how current research and development on a trusted infrastructure solution, including server, network and management, can provide interfaces to the cloud, such that data processed and stored on the cloud and flowing between cloud services in different security domains is seamlessly encrypted as it leaves a security domain defined by the enterprise.

We start by building the foundation of a Trusted Cloud right into the servers by employing a trusted hardware anchor which is capable of integrity checking and remote attestation. We build on it as a piece of hardware which measures the other hardware and software of the server during booting to ensure the integrity of the server. Moreover, via remote attestation the hardware anchor can be used to verify the integrity of the server towards a remote party (the customer or a management service).

The core piece of software the hardware anchor has to check is the security kernel [HASK08] and the hypervisor as a part of it. The security kernel is used to enforce our isolation requirements. It is responsible to encrypt the data of the customers as it is stored. During computation the data in the VMs is processed in plain text. The hypervisor isolates the VMs from each other but can itself access all the memory within the VMs. To secure the hypervisor being abused by a cloud administrator to peek into the VMs of customers we propose that the API of the hypervisor has to be tamed by the security kernel. The kernel should only offer a limited API (e.g. to start, stop and migrate VMs) but not to dump the memory of VMs. With such a management API in place there is no need for an almighty root account for administrators. The management can be done remotely via a trusted cloud management component using this API. The hardware anchor of the servers and the management component can be employed to build a trusted channel (encrypted, mutually authenticated and mutually integrity checked) between the management component and the servers. This scenario is depicted in **Fig. 3**.

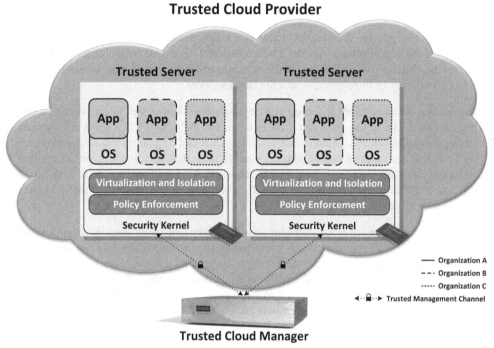

Fig. 3: Example of a Trusted Cloud Provider

As the hardware anchor Trusted Computing technology as proposed by the Trusted Computing Group [TCG11] could be used, e.g., the Trusted Platform Module (TPM) [TPM11].

3 Integration of Internal IT Infrastructure

Once such a trusted cloud infrastructure is available, one can go one step forward and not only isolate different customers but also push isolation principles into the organizations of the customers. Within an organization, there are typically different departments, like human resources, accounting, development and customer relations. These have different security requirements on the data they process, reaching from personal data to company secrets. These security domains should be kept separate and information flows between them should be strictly controlled. This concept is known as Trusted Virtual Domains (TVDs) [GJP+05].

Trusted Virtual Domains build an isolated virtual infrastructure on shared resources and thus fit into the cloud computing paradigm. Among the strengths of TVDs is the transparent data protection and enforcement of information flow policies - platforms and users logically assigned to the same TVD can access distributed data storage, network services, and remote servers without executing any additional security protocols, while resources belonging to different TVDs are strictly separated. Those resources remain inaccessible for unauthorized participants.

Information flows between TVDs are only allowed if they confirm to the security policy of the organisation. TVDs are realized by the same means as described above for the trusted cloud infrastructure: TPMs as a hardware anchor and for remote attestation, a secure hypervisor and a security kernel to govern isolation and information flows between TVDs and a central management component to manage the security policies. The only difference is, that the management component for the organisation's internal TVDs should be controlled by the customer himself and not by the cloud provider. This management component acts as an interface between the organization's internal IT infrastructure and the cloud services.

All devices from mobile phones to laptop and desktop computers as well as on-premise serves which access the TVDs in the cloud also have to be part of the same TVD security mechanisms and management. Only then a coherent end-to-end security can be guaranteed. As mentioned in Section 1, current examples of hacker attacks [Alpe11] show that infecting and remote controlling end users' desktops is an important goal for attackers. So, being able to use full functional and still usable TVDs on a desktop-level is another building block in enabling SMEs to reach compliance with IT security policies.

Since resources always remain inaccessible for unauthorized participants, even data that is stored on mobile storage devices is automatically protected by encryption. Those data can only be decrypted within the same TVD the device has been assigned to. Hence, users cannot forget to employ encryption, and data on flash drive cannot be used outside the TVD. A Trusted Desktop solution as depicted in **Fig. 4** supporting a Trusted Cloud, centrally managed by a trusted management component should complete the whole picture of a continuous secure and trustworthy cloud infrastructure. This is a first step towards continuous trustworthy infrastructures and services.

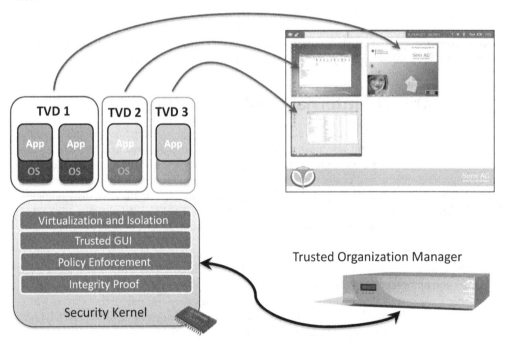

Fig. 4: Trusted Platforms at the Endpoints – TrustedDesktop

In **Fig. 5** such an integrated infrastructure is depicted. The Trusted Organization Manager is in charge to manage the internal infrastructure as well as to push the security policy to the Trusted Cloud Management Component which itself pushes the information to the Trusted Servers. The chain of trust is maintained by mutually ensuring the integrity of all trusted components via remote attestation and communicating via trusted channels. On the organisations side we exemplified the devices by a Trusted Desktop. As desktop virtualization is already commonly used today (e.g. to simultaneous use Windows and Linux programs on the same desktop or even laptop), the same architecture as described for the Trusted Server can be used. As [FGSS11] shows this also extends to mobile devices.

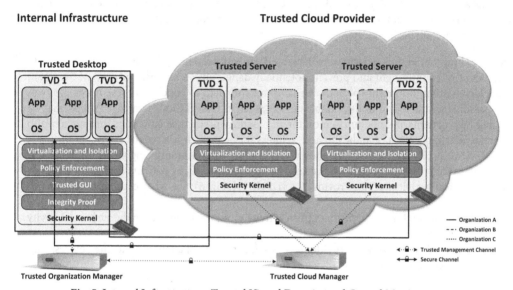

Fig. 5: Internal Infrastructure, Trusted Virtual Domains and Central Management

4 Example Project Use Case

In this section, a home healthcare use case motivate how future cloud services may look like and why innovative security, trust mechanisms and functionality of a Trusted Cloud as shown before are needed.

4.1 Home healthcare

Healthcare services are used in the cloud for several years now (e.g. several examples could be found in the U.S.) but many security and privacy related requirements such as privacy management, where the patient will be able to configure his privacy settings for deciding who can access his data, are not in place by now. Empowering patients, allowing a continuous home-monitoring and improving links between health professional and patients will have a significant impact in patient management.

In a home healthcare system IaaS is used rather than having dedicated IT infrastructure within the hospital. Most of the entities involved in such a system are relatively static. Flows of information do not change dynamically. The hospital can define interfaces accessible to different entities within its operations. For example, they can host a drug inventory system and configure it to be accessible to its pharmacy department or a patient registry system that is accessible to the registry staff. The cloud provider specifies well defined interfaces into the virtual infrastructure.

One example of a home healthcare application using such interfaces may be a drug therapies management service, used for drug prescription and anonymous drug delivery, improving compliance with doctors' recommendations. Other involved services could be a patient management portal and a personal diary. All those services need information flows between different organizational and security domains with different security and privacy related requirements. Therefore isolation mechanism and information flow control through policies and enforcement in a trusted security service are designed.

Here we show that in the scenario were depressed patients need home healthcare services, able to early identify, counter fight and prevent potentially dangerous situations. The current treatment model, consisting in monthly periodic visits, is not sufficient to cope with these needs. Innovative personal wearable and non-wearable devices, such as from TClouds partner Philips, may be used to help patients and doctors to monitor and identify predefined situations through a health management application of an health and wellness service which has special interfaces for those new devices. A physical activity monitoring service provides a monitoring system that collects and analyse data from those devices. Data can be inserted directly by patient's device, the patients, or by a Physical Activity Service Provider (cf. [DPNB11], Fig. 6). So, two use cases of this scenario may be:

- Patient uploads her activity data from activity monitoring devices to the Physical Activity Service Provider.
- Physical Activity Service Provider receives data from the patient monitoring devices, analyse it and provide relevant advice to the patient.

TVDs may be used here as the preferred isolation mechanism as described in Sections 2 and 3. This result in a TVD-based Trusted Cloud Infrastructure, servers and data are always isolated.

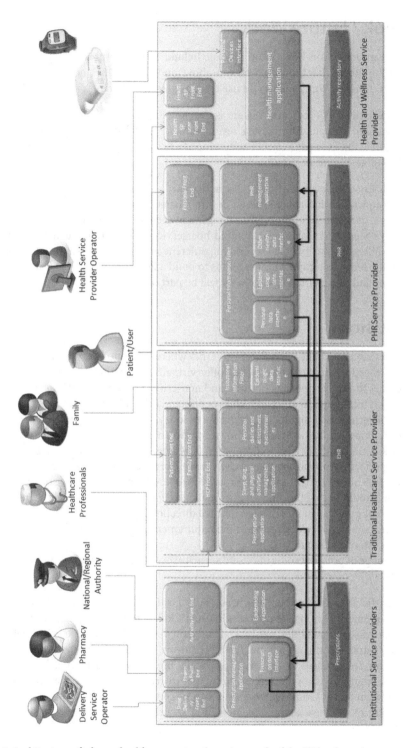

Fig. 6: Architecture of a home healthcare system (ongoing work of the TClouds project partners)

5 Outlook / Future Work

In this paper we focused on how to build trusted cloud infrastructures by employing trusted computing technologies. Both projects shown above and its activities consist of much more mechanisms, techniques, components and use cases as presented here.

In TClouds a Clouds-of-Clouds middleware is developed to further improve the resilience by replicating data and computation among several clouds provided by different vendors. With DepSky [BCQ+11] the TClouds Project has developed a first prototype for resilient storage building on the Cloud-of-Clouds paradigm.

In the TClouds use cases of home health care and Smart Lighting the stakeholders and services are statically known. The information flows do not change in a dynamic way. In the Emergent project however, the use case of an urban management scenario exemplifies a fast and dynamically changing system and aims at coherent ad hoc service composition. Such a scenario is in need of many different security policies covering different aspects of the compound service. One major goal of the security activity in Emergent is to build a Policy Language Toolkit. TVD-based security policies and information flow policies will be part of this.

6 Conclusion

Trusted Cloud Computing aims at a Future Internet where federations of standardized resilient and privacy-protecting infrastructure clouds offer virtualized computing, communication, and storage resources that allow hosting of critical and non-critical systems worldwide. Realizing this vision focuses on technological aspects, such as open standards and privacy frameworks. Security and privacy concerns pose a significant risk towards todays IT infrastructures and services, and also to Cloud Computing, but at the same time they offer tremendous opportunities for businesses to provide solutions and services in order to make Cloud Computing and thereby enterprises secure and to protect the privacy of users. For instance, Forrester Research expects cloud security to grow into a $1.5 billion market and to approach 5 % of the overall IT security spending by 2015 [Penn10]. While today encryption and identity management represent the largest segment of this market, particular growth can be expected in three directions:

- securing commercial clouds to meet the requirements of specific market segments
- highly customized secure private clouds
- a new range of providers offering cloud security services to add external security to public clouds.

Critical infrastructures of the future, such as Smart Grids, intelligent power distribution and management, or Smart Lighting are use cases Trusted Cloud Computing is aiming at. Consisting of a multitude of distributed nodes, networked based on the IP protocol, Smart Grids will benefit from existing, mature technology and proven mechanisms. Cloud Computing technology is seen as an enabler for Smart Grids or at least dramatically improves its usability and performance. Using Cloud Computing is a requirement to be met to reach new business models, flexibility and cost-savings in Smart Grids. However, such an undertaking should not be adopted blindly without thinking about consistently implemented IT security.

In the future, even more and more mobile and autonomous entities are accessing the cloud, so the concept of TVDs should be used on mobile user devices, such as smartphones and tablets as well as the cloud services. Then a coherent level of security can be guaranteed.

The overall solution resulting of research and development done in both projects introduced in this paper is one that establishes security guarantees on the data stored by enterprise platforms on infrastructure clouds and cloud services. This is designed and realized without affecting the enterprise workflows and builds up trust in public cloud services.

From our point of view the main goals for success of Cloud Computing related to IT security are:

1. Strong authentication (of each entity)
2. Secure virtualization (strong isolation)
3. Trusted platforms (reliable integrity verification)

Most of today's so called hacker attacks have shown that authentication by username and password is unsecure, especially in the Internet where public cloud services are within reach of everyone. So strong authentication, which means multi-factor, cryptographic authentication, is a requirement to be reached when using cloud computing. A trustworthy virtualization allows strong isolation of IT-systems, data and information which are belonging to different stakeholders/organizations. Trusted platforms allow companies a reliable integrity verification of cloud platforms. Trust in possibly false pretences of cloud providers or certificates gets a minor matter.

Acknowledgements

We thank all TClouds partners for substantial and very helpful input to our section, especially the authors of [DPNB11] use case for input and the picture of the home healthcare architecture. This research has been partially supported by the TClouds project (http://www.tclouds-project.eu) funded by the European Union's Seventh Framework Programme (FP7/2007-2013) under grant agreement number ICT-257243.

The work presented in this paper was partially performed in the context of the Software-Cluster project EMERGENT (www.software-cluster.org). It was partially funded by the German Federal Ministry of Education and Research (BMBF) under grant no. "01IC10S01". The authors assume responsibility for the content.

References

[Alpe11]   Alperovitch, Dmitri: Revealed: Operation Shady RAT, McAfee Labs, 2011. Available online at: http://www.mcafee.com/us/resources/white-papers/wp-operation-shady-rat.pdf

[BCQ+11]   Bessani, Alysson; Correia, Miguel; Quaresma, Bruno; André, Fernando; and Sousa, Paulo: DepSky: dependable and secure storage in a cloud-of-clouds. In Proceedings of the sixth conference on Computer systems (EuroSys '11). ACM, New York, NY, USA, 2011, p. 31-46.

[CaHo09]   Catteddu, Daniele; Hogben, Giles: Cloud Computing - Benefits, risks and recommendations for information security, European Network and Information Security Agency (ENISA), 2009. Available online at: http://www.enisa.europa.eu/act/rm/files/deliverables/cloud-computing-risk-assessment/at_download/fullReport

[DPNB11] Deng, Mina; Petkovic, Milan; Nalin, Marco; Baroni, Ilaria (Philips Research Europe, The Neth-
          erlands; Scientific Institute Hospital San Raffaele, Italy), 2011 IEEE CLOUD international con-
          ference, 2011

[DrMe11] Grance, Timothy; Mell, Peter: The NIST Definition of Cloud Computing (Draft). U.S. Depart-
          ment of Commerce, 2011. Available online at: http://csrc.nist.gov/publications/drafts/800-145/
          Draft-SP-800-145_cloud-definition.pdf

[FGSS11] Feldmann, Florian; Gnaida, Utz; Stüble, Christian; Selhorst, Marcel: Towards A Trusted Mobile
          Desktop. Proceedings of the 3rd International Conference on Trust and Trustworthy Comput-
          ing (TRUST'10), 2010

[GJP+05] Griffin, John Linwood; Jaeger, Trent; Perez, Ronald; Sailer, Reiner; van Doorn, Leendert; and
          Caceres, Ramon: Trusted Virtual Domains: Toward secure distributed services. In Proceedings
          of the 1st IEEE Workshop on Hot Topics in System Dependability (Hot- Dep'05), June 2005.

[HASK08] Sirrix AG: High-Assurance Security Kernel Protection Profile (EAL5), according to the Com-
          mon Criteria v3.1 R2, 2007, certified by German Federal Office for Information Security (BSI),
          2008.

[Penn10] Penn, Jonathan: Security and the cloud: Looking at the opportunity beyond the obstacle, For-
          rester Research, October 2010.

[Soft11] „Software-Cluster", Software-Cluster Koordinierungsstelle, c/o CASED - TU Darmstadt, 2011,
          http://www.software-cluster.org

[TCG11]   "Trusted Computing Group", http://www.trustedcomputinggroup.org

[TClo11] Trustworthy Clouds (TClouds) - Privacy and Resilience for Internet-scale Critical Infrastruc-
          ture, coordinated by Technikon Forschungs- und Planungsgesellschaft mbH, 2011, http://
          tclouds-project.eu/

[TPM11]   Trusted Computing Group (TCG), TPM Main Specification, Version 1.2, Revision 116, March
          2011.

Awareness, Education, Privacy & Trustworthiness

Information Security Awareness Campaign "Sicher gewinnt!": A Joint Action of the German Federal Administration

Käthe Friedrich[1] · Lydia Tsintsifa[2]

[1]Federal Academy of Public Administration
at the Federal Ministry of the Interior
Willy-Brandt-Str. 1, 50321 Brühl, Germany
kaethe.friedrich@bakoev.bund.de

[2]Federal Ministry of the Interior
Alt-Moabit 101 D; 10559 Berlin, Germany
Lydia.Tsintsifa@bmi.bund.de

Abstract

Information security is decided every day in every workplace. The human factor can constitute the weakest link in an information security framework. Improvement of the technical security measures shifts humans more and more into the target of attackers in order to compromise the information assets of an organization. High personal awareness of information security risks and well-trained security managers therefore constitute the first line of information security defence. To achieve this aim, a significant change in user perception and the establishment of an organizational information security awareness culture are necessary. This includes the users' comprehension and application of information security measures in an effortless and intuitional way.

This article provides an overview of our experience in conceiving and implementing an effective Awareness Security Campaign for a very heterogeneous and decentralized, large organization, as is the federal administration.

1 Introduction

The rapid pace of changes in information technology and the increasing dependence on it have made information security requirements within the federal administration increase continuously in the recent years. A variety of threats and security problems can be avoided by the use of technical defence systems. However, this is not sufficient to prevent information security incidents.

The human risk source is now considered to be at the forefront of information security risks [KES]. Moreover, the responsibility of the individual grows with increasing information security demands.

1.1 Framework conditions for information security awareness in the federal administration

In 2007 the federal administration adopted a unified information security strategy to implement the objectives of the "National Plan for Information Infrastructure Protection in Germany" in the area of Information and Communication Technologies [BMI1]. This included creating an institutional structure for information security for the entire federal domain. Thus, information security officers were appointed in each federal public agency. Furthermore, a unified information security management system, based on the application of the BSI Standards for information security [BSI1] and the IT-Grundschutz Catalogues [BSI2], has been made mandatory for the federal administration.

To meet the recommendations, all federal authorities had to implement appropriate information security awareness and training measures. These recommendations are also put to the forefront by the new Federal Cyber Security Strategy for Germany, published in February 2011 [BMI2].

The need for a concerted awareness campaign of the federal administration has been identified as a priority action within the framework of the joint information security strategy. Budget autonomy and distributed responsibility for information systems, high diversity of security requirements and a very large variety of tasks posed a challenge, though. To handle it efficiently, a comprehensive awareness campaign that builds on the common circumstances and conditions of the federal administration, has an organization branding and yet leaves room for adjustments to individual requirements was needed.

In early 2009 the "Act to Safeguard Employment and Stability in Germany" made it possible to set up a package of measures to improve IT and information security, the "IT Investment Programme", as part of the Recovery Plan mandated by the Federal Government. This provided the opportunity for the federal agencies to get access to a common budget for different purposes. As the improvement of information security was a main focus of the programme, the financing of a joint awareness campaign was approved, with a funding of € 3 million.

1.2 The Federal Academy of Public Administration

The planning and implementation of the awareness campaign "Sicher gewinnt!" ("security wins") is carried out by the Federal Academy of Public Administration (Federal Academy, "BAköV") in cooperation with the Federal Office for Information Security (BSI).

The Federal Academy was founded in 1969 as a central training body of the Federal Government. Working closely with the federal administration, industry and academia, the Federal Academy is responsible for providing practice-oriented advanced training for federal administrative staff and for advising agencies in personnel development and training matters.

For nine years, the Federal Academy has been offering IT training. Since 2006 also the training series "Information security officer in the public administration" has been offered in cooperation with the BSI. This is structured in three levels and can be completed with a certificate degree, which is recognized and meets the quality requirements for IT security managers in the public administration. Information security officers of the federal administration are recommended to successfully complete an appropriate training programme before taking up their duties.

Federal IT-focused trainings

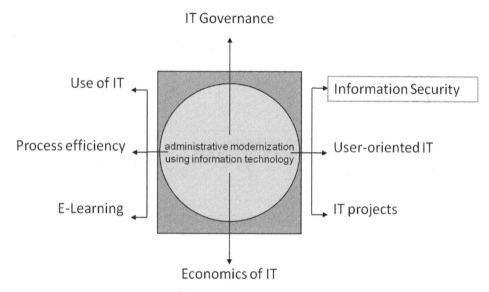

Fig. 1: The structure of the IT training offered by the Federal Academy.

The concept of training and certification of "IT security officer in the public administration" has been also adopted by the University of Applied Sciences North-West Switzerland Olten, the University of Applied Sciences Wildau, the Cooperative State University Baden-Württemberg and the University of Cooperative Education Gera.

Furthermore, the Federal Academy offers also information security trainings for IT administrators and awareness courses for IT users.

2 Compilation and commissioning of services

The main concern of the campaign "Sicher gewinnt!"was to give each agency the opportunity to plan and adapt its measures according to its needs and culture. It is clear that awareness-raising can be successful only if its messages reach the individuals and the learning processes work in an emotional and motivating way.

Although the planning time provided was very short, the Federal Academy managed to plan, compile and procure a well-concerted package of awareness modules, which could start within a few months. The following factors have contributed decisively

- The Federal Academy had already conceived a plan for the compilation of the campaign. The basic structure and content of the campaign as well as the concept of central modules had already been set up. As a result, a call for tender could be launched for certain parts immediately.

- A flexible model for the commissioning of services, the "three-partner model", which is often used in the federal administration, could be applied. The process is illustrated below:

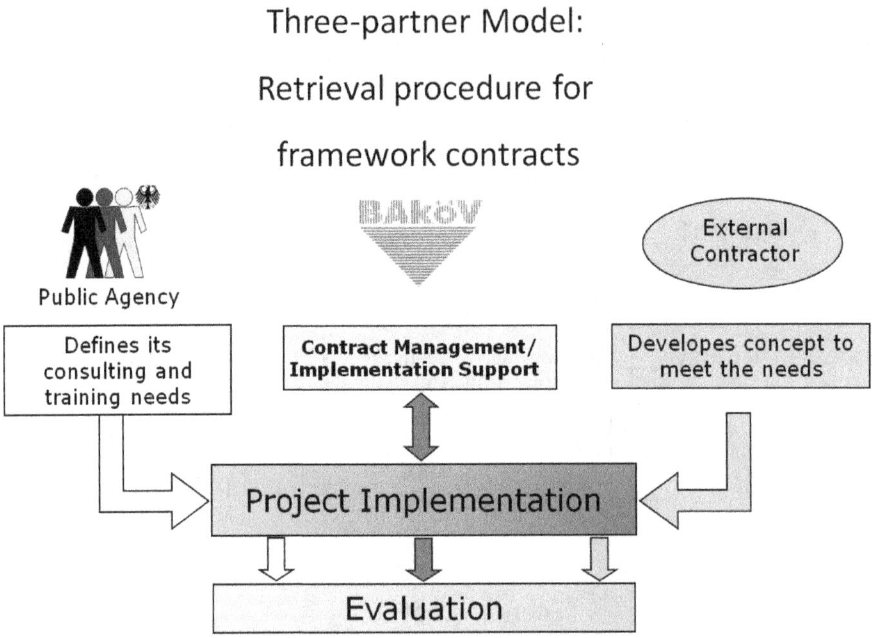

Three-partner Model:

Retrieval procedure for

framework contracts

Fig. 2: Processes within the "three-partner model".

The Federal Academy provides a framework contract for the implementation of services in the field of information security awareness. The control and coordination of these contracts is carried out by the Federal Academy. For the retrieval of the services, public agencies place individual orders directly at the Federal Academy.

The use of the "three-partner model" helps achieve a centralized and efficient supply as well as a target-oriented adaptation of services, since the agencies define their needs themselves.

The framework contracts include the following services:
- Support in individual preparation, planning and implementation of actions in the agencies. This includes events for specific target groups, such as managers or IT professionals, as well as the design of flyers and posters or the evaluation of awareness measures.
- Seminars on "Information Security at Work", adapted to the needs of the respective agency.
- Creation of awareness modules (seminars, events etc.) and other material (documents, media).

3 Structure and contents of "Sicher gewinnt!"

To meet a wide range of the individual agencies' needs, the campaign has been conceived to include adaptable modules. These vary from planning tools, awareness and training modules and instruments, to communication material and interactive elements. All of them can be customized to the needs of an agency.

The initiative is structured as follows:

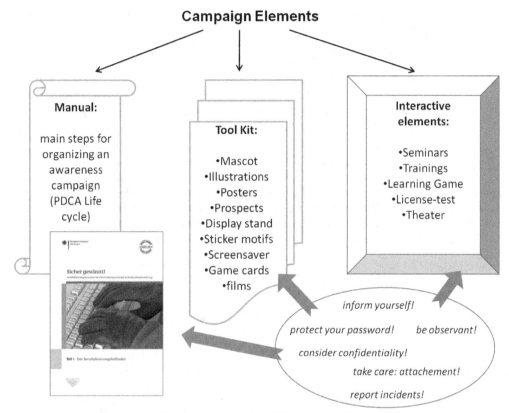

Fig. 3: Main elements of "Sicher gewinnt!".

- A guide [BAK2] provides IT security officers with the necessary information for participating in the awareness-raising initiative. It also explains the main steps for organizing and implementing awareness-raising measures. The guide is based on the BSI Standards for Information Security [BSI1] and on the ENISA publication "The new users' guide: How to raise information security awareness" [ENI1].
- A tool kit [BAK3] providing various methods, instruments and tools that can be used to plan, design and implement simple and effective awareness measures. It comprises basic instruments for requirements assessment, planning, communication and evaluation of the measures, basic material like pictures, flyers etc. as well as a list of references of existing tools and methods.
- Interactive elements and e-learning tools, consulting services and workshops on various subjects (topic-oriented courses, e.g. secure mobile communications, Internet threats as well as target-group-oriented modules (e.g. awareness-raising for managers, users, administrators), are also provided.

3.1 Tools for planning, implementation and evaluation

Furthermore, material assisting in the planning and implementation of the campaign "Sicher gewinnt!" is provided in the form of

- instructions for planning and implementation
- checklists for the organizational processes
- consulting support
- "The Campaign - Summary and outlook", an evaluation survey is currently being prepared. This module presents important outcomes and experiences as well as guidance for the further design of awareness activities.

3.2 Examples of modules

Some of the most successful elements of "Sicher gewinnt!" are described below:

- The educational game "cross through security": A mix of security quiz and train-to-train strategy game. It is based on 49 quiz cards and action figures. In two versions: as a live game in which players replace the characters, or as a board game.

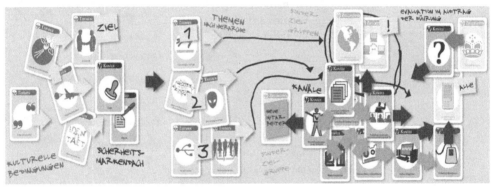

Fig. 4: Quiz cards "Cross through security".

- The world of learning: an online version to learn the secure handling of information and IT at work. The goal is to learn the basic IT security measures and apply them in practice.
- The "Federal Information Security Licence" (BISS): To get the BISS, an appropriate online test has to be passed. A high participation rate in the acquisition of the BISS demonstrates that the campaign is widely promoted in an agency.
- Events / Theatre / Movies: What is more convincing than the real world? Nothing! Live demonstrations effectively support the communication activities of the IT security officer.
- Password Theatre - a theatre improvisation: A way to introduce the topic of information security in an extraordinary way. These events also offer the opportunity to enrich special festivities with an information security awareness element. The show formats are characterized by spontaneous comedy, verbal wit and slapstick, peppered with numerous musical interludes. Everything is born improvised in front of the audience.

3.3 New modules planned

The campaign is being constantly adapted to the experiences and to current developments in information security. It is planned to revise modules concerning the following areas:

Positioning of the agencies in terms of information security:
- Current developments (trends) involving information security risks
- Responsibility for the management of information security (including legal issues) and the model effect of management in terms of awareness
- Information security and privacy in the agency
- Dealing with sensitive information of the agency
- Reaction and communication of incidents, preparation for emergencies

Information security aspects of information technologies
- Use of mobile storage media
- Use of mobile IT (phone, laptop, Tablet PC)
- Private and business use of Internet and e-mail
- Cloud computing and IT

4 Implementation

"Sicher gewinnt!" started in January 2010 with the provision of basic framework contracts for services to prepare and implement information security training and awareness-raising activities. The entire "kit" for the awareness campaign could be deployed within months.

4.1 Communication of "Sicher gewinnt!"

In order to reach a wider audience, target groups have been identified and multiple communication channels have been used. Involving the management has been an important component of communication. To achieve this, the Federal Government Commissioner for Information Technology initiated communication about the awareness campaign by sending letters to the management of the federal agencies. The Federal Academy informed security officers and human resources managers at an early stage about the campaign and the possibilities of commissioning. News, such as the availability of new modules, are being communicated regularly. Information material (flyers, posters, announcement texts for the intranet etc.) for the campaign communication within the agencies was also provided. The variety of communication channels and media used corresponds to those presented in [ENI1].

4.2 Deployment and range of the campaign

Due to the high response, the total amount available of € 3 million was allocated within the first year. So far, almost 100 agencies have logged over 1,600 man-days for consulting support on raising awareness and carrying out events with executives and IT professionals. By the end of the project in November 2011, over 40,000 staff are expected to have participated in these activities. In particular, all participants will have attended the series of seminars "Information Security at Work" on basic security skills of users.

Some 2,500 employees have successfully acquired the "Federal Information Security Licence" (BISS).

In addition to seminars and information sessions with live hacking, high-level management and state secretaries have been involved in discussions and events on information security awareness topics. Of particular interest are actions where the Minister and the executive management attended an information session on current information security threats including a live hacking demonstration. In the context of addressing high-level management, also the Forum of the Federal Academy for the presidents of the agencies was used to present a live hacking event, focused on mobile security. These events were particularly well received, and many agencies have also used them to address their employees. In 2010 a total of 5,000 staff participated in information sessions with hacking demonstrations.

Furthermore, the Federal Ministry of the Interior provided additional funds to enhance the part of the awareness campaign addressed to the executive management. 45 agencies have benefited from this measure.

5 Assessment and Outlook

"Sicher gewinnt!" is currently being implemented very successfully. The developed tools and modular design provide a central pool and ensure an efficient continuation of the awareness campaign. Tailored measures have proven very effective for the agencies. Even though the initial common budget is now exhausted, the modules can be easily booked from each agency according to its needs and budget. As they are being centrally managed by the Federal Academy, new modules, which are developed individually in the federal domain, can be added to the existing portfolio and made available for other federal agencies.

The feedback given to the campaign shows that users like the practical content of the modules and the tips for the private use of IT. In several cases the campaign directly led to the implementation of specific security measures, such as the use of privacy filters on laptops, as a result of a higher motivation and a better understanding of security risks.

Principal insights leading to an improvement of the campaign were:
- In order to ensure sustainability, high-level management has to be addressed with adequate information and involved in the implementation of measures.
- Opinion leaders also need to be involved to address and support the awareness issues to amplify the effect of the measures.
- Awareness modules for IT professionals have to highlight their special role within the information security process to be effective.
- Additional information to current topics meets high demand. Enhancements (e.g. on mobile computing and social engineering) are being prepared.

Within the scope of maintenance and improvement, the results to date and valuable lessons learned will be made available in the form of a booklet. It will also include information for the further design of awareness measures.

Central financing of the campaign has proved effective and led to resource-efficient design, planning and implementation. A further positive effect was the establishment of a common branding for the joint awareness campaign of the federal administration. Through the close monitoring by the Federal Academy, experience is being centrally collected, evaluated and integrated in the review and improvement process.

The campaign will be continued. Further central financing of the campaign would significantly contribute to consistently continuing and improving the awareness measures taken.

6 Conclusion

With the awareness campaign "Sicher gewinnt!" an important contribution to enhancing the information security of the federal administration has been provided, as part of the IT Investment Programme. The Federal Academy in cooperation with the BSI made available a well-concerted package of services and modules to raise awareness of information security. Nearly 100 agencies deployed the campaign and benefited from it. The Federal Academy and the BSI gained experience in the approach and implementation of joint information security awareness and training measures.

A central insight from the experiences made is that the organization of events and meetings with a participation of the high-level management constitutes a key step to deepen the consciousness of management for its essential responsibility for information security. In this context, events with live hacking demonstrations proved particularly successful.

Information sessions for all employees, especially live events, have generated clear and lasting impressions to raise awareness. Also the offer of a standard seminar on "Information security at work", adapted to the needs of the relevant agency, has found a high demand.

The use of a centralized service retrieval model has contributed considerably to the efficiency of the project. A large part of the federal agencies adapted the measures to their own circumstances and requirements. The flexible and modular structure of the campaign also facilitates its further continuation: it enables the participating agencies and the Federal Academy to contribute new modules and to use the gained experience to enrich the package.

References

[BMI1]   Nationaler Plan zum Schutz der Informationsinfrastrukturen (NPSI) http://www.cio.bund.de/SharedDocs/Publikationen/DE/IT-Sicherheit/npsi_download.html

[BMI2]   Cybersecurity http://www.cio.bund.de/DE/IT-Sicherheit/CSS/css_node.html

[BSI1]   BSI Standards 100-1, 100-2, 100-3, 100-4 https://www.bsi.bund.de/DE/Themen/ITGrundschutz/ITGrundschutzStandards/ITGrundschutzStandards_node.html

[BSI2]   IT-Grundschutz Catalogues https://www.bsi.bund.de/DE/Themen/weitereThemen/ITGrundschutzKataloge/itgrundschutzkataloge_node.html

[BSI3]   IT-Grundschutz Module B 1.13 „IT security awareness and training" https://www.bsi.bund.de/ContentBSI/grundschutz/kataloge/baust/b01/b01013.html

[ENI1]   ENISA publication "The new users' guide: How to raise information security awareness" http://www.enisa.europa.eu/act/ar/deliverables/2010/new-users-guide

[BAK1]   Webseite "Sicher gewinnt!" www.bakoev.bund.de/sicher-gewinnt, BAköV 2011

[BKA2]   Sicher gewinnt! Teil I Der Sensibilisierungsleitfaden, BAköV 2011

[BAK3]   Sicher gewinnt! Teil II Der Werkzeugkasten, BAköV 2011

[KES]   <kes>/Microsoft-Sicherheitsstudie 2010 http://www.kes.info/archiv/material/studie2010/index.html

Pebkac revisited – Psychological and Mental Obstacles in the Way of Effective Awareness Campaigns

Dr. Johannes Wiele

TÜV Rheinland i-sec GmbH
johannes@wiele.com

Abstract

When sometimes even elaborated information security awareness campaigns simply do not work, the reason may be that the security specialists who designed them did not pay attention to some very special human factors which make it difficult to change the behavior of certain target groups within an organization intentionally. This article discusses three of them: Memes, reactance and heuristics.

1 Introduction

From the IT technicians' point of view, end users in an organisation are strange components permanently endangering the smooth operation and the security of the information technology systems installed. Users are hard to configure. The way they operate and use technology drives IT personnel of the old school mad. This is how the pebkac acronym evolved: "Problem exists between keyboard and chair" for ages seemed to be the perfect answer to many IT problems which would not exist – well, if IT systems would work and could be left alone without those annoying people attempting to work with them in unpredictable ways.

1.1 The stupid user

"Pebkac" also means: "Users, if they are not IT specialists, in general are stupid". In Germany, two other acronyms flourish among IT nerds: The "Dummuser", which simply means "stupid user", and the "DAU", "Dümmster anzunehmender User". The latter one could be translated as "worst case stupid user", which in many IT departments was a very common expression to rate the intelligence of the average employee allowed to use a computer. Apparently, the benchmark used in these cases was a pure technological one. Natural human behaviour or business needs were not taken into account.

When information technology still was rocket science to the organizations which implemented it, the technicians' view of how human-computer interactions had to be organized was seldom challenged. Technicians easily managed to force managers and end users to accept IT related organizational and technical working conditions as well as security measures which were only optimized for technical perfection. Usability aspects or business needs had to stand back.

N. Pohlmann, H. Reimer, W. Schneider (Editors): Securing Electronic Business Processes, Vieweg (2011), 88-97

Today, to a certain extend IT has lost its exceptional position within organizations. To most managers, IT is just another asset and resource which has to function perfectly to support business processes. Information technology has to fulfil the needs and demands of the users. IT departments had to give up parts of their authority, and in many companies CIOs do not have direct access to the top management level any more.

But pebkac is still around, especially in the areas of information security and data protection. Today, compliance is one important motivation to rate human beings as the worst security problem and as the weakest link of the security chain. Compliance means to adhere to norms and standards, which for an organization implies complete control and documentation. In this context, again the human users and their unpredictable behavior form annoying factors which withstand the ideal of a perfectly manageable organisation.

1.2 Investment needs

Another reason to have a closer look at the pebcak aspects of information security again is much simpler. Most organizations today have deliberately invested in security technology and successfully run systems good enough to mitigate most of today's IT risks. But if managers look for the remaining vulnerabilities, most of them have to admit to themselves that at the same time they have neglected internal human factor measures like awareness and empowerment campaigns. In recent studies, awareness strategies and measures against social engineering are often to be found at the top of the to-do lists of IT security departments.

But the fact that today most managers and security specialist are fully aware of human factor risks does not automatically mean that the measures taken by them are as professional as the technical ones. To minimize pebkac problems, you have to understand the creature between keyboard and chair really well. Psychological, cultural and communicational aspects have to be taken into account. Unfortunately, science has just started to deal with these matters, and IT personnel being in place nowadays today in most cases has never learned how to get positive influence on human beings. Because of this situation, awareness campaigns sometimes fail miserably. The target groups do not react to them the way the security specialists expect it.

Taking all this into account, the interpretation of the pebkac phenomenon has to be changed: The problem between keyboard and chair does not exist because the creature to be found there is defective. It exists because most of today's CSOs and CIOs never have read the manual for human beings and do not listen well enough to those who did.

This article aims to add three chapters to the human factor manual of information security: Memes, reactance and heuristics. Each of these three phenomena is strong enough to partly or even completely undermine the effectiveness and success of awareness measures. The article will describe how exactly these factors often stand in the way of awareness-raising efforts, and it will make suggestions how to deal with them. The work is based on recent research and work in progress.

2 Memes

Memes are self-propagating ideas [Lync96], concepts, behaviours, styles or taboos that spread easily from person to person within a regional or organizational culture because they simply perfectly fit into it.

The meme idea itself is an application of the Darwinian algorithm of replication and survival of the fittest to cultural science. It implies that ideas can have a life of their own and spread through society a little bit like how the genes propagate themselves through the biological world. An individual does not actively accept or develop memes. An individual hosts them like viruses because he or she cannot withstand them. There is still an ongoing scientific discussion if memetics as a science have to be taken for earnest or if they are just an unqualified approach to darwinize culture [Aung00], but meanwhile memes have proved to be helpful to explain at least some cultural and intercultural phenomena which still are unsolved mysteries to the world of research.

Why, for example, did the song "Happy birthday to you" spread around the world without being stopped by any national or cultural border? It looks like in every culture of the world there simply was a strong need for such a song which makes it so easy to address a birthday child either as a group or as an individual with friendliness and without any disturbing associations.

Why do digital natives so easily embrace the idea of producing electrical power by solar cells or windmills and sharing it though a power grid, while at the same time members of the elder generation feel deeply uneasy about a world in which power supply does not rely on huge traditional power plants? It seems to be that younger people easily transfer the idea of networking, which they experience in the world wide web, to the power production and consumption business [Müll11]. The modern idea and practice of technology based networking as a risk-minimizing life assurance technique can be understood as a meme.

2.1 Pebkac as a dangerous meme

Did you notice that this very article is about a meme, too? The cultural ecosystem of the "Pebcak" idea is the intellectual world of old-fashioned IT engineers. Let's drill a little bit deeper into this environment.

At university, IT engineers learn that information technology is based on physics and mathematics. They understand that a perfect IT environment would always work and react in a predictable way. This is the first reason why technicians easily accept the rating of the human user as a disturbing factor to perfection. Furthermore, the typical education of an IT engineer at least in the past decades did not include any psychological or communicational skills. The manual of human behavior was not part of the IT and informatics curriculum. This started to change about five years ago, but most IT specialists working in organizations today do not have any interdisciplinary experiences including psychology or communication science.

In addition to that, informatics or IT studies are often deliberately taken up by individuals who do not like social science, psychology or philosophy because to them these disciplines look somehow woolly and imprecise. They like to work on technical environments which can be designed and configured to work perfectly. From their point of view, in their professional environments non-technical users are not only a threat to the technical ecosystem, but also to the problem solving model they prefer. This situation creates perfect conditions for the growth of the pebcak meme. For IT specialists, it is a meme which provides self-assurance and coherence of their view of the world. This is the bait which makes them accept and the hook [Brei02] which makes them propagate the meme without even thinking about it in detail. As memes form groups of related self-propagating ideas called "memeplexes" in the same individual or in groups of individuals, the pebcak idea produces conclusions like the one that it is impossible to educate non-technical users and that an invest into awareness campaigns is irrational.

Taking this into account, it is understandable why changing IT departments into service-oriented business units is still such a hard job today. You cannot stop a meme by order or by an one-hour-presentation. From the point of view of an awareness specialist, the pebkac meme – or DAU meme, if you are in Germany – is one of the biggest obstacles to overcome when trying to convince an organisation to invest into human factor information security measures. It also stands in the way of awareness campaigns which have been already started (Fig 1.), as it entices IT departments to completely refrain from human factor measures and to cast doubt on them.

2.2 Memes at management level

Before stepping into the countermeasures discussion, let us have a look at a few other memes in the way of successful awareness campaigns. Some of them are located at management level.

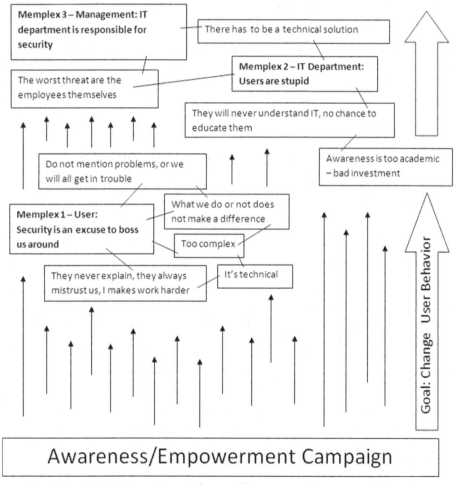

Fig. 1: Organizational memplexes in the way of Awareness or Empowerment Campaigns

One of them is the idea that about 80 percent of the threats to the information security of an organization come from inside and that they are intentional. When I first wrote about this idea several years ago, I did not know about memes and simply wondered why the 80-20-rule flourished so easily among management boards and at conferences without any significant statistical study confirming it [Wiel06]. A little bit later, when I discussed the phenomenon with scientists, I learned that human beings have a strong tendency to believe that natural and social phenomena can be described by dividing them into parts of 80 percent of one kind and 20 percent of the opposite kind.

I also found out that there is a simple reason why managers tend to believe that they cannot put trust into their employees: For them it is much easier to understand the potential motivation of an inside attacker than the motivation of a traditional hacker or an industrial spy. In most cases, managers know very well that they themselves from time to time produce disgruntled employees and how those individuals would probably react, because as members of the same organization managers can easily put themselves in the position of their own victims. In addition to that, managers learn to adhere to compliance requirements which say that only an organization completely under management control is a good one. Both aspects add to a tendency not to empower the staff to improve information security but to invest in surveillance.

Especially managers of the elder generation who started their career long before information technology became the most important asset of modern organizations also still tend to think that information technology and information security are pure technical phenomena. As a result, they hold their IT departments responsible for all information security and data protection issues. This concept perfectly fits to the technicians` view of the world and makes the life of human factor specialists even harder.

Fig 1. shows that the memes mentioned in this article may cause the propagation of strong counterparts within the culture of the average users. Employees who find themselves mistrusted and mainly estimated as a risk factor by their managers, and in addition to that find themselves being laughed at by IT personnel will easily develop the idea that it is best to step away from any information security task. If the staff shares the opinion that "they do not take us for earnest and they just want to control us", a behaviour change towards organizational commitment for information security is hard to achieve. In a culture corrupted by memes like that, reactance effects will probably ruin most information security measures which rely on the cooperation of the employees.

Often there are also memes in the way of an effective awareness campaign that are not at all related to IT. Some companies for example host an undiscovered but widely accepted self-distributing "keep your mouth shut and accept every order"-maxim. In Germany, in former times the Bosch corporation was well-known for a flourishing meme like this. It even formed a rhymed saying: "Ich schaff beim Bosch und halt die Gosch". For ages it was passed from employee to employee and from foreman to apprentice. As Bosch was one of the biggest employers of the region, the meme also was passed from parents to children.

At first sight, a meme like this may look like a beneficial one, as it forces individuals to perfectly follow policies. But it also makes it difficult to empower staff members to withstand industrial espionage, because to activate employees as sensors against social engineering and other espionage attack techniques, you have to create an atmosphere which motivates individuals to report suspicious incidents to security personnel [Wess11]. If "keeping ones mouth shut and wait for orders" is a widely accepted maxim within the staff, an awareness specialist commissioned to launch a campaign will find himself or herself in front of a huge challenge.

2.3 Memeplexes are strong

So awareness specialists have to know the memeplexes of an organization well before they start an awareness campaign. This is not easy to achieve, as common tools like employee surveys do not always reveal cultural aspects which are so deeply interwoven with the organizational practice that staff members even do not talk about these aspects any more. In-depth interviews are more promising tools. To find out about the memes flourishing in an organization, even asking family members of employees or former employees would be a good idea as those people have a unique outsider position aligned with unique insights.

If possible, awareness specialists should then design tailored measures which are so adequate to the company culture that they form new information security and data protection memes themselves. Finding opinion leaders to spread new ideas is an important prerequisite for that. Starting with a group of people within the organization who can more easily be infected with new ideas and to address them by an insider who cooperates is also a good idea [Konz11].

But can the power of existing memes be broken? This is not easy at all, as memes deeply root in organizational culture. One technique is to find them, show them up and to discuss them frankly as problems in the way of a certain project. It is also suggested to deliberately trivialize them, but this would have to be done in a very sensitive way. If certain memes really are a part of an organizational culture, perhaps too many employees will be annoyed by being laughed at their maxims or shared ideas.

3 Reactance

Reactance as a psychological phenomenon is defined as a strong emotional reaction in direct contradiction to measures, policies or regulations which reduce or eliminate specific behavioral freedoms. If an individual feels that he or she is pressured to behave only in a predefined way and to give up the freedom to choose alternatives, often he or she immediately adopts an attitude or behavior which is contrary to what was intended by those who issued the rule or policy which caused the irritation. Most information security specialists know the effect very well, and they complain about it as a factor which often undermines security or data protection optimization processes. Typically, policies like banning the use of USB devices or blocking access to certain internet services lead to reactance. Reactance will more likely occur if an organizational culture is affected by mistrust and excessive control or surveillance.

Reactance is a human constant you can count on. And whenever you reduce freedom, if there are more than just a few people subject to the change, one cannot avoid dealing with it.

3.1 Into a spiral of annoyance and mistrust

Astonishingly, when reactance arises, managers and IT security specialists tend to increase the pressure which caused the effect. Doing this, they enter a spiral of unwanted actions and reactions which sometimes ends up with a complete collapse of any fruitful cooperation between the IT security department and the staff of a company [Wiel11].

Unfortunately, reactance can not only be seen among individuals who really loose a freedom they were used to take advantage of. If, for example, the use of USB sticks is banned, often even individuals will react badly to that who never planned to use USB. The reason is that freedom also means to be able to do new things, and whenever a human being feels that his or her room for development decreases as a result of someone else's decisions, reactance will likely occur.

Sometimes, reactance shows its effects not as a direct reaction to the original cause. If for example in a company new security measures eliminate certain ways of doing work at home, employees may completely stop to do additional and perhaps unpaid work for their employer even if they still could do it by accepting a slightly more complicated method. They simply are annoyed because they feel patronized. In this case, a bad reaction to the IT security policy does not have a negative effect on information security itself, but it reduces productivity all over the company.

3.2 Explain, take for earnest and prefer regulation

The only way to avoid reactance is to take the human will to act freely for earnest and to address the problem early enough. If certain freedoms have to be reduced, it is the duty of those issuing the related policies to justify the means to those who have to follow them. If there really is a need for a security measure, there normally should be no problem to induce a consensus on the matter. To simply increase the pressure on employees to force them to accept annoying constraints is a typical technical approach. It does not work if applied to human beings.

Furthermore, it is extremely helpful to present alternatives to familiar procedures that have to be given up for security reasons. If, for example, the use of personal USB devices has to be banned, handing out secure devices registered by the company is a measure which demonstrates that the organization knows about and acknowledges the will of the employees to use USB devices for legitimate business purposes. If access to certain internet services at the workplace has to be blocked, a company may install terminals isolated from the internal network in the break room to provide less limited web access without exposing the organization's resources to risks arising from the internet.

Another approach is not to rely on bans but on regulation. If for example employees of a certain company tend to take files with them in the evening to continue work at home, this could be allowed without any restrictions as long as the information copied appears not to be classified as confidential or as long as the amount of data does not exceed a certain limit. At the next level, if an individual actually tries to copy confidential data or if the amount of data to be transferred looks suspicious, a data leakage prevention system may be programmed not to block the activity automatically, but to inform the employee about the related risks and to allow the procedure only if the individual accepts that the incident will be recorded and reported. Thus, legitimate actions will not be obstructed, errors will be prevented, loyal employees will not be annoyed –

and in addition to all these advantages, data leakage prevention configured to cooperate with the users works as an effective awareness raising tool.

4 Heuristics

Human heuristics are partly experience-based, partly hardwired short-cut techniques for problem solving. They are automatically used when analysing a problem is too difficult or impractical for an individual because there is either too much information or a lack of information in a certain situation. Heuristic decision making also jumps in whenever an individual finds himself or herself under pressure, especially under time pressure – a situation often to be found when non-experienced users are dealing with technical problems or when they get under the influence of social engineers who know very well how to force their victims into heuristics by issuing pressure.

It is important to accept that heuristics are based on millenniums of human experience and can never ever be switched off. Without them, especially in dangerous situations like an impending car accident individuals would not be able to react to the situation succesfully, as analyzing the case would take far too long to survive it.

Unfortunately, if applied to information technology and modern communication, some of the heuristic problem solving strategies proven again and again for world ages suddenly get dangerous:

- Sympathy. In the real world where you can take your time to decide whether you like a person or not, relying on sympathy was a good strategy to find allies you could easily work with to fend of enemies. Today, on the web and on the phone, an attacker can easily forge trustability and sympathy. Indirect communication hides most of the signs which normally allows individuals to rate their counterpart well.
- The tendency to adhere to authority. In former times, it was a life assurance to take up a subordinate role to a stronger or more experienced individual. Today, faking authority especially on the phone is as easy as forging sympathy, especially if time pressure can be added.
- Reciprocity. If someone gives you a present or does you a service, you immediately develop a strong desire to give something back. This is one of the bases of human society, but unfortunately this effect can also be used for manipulation. Social engineers for example may get influence on an IT user by solving IT problems they deliberately caused themselves before, and providing a manager with information about competitors in a bar or at the golf range makes him or her more willing to talk about internals himself or herself.
- Social proof. Individuals tend to adopt practices other individuals in a given environment seem to adhere to successfully. So if a social engineer claims to a newly hired employee that within an organisation it is common practice to share certain types of confidential information, the victim will probably tend to join in.
- Sure gain heuristics. If two goals seem to be in the way of each other, an individual usually prefers to follow the one which is more easily to achieve and which provides a sure gain. A predator will always prefer hunting a small but weak pray to entering an energy-sapping fight with a bigger but stronger animal which might be able to escape. Today, what will an employee do if he or she has the chance to close a big deal by just

sending out a contract file, if he or she at the same time discovers problems with the security software of his or her notebook? Wait for support and risk the deal or send the file out?

These are just a few examples of heuristics which make it difficult to change behavior by awareness raising campaigns. Even if the target group understands and internalizes the risks covered by a campaign, the individuals will lose their ability to use their newly gained knowledge and sensibility again as soon as in a certain situation they get under pressure and heuristic decision making takes over. Because of this, every attempt to force individuals to analyse dangerous situations cold-bloodedly under any circumstances is doomed to failure.

As there is no chance at all to take away heuristic decision making methodology from human brains, security specialists have to find ways to reduce the risks related to it. The only way to overcome the problem is to provide an easy way out of situations in which individuals detect that they get under pressure and in which they feel unable to analyse what is going on. This is one of the reasons why in production environments emergency buttons are installed.

A suitable equivalent to emergency buttons suitable for office IT environments is a helpdesk which listens to any security problem in a friendly manner and provides help and re-assurance, for example if an employee finds himself or herself under pressure of a person who claims to be the top manager of an overseas branch and urges him or her to immediately hand over confidential business data. To implement such a helpdesk can even help to mitigate industrial espionage risks if accompanied by very special organizational measures and targeted training efforts [Wess11].

5 Conclusion

The pebkac phenomenon has to be reinterpreted. It does not exist because users a stupid, it occurs whenever information security personnel does not understand human psychology and does know how to communicate with users. Today, as technical security has reached a high stage of development, it is time to address human security risks as professionally as the technical ones. To achieve this, communication between users, managers and IT security specialist has to be improved and psychologists and communication specialists have to be added to the information security teams.

In addition to that, awareness raising efforts have to pay more attention to cultural and mental obstacles which make it difficult to improve security by just imparting knowledge and the necessity of caution. To change human behavior effectively, close looks at interrelations between organisational cultures and human characteristics are a prerequisite.

References

The format of the title References is determined by the style „Literature".

Please use for your bibliography the style „Literaturetext":

[Aung00]   Aunger, Robert (ed): Darwinizing Culture. The Status of Memetics as a Science. Oxford University Press 2000.

[Brei02]   Breitenstein, Rolf: Memetik und Ökonomie. Wie die Meme Märkte und Organisationen bestimmen. LIT 2002. (http://www.sozialer-datenschutz.com/uploads/Memtheorie/Breitenstein_-_Memetik_und_%C3%96konomie_-_ISBN_3825862461.pdf)

[Lync96]   Lynch, Aaron: Thought Contagion. How Belief Spreads Through Society. Basic books 1996.

[Konz11]   Konz, Franziska: Changing and influencing organizational culture through memes. Unpublished Assignment, Karlshochschule International University, 2011.

[Müll11]   Müller, Johannes: Identification of memes forwarding Smart Energy. Unpublished Assignment, Karlshochschule International University, 2011.

[Wessl11]   Weßelmann, Bettina: Interne Spionageabwehr. In: kes 1/2011, p. 66-69 (http://www.kes.info/archiv/online/11-1-066.htm).

[Wiel06]   Wiele, Johannes: Zweifel am Innentäter-Primat. Der „innere Feind" ist ein Marketing-Tool. In: LANline 3/2006. (http://www.lanline.de/fachartikel/zweifel-am-innent%C3%A4ter-primat.html).

[Wiel11]   Wiele, Johannes: Vertrauensfragen. Unternehmenssicherheit und Führungspraxis. In: DuD 7/2011, p. 472-475.

I'd like to thank the members of my 2010 Evolutionary System course at the Karlshochschule International University, Karlsruhe – Jane Ding, Veronika Dinius, Lisa-Maria Häberle, Franziska Konz and Johannes Müller – as it was during this course when I learned how to apply memetics to the human factor topics of information security.

Building a Long Term Strategy for International Cooperation in Trustworthy ICT

James Clarke[1] · John C. Mallery[2]

[1]Waterford Institute of Technology, TSSG, Carriganore campus
Carriganore, Waterford, Ireland
jclarke@tssg.org

[2] Massachusetts Institute of Technology, Computer Science &
Artificial Intelligence Laboratory, Cambridge, MA, United States
jcma@csail.mit.edu

Abstract

This position paper contains a description of a recently held session organised by the FP7 Coordination Action BIC [1] project (Building International Cooperation in Trustworthy ICT) during the SysSec workshop on 6th July 2011 [2]. The goal of the BIC project is to bring together the global research community with the aim of determining mutually beneficial and urgent topics for international collaboration on the research and development of Trustworthy ICT. The session was entitled Building a long term international cooperation strategy in Trustworthy ICT: System Security and Cyber-Defence: Requirements for an international approach to technological challenges and open issues. The purpose of the session was to address the scope and priorities, and initial planning considerations for international collaboration on R&D towards trustworthy ICT and, as part of that, to explore international cooperation required within Frameworks for Data Exchange, as a specific enabler for collective defence and response to cyber attacks.

1 Introduction

During the past four years, there has been a steady, structured international consultation and resultant collaboration process that has built significantly across the international program management and researchers engaged within ICT Trust and Security areas. During 2008 – 2010, the Coordination Action INCO-TRUST project [3] established a framework for collaboration between EU program managers and research communities within Trustworthy ICT and the Countries USA, Japan, Australia, South Korea and Canada. In addition to a number of dedicated networking sessions and other events around the globe, there were two large scale workshops bringing together the programme management and research communities to prioritise the themes of ICT trust and security research that would benefit from international collaborations. Over its lifetime, this project has been highly successful in establishing consensus and co-operation between the research and industrial leaders and program management decision makers in these countries.

N. Pohlmann, H. Reimer, W. Schneider (Editors): Securing Electronic Business Processes, Vieweg (2011), 98-108

Within the recently started BIC Co-ordination Action (January 2011), the successful models already progressively developed by the INCO-Trust partners will be used to engender co-operation of EU researchers and program managers with their peers in emerging countries, namely Brazil, India and South Africa. The action will facilitate a technical and program level catalyst for engagement, collaboration and networking activities internationally. The BIC countries represent significant information economies through the scale and sophistication of their growing ICT sectors. Based on initial contacts, the emerging states clearly recognize the EU's value for ICT interactions and are actively committed to engagement.

In addition, the BIC project will provide continuity and bring together a truly global collaboration with the participation of the already established connections from the INCO-TRUST project. This will be accomplished by the establishment of an International Advisory Group (IAG) and an Annual Forum on Trustworthy ICT. The IAG will provide a dedicated forum to address trust & security issues of global relevance. If successful, Europe has a unique opportunity to establish a vision that reflects the European technical, societal and economic values for future global solutions.

2 Topics for International cooperation

The international research communities have worked together and identified several high impact, strategic and tactical research topics as a result of the common effort of project stakeholders and participants in the discussions and workshops over the four years. These reports can be found in the impacts section of the INCO-Trust web site [4]. Whenever considering research topics, the INCO-Trust consortium partners in their interactions with the involved participants from the USA, Canada, Japan, Australia, South Korea and, of course, the EU, have always placed in the forefront of any discussion the impact of proposed research topics.

INCO-Trust has always sought to maximize scientific results and societal impacts from a global perspective beyond the limits of the technical and research community, foreseeing repercussions on social agents and policy makers.

The second INCO-Trust workshop held in May 2010 [5] focussed on development of an International Cyber Data Exchange System, which is critical issue for international cooperation. Such defensive coordination could dramatically improve defensive understanding and coordination resulting in biasing the work factors for cyber attack and defence in favour of defenders. The international system could be used for data exchange related to cyber crime, attack patterns and best defence practices. Additionally, bringing together of the ICT trust and security communities around the requirements of a data exchange scenario can motivate relevant research and international collaboration opportunities. Rather than forward chaining from current cyber research alone (deduce scenario from security capabilities), this scenario driven approach enables backward chaining from data exchange requirements to enabling research and development. Research aimed at filling capability gaps benefits from focus and prioritization, which is more appropriate for selection of the relevant technical challenges and opportunities. This task-driven approach would also lead to a much better understanding of the data itself: what data makes sense to exchange, what are impacts, what are the collection issues, and what sequence of data domain for ramp up.

Additional benefits would be gained from an international system for data exchange. Some examples include:

- **Trends** on cyber statistics across the OECD could be available;
- **Anti-crime measures related to c**yber crime targets, vectors, methods, counter-measures could be available;
- **Early warnings** could be enhanced with integrated detection capabilities, signatures and anomaly recognition for analysis;
- **Closing defensive gaps** enabled with comparison of defensive coordination and best practices;
- **IP Protection** enabled with detection and prevention of industrial espionage;
- **Expertise integration** possible with a focus of collective expertise on important cyber data and analysis tasks;
- **International Collaboration and coordination** will reduce defensive gaps across the OECD and build crisis response capacity; and
- **Research and development coordination** will be enhanced through leveraging and combining task-relevant national expertise.

3 The BIC session during the SysSec workshop

Due to the nature of the SysSec event in which the BIC session was held and its participants expertises in systems and network security, the organising committee of the BIC session mainly focussed on an international strategy mainly for the topic of International Data exchange as described in section 2 above.

The exchange and sharing between responsible states and organisations of information and intelligence on cyber-attacks is seen as an essential component of collective cyber-defence against malicious action (as well as accidents and flaws). It is central to the ability to anticipate and respond: longer-term in the preparation of strategic, collective defensive measures, and short-term in recognising, isolating, and recovering from, attack – threatened or actual.

The two hour session was structured around the following topics related to the development of an International Data Exchange Architecture.

3.1 Motivation and Vision

The quantity and seriousness of cyber attacks have been clearly growing over the past six years and have surged over the last three months. Although there have been real improvements in enterprise cyber defences, threats have been outpacing them. Recent attacks have ranged from spear phishing email accounts to gain footholds into organizations, infiltration of international economic institutions (possibly with insider advantage), and other neo-mercantilist industrial espionage. Added to these are growing ideological hacktivism and a potential threat of cyber terrorism against critical services and infrastructures as terrorist continue to use the Internet to recruit and coordinate.

Cybersecurity is now receiving high priority for international collaboration. Some recent examples are highlighted here:

- EU–US INCO-Trust workshop of May 2010 [6],

- Munich Security Conference, 4-6ᵗʰ February, 2011 [7]
- US-UK Cyber Communiqué of 25th May 2011[8],
- Recent accession to the Budapest Convention on Cybercrime [9],
- 28th Annual International Workshop on Global Security on June 16, 2011 [10], and
- Vienna Security conference, 1ˢᵗ July 2011 [11].

A key message throughout all of these events is the acknowledgement that international cooperation is nascent and a more global approach is urgently needed because there is ultimately just one, single global information environment, consisting of the interdependent network of information technology infrastructures, including the Internet, telecommunications networks, computer systems, and embedded processors and controllers.

It is essential that we have the ability to conduct comprehensive intelligence collection and evaluation on any developing situation that threatens our cyberspace activity, followed by near-simultaneous processing, exploiting and disseminating of the information. This depends on collaboration, data exchange and sharing (and also knowledge sharing) between countries. We need comprehensive research towards international intelligence, surveillance, and reconnaissance (ISR) in the cyberspace domain. The anticipated benefits of an international data exchange system include:

- **Data exchange and sharing capabilities** for monitoring of trends with availability of retrodictive cyber statistics across the OECD; enhanced anti-crime counter-measures better identifying cyber crime targets, vectors, methods, and counter-measures; closing defensive gaps with better defensive coordination and best practices; and enhancement of IP protection with the detection and prevention of industrial espionage.
- **Expertise integration** to focus collective expertise on important cyber data and analysis tasks.
- **Collaboration and coordination** reducing defensive gaps across the OECD and better crisis response.
- **Research and development coordination** to leverage and combine national expertise.

Table 1 enumerates asymmetries within cyber attack and defense that today disproportionately favor the attacker. The attacker benefits from the initiative (A) and the large defender value at risk (B), whereas the defender controls more knowledge (L), architects the systems (M) and the criminal justice system (N). In between (C – K), the attacker has many advantages but international data sharing and defensive coordination can deny advantage to the attacker by improving communication (F), enhancing situational awareness (G), providing mechanisms for coordination (I), speeding up decision cycles (J), increasing agility (K), encouraging more defensible architectures (M) and supporting or incentivizing defensive coordination with the legal system.

Table 1: International data exchange can reduce asymmetries between attack and defence.

	Mode	Attacker	Defender
A	Initiative	Chooses the best place, time and means of attack	Must defend everywhere, all the time, against any attack
B	Value At Risk	Small (terror or criminal actors)	Large
C	Code Size	Small (often 100s of lines)	Large (>20-50 million lines)
D	Software Control	High	Supply chain ➔ Low
E	Software Abstraction	Good, integrated for purpose	Poor, evolutionary tower
F	Communication	Organized around attack ➔ Good	Organized around products ➔ Poor
G	Situational Awareness	High	After-market bolt-on ➔ Low
H	Accountability	Low (terror or criminal actors)	High
I	Coordination	Small group ➔ high	Non-scalable ➔ low
J	Decision cycle	Fast	Slow
K	Agility	High (apparent)	Low
L	Domain Knowledge	Low, narrow & concentrated	High, broad but diffuse
M	Architectural Control	Low	High, but slow
N	Legal/Justice Systems	Low	High, but slow & political

3.2 Threats and Actors

Drawing upon his work in the FP7 projects WOMBAT [12] and SYSSEC [13], Sotiris Ioannidis of FORTH in Greece presented the current situation on threat actors and provided an overview of their capabilities, threat models and assessment of the consequences of breaches or disruptions and their criticality. He stressed that in order to improve our knowledge about malicious code, we must work together on international data exchange especially on malware and to enable increased and better analysis results for context consolidation. This would enable the community to understand malware activities and trends. In order to improve our posture against these threat actors, this work can be supported by technologies and tools developed within these projects including new sensors for data acquisition (wireless, …) and new analysis techniques (code, context, …). The speaker highlighted a number of proposals for new technologies for enterprise and home-use and for new practices (CERTs, ISPs) and regulations.

The speaker focussed on the approach taken by the WOMBAT project, whose goal was the collection of information and alert data from multiple sources to learn something about the attacks. The motivation behind this was to understand the attackers and the enemy as cybercrime has become a huge business. We need to understand better what they were doing by collecting, sharing, manipulating and analysing the collected data. However, it is recognised there are a number of issues when collecting data, including monetary disincentives of sharing data (someone could be looking to make money with it); and of course, privacy issues. WOMBAT pushed for the sharing of this data to give the ability to investigate malware and how the threat actors operate.

The first step in the WOMBAT process is data acquisition and collection of the data. The next step was the enhancement of the data to better visualise and contextualise of the data. This enabled more intensive data mining to understand the threats better and allowed the project to then build better tools in a feedback loop. The tools must be dynamic with the services being developed further with more enhancements. The project was able to promote the tools to industry, who were very supportive of the ideas and algorithms and have utilised them into new services. The project strived for a common API that could be adapted by others with different data sources and an interest in examining the data. There has been significant knowledge transfer to the security industry into their security projects and the project has made a great deal of impact and improved the knowledge of malware and threats by looking at the raw data and harvesting of this data via the new tools developed including new sensors used to collect the data.

The speaker concluded with lessons learned within the WOMBAT project. The TRIAGE framework enables multi-dimensional analysis of security events. It has been applied to several data sources and led to interesting findings that will improve our ability to counter the many threat actors that are out there. The framework has been used and is being transferred within Symantec. Publications of these lessons contributed significantly to the visibility of WOMBAT, which finished a few weeks ago.

3.3 Technologies to support an International Data exchange architecture

The aim of this technical part of the session was to continue the work that was started during an earlier INCO-Trust workshop in May 2010, specifically on jointly developing a Secure International Data Exchange Architecture for Cybersecurity outlined by the *Technical Challenges for Transnational Repositories* session [14]. Such a capability would reduce defensive gaps across the contributing states, and build crisis-response capacity and an international system for data exchange related to cyber crime. This would include attack patterns and '*signatures*', best defence practices, and response and recovery – individual and collective. This would greatly improve defensive understanding and coordination resulting in biasing the successful work factors for cyber attack and defense in favor of defenders.

At the workshop in May 2010 and in follow up iterations between the participants, as shown in **Figure 1**, a straw-man architecture was generated and this was described in more detail at the BIC session. Due to the duration of the session, it wasn't possible to get into very technical discussions but instead focus on bringing this work to the next level and commitment to the research and development coordination, which will enhance the outcomes through tactical planning, leveraging and combining task-relevant national expertise.

Malicious actors[1] in cyberspace actively exploit the shortcomings in the ability of defenders to coordinate their activities. They can rerun the same attacks against different countries, sectors and organizations so long as cyber data and countermeasures are not being shared effectively.

An architecture for international and cross-sector sharing of cyber threat and attack data will ensure a more effective collective cyber defense than countries, sectors or organizations might otherwise achieve individually.

---

1   cyber criminals, adversarial national intelligence agencies, hacktivists, and cyber terrorists for starters

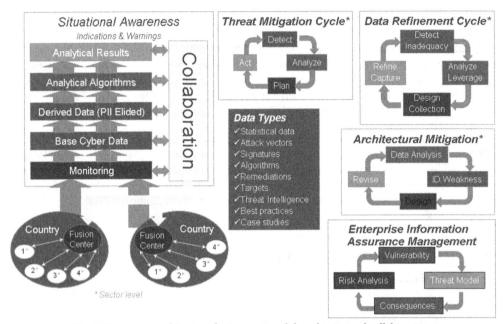

Fig. 1: Straw man architecture for international data sharing and collaboration.

Figure 1 illustrates an international cyber data sharing architecture that integrate data from multiple countries and sectors and returns collaboratively produce analytical products and threat mitigation techniques. Country fusion centers integrate country information and expertise internationally. Within each country and across its sectors, shared monitoring infrastructures capture base cyber data at sources. This data is processed to remove personally identifiable information (PII) before being analyzed using shared algorithms to produce results fed back into shared situational awareness. The architecture supports sector-based threat mitigation cycles as well as enterprise information assurance management of value at risk. The architecture supports learning modalities like data refinement to improve data capture, analysis and utility in threat mitigation. Based on knowledge gained about vulnerabilities and attacker vectors, the architecture helps drive improvement of enterprise and infrastructure architectures to improve defensibility.

This kind of sharing scenario can drive research along many trajectories. The type of data collected needs to be effective and offer leverage for cyber defense. Large-scale analytics over the data need to reveal important patterns in real time and lead to timely threat mitigation. Given an effective sharing architecture, major malicious actors will endeavor to corrupt the data and subvert its operation, and so resilient and trustworthy engineering will be needed for all components from sensors to hosts, monitoring, analysis and mitigation actions. At the same time, PII and enterprise information must be protected to respect important societal values and incentivizing sharing. Difficult technical, legal and administrative challenges in international authentication, authorization, encryption and remote policy enforcement must be overcome to reach higher levels of trust and sharing necessary for weaponizable data like critical infrastructure attacks and mitigations.

We need to look at optimising the integration of both technical and economic perspectives to favour defensive interventions that disrupt malicious business models. Figure 2 illustrates the limited scope of conventional technical approaches to cyber defense. By integrating understanding of the attack business model, defenders gain additional opportunities to disrupt the attacker anywhere on his value cycle using passive or active means. Additionally, the resources, capabilities and motivations of the attacker provide constraints on the range of technical defenses necessary for effective defense.

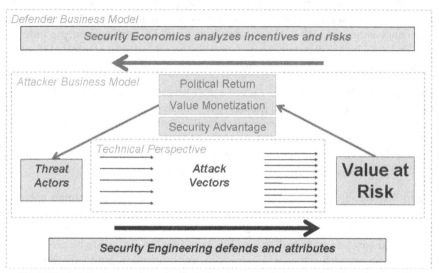

Fig. 2: Optimising integration of technical and economic perspectives for cybersecurity.

3.4 Legal, Regulatory, privacy environment challenges

A globally recognised expert on the legal, regulatory and privacy challenges, Ms. Jody Westby, Esq., presented the problem areas that arise from the complex legal and regulatory situations when dealing with data collection and sharing specifically for the purposes of the security and protection of cyberspace. As cyber security R&D increases and the attacks become more complex, organizations are becoming more concerned about the legal and policy considerations associated with R&D projects. However, guidance on the legal, regulatory and privacy issues is scarce and highly complicated and global in nature. This is coupled with a highly inconsistent legal framework making it difficult for research organisations to understand.

In order to improve the situation, the Department of Homeland Security's Cyber Security R&D Division funded a project entitled "New Frameworks for Detecting and Minimizing Information Leakage in Anonymized Network Data." Within this project, a tool was developed by Ms. Westby entitled The *Legal & Policy Tool Chest for Cyber Security R&D* (*Tool Chest*). Ms. Westby described the Legal & Policy Analysis Tool Chest, which is a comprehensive set of three tools that may be used both to help analyze the legal and policy implications associated with the use of traffic data in cyber security R&D and to mitigate identified risks:

1. Legal Analysis Tool on Obtaining & Using Network Communications Data (Legal Analysis Tool) focuses on obtaining, using, and disclosing intercepted and stored communications data.

2. Privacy Tool on Using Network Communications Data (Privacy Tool) focuses on the relevant privacy legal considerations with this data.

3. Protection Measures Tool contains sample contract clauses and memoranda of agreement that can be used by researchers and their organizations to mitigate legal risk.

While the privacy tool is based on U.S. Laws, Ms. Westby stressed that it also takes into account foreign privacy issues, especially in regard to the EU. The Privacy Analysis Tool explains these legal and policy privacy considerations and provides a decisional framework to guide researchers and institutional review boards (IRBs) through the process of determining (1) whether a dataset has privacy issues associated with it, (2) whether these issues are fatal and may preclude the use of the data, and (3) whether certain privacy issues may be mitigated or eliminated through anonymization or other de-identification techniques.

Ms. Westby presented the *Legal Guide on Cyber Security Research on Botnets (Botnet Legal Guide)*, which was developed in order to extend the *Tool Chest's* analysis and examine the myriad of legal issues associated with this particular type of research. The *Botnet Legal Guide* also was funded by DHS's Cyber Security R&D Division and developed by Ms. Westby as a component of a technical research project led by Georgia Institute of Technology on "Countering Botnets: Anomaly-Based Detection, Comprehensive Analysis, and Efficient Mitigation."

According to Ms. Westby, the *Tool Chest* and *Botnet Legal Guide* are companion publications that provide the cyber security research community with a central repository of definitions, descriptions of the laws, worksheets, decisional frameworks, tables simplifying privacy provisions and penalties, and conclusions regarding how U.S. laws apply to datasets to be used in research projects and impact research activities. International considerations, especially with respect to privacy and cybercrime laws, present challenges for researchers that require careful and joint analysis. The *Tool Chest* and *Botnet Legal Guide* offer a positive step toward helping researchers, IRBs, legal counsel and management better understand the legal issues associated with research projects and the data used in them.

In conclusion, Ms. Westby stressed the need for international collaboration between the legal and technical communities, particularly with respect to exploring the extraterritorial reach of laws and inconsistencies in legal frameworks. Researchers particularly need to better understand critical jurisdictional differences in the global legal framework for interception, privacy, and cybercrime. Programs such as PREDICT[2] that include the legal analysis of datasets that are offered to researchers help build confidence that data used in research efforts will not run afoul of the law, but they do not address the legality of the activities undertaken by researchers when using the data. The development of best practices with respect to certain research activities would make a significant difference toward encouraging legal conduct in R&D projects. More information on this work can be found in a recently published paper by Ms. Westby in the proceedings of the Building Analysis Datasets and Gathering Experience Returns for Security (BADGERS) 2011 Workshop, Apr. 10, 2011, Salzburg, Austria (part of EuroSys 2011) [15].

---

2 PREDICT is an acronym for the Protected Repository for the Defense of Infrastructure Against Cyber Threats sponsored by the U.S. Department of Homeland Security (DHS) Science & Technology Directorate's Cyber Security R&D division,

4 Conclusions

A number of conclusions emerged from the BIC session held at SysSec. These included:

- *Research required on technical enablers:* The enablers for a secure international data exchange architecture eg. cryptography based obfuscation, sensors on the network, monitoring traffic capabilities, privacy protecting identity management, amongst others.
- *Integration of technical and economic perspectives:* to optimize defensive interventions for the disruption of malicious business models.
- *Sharing Incentives:* Research is needed on incentivizing data sharing and collaboration across entities, sectors and countries. Basics of how we share recognizable data, especially on critical infrastructures and across different countries. eg. share patterns for recognizing advanced persistent threats without losing efficacy if they are exposed. What obfuscation and security measures would make patterns easier to share?
- *Collection Prioritization:* Methodologies are needed for identifying and prioritizing data for collection in order to yield high leverage against cyber threats across different time.
- *Learning and Agility:* Data sharing and collaboration needs to evolve rapidly to keep pace with threats.
- *Resilient Sharing Architecture:* Research needs to produce a defensible architecture for sharing and collaboration.
- *Integration of technical and legal requirements:* The need for international collaboration between the legal and technical communities, particularly with respect to exploring the extraterritorial reach of laws and inconsistencies in legal frameworks.
- *Trust:* Data sharing and collaboration will only be a good as the confidence participants have in the ability of the architecture to enforce access control and dissemination policies.

The BIC session concluded with a call for position papers for a longer event to be held in Quarter 4 of 2011 in order to develop and refine visions of such an architecture and use these conceptualizations to identify and prioritize what is needed in the medium- and long-term research. Some examples of the types of desired topics for position papers were highlighted.

- What kind of data sharing and collaborative analysis architecture could be built with today's technologies and operational knowledge?
- Who are the current actors around the globe and what are their approaches and can these be leveraged and harmonized together?
- What are the gaps?
- What research would be needed to build a better architecture in the 5-10 year time frame?
- Who are the actors needed to carry out this research and where are they from?
- What organizational modes are necessary for this research to proceed most expeditiously?
- What funding sources and mechanisms can be mobilized to support the joint international efforts required?
- In order to better motivate countries to contribute and support the effort, we should highlight the rationale and motivation for designing and building sophisticated architectures for international cyber data sharing, collaborative analysis, and collective defense. For example,
  - Dramatically improve defensive coordination to move the economic advantage away from offense in favour of defence;
  - Create shared real-time situational awareness;
  - Identify cyber data for sharing together with leverage scenarios and collection issues;
  - Motivate targeted research to enable effective collection, sharing, analysis and response.

- A number of technical aspects were highlighted when going through the straw-man architecture for coverage at the next longer workshop expected in Q4 2011. These included:
- The enablers for a secure international data exchange architecture eg. cryptography based obfuscation, sensors on the network, monitoring traffic capabilities, privacy protecting identity management, amongst others.
- Basics of how we share recognizable data, especially on critical infrastructures and across different countries. eg. share patterns for recognizing advanced persistent threats without losing efficacy if they are exposed. What obfuscation and security measures would make patterns easier to share?
- Architecting for leakage and resilience under compromise.
- Integration of technical and economic perspectives to optimize defensive interventions that disrupt malicious business models.

5 Acknowledgment

The BIC project is funded under Call 5 of FP7 ICT and began on 1st January 2011 with a duration of three years. The project is supported by the European Commission DG INFSO, Unit F5 ICT Trust and Security Research [16].

References

[1] BiC project web site http://www.bic-trust.eu/

[2] SysSec workshop http://www.syssec-project.eu/events/1st-syssec-workshop-program/

[3] Inco-trust WEB SITE http://www.inco-trust.eu/

[4] http://www.inco-trust.eu/incotrust/general/project-impact.html

[5] Clarke, James, Wright, Rebecca, et al., "D4.2 INCO-Trust 2nd Workshop report", available at http://www.inco-trust.eu/incotrust/general/project-impact.html

[6] http://www.cs.rutgers.edu/~rebecca.wright/INCO-TRUST

[7] http://www.securityconference.de/Home.4.0.html?&L=1

[8] https://update.cabinetoffice.gov.uk/sites/default/files/resources/CyberCommunique-Final.pdf

[9] http://conventions.coe.int/Treaty/Commun/QueVoulezVous.asp?NT=185&CL=ENG

[10] Remarks at the 28th Annual International Workshop on Global Security, Paris, France 16th June 2011 http://www.defense.gov/speeches/speech.aspx?speechid=1586

[11] International cooperation "at nascent stage" - U.S. Secretary of Homeland Security Janet Napolitano, Vienna, 1st July 2011. http://www.reuters.com/article/2011/07/01/us-cybercrime-idUKLDE75T1CC20110701

[12] WOMBAT project web site http://www.wombat-project.eu/

[13] SysSec project web site http://www.syssec-project.eu/

[14] Mallery, John C. "Straw Man Architecture for an International Cyber Data Sharing System," position piece, INCO-TRUST Workshop On International Cooperation In Security And Privacy: International Data Exchange with Security and Privacy: Applications, Policy, Technology, and Use, New York: New York Academy of Sciences, May 3 - 5, 2010. http://www.cs.rutgers.edu/~rebecca.wright/INCO-TRUST/position.html

[15] Badger workshop site http://iseclab.org/badgers2011/

[16] DG INFSO Unit F5 web site http://cordis.europa.eu/fp7/ict/security/

Emerging Threats
in 21ˢᵗ Century Cyberspace

Vaclav Jirovsky

Faculty of Transportation Sciences
Czech Technical University in Prague
Konviktská 20, 110 00 Prague 1
jirovsky@fd.cvut.cz

Abstract

Ongoing rapid development in information technologies and increasing dependency of the mankind on cyberspace creates new emerging threats more dangerous than ever before. Retail and e-shop attack will outpace attack targeting banks and financial institutions while hospitals become the most exploitable issue. Identity theft will dramatically increase losses of e-shop operators and increase number of subsidiary court cases.

The dependency of mankind on the computers and computer networks will decrease his alertness creating him an easy target. Social networks such as Twitter and Facebook are extending their services for third party development through the use of application programming interfaces (APIs). The social engineering in majority using data from social networks will enter a new era of internet exploitation utilizing sophisticated virtual identities covered by L2 anonymizers and methods of artificial intelligence. Also there is an expectation of growing privacy right violation by governments and governmental agencies in the name of cyber defense. Also big corporation will collect and process the data which, collected in the large amount, could lead to the violation privacy rights.

The Virtual Environment will be specifically targeted by cybercriminals and cyberterrorist resulting in new way of attacker strategies. The complexity of Virtual Environment creates room for new sophisticated attack and large data storages in clouds make data pirates' life easier. The exploit will be more focused to cause physical or other sensitive damage by penetrating the lowest levels of systems. The mobile cell phones and PDA becomes natural target mainly by misleading users to download so called "trusted application" software. Using many different communication channels like wi-fi, GSM or Bluetooth, the mobile device became very sensitive to outer attacks.

1 Life in the Cyberspace

The mankind had created the technology. The technology creates internet. New technology environment, new actors and new models of social behavior has given rise to unexpected and as yet to be described social phenomena. The mankind set up a new "virtual dimension" of his own life while although he is not able to coop with such an environment using his old naturally developed habits.

The decentralized nature of the cyberspace, without any formally centralized "governing" authority, seems to impart a highly democratic quality to this world. However, while appearing democratic, the cyberspace is more akin to widespread anarchy which, if not limited by technological rules, may in fact annihilate the cyberspace or make it unusable. The functionality of the cyberspace is ensured

N. Pohlmann, H. Reimer, W. Schneider (Editors): Securing Electronic Business Processes, Vieweg (2011), 109-119

by mutual agreement among administrators, who adapt their manners to the majority. We can say that cyberspace is "driven" by its users and their general sense of morality and ethics.

Several features of the cyberspace, arising from the characteristics mentioned above, facilitate illegal activities in the cyberspace. The most important one is a non-transparent environment due to the technological complexity of the system. This technological "shadow" gives a sham sense of safety to the criminal, since the crime scene knows him only by his virtual identity. The potential for existence of a virtual multi-personality in the cyberspace, anywhere and anytime, is a stimulus for creation of different virtual groups and virtual communities. By communication, presentation of personalities in the virtual space and coordination of their activities, we can view formation of different subcultures. At the same time, having more than one subculture in the unique virtual space, there are conditions for subcultures to encounter, quarrel and combat each other. Such combats are either retroactively exposed or mirrored in the real world, with all the consequences of the virtual events.

With increasing usage of internet and mankind dependency on the electronic media we can observe two main groups of reasons of risk
- mankind dependency on cyberspace and addiction to the cyberspace, where main vulnerability creates mankind psychic;
- technological vulnerabilities, where majority of reasons is formed by hidden errors in manufacturing, software or hardware design or implementation of electronic means.

The main driver of the first group is mankind psychic, its tendency to trust more to presented virtual explanation then to rational facts. Simple deceptive mechanisms are very effective especially in the category of regular users who have no or little knowledge of internet security and high trust to the magic digital media. The various studies dealing with network addiction are described in [YOUN97], but without specific correlation to the threats created by virtual communities or individuals.

Technological vulnerabilities, as a major driver of second group were mainly tools or pathway how to enter the mankind secrecy, change internal environment of the computer system to cheat the user or to scare him. As time is going we see the further improvement of this technique hitting the society much deeper by causing physical pain or damage.

Significant branch of future threats combine both symptoms using technological vulnerabilities to misuse mankind dependency or, in the worst case, misuse the mankind dependency to create technological vulnerability. As a conclusion of this approach we have to state that it is necessary to study not only technological aspect of the cyberspace but the social impact and psychological influence will become a required part of the research. Speaking in strictly technical manner we have to study complex system of systems where mankind and his reactions create non-negligible part of description and analysis.

1.1 Population of cyberspace

The development of global communication technologies created new space for individual activities and new dimensions in the socialization of mankind. The experiences of the individual, obtained during his stay in the cyberspace, influence his psychic, social behavior, his practice and evaluation of society's values. The influence of technology and of the cyberspace's effects on mankind is manifestly evident. The population and organization of the cyberspace results from projection of the real population into virtual identities, by using specific languages and means of communication, bereft of nonverbal expression or perception. This suppresses the social effects of the communication while increasing the feeling of safety of being in cyberspace. As a consequence, we can observe noticeable changes in human psyche and health when his stay in the cyberspace is long enough. New types of experience obtained in the virtual world and being part of virtual communities or subcultures, lead to a clash of virtual and real personality [JIRO10].

The decentralized nature of virtual world produces the forms of organization of individuals into groups. Virtual communities or subcultures are organized around topics rather than within national boundaries. The existence of virtual groups on the internet has been the subject of psychological and sociological studies, but the focus has been usually on how reality is reflected in the virtual world (eg. [DOUG07]) or on the characterization of virtual groups according to technology usage (eg. [BRHO07]). Other social science studies have examined the effects of internet usage on the formation and maintenance of personal relationships, group memberships and social identity, mainly as psychological aspect of user's well-being (eg. [BAMC04]). The effectiveness and dynamic of virtual community work has also been studied (eg. [WABJ02]).

1.1.1   Virtual Individuals

In general, we surprisingly find that most individuals do not need to fulfill their ambitions in the real world. They are quite satisfied with only a virtual resemblance of the fulfillment of ambition [JIRO08]. As such, the difference between virtual and real experience becomes reflected in virtual and real behavior[1]. While symbolic experience cannot offer a full experience of reality, it does minimize risks for the individual in the cyberspace. Moreover the individual can express himself in different roles within communities, changing age or gender when carrying out one's own image of his personality [HUCI00]. With cognizance of immortality in cyberspace the addictive person anchors this perception in such a way that it lately transferred to the real world and suppresses the instinct for self-preservation. The behavior of the respective individual could become more aggressive or violent[2] in the view of his own perceived immortality [KYL+09].

On other side, while humans cannot use their natural habits in the virtual space, their perceptions are not adapted to the virtual world yet and so are continuously sustaining improper notions of ethics, morality and law in the virtual world. The perception of identity, quite different in real life, leads to the virtualization of the individual and of society in the virtual world. We can introduce simple taxonomy to the population of virtual world by defining following types of users

- regular users of the virtual world, who are not exhibiting any addiction to the internet;
- "happy users", who explore features of the virtual world and then use online activities as a tool to enhance their lives in real world;
- users with addiction to the virtual world, who are entirely captivated by the virtual world and exhibit dependency;
- developers – professionals who are continually contributing to the technology's progress while retaining resilient personalities;
- abusers, misusing the virtual world for criminal and other illegitimate activities.

---

1 For example, to release aggression against an enemy, it is sufficient in many cases to just destroy the symbol of the enemy. Similarly, many individuals could satisfy their ambitions just through symbolic resemblance in virtuality of cyberspace.
2 The perception of immortality is often accompanied by perception of abilities and attributes which belongs to the virtual personality created e.g. in network game. Later projection of such an attributes could expose itself in the real life as a verification of virtual experience – e.g. using a gun the same way as in the virtual world.

This last group – the abusers, forms a growing virtual world community moving criminal activities from the real world to the virtual world[3].

1.1.2 Virtual Communities

Virtual communities recognized in the virtual world are global, a society of virtual individuals without boundaries, linked by similar ideas, religion, political opinion, experiences, interest etc. The behavior of communities which create threats in cyberspace is often politically or religiously motivated. We can find also business-oriented communities on the internet – virtual corporations in the virtual world targeting market segments and created by its users freely or "on contract" basis.

Besides hackers' communities known to exist only on the internet, the chatters' and internet gambler's communities would be the second largest one. Also communities grown around social networks servers becomes significant cyberspace entity but, on other hand also subject of mass manipulation. Even the internet addiction in this case could not be as strong and helps to form some kind of social group based on sharing of common communication media. Nevertheless persons addicted to social networks exhibit restlessness when not on the internet similarly internet gambles community.

Contrary to "peaceful" communities where jeopardy to the society remains more than less in addiction to cyberspace and accompanying psychic and social impact, the criminal communities are targeting the cyberspace directly, more focusing on combating and fighting in the cyberspace. They will have much more impact on the day-to-day life of society and the individual when misusing his addiction or careless. Beside of typical criminal acts as data theft or phishing there can be observed an important grow of politically motivated acts as is publishing of stolen confidential information or cyber terrorism. The global interconnection of criminal a terrorist groups together with formally presented great common goals[4] creates possible threat to the public, when mirroring such a situation in real world

1.2 Addiction to the Virtual World

The escape from cruel reality into the virtual world where there is less need for compromises, where one can behave arbitrarily according to one's wishes, can result in disintegration of the personality [JIRO08]. Unhappy and unsatisfied individuals, yearning for a simple, understandable world, where they can realize their dreams, discover opportunities in the welcoming environment of virtual world, however at the price of the total absorption of their personalities.

It is a reality that the virtual world and the internet have a great impact on human psychology. Seeking of virtual communication and relationships is often a response to low satisfaction in the real world. Troubled personal relationships in the real world lead to frustration and preference for virtual relationships, where one seems to find more understanding and a higher enrichment of life. The virtual world becomes for the addicted person so attractive after while that he would be willing to sacrifice his own real life, reducing it to basic physiological needs.

---

3 The reason is not only the complexity of systems with many vulnerabilities and abundant targets, but also the increasing value of information as regular social and economic activities gets transferred more and more into the virtual world infrastructure, and because of the difficulty of investigation of digital crime.

4 These goals usually phrase the old common symbols of technology generation like protests against corporation or freedom of speech etc.

The Websense [WEBS07] found that 25% of employees who are working on the internet exhibit symptoms of internet addiction. Moreover, the dependency is supported by compulsive use of computer applications while working. Current company information systems force human to interact by e-mail and with databases. While this increases company productivity the work process is depersonalized and reduced to communication with computer via keyboard and display. Steeped in such an environment it is not surprising that employees search for personal entertainment in the same way – with their computers via the internet[5], little by little becoming addicted.

Net addiction is arguably one of the most risky security threats. The addictive individual believes more in the information and relationships gained in the virtual space than in real life. The communication in virtual space expresses high levels of virtual exhibitionism, and the addictive person in a virtual environment tends to release more information than he would do in real life. Following misuse of revealed information collected from different sources of activity, an addictive individual can cause damage to his employer, partner or even to the state.

Addictive persons feel that their own personal exhibitionism in the virtual environment as something very natural and normal. Social networks and social webs are examples of such exhibitionism. We noticed a case when several ministers of the Czech government exhibited themselves on the Facebook website, releasing a lot of information about themselves using nickname [KOKU08]. Later, when they have interviewed by journalists about such an activity, they defended themselves as very advanced persons using Facebook as a modern communication medium[6].

1.2.1 Netholism and Netmania

Dependency on life in the cyberspace was originally noted by Ivan Goldberg at PsyCom.Net [GOLD95]. The Internet Addiction Disorder (IAD), or internet overuse has been defined as pathological computer use that interferes with daily life. Clinical psychologist Kimberly Young, supports the existence of the phenomenon [YOUN96]. We can, in fact, see an increasing incidence of events caused by internet addiction mainly in Asian countries where internet cafés are frequently used and mental or physical effects are publicly displayed. In the United States and Europe games and virtual sex are accessed from the home, so any attempt to measure the phenomenon is obscured by shame and denial [BLOC07]. The most advanced stage of IAD is usually referred to as "netholism" or "netmania". Interesting research results have been published in South Korea [AHND07] where a series of 10 cardiopulmonary-related deaths in internet cafés and a game-related murder had been reported.

The terminal stage of internet addiction is often called "Jekyll-Hyde syndrome" [JIRO07], when individual's personality disintegrates by living in both worlds, virtual and real, without ability to separate them. Gradual transition from real to virtual world accompanied by resignation from the real surrounding world is a visible symptom of Jekyll-Hyde syndrome. Total addiction to the internet relationships, loss of ability to suffer and resist the cruelty of real world is often accompanied by suicide attempts.

---

5 The most frequently non-task-related activities are online shopping, reading of news and magazines, web erotica and pornography and gambling. Interestingly, over 70% of visits to erotic server pages happen between 9 a.m. and 5 p.m. and more than 60% of internet shopping is done from company computers.
6 On other hand, it should be noted that social networks and social websites are very effective public relations tools for voting campaigns or influencing public opinion for various purposes.

1.2.2 Cyberspace Addiction Disorder Treatment

The Internet addiction disorder is a relatively new phenomenon, so there is little research on the effectiveness of treatment procedures. Some psychiatrist advocate abstinence from the Internet, others argue that such a treatment may be unrealistic. As society becomes more and more dependent on computers it will be difficult for a computer-literate person to avoid using the Internet.

If a person's Internet addiction disorder has a medical dimension, then such treatment as an antidepressant or anti-anxiety drug may help. Psychological interventions may lead to change of the environment to alter associations that have been made with Internet use, or decrease the reinforcement received from excessive Internet use. Treatment appears to be effective in maintaining and changing the behavior of people drawn to excessive use of the Internet. If the disorder is left untreated, the person may experience an increased amount of conflict in his or her relationships.

Also the prevention is important. If a person experience difficulty with addictive behavior, he or she should be cautious in exploring the types of application that are used on the Internet. Also it is important that mental health workers should investigate ways in which to participate in the implementation of new technology rather than waiting for its aftereffects.

2 Technological vulnerabilities

Computers, computer systems and Internet are so complex that it is impossible to keep it without errors and mistakes. Graph in **Fig. 1** demonstrate rise of vulnerabilities reported during period 1995 – 2011, where sharp increase of vulnerabilities in the middle of first decade this century is observable[7]. As a reaction to the number of vulnerabilities reported security measures has been accepted at software developer's side as well as at server operation side leading to decreasing statistic from the 2007 onward.

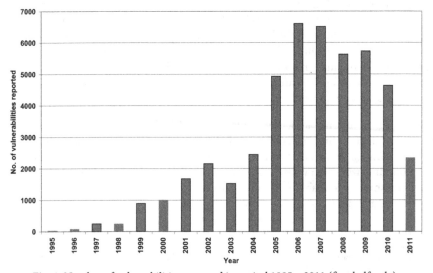

Fig. 1: Number of vulnerabilities reported in period 1995 – 2011 (first half only)

7   Data according to National Vulnerability Database - http://nvd.nist.gov/home.cfm

The attack models have not been significantly changed from past, nevertheless weakness and vulnerabilities of code allows the attacker to place specific type of attacker to different place of the code. The most used attack models remains in improper neutralization of special elements used in an SQL Command, so called SQL Injection, or in an operation system command, so called OS Command Injection. In the Top-Ten of attack method used in 2010/2011 we can list following

- copying buffer without checking size of input, so called Buffer Overflow, which is classical methods of penetration into system,
- Cross-site Scripting dealing with improper neutralization of input during web page generation,
- missing authorization of user accessing the site or authentication for critical function when particular application is running,
- one of the most irresponsible errors of programmers - use of hard-coded credentials. It is surprise that such a simple fault is gaining high position in the statistic,
- missing encryption of sensitive data like password files etc.,
- reliance on untrusted inputs in a security decision or unrestricted upload of files with dangerous type, where both events are basic violation of security policy etc.

Other less frequently used methods are CSRF (Cross-Site Request Forgery), execution with unnecessary privileges or so called Path Traversal which is improper limitation of a pathname to a restricted directory.

2.1 Cloud Computing Security

The most significant shift in information technology is represented by cloud computing. Even it could be felt as innovated comeback of large computing centers with remote terminal connection, reaching the point where computing functions is presented as a utility is promising innovations. Nevertheless, customers are both - excited and nervous of cloud computing. They see opportunities to reduce capital costs, however at the same time are concerned about the risks of cloud computing if not properly secured. The perception of loss of direct control over systems is nightmare of large companies as well as for SME's.

There has been much debate about threats to cloud computing where many issues, such as provider financial stability creating significant risks to customers has been discussed. The cloud computing and its shared, on-demand nature. The security of shared system is already tough task and "security by obscurity" will never work in this case. The users "do not know what you do not know" which makes them nervous, loosing confidence in cloud computing.

Also shared technologies mean shared risk. Virtualization allows multiple companies to share assets and applications across a single piece of hardware. Unfortunately, it is yet another way data can get into the wrong hands. Fear of abuse and nefarious use of cloud computing, malicious insiders and insecure application programming interfaces are main sources of user's hesitation. As a matter of fact, if provider will not be able to present its security policy including clear security perimeter model and satisfy customers with high availability and reliability of resources provided, the cloud computing will remain a risky business.

An important part of the cloud computing usage will be legal and regulatory issues. In this case it is clear that customer cannot always trust to cloud provider's employees. There is no uniform level of assurance or background checks among cloud providers, nor is there often much visibility into hiring standards or practices. The only measures which can be taken on customer side remain in enforcing strict supply-chain management, conducting a comprehensive supplier assessment and specifying human resource requirements, all as part of legal contracts. Also it would be useful to insist on transparency into overall information security and management practices, as well as compliance reporting.

2.2 Attack on physical systems

There are many types of malware wreak havoc on computers, but there is a rising concern that the damage done could also cause the destruction and malfunction of physical systems including critical infrastructure and even information technologies deployed in the critical application[8]. While there are differing opinions in terms of how real this threat to physical systems is, we should demonstrate real attack on physical layer of critical application implemented in worm Stuxnet.

Worm Stuxnet has been discovered in June 2010 but got wider attention in July when the true purpose of worm was discovered. It has been called a military-grade guided cyber missile and a hyper sophisticated cyber weapon. Among others targets, the main focus was directed to industrial control systems, where worm can modify code on programmable logic controllers that drive industrial processes. The worm was exceptionally long with unpacked main module over 1 Mbyte, contains approximately 10 executable components and can injects itself into multiple processes, using global mutual exclusions and an RPC server for coordination and communication. Siemens reported that as many 24 of its customers had been infected by Stuxnet [HTTP11]. Even number 24 looks very small we have to understand that by attacking physical layer of PLC, the physical damage had been done to targeted system, sometime repairable with difficulties only[9].

The move towards smart grid, or more automated power grids, is ongoing. Everyone is looking forward to its benefits, including greater efficiency and reliability, the simpler incorporation of renewable energy sources and lessen environmental impact. However, as more data are transferred via Internet and reliant on digital communications, it is being opened up to greater risk. As the grid matures, it will be important to devise a defense supervisory system that can efficiently process myriads of data to evaluate system status, identify failures, predict threats, and suggest remediations [KHLF10].

Similar attacks that target physical systems could be expected in the healthcare industry, which operate under different regulatory framework than other industries. If an infected device is used in patient care, because of the regulatory risks and potential litigation involved in modifying computer systems that interact with medical devices, some facilities may choose not to patch known infected systems. The compromise of medical systems could be a result of cyber attacks. According to SecureWorks, attempted hacker attacks launched against their healthcare clients nearly doubled during the last quarter of 2009 [HTTP10].

---

8 By critical applications are understood application which can directly jeopardize human life or create damage of substantial size.

9 The physical damage on Iran centrifuges used in nuclear industry had been reported with no other impact on human life. But the same system are used in control of trains, large power generators etc. where physical damage could be much larger including human life loses.

3 Emerging Threats and Attacks

The new century brought some new look onto threats in cyberspace. The increase in attacks coupled with economic strains that cause many enterprises to cut security budgets have many skeptics predicting the start of the century as a worse period for security breaches. Surprisingly, the software and hardware manufacturers had accepted many security measures causing decreasing trend in number of vulnerabilities. On other site, the cyberspace battles had professionalized exhibiting support from organized criminal and terrorist group as well as from military units and states. The increase in digital espionage and state sponsored attacks could be observed as well as closer correlation among affairs in real world and activities in cyberspace. Hactivism had changed its face digging deeper into hidden files and servers later exhibiting gained "classified materials" on the internet, often as a tool for government or governmental agency blackmail. Social network became source of protest, either as part of regular civil disobedience or as a communication means when organizing meetings or demonstration. On other hand, social network serves as a perfect tool for public opinion manipulation, spreading of disinformation and political campaign.

As it has been said, the emerging threats will concentrate in two domains – misuse a human cyberspace addiction and dependency, including high level of trust in electronic media and technology threats targeted to low levels of architecture.

3.1 Social Engineering

The social engineering in new fashion will become one of the main raising threats of the future. Contradiction security measures and "excellent customer services" mostly confuse employees already bombarded by large amount of other company standards and rules. Most traditional social engineering attacks capitalize on this vulnerability. Note many of these attacks could actually be originating from foreign terrorist groups, some of which are funded by foreign governments. So, many of the people attacking us are in a sense just showing up for work each day. But anyway there could be recognized few outstanding trends

- Phishing –attacks usually done via e-mail asking addressee to visit a website and input confidential information. If a customer responds, then the perpetrator succeeds. New versions of attack are gaining directly on paid services already contracted by customer e.g. high rate SMS service used for erotic services or sponsoring SMS. The other types of fishing are using different masquerading – e-mail message appearing to come from your employer (Spear Phishing) or specifically target executives or Board members using their biographies (Whaling);
- Vishing (voice phishing) or SMiShing – when confidential information is solicited over the phone instead of e-mail or by using SMS text messages.

New gold age of social engineering is naturally growing from human dependency on information technologies and confidence in electronic means and technology.

3.2 Malware

Malware includes viruses, worms, spyware, Trojan horse programs, etc. Malware has been a steady contender as a top threat for the past several years, and will stay on top list of threats for further period. While it is not a new threat concept, many enterprises still do not have adequate controls to reduce the risk to a manageable level, but new types of malware are introduced daily. Important is an observation mentioned above on specific type of malware targeted to the lowest levels of the system.

3.3 Mobile devices

There is increased marketing pressure observable to support more mobile devices on the network and thus creating new rising threat. Even many enterprises tried to standardize on one type of phone there could be seen a push usually coming from upper management to support other mobile devices as the iPhone and other smart phones. Vulnerabilities in smart phones continue to be found, new patches are released. However for most smart phones and their users the update of software on smart phone turns into a manual process. As had been discovered, some smart phones have built-in functions which make easier to gather personal data into dedicated servers – e.g. data describing location of the phone are sent to server.

4 Conclusion

With increasing usage of internet and human dependency on the electronic media is growing. The human psychic not prepared to new untouchable virtual world exhibit difficulties in dealing with entities in cyberspace. This mankind dependency on cyberspace and addiction to the cyberspace, create one of the main vulnerabilities in cyberspace, which could be misused not only by criminals but also by enterprises or politicians. Other issue is deep targeted malware, technological vulnerabilities on the lowest levels of systems. There are not only hidden errors in manufacturing misused by attacker but also poorly designed software or hardware or incorrect implementation of electronic means.

There are expected three emerging threats – new means of social engineering, new deep targeted malware and mobile devices vulnerabilities. All three will create main problem area in security of information and telecommunication networks as well as in control systems where final impact could be fatal. To defend systems and humans is a huge task for the future based on continual education of users and increasing security measures in design, manufacturing and deployment.

References

[JIRO08] Jirovsky V.: „Kyberprostor", Paper presented at the meeting of the state attorneys and judges on problem of cyber criminality, Kromeriz, Czech Republic, July 2008

[JIRO10] Jirovsky V.: „Society in a Virtual World" in Security in Virtual Worlds, 3D Webs, and Immersive Environments: Models for Development, Interaction, and Management, IGI Global, 2010

[DOUG07] Douglas K. M.: „Psychology, discrimination and hate groups online", in Oxford Handbook of Internet Psychology, pp. 155 – 163, Oxford University Press, Oxford 2007

[BRHO07] Brandon P. D. & Hollingshead A. B.: „Characterizing online groups" in Joinson A. N., McKenna K. Y. N., Postmes T., Reips U.D (Ed.), Oxford Handbook of Internet Psychology (pp. 105 – 119). Oxford University Press, Oxford 2007

[BAMC04] Bargh J. A., McKenna K. Y. M.: „The Internet and Social Life", Annual Review of Psychology, Vol. 55, pp. 573-590, February 2004

[WABJ02] Walther, J.B., Boos M., Jonas K.J: "Misattribution and attributional redirection in distributed virtual groups", in Proceedings of the 35th Annual Hawaii International Conference on System Sciences, IEEE Conference Proceedings, Hawai 2002

[YOUN97] Young K. S.: "What Makes the Internet Addictive: Potential Explanation for Pathological Internet Use", Paper presented at the 105th annual conference of the American Psychological Association, Chicago, August 15, 1997

[HUCI00] Hučín J." "Droga jménem internet", Chip CZ 7/2000, pp. 7 – 9, Prague 2000

[KYL+09] Ko C., Yen J., Liu S., Huang C., Yen C.: "The Associations Between Aggressive Behaviors and Internet Addiction and Online Activities", in Adolescents, Journal of Adolescent Health, Volume 44, Issue 6, pp 598-605, 2009

[KOKU08] Kottasová I., Kubita J.: "Čestí politici vnikli na Facebook. Zatím dva." Hospodarske noviny, Prague, May 12, 2008.

[WEBS07] Websense: "Information Protection and Control: Targeting the Insider Threats", Wesense, 2007, Retrieved September 9, 2008, from www.bitpipe.com

[GOLD95] Goldberg, I.: "Internet Addiction Disorder (IAD)", PsyCom.Net, 1995, Retrieved January 7, 2001 from http://web.urz.uni-heidelberg.de/Netzdienste/anleitung/wwwtips/8/addict.html

[YOUN96] Young, K.: "Internet Addiction: The Emergence of a New Clinical Disorder", Paper presented at the 104th annual meeting of the American Psychological Association, Toronto, Canada, August 15, 1996

[BLOC07] Block J.J: "Pathological computer use in the USA", in International Symposium on the Counseling and Treatment of Youth Internet Addiction, pp 433-447, Seoul, Korea, National Youth Commission

[AHND07] Ahn D. H.: "Korean policy on treatment and rehabilitation for adolescents' Internet addiction", in International Symposium on the Counseling and Treatment of Youth Internet Addiction. p 49-52, Seoul, Korea, National Youth Commission, 2007

[JIRO07] Jirovsky V.: "Kybernalita – kybernetická kriminalita", Grada Publishing, Prague 2007

[HTTP11] http://support.automation.siemens.com/WW/view/en/43876783, Siemens Web Site, Downloaded June 2011

[KHLF10] Khurana H., Hadley M., Lu N., Frincke D.: "Smart-Grid Security Issues", IEEE Security & Privacy, pp. 81 – 85, January/February 2010

[HTTP10] http://www.secureworks.com/research/newsletter/2010-01/, SecureWorks Web Site, Downloaded June 2011

Smart Grids, Mobile & Wireless Security

Security Policy Automation for Smart Grids: Manageable Security & Compliance at Large Scale

Ulrich Lang · Rudolf Schreiner

ObjectSecurity
Cambridge, UK, and Palo Alto, CA, USA
{ulrich.lang | rudolf.schreiner}@objectsecurity.com

Abstract

A smart grid is an electricity network that has been infused with information and digital communications technology to provide greater control, stability, reliability and flexibility of the power grid. Technology has been added from the consumer premise which includes appliances, thermostats, home energy managers and load control switches all the way back to the generation facilities. The combination of these technologies could potentially optimize demand management, save energy, reduce costs, increase reliability, connect alternative and home-generated energy sources to the grid (i.e. transmitting a bi-directional flow of energy), and evolve into a powerful platform for new business opportunities. In order for smart grids to achieve all objectives, cyber security and risks (e.g. cybercrime or cyber warfare) and privacy concerns must be overcome. The smart grid adds new entry points to the older technologies that are already vulnerable but were previously protected from exploit by physical isolation. Theoretical concerns have become practical realities as a number of vulnerabilities in the smart grid and power complexes have been exploited. After a general introduction to smart grids and smart grid security, this paper analyses security (control) and compliance (visibility) requirements for smart grids. In order to justify the need for security policy automation, the paper focuses on the hard-to-implement least privilege, information flow enforcement, and security incident monitoring/reporting/auditing requirements. The paper then presents "model-driven security policy automation" (control) and "model-driven security incident monitoring/analysis automation" (visibility) within the context of smart grids, and explains how alternative approaches such as identity and access management and authorization management are necessary but not sufficient on their own. The presented "model-driven security" (MDS) policy automation solution uniquely helps solve the challenge of capturing, managing, enforcing, and monitoring/analysing fine-grained, contextual technical authorization policies for small to large scale smart grids.

1 Smart Grids

Smart grids are being promoted by many governments as a way of addressing energy independence, global warming issues, emergency resilience issues, and the attempt to phase out nuclear power in several countries. A smart grid is a form of electricity network combined with information technology – across generation at power plants, distribution and transmission along electrical lines, and delivery and consumption at the customer homes or businesses of a utility. A smart grid transmits electricity intelligently using two-way digital communications to continuously monitor the bi-directional flow of electricity and to control a number of devices across the grid,

N. Pohlmann, H. Reimer, W. Schneider (Editors): Securing Electronic Business Processes, Vieweg (2011), 123-137

including appliances at consumers' homes; this could potentially optimize demand management, save energy, reduce costs, increase reliability, and connect alternative energy sources to the grid – if the risks inherent in executing massive information technology projects are mitigated. The smart grid is envisioned to integrate today's electrical grid with large scale deployments of Information and Communications Technologies (ICT) and smart meters. Smart meters support quick and precise measuring and information gathering to allow easy, real-time control of electricity consumption (e.g. power, heating, and cooling devices, and appliances). One of many examples for the use of smart grids is that new technologies (e.g. electric vehicles, air conditioning and household appliances) will require more intelligent energy demand management, as well as involvement of users (e.g. through home automation). Because the final end-state is still unknown, today's smart grid rollouts can be viewed as the deployment of a general energy ICT platform that forms the basis for future energy-related applications. Because smart grids can potentially mitigate growing energy and environmental concerns, significant investments are being made. For example, the worldwide smart grid market in 2009 was $69 billion, with tens of millions of smart meters installed across the world. By 2014, it could reach about $170 billion. In the U.S., a chunk of the federal stimulus spending in 2009-10, some $3.4 billion, was directed to investment in, and modernization, of smart grids [Rick09]

Relevant for this paper, from an IT perspective, the authors expect that smart grids will have several unique features compared to "normal" IT environments, including: critical infrastructure reliability expected; extremely large scale/distribution/interconnectedness; many embedded devices (e.g. smart meters, SCADA based devices); many stakeholders involved; dynamic stakeholder roles (e.g. buyer, seller); increasingly dynamic/agile interactions between stakeholders; many utilities have very immature security practices or security practices that are not being included in the solutions development processes. This is mostly due to the lack of need prior to the incorporation of technology and network connectivity. Many projects are advancing through the lifecycle to the point of deployment before security is aware of what has happened.

2 Smart Grid Cyber Security

The smart grid vision can only become a reality if cyber security risks are sufficiently mitigated. This is because power grids are absolutely critical infrastructure – if power goes down for extended periods, the affected geographic area stands still. New cyber security challenges (e.g. cybercrime or cyber warfare) become a major risk factor due to the convergence of the information technologies (IT) with the electric power grid, the critical reliance on IT for smart grids, and the fact that parts of the smart grid will be connected to the internet (which makes them susceptible to many of the same malicious attacks that regularly occur against computer networks outside the electrical and energy sectors). The smart grid technologies are introducing in many cases millions of new points of entry into the electric grid by placing meters on every home that have connectivity back to the corporate network and its infrastructure. Some organizations are making attempts to ensure that the paths to the critical cyber assets are separated from the advanced metering infrastructure (AMI) networks, but others just do not appear to understand the risks.

There are also increased privacy concerns, as smart meters and other tools could leak personal and financial data on a consumer to utilities and attackers alike. Many organizations are not transmitting the account information over the networks, where the major issues lie in the usage information itself. Usage information could lead someone to be able to identify patterns that may lead them to know when the consumer is present or away from the premise. However, because of a potential of lack of understanding of how their networks may be interconnected a utility could potentially expose its entire network to the AMI environment creating a vector to their critical infrastructure.

This changing environment poses a major challenge to power utility IT departments, which are not ICT/internet focused and currently mostly operate closed tried-and-tested legacy main-frame/server systems. In general, there is often a "culture gap" between the employees of IT shops and those of electrical and other infrastructure facilities, and government regulators.

A few examples of potential risks associated with the evolution of the smart grid include [Nist10]:

- Greater complexity and interconnectedness increases exposure to potential attackers and unintentional errors;
- Previously closed networks are now opened up and may span multiple smart grid domains ("system of systems"), which increases the attack surface and the risk of cascading attacks;
- More interconnections increase "denial of service" and malware related attack risks;
- Increasing number of attacker entry points and paths as the number of network nodes increases;
- Increased potential for data confidentiality and privacy breaches due to more extensive data gathering and two-way information.
- In deregulated areas the utility may not have control over the devices being utilized on the AMI or Home Area Network and therefore do not control the security requirements for those devices or even the kinds of devices that may be introduced to the environment.
- Unauthorised privileged access to AMI could provide the opportunity to send control commands or create denial-of-service in order to prevent the utility from issuing control commands
- Unauthorized access to meter could be exploited in many ways, e.g. readings could be altered for monetary benefit, spoofing the meter and injecting bogus responses to utility command as in denial-of service attacks, forging meter readings to gain monetary benefits

Vulnerabilities might allow an attacker to penetrate a network, gain access to control software, and alter load conditions to destabilize the grid in unpredictable, potentially safety-hazardous ways. A cyber-attack aimed at energy infrastructure "could disable trains all over the country and it could blow up pipelines. It could cause blackouts and damage electrical power grids so that the blackouts would go on for a long time" [Clar10]. A hacker with a basic knowledge of electronics and a few hundred dollars in hardware could interfere with, and get control over, the smart me-ters that are essential to managing the two-way interaction.

Theoretical concerns have become practical realities, as a number of exploits involving smart grids and power complexes have taken place. In particular in 2010, Stuxnet [Wiki11], a sophisti-cated malware attack that targets Siemens WinCC, industrial control software popular in the util-ity sector and other industries, via a Microsoft Windows vulnerability, infected at least a dozen systems worldwide (and specifically suspected nuclear weapons facilities in Iran) and represents the first publicly-known rootkit to specifically target industrial control systems. There are many other reported attacks on industrial control systems, e.g. [Cbsn10] [[Sans08]. Electric Power Re-search Institute (EPRI) has compiled a database of more than 170 infrastructure cyber incidents [Epri11].

But as illustrated by a 2003 blackout in the US, cyber security must address not only deliberate attacks, but also inadvertent compromises of the information infrastructure due to user errors, equipment failures, and natural disasters. Another classic failure example was the 1999 explosion of a pipeline in Bellingham, WA, USA where the computer monitoring systems failed to detect the build-up of pressure within the fuel line – the resulting explosion killed three, and the busted line spilled gasoline into nearby creeks, resulting in $45 million of damage. Another challenge is that it is also not always easy to apply traditional IT security tools and processes such as routine software patches or upgrades to control systems. For example, penetration testing has been known to destroy the firmware or disrupt the control systems of infrastructure facilities, and maintenance of anti-virus software on such facilities has disrupted control devices and triggered denials of service. Installation of software patches has prevented shutting off the pumps of water utilities, while software for other infrastructure cannot be patched while the facilities are in operation. Inadvertent incidents have even forced nuclear power plants to fall back on auxiliary power. [Harr10]. Fortunately, despite the exploits that have occurred and can occur, malicious or inadvertent, cyber threats to the electrical grid and other infrastructure elements are still at early stages. This fact hopefully will allow companies and government agencies the time to take countermeasures to minimize the threat. Most of the steps that have been proposed mirror those that have been taken to better secure the IT industry against malicious attack.

However, the introduction of these technologies to the electric sector also presents opportunities to increase the reliability of the power system, to make it more capable and more resilient to withstand attacks, equipment failures, human errors, natural disasters, and other threats. Greatly improved monitoring and control capabilities must include cyber security solutions in the development process rather than as a retrofit.

Governments around the world are working on standards and best practice guidance to educate, guide, and to raise awareness. For example, the North American Electric Reliability Corp. (NERC) [Nerc11] is a non-profit organization of industry working groups and utilities. It is formulating some Critical Infrastructure Protection (CIP) standards to ensure reliability of power systems in North America. The Federal Energy Regulatory Commission (FERC) [Ferc11], an independent agency that regulates transmission and transport of electricity and energy commodities, provides oversight for NERC. NERC currently only focuses on generation and transmission (for North America). There is conversation about setting standards for distribution, but they have not been concluded yet.

As a consequence of these security and privacy related challenges, the market for security-related expenditures on smart grids is growing fast, by about one-third a year, and is forecasted to reach $4 billion annually by 2013. A report released in 2010 by Pike Research [Pike10] estimated that utility companies worldwide will spend $21 billion by 2015 on smart grid cyber security. As a relatively new field, infrastructure cyber security must begin to embed state-of-the-art security (adapted from other industries with more mature cyber security) into it architecture, as part of the design and development process, rather than as a retrofit.

3 Smart Grid Security & Compliance Requirements

This section analyses the main security and compliance requirements presented in guidance documents for smart grids related to this paper's topic, security policy automation.

In particular, as the smart grid emerges, it will be necessary to improve control and visibility in line with recommended guidance (e.g. US NERC CIP, and US NIST IR 7628):

- **Control:** Enforce technical security policies across the millions of devices (including many control systems, meters, substations etc.) across an ever-changing, interconnected IT landscape
- **Visibility:** Show that the technically enforced security policies support compliance with recommended guidance.

Smart grids have some unique security and compliance requirements compared to most traditional IT environments, including the need for:

- message authentication and authorization to millions of devices
- tamper resistance and physical device security due to the large number of devices in uncontrolled environments
- least privilege access controls between interconnected devices to prevent attack points from scaling across a large number of devices, and to compartmentalize distributed attacks
- mechanisms to meet power utility specific legal security and privacy requirements
- auditability and metering without compromising privacy regulations
- highly secure and automated policy update, certificate management and configuration management across the network even for embedded devices, because there will be too many devices to manually manage
- high availability, which rules out a number of slow or CPU/network performance hungry security mechanisms
- high reliability and assurance because smart grids will be critical infrastructure and an attractive attack target
- security beyond the network layer to cover all layers (incl. the application layer), because fine-grained, contextual least privilege access control and information flow control cannot be effectively implemented purely on the network layer
- prevention of social engineering attacks, e.g. through security policy and configuration automation that takes humans out of the loop
- security of consumer usage information on millions of devices

To achieve these complex requirements, security will need to be designed into the smart grid architecture right from the beginning – because retrofitting security after the system has been designed and built will be more costly and less effective.

Unfortunately, many of the companies that are producing the solutions for meter management have not incorporated security messages in their product beyond simple physical breaches of the equipment. Utilities will have to request modifications of the products to be able to capture security information that would provide sufficient forensic value.

3.1 Security Requirements Guidance for Smart Grids

In the US, North American Electric Reliability Corporation (NERC) Critical Infrastructure Protection (CIP) [Nerc11] is the foremost recommended guidance for protecting power grids against cyber-attacks. It is soon expected to fully apply to all aspects of smart grids.

In this paper, we will focus on another major publication, US NIST's 537-page "Guidelines for smart grid Cyber Security" (NIST IR 7628) [Nist10] security requirements and risk assessment framework[1].

The guideline includes high-level security requirements, a framework for assessing risks, an evaluation of privacy issues at personal residences, and additional information for businesses and organizations to use as they craft strategies to protect the modernizing power grid from attacks, malicious code, cascading errors, and other threats. Its reference architecture with 6 functional priority areas across 7 domains and 46 actors identifies 137 interfaces—points of data exchange or other types of interactions within or between different smart grid systems and subsystems. These are assigned to one or more of 22 categories on the basis of shared or similar functional and security characteristics. In all, the report details 189 high-level security requirements, which are grouped in 19 families, applicable either to the entire smart grid or to particular parts of the grid and associated interface categories.

The report also includes a description of the risk assessment process used to identify the requirements, a discussion of technical cryptographic and key management issues across the scope of smart grid systems and devices, initial recommendations for addressing privacy risks and challenges pertaining to personal residences and electric vehicles. It also includes an overview of the process that the Cyber Security Working Group (CSWG) developed to assess whether existing or new standards that enable smart grid interoperability also satisfy the high-level security requirements included in the report, and summaries of research needs.

It covers the following families of recommended security requirements for smart grids: Access Control, Awareness and Training, Audit and Accountability, Security Assessment and Authorization, Configuration Management, Continuity of Operations, Identification and Authentication, Information and Document Management, Incident Response, smart grid Information System Development and Maintenance, Media Protection, Physical and Environmental Security, Planning, Security Program Management, Personnel Security, Risk Management and Assessment, smart grid Information System and Services Acquisition, smart grid Information System and Communication Protection, smart grid Information System and Information Integrity. The document also discusses smart grid Cryptography and Key Management Issues.

Several controls recommended in NIST IR 7628 directly relate to the topic of this paper, security policy automation for smart grids. Particularly relevant are least privilege and information flow enforcement:

3.2 Least Privilege

The recommended control "Least Privilege" (NIST IR 7628 - SG.AC-7) requires that "the organization assigns the most restrictive set of rights and privileges or access needed by users for the performance of specified tasks", and that "the organization configures the smart grid information system to enforce the most restrictive set of rights and privileges or access needed by users"[2]. In

---

1 Many other important regulations, standards, and guidance also applies to smart grids, such as PCI-DSS for payment card processing, but theoe are not discussed in this paper.
2 The section of the document also offers the additional considerations relevant to the discussion of this paper, in particular that "the organization authorizes network access to organization-defined privileged commands only for compelling operational needs and documents the rationale for such access in the security plan for the Smart Grid information

other words, a caller should only be granted access to a resource if that caller has a need to do so in the specific context, for example a particular step in a business process, or a particular system situation such as emergency level.

What this specifically means is that a dynamic access control "whitelist" (i.e. stating what is allowed, vs. "blacklists" that state what is not allowed) needs to be available that enforces the that policy requirement. Static access control models such as identity-based access control (IBAC) or role-based access control (RBAC) [FeKu92] are not sufficient access mechanisms because they do not capture such context in the policy [Lang11a, Lang11b]. As a result, virtually all IBAC/RBAC implementations, including traditional Identity and Access Management (IAM) technologies, are insufficient on their own. Attribute-based access control (ABAC), as for example standardized in OASIS eXtensible Access Control Markup Language XACML) [Oasi05], help add this missing context and other additional expressions to the policy. The flipside of ABAC is that those fine-grained contextual authorization policies are extremely difficult, time-consuming, and error-prone for human administrators to manually author and maintain.

This paper will describe further below how model-driven security can solve the ABAC manage-ability challenges.

3.3 Information Flow Enforcement

The recommended control "Information Flow Enforcement" (NIST IR 7628 - SG.AC-5) requires that the smart grid information system enforces assigned authorizations for controlling the flow of information within the smart grid information system and between interconnected smart grid information systems in accordance with applicable policy. Information flow control regulates where information is allowed to travel within a smart grid information system and between smart grid information systems. As example implementations, the document mentions boundary protection devices that restrict smart grid information system services or provide a packet-filtering capability.

This section of the document also offers a number of supplemental considerations. Particularly interesting for the discussion in this paper, the guidance recommends "dynamic information flow control allowing or disallowing information flows based on changing conditions or operational considerations"[3].

As already mentioned in the previous subsection, IBAC and RBAC are insufficient on their own, and due to the inherent changing ("agile") nature of today's interconnected IT landscapes ("system of systems"), ABAC policies would need to be constantly manually updated to be correct after "system of systems" changes, resulting in a policy management nightmare [Lang10a]. There are a number of other problems with ABAC, e.g. challenges around authorization delegation across service chains and impersonation, which can be solved using authorization-based access control (ZBAC) [KaHD09], which uses authorization tokens and federated authorization token servers.

---

system", and "the organization authorizes access to organization-defined list of security functions (deployed in hardware, software, and firmware) and security-relevant information".

3 Other considerations not directly related to the discussion in this paper include enforcement based on explicit labels on information, source, and destination objects, organization-defined security policy filters, human policy filter review, privileged administrator policy filter configuration

This paper will describe further below how model-driven security can solve the unmanageability problem of ABAC and ZBAC.

3.4 Security Incident Monitoring, Reporting, Auditing

Related to achieving visibility, numerous recommendations for incident monitoring, incident reporting, and auditing are spread throughout the NIST IR 7628 document. For example:

- "smart grid Information System Monitoring Tools and Techniques" (SG.SI-4) requires that "the organization monitors events … to detect attacks, unauthorized activities or conditions, and non-malicious errors" based on the organization's "monitoring objectives and the capability of the smart grid information system to support such activities". The supplemental guidance states that this can be achieved through a variety of tools and techniques (e.g., intrusion detection systems, intrusion prevention systems, malicious code protection software, log monitoring software, network monitoring software, and network forensic analysis tools), and can include real-time alerting
- "Incident Monitoring" (SG.IR-6) requires that "the organization tracks and documents … security incidents", maybe using "automated mechanisms to assist in the tracking of security incidents and in the collection and analysis of incident information".
- "Incident Reporting" (SG.IR-7) requires incident reporting procedures about what is an incident, granularity of incident information, who receives it etc., again potentially employing "automated mechanisms to assist in the reporting of security incidents".
- "Auditable Events" (SG.AU-2): to identify events that need to be auditable as significant and relevant, requires the development and review of a list of auditable events on an organization-defined frequency, including execution of privileged functions
- "Audit Monitoring, Analysis, and Reporting" (SG.AU-6) requires audit record reviews and analyses to find and report inappropriate or unusual activity, potentially employing automated, centralized analysis tools.
- "Audit Reduction and Report Generation" (SG.AU-7) supports near real-time analysis and after-the-fact investigations of security incidents, e.g. by automatically processing audit records for events of interest based on selectable event criteria
- "Audit Generation" (SG.AU-15) recommends audit record generation capability, potentially from multiple components into a system-wide audit trail that is time-correlated.
- "Remote Access" (SG.AC15) mentions automated mechanisms to facilitate monitoring and control of remote access methods.

In the context of the fine-grained contextual authorization mentioned earlier, incident monitoring, reporting, and audit are intrinsically intertwined with authorization. Monitoring, reporting, and audit tools will need to know the specific authorization policies in order to decide whether behaviour is in fact suspicious or not. This differs dramatically from traditional monitoring approaches which mainly monitor for generic vulnerabilities (i.e. the same vulnerabilities occur for a particular technology, rather than for a particular business) and thus do not need to know any specifics about the organization's business processes in order to flag an incident. The authors call control and visibility for generic vulnerabilities "security hygiene" to distinguish them from organization-specific policy enforcement and monitoring.

This paper will describe further below how model-driven compliance can solve the policy-driven monitoring challenge for authorization management.

4 Model-Driven Security Policy Automation for Smart Grids

This section describes how authorization policy implementation can be automated using model-driven security.

4.1 MDS: Model-Driven Security

Since 2002, the authors have implemented "model-driven security" (MDS) [Lang11b], the use of model-driven approaches to automate the generation of technical security policy implementation from generic security requirements models. Numerous publications are available, e.g. [Lang10b, [RiSL06]. Model-driven security solves the challenge that manually translating security policy & compliance requirements into effective technical implementation is difficult, expensive, and error-prone - especially for interconnected, agile, large-scape software application landscapes such as smart grids. The main challenges are:

- Where do concrete policy requirements (based on the rather vague guidance documents) come from?
- Who can reliably write the matching technical policy rules?
- Who can reliably and cost-effectively maintain them despite dynamic changes?
- Who can verify policy correctness & compliance?

The authors' definition of model-driven security (MDS) is as follows [Lang11b]: MDS is the tool supported process of modelling generic, human-understandable security requirements at a high level of abstraction, and using other information sources available about the system produced by other stakeholders (e.g. mashup/orchestration models, application models, network topology models[4]). These inputs, which are expressed in Domain Specific Languages (DSL), are then transformed into enforceable security rules with as little human intervention as possible. It also includes the run-time security management (e.g. entitlements / authorizations), i.e. run-time enforcement of the policy on the protected IT systems, dynamic policy updates and the monitoring of policy violations. MDS helps develop, operate and maintain secure applications by making security proactive, manageable, intuitive, cheaper, and less risky.

This model-driven security policy automation approach forms a critical part[5] of any authorization management, entitlement management and identity & access management (IAM) strategy. Through its integration with system/application specification tools (e.g. modelling, orchestration, and development tools) also enables a secure application development lifecycle at development time right from the beginning – dealing with policy abstraction, externalization, authoring, automation, enforcement, audit monitoring and reporting, and verification.

The only fully fledged model-driven security product currently in the market is ObjectSecurity OpenPMF [Obje11a, Obje11b], which automates application security policies for access authorization and incident monitoring. Unlike any other application security policy management product in the market, OpenPMF automates the process of translating human-understandable security & compliance requirements into the corresponding numerous and ever-changing technical authorization policy rules and configurations. In addition, it proactively enforces ("whitelisting")

---

4 Asset tracking tools can replace modeling/orchestration tools for the purposes of model-driven security.
5 Other important aspects to consider are network segmentation, incident monitoring, vulnerability analysis & testing

decentralized access decisions[6], and continuously monitors for security incidents (incl. at the application layer). OpenPMF involves five steps:

- Configure intuitive business security requirements: Security professionals can configure and audit generic application security requirements in OpenPMF, including access and monitoring policies. No need to be an application specialist. The Human-Machine Interface (HMI) to configure model-driven policies is similarly intuitive and visual as process modelling and enterprise architecture tools.
- Generate matching technical security policies automatically: Application developers can implement application specific technical application security at the click of a button. OpenPMF automatically analyses your software as it is being written or updated, and generates fine-grained access and audit policies. No need to be a security specialist.
- Enforce technical security policies transparently: At runtime, OpenPMF's local protection agents underneath all applications automatically intercept and check all application communications before they are forwarded to the application.
- Audit technical security policies transparently: At runtime, OpenPMF also automatically monitors and collects incident alerts and analyses them for compliance purposes. The collected information can be configured through fine-grained audit policies. In large-scale deployments, OpenPMF's analysed alert information is provided to third-party monitoring tools, to ensure there is a single HMI for operators to be concerned with. There is also a basic built-in HMI for incident monitoring for small-scale or development purposes.
- Update technical security policies automatically: OpenPMF agile policy automation uniquely makes policy management and implementation manageable for today's rapidly evolving interconnected applications (e.g. agile SOA with BPM, agile cloud infrastructures

OpenPMF stands for "Open Policy Management Framework" because it is based on open standards where possible (e.g. Eclipse EMF, and web app server security APIs, XACML, syslog), and because it is designed as a customizable, future-proof toolkit so it can be easily expanded to both legacy devices and new kinds of devices from different vendors.

OpenPMF automates policy management even for complex, large-scale environments such as smart grids, as well as agile Service Oriented Architecture (SOA) [LaSc07, Lang10c] and cloud [Lang10a/b/c, Lang11a] application platforms. Developed since 2002, OpenPMF is useful for protecting smart grids because it has already been successfully used in other highly regulated, critical, large-scale sectors such as defence, healthcare, air traffic management, and telecoms. Thanks to its decentralized architecture, OpenPMF supports authorization management and enforcement across several trust domains (e.g. across multiple companies' networks, or intra-company network segments), and across multiple devices. As mentioned earlier, ZBAC should be used to achieve scalable and manageable cross-domain authorization management.

MDS is well suited[7] to implement authorization policy implementation for smart grids in an automated, flexible, reliable, and cost-effective way. Figure 1 shows how smart grid system models (e.g. from asset tracking/monitoring tools, development tools, deployment/orchestration tools) and security requirements models (captured within OpenPMF) are used to generate fine-grained,

---

6 For scalability, availability, and robustness reasons, OpenPMF's Policy Decision Points (PDPs) are typically deployed decentralized and collocated with the Policy Enforcement Points (PEPs) on each protected systems.
7 Based on the authors' experience gained from being part of several smart grid alliances and centers of excellence, and from informal knowledge exchange with security staff at power utilities and smart grid vendors.

contextual technical access rules. These technical rules are then distributed to local policy decision and enforcement points, where they are automatically enforced at runtime on all traffic.

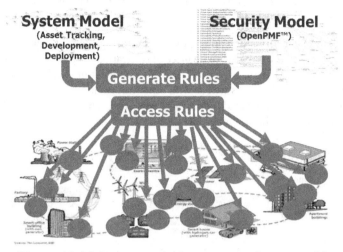

Figure 1: Model-driven security policy automation for smart grids[8]

4.2 MDSA: Model-Driven Security Incident Monitoring and Analysis Automation

As authorization becomes increasingly fine-grained and contextual, authorization incident monitoring and analysis also need to be policy-driven. This is because the authorization policy determines to a large extent what behaviour is deemed to be an incident.

In the simplest case, any blocked access requests should trigger an incident alert in real-time (this is implemented in OpenPMF by default). Furthermore, customized incident monitoring policy rules can be specified in OpenPMF to trigger customized incident alerts. But just creating such incidents is not enough. This is because security administrators typically get flooded by an unmanageably large number of irrelevant alerts to and cannot prioritize and filter alerts based on the policy requirements to find and respond to the truly important situations.

To solve this problem, the authors have implemented an automatic model-driven correlation engine called "Model Driven Security Accreditation (MDSA)" [LaSc09]. MDSA was originally invented for automating large parts of the compliance and assurance accreditation management processes (e.g. Common Criteria) to achieve reduced cost / effort, and increased reliability / traceability. MDSA automatically analyses and documents two main compliance aspects:
- Does the actual security of the "system of systems" at any given point match with the stated requirements? MDSA is a system and method for managing and analysing security and information assurance requirements in reusable models, and for (mostly) automating the verification of the traceable correspondence between incident alerts, functional models, security models, and requirements models.

---

8   Background images for Figure 1+2 top: © ObjectSecurity, bottom © GridWise Alliance

- Do any changes to the system of systems impact the current accreditation? MDSA automatically identifies changes to any aspect of the system of systems, and evaluates whether changes impact the current accreditation and whether manual corrections and re-accreditation are required.

Figure 2 shows in simplistic terms how local policy monitoring points generate incident alerts based on the policy (implemented in the same piece of software that contains the policy decision and enforcement logic). These alerts are centrally collected and automatically correlated with the various system and security models, as well as with other information (this is described in detail in [LaSc09]). The result is a consolidated report that correlates each incident to the affected security requirements and parts of the system.

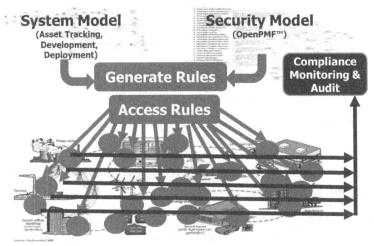

Fig. 2: Model-driven security incident monitoring and analysis automation for smart grids[9]

4.3 Example Use Case Scenario

This section outlines a basic use case scenario to illustrate how the described solution works: Assume the following policy statement that includes least privilege, information flow control, and incident monitoring / analysis: A power utilities' customer service staff should only be able to initiate the electricity shutoff at a smart meter (by sending a web service request to a web service that deals with the shutoff) if the corresponding customer requested termination of service or has not paid for their electricity usage, and an incident alert detailing the shutoff should be automatically generated by the meter and analysed by the operator. Also assume a Service Oriented Architecture (SOA) where the customer service staff uses a browser-based web application that is orchestrated from numerous web services using business process modelling (BPM) orchestration tool. While on the phone to the customer, the BPM tool guides the staff through a defined multi-step business process through several webpages. The steps are: get customer information, verify balance or shutoff request, verify meter correctness, instruct smart meter infrastructure to shut off electricity. Note that it is intended that this workflow could change frequently to reflect

---

9 Background images: top: © ObjectSecurity, bottom © GridWise Alliance

changes in the way the business is run. The five steps of model-driven security (as implemented in OpenPMF) now look as follows:

- Policy model configuration: When the system is designed, built, and deployed, security specialists capture the security requirements in a Domain Specific Language (DSL), a modelling language that uses the concepts configured specifically for the requirements of power utilities (e.g. smart meters, smart meter shutoff service, customer payment information). This can be done using a visualisation or a model editor. It is important that these policy models are specified generically and close to human thinking (i.e. close to the policy description above.

- Technical policy generation (MDS): Next, the model-driven security tool automatically analyses the security policy model, the BPM orchestration model, and other information, and automatically generates the policy rules for each node. For example, the rules generated for the shutoff web service will include e.g. "only accept the shutoff request if it is secured and comes from a known customer service system node and from the correct network segment, and from an authenticated and authorised customer service staff, and only if that staff's web application is currently going through the business process involving the customer whose meter is going to be shut off, and only if there is a shutoff request or non-payment notice on that customer's account, and only if the business process is currently at the 5th (example!) step (the shutoff step) in the business process, and only if there is no emergency or crisis situation on the network; in this case an incident alert should be generated for analysis and auditing purposes" etc. As opposed to authentication-based or role-based access control, such a contextual, fine-grained authorization rule implements real least privilege access control. Once all the rules have been generated, they get automatically distributed to Policy Decision Points (PDPs) on each protected system for localized decision making.

- Technical rule enforcement: Whenever a message arrives at a protected system, the PDP automatically evaluates the policy and makes a decision whether to grant or deny the request. The Policy Enforcement Point then preventatively enforces that decision by potentially blocking the message.

- Incident monitoring & analysis (MDSA): A Policy Monitoring Point (PMP) also generates alerts if needed based on the policy, or based on incidents (such as unauthorized blocked requests). Using model-driven approaches, alerts information can now be automatically be analysed and correlated with the specific requirements in the model – this minimizes irrelevant information and enables more accurate decision-making in near real-time.

- Automatic updates: Whenever the system changes, the rules can automatically be updated. For example, if the business process for the customer service staff changes to include an extra step where the supervisor authorizes each shutoff request, or if the customer service staff has to get authorization before viewing customer payment information, then the BPM service orchestration will change and the shutoff step in the business process may now be somewhere else in the workflow. The technical policy on the shutoff web service should then for example be automatically configured so that the correct step is not step 5 anymore but, say, step 9 in the process sequence, and that, for example, a valid delegated authorization token from the supervisor must be attached to the request. Because model-driven security generates technical rules automatically from generic models, these rules can be updated and deployed automatically if such changes occur, which minimises security policy management.

While this example is deliberately simplistic and hypothetical, model-driven security is being implemented in several critical sectors with security requirements similar to smart grids, such as defence [Obje11b], air traffic control [Obje11c], and crisis management [Obje10], and is considered for health IT and government cloud computing.

5 Conclusion

This paper explains why smart grid architectures needs to be designed to include state-of-the-art model-driven security (MDS) approaches to control (using "model-driven security policy automation") and visibility ("model-driven security incident monitoring/analysis"). Recommended controls such as least privilege, information flow enforcement, and policy-driven monitoring/ analysis can only be effectively implemented at the very large scale of a smart grid by using a combination of MDS with fine-grained, contextual authorization management (AM) and identity & access management (IAM). The paper explains why AM and/or IAM on their own are insufficient mechanisms. MDS needs to be designed into the architecture right from the start to ensure that the architecture is geared to support MDS. The actual deployment roadmap can then be implemented gradually based on a low-risk "start small, think big" approach (similar to how the smart grid itself is rolled out). While some degree of customization is to be expected due to the uniqueness of smart grid technology platforms (e.g. many embedded and legacy devices, unique security requirements), the authors have proven the approach in other critical infrastructure projects. The paper also outlines OpenPMF, the authors' MDS reference technology, which can be deployed for smart grid. The mentioned OpenPMF's cloud "policy as a service" approach, which centralizes policy requirements in a cloud service, is expected to also add value in a smart grid environment when deployed as a private cloud service.

Acknowledgements

The authors would like to thank the following individuals for their comments and suggestions on the final draft of this paper (in alphabetic order): Christine Hertzog (Smart Grid Library), Amir Khan (consultant for Portland Gas & Electric), John Reynolds (Integrated Architectures), and Jeffrey J. Sweet (American Electric Power).

References

[Cbsn10]   CBSNews. "Cyber War: Sabotaging the System". cbsnews.com/stories/2009/11/06/60minutes/main5555565.shtml. June 15, 2010

[Clar10]   Clarke, R. A. "Cyber War: The Next Threat to National Security and What to Do About It". ISBN: 0061962236. April 2010

[Epri11]   Electric Power Research Institute website. epri.com. 2011

[FeKu92]   Ferraiolo, D.F. and D.R. Kuhn. "Role-Based Access Control",. 15th National Computer Security Conference. pp. 554–563. October 1992

[Ferc11]   Federal Energy Regulatory Commission (FERC). website. ferc.gov. 2011

[Harr10]   Harris, S. "Smart Grid Security Overview". Blog post. cissp.logicalsecurity.com/network-security/cissp/smart-grid-security-overview. December 2010

[KaHD09] Karp, A. H., H. Haury, and M. H. Davis. "From ABAC to ZBAC: The Evolution of Access Control Models", HP Laboratories, HPL-2009-30, 2009

[LaSc09] Lang, U. and R. Schreiner. "Model Driven Security Accreditation (MDSA) for Agile, Interconnected IT Landscapes", Proceedings of WISG 2009 Conference, November 2009

[Lang10a] Lang, U., "Security Policy Automation: Improve Cloud Application Security ROI" ISSA Journal, October 2010

[Lang10b] Lang, U. "Cloud & SOA Application Security as a Service" Proceedings of ISSE 2010, Berlin, Germany, 5-7 October 2010

[Lang10c] Lang, U. "Authorization as a Service for Cloud & SOA Applications", Proceedings of the International Workshop on Cloud Privacy, Security, Risk & Trust (CPSRT 2010), Collocated with 2nd IEEE International Conference on Cloud Computing Technology and Science (Cloudcom) CPSRT 2010, Indianapolis, Indiana, USA, December 2010

[Lang11a] Lang, U., "Model-driven cloud security", IBM developerWorks online publication. ibm.com/developerworks/cloud/library/cl-modeldrivencloudsecurity/index.html?ca=drs-, 02 February 2011

[Lang11b] Lang, U. Security "Policy Automation and Model Driven Security", blog. modeldrivensecurity.org, 2011

[LaSc07] Lang, U and R. Schreiner. "Model Driven Security (MDS) management and enforcement to support SOA-style agility". Proceedings of the Information Security Solutions Europe (ISSE) conference, Warsaw, Poland, 26 September 2007

[Nerc11] North American Electric Reliability Corporation (NERC). website. nerc.com. 2011

[Nist10] National Institute of Standards and Technology. "NISTIR 7628: Guidelines for Smart Grid Cyber Security", csrc.nist.gov/publications/PubsNISTIRs.html#NIST-IR-7628, August 2010

[Oasi05] OASIS, "Extensible Access Control Markup Language (XACML)", OASIS Standard, 2.0, xml. coverpages.org/xacml.html, March 2005

[Obje10] ObjectSecurity. "ObjectSecurity part of 3-year EU FP7 crisis management R&D project "CRISIS", Press Release, 09 June 2010

[Obje11a] ObjectSecurity. OpenPMF website. openpmf.com, 2000-2011

[Obje11b] ObjectSecurity. "ObjectSecurity and Promia implement XML security features for next-generation US military security technology", Press Release. objectsecurity.com/doc/20100430-object-security-promia-navy-soa3.pdf, April 2010

[Obje11c] ObjectSecurity. "ObjectSecurity Awarded Joint Air Traffic Management Study on SWIM Civil-Military Interoperability", Press Release, 08 July 2011

[Pike10] Pike Research. "Smart Grid Cyber Security". pikeresearch.com/research/smart-grid-cyber-security,2010

[Rick09] Camille Ricketts. "Green Beat: U.S. smart grid market poised to double by 2014"., venturebeat.com/2009/12/16/u-s-smart-grid-market-poised-to-double-by-2014, December 16, 2009

[RiSL06] Ritter, T, R. Schreiner, U. Lang. "Integrating Security Policies via Container Portable Interceptors", IEEE distributed systems online, (vol. 7, no. 7), art. no. 0607-o7001, 1541-4922, July 2006

[Sans08] SANS Institute. "SANS NewsBites - Volume: X, Issue: 5, January 2008". sans.org/newsletters/newsbites/newsbites.php?vol=10&issue=5&rss=Y, January 2008

[Wiki11] Wikipedia. "Stuxnet", en.wikipedia.org/wiki/Stuxnet, 2011

Consumerization: Consequences of Fuzzy Work-Home Boundaries

Patrick Koeberl · Jiangtao Li · Anand Rajan · Claire Vishik ·
Marcin Wójcik

Intel Corporation
{patrickx.koeberl | jiangtao.li | anand.rajan | claire.vishik | marcinx.wojcik}@intel.com

Abstract

The paper discusses the phenomenon of consumerization of IT, the use of consumer devices in the work environment to perform ordinary work tasks. We analyze representative threats connected with consumerization as well as some of the common consumerization scenarios and discuss architectures and other mitigation approaches that can help address the issues associated with consumerization in the current and future generations of computing devices. We outline research areas that could represent the next generation R&D agenda and provide technology answers to some security issues associated with consumerization. Much of the focus of the paper is on mobile smart phones because this environment makes it easier to highlight the security problems of consumerization. But many of the vulnerabilities and potential mitigations we describe and mitigations we outline apply to mobile PC platforms, tablets, and mobile handsets.

1 Introduction

The advent of multiple connected devices is not a new phenomenon. But with the simultaneous increase in power and connectivity of consumer mobile devices, their ubiquitous use begins to strongly affect adjacent environments, including the work space. Increasing diversity of currently available consumer devices forming a compute continuum as illustrated in Figure 1, currently exercises direct influence on IT practices and requirements for the new generations of devices. Just as the boundary between the Internet and Intranet continues to grow fuzzier, so the boundary between the work environment and consumer environment is now becoming diluted. The phenomenon that is sometimes called consumerization – pervasive use of consumer devices for organizational tasks, for which they were not designed or configured – has reached proportions where it needs to be addressed more systematically. The devices in question – smart phones, netbooks, iPads, e-readers – are architected and configured differently from each other and provide varying levels of security protection for the user data that they contain and exchange, but they frequently work in concert with full computing environments (e.g. laptops) that are adapted for organizational environments. Sometimes, when ultra mobility is necessary, mobile devices of various kinds are used as alternatives to access more secure computing environments. More frequently, the necessity for greater mobility or execution of a certain task has become a matter of choice rather than necessity. An increasing number of organizations now permit the employees to bring to work devices of their choice as main or supplementary work tools.

N. Pohlmann, H. Reimer, W. Schneider (Editors): Securing Electronic Business Processes, Vieweg (2011), 138-153

As a result, organizational use of consumer devices and the number of dual-use devices has increased significantly, even in some higher security environments. Typically, protection measures in organizations focus on types of devices, by creating rules on how a certain type of platform can be used in the work environments. Frequently, configurations of official mobile devices are made more secure. But the over-riding issue remains: security policies and requirements are mapped to devices that were not architected for these policies and these requirements. And we do not yet have conceptual models to permit us to design new devices with diverse use environments in mind. There are also limited techniques to ensure we take into consideration the fact that these devices interact with other devices and access diverse networks while also participating in secure transactions or storing data securely. Ideally, consistent architectures and levels of security protection combined with agility need to enable the new generation of connected devices. In practice, we need to start with a thorough analysis of dynamic threats and environments characterizing today's computing spectrum and use the learning as the first step to bringing more consistency into the area of security research.

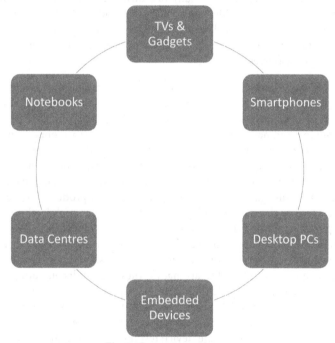

Fig. 1: Compute continuum

In research, some work has been done to evolve architectures that support the use of the same platform in environments with varying security requirements. For example, domain isolation was suggested as an approach to separate work and home environments, and virtualization is increasingly perceived as one of the solutions for this growing problem. Approaches to building secure operating systems have been evaluated, and work on security ontology that spans multiple domains has been attempted (see [EkFe09]). But the rapidly increasing diversity of devices will soon make these approaches difficult to sustain.

2 Emerging Requirements for Multi-Use Mobile Devices

Today, accessing, sharing, gathering, manipulating, and analyzing information is an important issue from the economic, social and cultural perspective. This information "juggle" constantly increases demands for computing power, bandwidth and storage resources. In many cases, the newest technologies and applications emerge in consumer environments and then are introduced into the organizational environment, forcing IT departments to re-evaluate access and usage policies, and also re-consider the levels of support that are provided. There are a sufficient number of new features in the new consumer devices to make them attractive tools to perform crucial tasks in today's dynamic and mobile workforce. At the same time, we observe the convergence of electronic devices, e.g., mobile handsets and PDAs, using the same types of applications and similar interfaces. While some organizations continue to resist dual- use devices or supporting devices originally designed for consumer markets, many organizations have introduced new policies, permitting employees to purchase a wider range of devices and platforms as primary computing and communication tools and even allowing employees to bring the devices they chose and purchased themselves to work, to be set up, to the extent possible, as work devices with complete access to most enterprise resources.

Consumerization of IT has received a lot of coverage lately, predominantly in trade publications, and achieved enough visibility to become one of the latest technology trends. Although consumerization is not limited to mobile handsets used in work environments, mobile telephones receive the greatest publicity in conjunction with consumerization. Modern mobile terminals are not only phones used for voice communication, but they have evolved from simple, single purpose devices to advanced, sophisticated multi-purpose communication, productivity, and entertainment platforms. They can handle a wide range of applications from simple notepads and messaging to complicated 3D on-line games. Their capability to support productivity applications has improved in the past two or three years. In general, state-of-the-art mobile phones are close in functionality, though not in performance, to previous generations of mobile computers. Based on the introduction of new functionality on smart phones, it is reasonable to expect that the main security principles that have been applied for personal computers should now be applied to mobile terminals. Without adequate protection, threats that we know from full computing environments will become common in the mobile world. Similarly, principles of access control that have been accepted for PCs have to be adopted for smart phones. In the past, risks to voice services have been considered in mobile telephony. Today, risks of compromise of data and risks connected to leaking confidential information from the device terminal have become real. Moreover, with location services on mobile terminals, additional risks, to both security and privacy, arise that are not well understood. This is only one area of potential vulnerabilities, but the environment where some applications reside on mobile devices, some are located on Web servers, and multiple access mechanisms (Wi-Fi, WiMAX, 3-4G, Bluetooth, etc.) are supported is expected to expose the users to new types of attacks that we cannot anticipate.

In scenarios where professional and private worlds coexist, boundaries between them are becoming more and more diluted. We tend to use mobile phones as devices that help us deal with day to day tasks at work and at home. We download maps and slides and boarding passes to the phones, and maintain address books and email repositories, containing a range of data with different protection needs. Potentially, mobile telephones can play crucial roles to support security and trust.

Proposals to use telephones as pervasive and ubiquitous trust devices have been put forward, and the first applications of this type have been developed. The information that is accessible from mobile phones is located in various spaces: on servers on the World Wide Web, on email servers in the enterprise, on the SIM card, in the device memory, or on other communication or storage devices. Moreover, this information belongs to different environments: work and consumer. In both environments, frequently the same productivity and supporting applications are used. The strict separation envisioned in earlier work on domain isolation and virtualization may not offer sufficient protection as today's environment evolves.

In the old paradigm, approved communications and computing devices undergo numerous compatibility, security, and usability tests. Such scrutiny is not possible in the new paradigm where the employees can bring their own devices and enable them for some – frequently full – level of access. This enablement is sometimes of limited strength because the typical architectures of many modern mobile devices have not been developed with the idea of simultaneous use in business and consumer environments. This is a fundamental flaw that cannot be overcome with a new application layers or stronger configurations.

In this context, it is necessary to understand a new class of threats associated with dual use of devices and begin to address the development of architectures that could better support such usage patterns and act against the increased number of possible and likely attacks. The section below describes representative use cases and is followed by a section describing representative threats we believe are associated with this new environment.

3 Usage Scenarios

Several use cases are presented to highlight security problems connected with consumerization. This is not an exhaustive list of usage scenarios, but a selection that attempts to highlight some of the representative areas.

3.1 Consolidation of User and Work Applications on One Device

The user's preference to consolidate ownership and use of devices for work and personal tasks leads to their agreement to permit some level of IT stewardship of the personal devices to allow work access. On the enterprise side, there are new policies to permit dual-use devices if they are set up in accordance with IT requirements. As a result, the same device is used in conjunction with diverging security requirements and hosts data that is confidential alongside PII (Personally Identifiable Information) and sharable general purpose information. Enforcing access control and preventing information leakage are among the main remediation goals in conjunction with this scenario. In addition, a different maintenance paradigm is likely to apply to devices used in this way, affecting updates, upgrades, patching where applicable, download and use of applications, permissions with regard to access to device configuration and resources, and synchronization with IT maintained devices.

3.2 Use of Smart Phone Applications Designed to Access Enterprise Back-end Systems

Increasingly, the mobile work force needs seamless access to information contained in enterprise back-end systems from anywhere in the world, including locations where wireline or wireless connectivity may not be available, but sufficient mobile telephony infrastructure exists. The applications permitting such access have been designed for a variety of tasks, frequently implemented as thin smart phone clients (e.g. [LaTh11]). Access-control, potential access to confidential resources by unauthorized parties, data leakage, and use of non-protected storage for confidential information are among the risks associated with using of this class of applications. Additionally, the effect of location-based services on applications of this nature is an interesting avenue for investigation.

3.3 Use of NFC (Near Field Communications) enabled phones

As described in literature, e.g., [RKSH07], an NFC enabled smart phone is used for tasks at work and outside of work to check inventories and availability of products. Both security and privacy issues arise in this situation, as described in studies regarding the use of RFID in general. Potential intercept of sensitive information through NFC channels and other attacks initiated from this channel also represent a concern.

3.4 Use of Mobile Devices to Support Team Work

In enterprise and consumer environments, applications across the computing spectrum are used to support team work or group communications. Concerns about security, privacy, and confidentiality are associated with this type of use. Risks outlined above combined with known and new risks for social networking environments apply to this group of use cases.

3.5 Use of Mobile Devices for Document Storage

Electronic devices, from smart phones to e-readers are used as convenient and ultra-portable document storage tools to enable quick access to some documents in situations where battery power and use environment is not compatible with the retrieval from PC-like devices. Strong concerns for general information leakage are associated with this group of use cases, as well as risks of theft, access control concerns, and synchronization-related attacks.

3.6 Connecting from Mobile Devices Using Diverse Networks

Connectivity from the same devices can be achieved using different paradigms, e.g., WiFi and 3G, sometimes also WiMAX. Different connection types are associated with different protocols and different security features. The security consequences of multiple connectivity options in various mobile devices have not yet been studied. The weaknesses of each of the networking paradigms used for connectivity can form a foundation for potential security and privacy attacks.

3.7 Location-based Services on Dual-Use Mobile Devices

The use of location-based services on smart phones that are used for many activities associated with confidential or personal data is likely to introduce additional threats that need to be studied to improve current security models. Privacy concerns associated with location based services have been known for a while, but security concerns and possible attacks and vulnerabilities associated with knowing the location of a device have not been explored in the research environment.

4 Threats

4.1 Definitions

As we are describing security threats associated with the consumerization of IT, it is helpful to introduce some formal definitions. In [Info08], a threat is defined as "a potential cause of an incident that may result in harm to a system or organization", a vulnerability as "a weakness of an asset or group of assets that can be exploited by one or more threats" and a risk as "an effect of uncertainty on objectives." Usually standards define sources of threats in a particular context, but the definitions are basic and can be adapted to other use cases. In [ASMO], the following categories of threats for mobile networks and devices are introduced: loss of availability (flooding an interface, crashing a network element via a protocol or application implementation flaw), loss of confidentiality (eavesdropping, unauthorized access to sensitive data on a network element via leakage), loss of integrity (traffic modification, data modification on a network element), loss of control (compromise of a network element via a protocol or application implementation flaw, compromise of a network element via a management interface, malicious insider) and theft of service. In literature dedicated to security management of smart phones, e.g., [Land10], other categories of threats are proposed: threats from malware, social engineering, intercepting communications, direct hacking attacks, and theft/loss of devices. These categories apply to mobile terminals as well as networks and can be considered as threat scenarios for this new wave. Reasoning about threats is considered useful for some development models, and security and threat taxonomies have been introduced to support this.

4.2 Representative Threats

In this section we explore specific threat scenarios, see Figure 2, resulting from consumerization that are linked to the use cases outlined earlier. This is not a complete list of threats, and the intent here is to outline threats that are pertinent to many or most consumerization scenarios.

Fig. 2 Consumerization threats

4.2.1 Data Leakage

Loss of confidential and proprietary data, physical loss of devices, synchronization risks, removable media as well as leakage connected to unauthorized access to data stored on the device or intercepted in transit represent some of the threats associated with data leakage. Data and information leakage are linked to a range of situations, from those associated with lost and stolen devices (e.g., [MLL+10] to information leakage from hardware cache (e.g., [BoOr10]). The synchronization of data between mobile devices and corporate PCs poses a risk. Synchronization occurs over a range of local communication channels (WiFi, USB, IRDA, Bluetooth), typically using specialized (and in many cases proprietary) applications. Mitigations involving some form of data filtering such as content based filtering are difficult to apply in this scenario. Some novel approaches to data sharing between environments have been presented in research, e.g., [MAF+11] or [MaWK08]. Data leakage is a risk for all the use cases in Section 3.

4.2.2 Location-based threats

Location-based studies usually focus on threats to user privacy (see, e.g., [Krum09]), and technologies for obfuscating or anonymizing location information have been proposed. Threats to privacy are real (see, e.g., a recently reported discovery that location information is stored unencrypted on some smart phones), but the security implications of access to location-based data are not clear because security threats associated with knowledge of the location of a device have not been thoroughly studied. Adjacent fields, such as security of geospatial data, have received some attention, e.g., [BTGD08], but the complexity of the data structures and usages in this area led to only a superficial evaluation of security risks. Additional work in this area is required that focuses on security. Possibilities for social engineering driven by the potential knowledge of the location of a device or platform also need to be studied. Location-based threats apply to most of the scenarios in Section 3.

4.2.3 Malware

Unlike full PCs and netbooks, smart phones and tablets frequently do not use tools and applications to protect them from malware. However, the latest Operating Systems on smart phones possess most of the features that Operating System for PCs are expected to have [BHB+10]. Rootkits have become a threat, and malware occurrences on smart phones are growing, although are still minuscule compared with malware in desktop computers [Land10]. In 2008, only 43 organizations reported malware contamination from smart phones [Land10], but this was before significant advances in smart phones technologies and before the advent of consumerization. The expectation is that the significant growth of malware instances on handsets will occur as the differences between mobile computers and smart phones continue to erode. Contamination by malware is a risk for all the use cases in Section 3.

4.2.4 Application Access to Resources

In most mobile Operating Systems, access to resources has to be confirmed by a user after installation of an application. In reality, users do not understand the implications of access that is granted and what kind of resources can become available to the application. Even if we assume a higher level of expertise in an average user, the level of granularity available for an application's access decisions would prevent educated users from making meaningful selections in many cases. This situation may lead to increased threats of data leakage from mobile terminals. We can imagine a scenario when a user of a dual-use device grants access to selected resources (e.g., contact information or messaging) enabling the application to leak data through internet connections. There is also a significant risk to privacy from data sharing via mobile applications.

5 Survey of Available Mitigation Approaches

5.1 User and Device Authentication

Access to corporate resources is typically achieved using user authentication mechanisms such as passwords combined with additional authentication factors. As the consumerization of IT builds momentum, the pressure from users to simplify the user authentication experience will increase. It can be argued that current approaches to strong user authentication such as strong passwords, client-side digital certificates and one-time passwords have usability and support cost challenges leading to a requirement for simpler, cheaper and more intuitive methods which maintain a similar level of security.

While the user authentication techniques prevent unauthorized users from accessing the corporate network, they do not prevent unauthorized devices from connecting to the network in the first instance. Device authentication mechanisms that are privacy friendly can prevent unauthorized network access by unknown devices and are important elements of any consumerization IT strategy.

While user authentication has experienced fast evolution, the development of new techniques for device authentication has been slower. Combining portable user authentication with the authentication of a device can improve access control in conjunction with most consumerization scenarios.

5.2 Remote Attestation

The ability to verify the integrity of a computing device's hardware and software configuration remotely, known as remote attestation, is a valuable mitigation against some malware threats. Anonymous and attribute based attestation protocols have been developed. Attestation can be supported by enabling a series of platform measurements that need to be securely stored. The measurements take the form of cryptographic hashes of the software and hardware configuration. Trusted Computing standards and related research work describe options for attestation, with Mobile Trusted Module [MTMS] providing built-in support for secure boot. Attestation can be static, i.e., it enables a device to be bootstrapped from a known-good configuration, but dynamic approaches are also known (see, e.g., [BHB+10]). Beyond Trusted Computing, other forms of attestation are possible, collecting representative proofs of status or security features of a device, an application, or a network. Defining novel forms of attestation is a promising research topic, and these technologies can solve some problems of consumerization, such as notifying the environment of the trustworthiness of dual-use devices.

5.3 Domain Isolation

Domain isolation is one of the common mitigation approaches to address security issues in consumerization and is enabled by virtualization technologies, allowing isolated environments to be run on the same hardware. Although more common in full computing platforms (PCs and servers), virtualization for handsets was proposed, prototyped, and implemented (see, e.g., [BBD+10]). Virtualization techniques allow the virtualized containers to be moved between hardware platforms, even during operation. In a typical scenario a company might prepare a virtualized environment and allow an employee to run this on the employee's hardware under some agreed policies. Virtualization technologies are still poorly supported in mobile platforms such as smart phones and PDAs. Recent attempts to solve the issue are still under development and require close cooperation with phone manufacturers, e.g., to install software needed for the virtualization. Nevertheless, in the future it might be possible to launch the isolated corporate container on a private mobile device and support features such as remote management and data deletion in the event of the device being lost or stolen. Security by isolation is also a basic principle applied in the experimental open-source Qubes OS [QUBE] based on the Xen hypervisor and Linux. This operating system is aimed at desktop and laptop computers, which is especially interesting from the user and corporate perspective in terms of consumerization. The security model is based on virtual machines called domains, which are isolated from each other and within which the user can host applications. If something happens with one of the domains, e.g., it gets compromised, others remain unaffected. The main drawback of the system is that the user has to decide how to partition applications on domains. New approaches to domain isolation can bring answers to many issues associated with dual-use mobile devices.

5.4 Content Based Filtering

Applying controls to the type of data transferred from corporate servers to employee devices is an important element of any data leakage prevention strategy. Traditional methods such as ACLs and file extension filtering go some way toward preventing data leakage, however these are not sufficient and some form of data filtering is preferable. Depending on the complexity of the filtering rule-set, content based filtering can be resource intensive and is in many instances applied at a centralized point on the network on a dedicated appliance. As a result, it is well suited to controlling data transfers from corporate servers to employee devices. However, in the case of a data transfer from a corporate PC to an employee-owned mobile device (such as during data synchronization) it is difficult to apply a content filtering approach. Moreover, in any environment, content filtering is potentially connected with privacy and user control concerns. These concerns need to be answered when developing new technologies in this area.

5.5 Network Separation

Non-employees visiting corporate facilities may have need to access local corporate resources. A typical approach to these cases is to implement separate networks for employees and non-employees, for example a wireless "guest network". This allows data transfer to non-employee devices to be controlled at a centralized point rather than relying on traditional ACL-based approaches. It is impractical to use network separation for dual-use devices, but learnings from implementations of this approach can inform new research directions that will benefit consumerization.

5.6 Device-Level Encryption

Encrypting the data resident on a mobile device is an important element of any data leakage prevention strategy. Mobile devices are particularly susceptible to loss or theft; in these cases robust encryption of the data stored on the device is effective in mitigating a range of attacks which attempt to access confidential data. Although authentication mechanisms (such as passwords) typically control access to the device, the device memory can in many cases be simply removed and subsequently read in an uncontrolled device. Such attacks can be mitigated by encrypting at the file or volume level. Note that during device operation, data typically exists in volatile storage (RAM) in unencrypted form. This poses a security risk, which can only be fully mitigated by applying encryption to processor memory accesses; an approach which is not typical today due to cost and performance considerations. Although not directly applicable to consumerization issues, research results from this area can bring new ideas to develop new more resilient device architectures.

5.7 Remote Data Wiping

The ability to remotely wipe data on the dual-use device can be viewed as a supplemental mechanism to device-level encryption. It has to be implemented in a privacy-friendly fashion. Remote Data Wiping in isolation is not sufficient to mitigate the data leakage threat since an attacker may succeed in removing the storage media before any data wiping operation can be executed. Nevertheless, the technique has value in reducing the risk of data leakage in some instances, e.g., by deleting corporate data when the mobile device doesn't 'check-in' with corporate severs after a pre-defined timeframe or by deleting corporate data when the mobile device doesn't "check-in" with corporate servers after a pre-defined timeframe or by deleting data that the employee no longer requires for his/her job. In order to consider the introduction of such a technique, policies need to be developed that will be compatible with the dual-use model and acceptable to the device owners.

6 Potential Novel Mitigation Approaches

In this section we review a number of novel mitigation approaches, illustrated in Figure 2, which may form part of an overall consumerization security strategy.

6.1 Context Aware Security

As devices gain the ability to obtain information about the environment in which they are operating, for example a device's location or whether other persons are in the user's vicinity, opportunities for improving security arise. As an example, methods can be devised for a device to restrict the display of confidential corporate information at locations other than the employee's home and workplace or adjust to the security rating of a network being used. Context awareness has not been studied as one of potential remedies for consumerization issues, and it is an interesting research topic to pursue in this context.

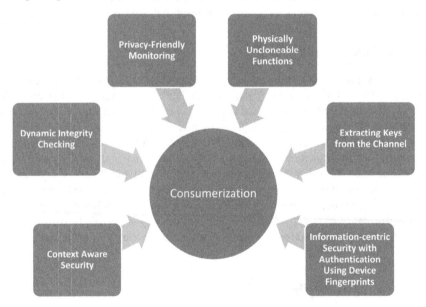

Fig. 3: Novel Mitigations

6.2 Dynamic Integrity Checking

While static integrity checking approaches such as that specified by the Trusted Computing Group [TRST] can support a trusted boot process from a known good software and hardware configuration, only dynamic integrity checks can prevent or detect runtime attacks such as those posed by stack and heap based buffer overflows. Dynamic integrity checks, for example those based on global invariants [KSA+09], control flow integrity [ABEL05] and the tracking of untrusted data (dynamic taint analysis) [DaSW09] could potentially provide a valuable extension of the integrity checking approaches based on Trusted Computing specifications.

6.3 Privacy-Friendly Monitoring

The users' behavioral patterns present opportunities for addressing some of the security concerns raised by consumerization. The idea is to define a unique template of user behavior that is meaningful, but not identifiable, and that is applicable no matter what kind of electronic device he or she uses. This pattern can be constantly checked with real-time data of user behavior and raise an alarm in the case of anomalous behavior, which could be an indication of unauthorized device use. Many new features in mobile devices, such as GPS, touch screens, sensors etc., might be used to create behavioral patterns. For example, with GPS coordinates we can create a location-based "sandbox", where all anomalies like travelling to different geographical locations might be reported. Another well known method which could be applied in this scenario is dynamic keystroke analysis. Each individual has unique manner and rhythm of typing on a keyboard, and this feature might be used to augment the behavioral pattern. Understanding of low-level user-specific behaviors enables a more device-agnostic approach to the consumerization problem. Finally, monitoring of low level execution events offers some possibilities to detect deviations from normal device behavior and define policies based on this information. In all the cases, privacy of users needs to be a strong concern in creating these technologies. Potentially, an anonymous construct confirming expected (though not identifiable) usage patterns may be part of attestation information.

6.4 Physically Unclonable Functions

Cryptographic techniques will form part of the solution to the security issues raised by consumerization. Encryption, decryption and authentication functions require key material to be stored securely, a requirement that can be challenging in the context of mobile computing devices. The typical price points and form factors of such devices rule out traditional key protection techniques such as environmental monitoring and protective device enclosures. A recently introduced security primitive, termed the Physically Unclonable Function (PUF) [Papp01], offers interesting opportunities for enabling lower cost authentication and secure key storage.

Silicon PUFs [GCDD02] in particular are of interest since they can leverage the high levels of integration possible with modern CMOS IC fabrication processes. Manufacturing variations of CMOS physical parameters, such as dopant-concentrations, transistor-dimensions and interconnect line widths, phenomena that are usually considered detrimental, are extracted by the silicon PUF and used to enable biometric-like authentication or cryptographic key generation functions. The key advantage of PUFs is that cryptographic secrets are no longer stored in any digital sense on the device, significantly raising the effort level for an attacker attempting to extract these secrets using invasive methods. In contrast, traditional techniques for storing cryptographic secrets rely on non-volatile memory such as flash, EEPROM or fuses. These may be vulnerable to key extraction attempts or cloning attacks where the secret is replicated in a target device. With regard to consumerization, PUF based techniques can become part of more secure authentication protocols or be used in other contexts, including domain isolation.

6.5 Extracting Keys from the Channel

As mobile devices become ubiquitous, the requirement for secure wireless communication between them and other devices will increase. Fundamentally, two devices wishing to communicate securely with each other must share a key, a requirement which encounters scalability problems when the number of devices is large. PKI is one solution to the key management problem; experience shows that there are also significant difficulties associated with large PKI deployments around scalability and usability. Another approach to establishing a common key involves combining pre-shared authentication credentials with a nonce transmitted in the clear. In this case, a compromise of the authentication credentials results in a compromise of previously encrypted messages. Both solutions are incompatible with dynamic mobile environments where devices may wish to communicate with each other in an ad-hoc, on-the-fly manner.

The nature of the wireless channel between two communicating mobile devices offers an interesting opportunity for establishing a secure link in the absence of a pre-shared secret. In [MTM+08] the properties of the wireless link are used to generate a common, secret cryptographic key between two devices. The properties are location specific and reciprocal. In other words, an eavesdropper attempting to extract the common key will experience different link properties such that no information about the key is revealed. The technique presents opportunities for improving existing wireless protocols, for example, rather than transmitting information in the clear during the establishment of the channel the link can be secure from the outset. It may be applicable to some consumerization scenarios.

6.6 Information-centric Security with Authentication using Device Fingerprints

Information-centric security is a term describing a process of shifting information or data protection responsibility from users or applications to the data itself. There have been a number of proposals in this area, e.g., [OLTS07]. In the context of information-centric security, it is easy to imagine data as a self-contained protected container with embedded security, policy and other necessary information. These packages can be shifted around hardware platforms and users whenever security requirements are met, for example, in the context of a trusted environment. To perform operations on this data, adequate trusted environments might be created with the use of virtualization and trusted booting methods. One approach is that taken by Qubes OS [QUBE]. Here, a user can create a virtual container and recreate an environment needed for a particular security level. It is worth mentioning, that apart from standard security methods like passwords etc., additional information like GPS location, working hours or mobile device user data might be used to increase the security level. Innovative and novel approaches might use as additional information a device's fingerprints, e.g., using Physically Unclonable Functions (PUFs) [GCDD02] to authenticate a device, or a group of devices and data containers. This mitigation, as some others described above, is an opportunity for future technologies due to current lack of widespread virtualization technologies available for smart phones. It can enable novel protocols that can improve and customize security requirements in the context of consumerization.

7 Conclusions and Future Work

Consumerization is a phenomenon that leads organizations to reassess their security policies and maintenance practices. It is an invitation to technologists to revisit not only the inventory of available and possible mitigations for the risks associated with the new phenomenon, but also to reassess security models used for the development of new security features and even the basic architectures of mobile devices that could support dual-use at work and at home without jeopardizing security. Although consumerization has not been thoroughly studied in a research context, it is likely to provide fertile ground for future projects.

The review of recent work in this paper highlights serious gaps in the current apparatus that can enable us to study phenomena such as consumerization. General threat models that address dual-use issues do not exist, and security models that can enable both policy and feature development in environments that support consumerization have not yet emerged. There is a general understanding of the issues associated with consumerization of IT, but this knowledge is derived from enterprise uses of technology and doesn't take into consideration changed usage models.

While the difficulties associated with managing consumerization are clear, the situation can also contain an opportunity to introduce semi-experimental technologies destined for the enterprise frameworks into consumer environments and increasing the general level of security in the ecosystem. Another opportunity is to gradually modify behavior of consumers to resemble the attitudes of enterprise users, a direction that also promises to increase the safety of the computing environment.

References

[ABEL05] Martin Abadi, Mihai Budiu, Ulfar Erlingsson, and Jay Ligatti. 2005. Control-flow integrity. In *Proceedings of the 12th ACM conference on Computer and communications security* (CCS '05). ACM, New York, NY, USA, 340-353.

[ASMO] ASMONIA Project, Threat and Risk Analysis for Mobile Communication Networks and Mobile Terminals, D5.1(I)-1.2, available at: http://www.asmonia.de

[BBD+10] Ken Barr, Prashanth Bungale, Stephen Deasy, Viktor Gyuris, Perry Hung, Craig Newell, Harvey Tuch, and Bruno Zoppis. 2010. The VCMware mobile virtualization platform: is that a hypervisor in your pocket?. *SIGOPS Oper. Syst. Rev.* 44, 4 (December 2010), 124-135.

[BoOr10] Garo Bournoutian and Alex Orailoglu. 2010. Dynamic, non-linear cache architecture for power-sensitive mobile processors. In *Proceedings of the eighth IEEE/ACM/IFIP international conference on Hardware/software codesign and system synthesis* (CODES/ISSS '10). ACM, New York, NY, USA, 187-194.

[BHB+10] Jeffrey Bickford, Ryan O'Hare, Arati Baliga, Vinod Ganapathy, and Liviu Iftode. 2010. Rootkits on smart phones: attacks, implications and opportunities. In *Proceedings of the Eleventh Workshop on Mobile Computing Systems & Applications* (HotMobile '10). ACM, New York, NY, USA, 49-54.

[BTGD08] Elisa Bertino, Bhavani Thuraisingham, Michael Gertz, and Maria Luisa Damiani. 2008. Security and privacy for geospatial data: concepts and research directions. In *Proceedings of the SIGSPATIAL ACM GIS 2008 International Workshop on Security and Privacy in GIS and LBS*(SPRINGL '08). ACM, New York, NY, USA, 6-19.

[DaSW09] L. Davi, A. Sadeghi, and M. Winandy, "Dynamic IntegrityMeasurement and Attestation: To-wards Defense against Return-Oriented Programming Attacks", *Proceedings of the 2009 ACM-workshop on Scalable Trusted Computing (STC)*. November 2009.

[EkFe09] Ekelhart, A and Fenz, S. Formalizing Information Security Knowledge. In *Proceedings of the 4thInternational Symposium on Information, Computer, and Communications Security*, (Sydney, 2009), ACM, 183-194.

[Info08] ISO/IEC, "Information technology -- Security techniques-Information security risk manage-ment" ISO/IEC FIDIS 27005:2008

[GCDD02] Blaise Gassend, Dwaine Clarke, Marten van Dijk, and Srinivas Devadas. 2002. Silicon physical random functions. In *Proceedings of the 9th ACM conference on Computer and communications security* (CCS '02), Vijay Atluri (Ed.). ACM, New York, NY, USA, 148-160.

[MLL+10] Jon Meling, Bjornstein Lilleby, Paul Levlin, Tor Erik Sonvisen, Stig Johansen, Dag Johansen, and Age Kvalnes. 2009. Gohcci: Protecting Sensitive Data on Stolen or Misplaced Mobile Devices. In Proceedings of the 2009 Tenth International Conference on Mobile Data Management: Sys-tems, Services and Middleware (MDM '09). IEEE Computer Society, Washington, DC, USA, 348-354.

[Krum09] John Krumm. 2009. A survey of computational location privacy. Personal Ubiquitous Com-put. 13, 6 (August 2009), 391-399.

[KSA+09] Kil, C.; Sezer, E.C.; Azab, A.M.; Peng Ning; Xiaolan Zhang; Remote attestation to dynamic sys-tem properties: Towards providing complete system integrity evidence, *Dependable Systems & Networks, 2009. DSN '09. IEEE/IFIP International Conference on* , vol., no., pp.115-124, June 29 2009-July 2 2009

[LaTh11] T. K. Lakshman and Xander Thuijs. 2011. Enhancing enterprise field productivity via cross plat-form mobile cloud apps. In *Proceedings of the second international workshop on Mobile cloud computing and services* (MCS '11). ACM, New York, NY, USA, 27-32.

[Land10] Max Landman. 2010. Managing smart phone security risks. In *2010 Information Security Cur-riculum Development Conference* (InfoSecCD '10). ACM, New York, NY, USA, 145-155.

[Mace10] John C. Mace, Simon Parkin, and Aad van Moorsel. 2010. A collaborative ontology development tool for information security managers. In *Proceedings of the 4th Symposium on Computer Hu-man Interaction for the Management of Information Technology* (CHiMiT '10). ACM, New York, NY, USA

[MAF+11] Petros Maniatis, Devdatta Akhawe, Kevin Fall, Elaine Shi, Stephen McCamant, and Dawn Song. 2011. Do you know where your data are?: secure data capsules for deployable data protection. In Proceedings of the 13th USENIX conference on Hot topics in operating systems (HotOS'13). USENIX Association, Berkeley, CA, USA, 22-22.

[MaWK08] Takashi Matsunaka, Takayuki Warabino, Yoji Kishi, Secure Data Sharing in Mobile Environ-ments, mdm, pp.57-64, The Ninth International Conference on Mobile Data Management (mdm 2008), 2008

[MTMS] Trusted Computing Group, Mobile Trusted Module Specification, available at: http://www.trustedcomputinggroup.org/resources/mobile_phone_work_group_mobile_trusted_module_specification

[MTM+08] Suhas Mathur, Wade Trappe, Narayan Mandayam, Chunxuan Ye, and Alex Reznik. 2008. Radio-telepathy: extracting a secret key from an unauthenticated wireless channel. In Proceedings of te 14th ACM international conference on Mobile computing and networking (MobiCom '08). ACM, New York, NY, USA, 128-139.

[OLTS07] Jon Oltsik, Enterprise Strategy Group, The Information-Centric Security Architecture, available at: http://www.emc.com/collateral/analyst-reports/esg-info-centric-security-architecture.pdf

[Papp01]   Pappu Srinivasa Ravikanth. 2001. *Physical One-Way Functions*. Ph.D. Dissertation. Massachusetts Institute of Technology. AAI0803255.

[QUBE]   Qubes: Strong Security for Desktop Computing, available at: http://qubes-os.org

[RKSH07]   Florian Resatsch, Stephan Karpischek, Uwe Sandner, and Stephan Hamacher. 2007. Mobile sales assistant: NFC for retailers. In *Proceedings of the 9th international conference on Human computer interaction with mobile devices and services* (MobileHCI '07). ACM, New York, NY, USA, 313-316.

[Schw04]   F. Swiderski and W. Snyder, *Threat Modeling*. Microsoft Press, 2004, ISBN 0735619913.

[Tayl03]   Ken Taylor and Doug Palmer. 2003. Applying enterprise architectures and technology to the embedded devices domain. In *Proceedings of the Australasian information security workshop conference on ACSW frontiers 2003 - Volume 21* (ACSW Frontiers '03), Chris Johnson, Paul Montague, and Chris Steketee (Eds.), Vol. 21. Australian Computer Society, Inc., Darlinghurst, Australia, Australia, 185-190.

[TRST]   Trusted Computing Group, available at: http://www.trustedcomputinggroup.org/

Smart Grid Privacy by Design: Ontario's Advanced Distribution System

Ann Cavoukian[1] · Michelle Chibba[1]

[1]Information and Privacy Commissioner of Ontario
2 Bloor Street East, Suite 1400, Toronto, Ontario, Canada, M4W 1A8
info@ipc.on.ca

Abstract

Building on our earlier Smart Grid privacy work [Cavo10] this paper demonstrates how Best Practices for Smart Grid *Privacy by Design* can be operationalized into Smart Grid systems. In Ontario, Canada, Hydro One is the largest electricity transmission and distribution company and already has an advanced metering infrastructure in place along with over 1 million smart meters deployed across its rural and suburban service area. The next logical step for Hydro One in implementing its long-term Smart Grid vision is to focus on their Advanced Distribution System (ADS). This paper outlines our collaborative effort with Hydro One and its Smart Grid vendor partners to proactively make privacy an essential design feature that figures prominently in the very architecture of the solutions being contemplated. Having a gold standard for privacy against which business requirements and processes can be mapped during development and implementation leads to choices in architecture and design that significantly reduce privacy risks, such as the unauthorized dissemination of personally identifiable information. The result is that consumer expectations of privacy *and* an improved electrical grid can indeed be achieved in unison, in a positive-sum manner.

1 Introduction

The rate of change in the electrical industry today continues to accelerate, as does the complexity of that change. With the evolution of the Smart Grid, Hydro One and local distribution companies are undertaking large, complex initiatives that will transform their technologies, processes and organization. Since the Smart Grid will potentially encompass the entire utility infrastructure, it is critical to ensure that the proposed solution meets not only electricity infrastructure needs, but also customers' needs.

Now that *Privacy by Design* has gained wide recognition in the North American and European energy sectors [NIST10] [Task11] [Euro11] [Arti11], the logical next step is to demonstrate that introducing privacy at this nascent stage of Smart Grid planning and development is essential and often less costly than trying to bolt it on after a breach occurs. With the guidance of the Information and Privacy Commissioner of Ontario, Canada, and the on-the-ground experience of Hydro One and its vendor partners, this paper demonstrates how to incorporate *Privacy by Design* considerations in the development and implementation of Smart Grid systems, product design, and energy information services and processes. Hydro One is utilizing its Living Lab as an initial deployment to confirm solution and process details, beginning with its major advanced distribution solution.

N. Pohlmann, H. Reimer, W. Schneider (Editors): Securing Electronic Business Processes, Vieweg (2011), 154-163

2 The Hydro One Smart Grid Solution in Ontario, Canada

Hydro One established a long-term vision in 2005 to increase innovation and continue its leading role in providing safe, reliable and cost-effective transmission and distribution of electricity from various supply sources to Ontario electricity users. The backbone of the Hydro One vision includes building the means to renew Ontario's power grid. In the first wave of this planned activity, a number of major system improvements were undertaken to enhance the performance of existing infrastructure, relieve internal congestion points, and deliver clean and renewable energy generation. Among these innovations was the introduction of an advanced metering infrastructure. Preparations for the next wave is already underway — the Advanced Distribution System (ADS).

Distributed generation sources will be primarily in the form of renewable energy such as wind, solar, and biomass. These advances, along with all the other characteristics of the Smart Grid, have the potential to bring significant benefits to Hydro One and its customers. However, implementing these improvements also implies significant changes in the operation of Hydro One's electrical system. Among the most important of these is the need to improve the analysis, automation, and remote control of the distribution grid. To achieve these improvements, Hydro One has been working towards a common communications infrastructure that will also support the four business requirements for the ADS program: a) optimize connection of distributed generation on the distribution network; b) improve distribution reliability and operations; c) optimize outage restoration and; d) optimize network asset planning.

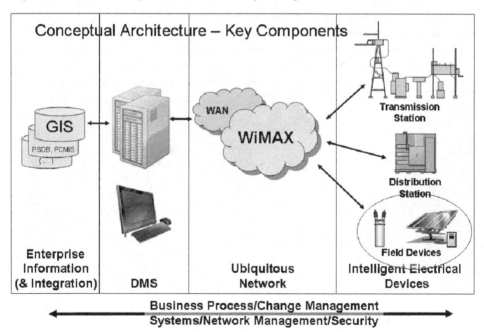

Fig. 1: Smart Grid Conceptual Architecture

Core components of Hydro One's ADS program are represented in Figure 1. The system that is used to automate and control an electrical distribution grid includes a central software component that is called a distribution management system (DMS) which acts as the "brain" of the ADS program.

A DMS is a suite of decision-support software applications which will assist Hydro One's control rooms and field operating personnel in monitoring and controlling the distribution system. This software system is a powerful network planning, analysis and operations tool that uses a detailed model of the grid, telemetry and information about power flow patterns to help manage the system in real time. Close integration of the DMS with other enterprise applications and data stores is essential. With the help of the DMS, Hydro One will demonstrate the ability to manage the increasingly complex network of consumer load and distributed resources, along with the existing centralized generation and traditional operating characteristics of the distribution system.

Adding intelligent devices, with automation where appropriate, is another core component of the program and includes an array of devices, equipment, and related software, such as intelligent power equipment (e.g. reclosers, switches, and relays) and monitoring and control devices and subsystems (e.g. power quality monitors, energy storage systems, intelligently controlled capacitor banks to provide voltage support, electronic fault indicators, and dynamic controllers). The ADS program also requires a communication network to facilitate communication with intelligent devices. This communication network is used for status and control messages, alerts, etc., to support management of the systems, and operations of the grid. To deploy this WiMAX communications network, Hydro One is using a nationally established licensed spectrum of 30 MHz in the 1800-1830 MHz range for the "Operation, Maintenance and Management of the Electric Supply" [Depa09].

Hydro One's first deployment stage of its Smart Grid for advanced distribution will include a subset of its service area in Southern Ontario known as the Living Lab. The figure below is an illustration of part of Hydro One's service area near Owen Sound, Ontario. Those solutions offering representative insights for the technology and processes to assist with future rollout will go first in the Living Lab area, followed by other areas in the province in order of priority.

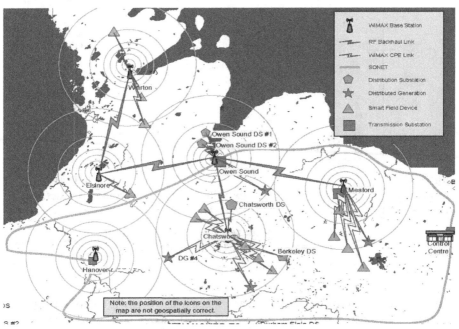

Fig. 2: Hydro one's Living Lab

As may be seen above, several features are being addressed, including substation automation, smart devices and communications network elements.

3 Operationalizing *Privacy by Design* into Hydro One's ADS

In *Privacy by Design: Achieving the Gold Standard in Data Protection for the Smart Grid*, a set of Best Practices for Smart Grid *Privacy by Design* were developed to aid organizations in understanding foundational privacy concepts that must be incorporated in to the Smart Grid. The Best Practices are as follows:

1. Smart Grid systems should feature privacy principles in their overall project governance framework and proactively embed privacy requirements into their designs, in order to prevent privacy-invasive events from occurring;

2. Smart Grid systems must ensure that privacy is the default — the "no action required" mode of protecting one's privacy — its presence is ensured;

3. Smart Grid systems must make privacy a core functionality in the design and architecture of Smart Grid systems and practices — an essential design feature;

4. Smart Grid systems must avoid any unnecessary trade-offs between privacy and legitimate objectives of Smart Grid projects;

5. Smart Grid systems must build in privacy end-to-end, throughout the entire life cycle of any personal information collected;

6. Smart Grid systems must be visible and transparent to consumers — engaging in accountable business practices — to ensure that new Smart Grid systems operate according to stated objectives;

7. Smart Grid systems must be designed with respect for consumer privacy, as a core foundational requirement.

3.1 Methodology

The successful development of any large-scale networked data system solution that involves or may involve personally identifiable information requires the adoption of a methodology that embeds privacy at the core of the solution's design. The methodology has to enable Hydro One to be able to trace privacy requirements from the inception of their business needs, to their fulfilment.

Transforming the Best Practices into a concrete reality for Hydro One and its Smart Grid vendor partners was a multi-step process. In general, this means starting with an incorporation of *Privacy by Design* into project governance at the earliest stages driving the development of business requirement and design processes, then following through to subsequently build and test systems for alignment with those requirements. This traceability then follows the hierarchy defined by Hydro One in their Enterprise Architecture Framework, which defines standards to be applied across various initiatives. This same methodology may be repeated to allow for the coordination of efforts across multiple delivery teams (vendors, project teams, sustaining organization, etc.) and disciplines (IT, power infrastructure, process design, etc.) to contribute to the success of Hydro One's initiatives and overall business objectives. This methodology provides a framework that may be tailored to the realities of the operating environment in order to meet the needs of the system, which in this case, is Hydro One's Smart Grid program with its initial deployment in the Living Lab.

In the context of the Best Practices for Smart Grid *Privacy by Design*, the first and most important artefact is the Architectural Decisions document. The Architectural Decisions document is a seminal project document that defines policies and principles, and documents the design decisions taken by the project. Specifically, it answers: What are the policies of the organization that will impact the deliverable? What are the design, building, testing and deployment principles that the project will adhere to? What solution deliverable decisions have been adopted, based on the requirements vis-a-vis the policies and principles?

For Hydro One's ADS Program, a risk assessment was conducted to specifically define the privacy and security requirements for the program. The risk assessment evaluated threat and vulnerability scenarios, the likelihood that the scenario could occur, and the impact of the scenario to Hydro One and its customers. Any applicable privacy requirements were created from the risk assessment and then incorporated into an overall privacy and security architecture.

3.2 Smart Grid Domains

Hydro One uses the concept of "Domains" to classify the possible implications for privacy in the Smart Grid, and to impose certain architectural decisions that will meet privacy requirements, while delivering the necessary functionality. The domains identified are: "Customer Domain," "Services Domain," and "Grid Domain," as illustrated in Figure 3.

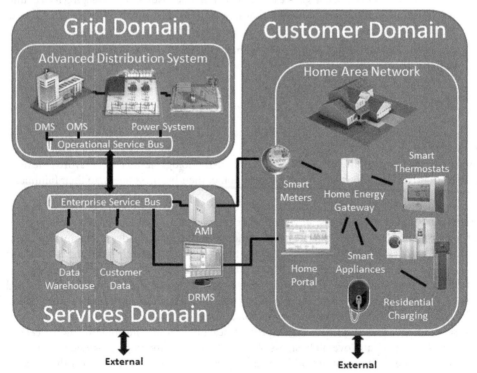

Fig. 3: Grid Domain, Services Domain, and Customer Domain

3.2.1   Customer Domain

The Customer Domain consists of all the devices associated directly with a customer's home. This includes: meters, customer-owned transformers and in-home equipment, be that a Home Area Network or otherwise, such as displays, thermostats, switches, etc. The meter is considered the demarcation point between the customer and Hydro One.

The Smart Grid and metering networks allow for more robust and economical demand management strategies, where information can be collected in real time to identify areas of demand, and properly tailored demand management programs allow for planned reductions in demand. When consumers enroll in such programs, questions inevitably arise such as: How is consumer information protected from the broader network? What limits can consumers place upon possible privacy intrusions and how can consumers withdraw from such programs? How can the devices in homes be connected to the actions within the Grid Domain without compromising privacy?

Specific to the ADS Program, to operationalize the Best Practices for Smart Grid *Privacy by Design* in the Customer Domain, Hydro One included design requirements such as the following as a result of implementing its project methodology:

- No data regarding a customer's identity will persist on any device from the meter to the Hydro One Services Domain — no personally identifiable information will be retained. The customer may choose, however, to purchase additional devices and disclose information to other third parties from their domain (the Customer Domain) which may contain personally identifiable information.
- No information sent to the Customer Domain from the Hydro One Services Domain will include any personally identifiable information that may allow unauthorized recipients to determine the association of the transaction to a specific person or place. All transactions will only include information necessary for the delivery of the information and the information necessary for the transaction to be completed. For a detailed discussion on Personal Information, please refer to our paper *Privacy by Design: Achieving the Gold Standard in Data Protection for the Smart Grid* [Cavo10].
- Any interface provided to the customer for the purposes of program subscription management (e.g. demand management) or power account management will utilize internet (Web) and voice service industry practices for identity management and information protection (e.g. appropriate provisions for the protection of the confidentiality, integrity, and availability of such information).

Customer Domain Applications may limit their interaction to within the customer's home, such as when the customer buys and configures a gateway about which the utility has no visibility or knowledge. In the event that these Customer Domain applications are integrated into the Services Domain of the utility, some of the critical privacy elements on the home portal front include: program enrolment and device provisioning; restricting access to authorized users, third party services and devices; limiting the retention of consumer data; future and upcoming demand response event notification; energy and economic value of customer participation in a program; as well as educating the consumer of the value of participating in other programs.

3.2.2   Services Domain

The Services Domain consists of technology, processes and data used in the delivery of utility services and programs to customers. This includes functions such as billing, power network planning, demand management programs, customer communication programs, etc. The functions within this domain depend upon data and control resources from the Customer and Grid Domains.

For example, meter readings are collected and used within the billing function and may be directly associated to a customer within the Services Domain. This same meter data may also be used for power network planning functions within the Grid Domain, but in a form that is typically not associated directly to a specific customer. Other examples are demand management programs which may request new settings for thermostats, or revenue management which may request the disconnection of service at a meter within predefined parameters. These functions, while associated to a customer in the Services Domain, are not closely associated in the Grid Domain.

Specific to the ADS Program, to operationalize the Best Practices for Smart Grid *Privacy by Design* in the Services Domain, Hydro One included design requirements such as the following as a result of implementing its project methodology:

- Access to any device in the Customer Domain from the Services Domain is restricted through authenticated and authorized services published within the Services Domain. All such access will be recorded.
- Direct access to any device within the Customer Domain must be authorized by the customer or customer's agent ensuring separation of duties. Access for a particular process or action is limited to the authorized action and duration. All direct access requests will be logged.
- All applicable systems will support role-based security. Only authorized Hydro One personnel may have access to systems that use customer information. This access is limited to the roles in which the personnel are authorized. This access is authorized and reviewed by designated managers and is managed by system owners.
- Management of all data storage systems must follow the appropriate industry practices.
- All requests made within this domain for an action within another domain will follow the identified operationalized design requirements in the target domain.
- All requests from other domains to this domain will follow operationalized design requirements from the requesting domain.
- All systems will save and archive information in accordance with agreements made between the customer and Hydro One.

The demand response management system (DRMS) will be designed with privacy at its core, while maintaining the ability to handle the following functions: receive demand response events from the Independent System Operator via an external connection; receive demand response events from the distribution management system; determine the appropriate demand response control for selected customers; transmit demand response events to the customer via the advanced metering infrastructure or via other communications method; and storage and retrieval of demand response event data in the data warehouse.

3.2.3   Grid Domain

The Grid Domain consists of all systems, processes and devices used for the management of the power network, to ensure the safe and reliable delivery of energy. From generators to high-voltage transmission lines, through substations to medium-voltage distribution lines, on through individual transformers and low-voltage cables, the grid delivers electrical energy to consumers.

Today's grid is monitored and controlled at a limited number of strategic points. Real time monitoring of electric system status occurs at transmission switching stations and substations, as well as substations feeding medium-voltage lines. A limited number of monitoring and control devices currently exist in the medium and low-voltage areas of the system. As the grid evolves into a smarter delivery system, the devices and systems that monitor the grid will grow, adding many more data gathering points. More sensors and smart switches will be added to the medium-voltage system. Smart meters and other intelligent electronic devices will provide monitoring, and limited control, in the low-voltage system.

Smart Meters, while a very important element of the Smart Grid, actually represent a small fraction of the overall grid. The vast majority of the Smart Grid has to do with the operation of the power network rather than pertaining to individual energy customers. Since such operations do not involve individual consumers, transmitters and distributers do not require any personally identifiable information for the operation of power network systems, and can thus be designed to have minimal privacy impact, if any. Since the monitoring and control of the grid does not require the use of any personally identifiable information under normal operations, privacy concerns remain practically non-existent.

Today, information in the Grid Domain is limited to network devices, their status, and their historical performance (e.g. aggregated load profiles, system conditions, operating peaks, maintenance information, etc.). As a result, the sources of data represent nodes on the network — not specific customers. In the future grid, some consumers may be required to be identifiable, in order to support bidirectional operations. For example, those who contribute distributed generation to the grid may need to be identifiable in order to ensure safe operations. While this is an important distinction, it represents the exception, not the norm, and such identification would be known and agreed to by the customer, as a condition of service.

The ADS uses aggregated average consumption profiles from a meter data system that is segregated from the commercial and personal information of the consumer. For purposes of analyzing the network, the location of the meter's connection to the grid is important, allowing the system to represent load along the length of a particular circuit aggregating load to transformers, substations and the entire system. However, parameters such as a consumer's name, address, and contact information are not relevant for load analysis (including feeder optimization and overload management) in the DMS. Similarly, outage and location data from smart meters is valuable to the Outage Management System (OMS) operator to verify and determine the extent of any outage; monitor service restoration and; facilitate communication to customers.

There are cases, though, where personally identifiable information of the consumer could be required by the Advanced Distribution System. For example, if a consumer has a distributed generation source, contact information may be required as a safety precaution in the event of an emergency. In such cases, appropriately authorized services in the Services Domain would be used to separate the personally identifiable information from the Grid management functions.

Specific to the ADS Program, to operationalize the Best Practices for Smart Grid *Privacy by Design* in the Grid Domain, Hydro One included design requirements such as the following as a result of implementing its project methodology:

- No data regarding a customer's identity will persist on any device within the Grid Domain — no personally identifiable data will be retained.
- Information regarding a device within the customer domain will be provided through authorized services within the Hydro One Services Domain.
- Access to a device within the Customer Domain must be performed through an authorized service within the Hydro One Services Domain.

The above design approach allows the information that is used by the DMS to perform network state estimation, load flow analysis, and several other advanced functions, to be carried out without the need for personally identifiable information.

4 Conclusion

Over the 100-year history of providing electricity, utilities have strived to attain the highest reputation in the reliability of electricity provision. In the next 100 years, they are also committed to keep up with the increasing pace of change in the industry, while continuing to look out for the customer's best interests, including the privacy of energy consumers' personally identifiable information.

Best Practices for Smart Grid *Privacy by Design* will be critical to the successful implementation of a fully utilized Smart Grid. Without the protection of consumer energy use data, lack of consumer confidence and trust will dampen consumer buy-in for the many enabled programs. The Smart Grid is a participatory network where all stakeholders, starting with the consumer, play a very important role in the solution's ultimate success. Energy consumers need to trust that their granular customer energy usage data, made available through the widespread deployment of smart meters and other Smart Grid devices, will be strongly protected.

Operationalizing Best Practices for Smart Grid *Privacy by Design* will become increasingly necessary as new smart devices are deployed in the Customer Domain, and as utilities and other service providers introduce more and more programs. By assessing the data needs associated with any new applications for the Smart Grid, engaging in data minimization, and only retaining the data when needed, strong privacy practices can be implemented. To achieve this, they need to be incorporated into Smart Grid requirements, business process analysis, architectural decisions, and design considerations, at each step in the planning and development. Such a process will result in the subsequent implementation of Smart Grid solutions that provide strong protections for confidentiality, integrity and systems availability, when and where applicable, thus achieving the positive-sum goal desired for electricity conservation, reform and good privacy — a true win-win solution that benefits all parties.

References

[Cavo10]   Cavoukian, Ann: Privacy by Design: Best Practices for Privacy (Eds.) ISSE 2010 Securing Electronic Business Processes, Vieweg+Teubner Verlag, 2010, p. 260-270.

[NIST10]   National Institute of Standards and Technology (NIST), U.S. Department of Commerce. The Smart Grid Interoperability Panel – Cyber Security Working Group: Guidelines for Smart Grid Cyber Security. Volume 2, Privacy and the Smart Grid (NISTIR 7628). National Institute of Standards and Technology (NIST), 2010

[Task11]   Task Force Smart Grids, Expert Group 2: Regulatory Recommendations for Data Safety, Data Handling and Data Protection. Task Force Smart Grids, 2011

[Euro11]   European Commission: Communication from the Commission to the European Parliament, the Council, the European Economic and Social Committee and the Committee of the Regions - Smart Grids: from innovation to deployment. European Commission, 2011.

[Arti11]   Article 29 Data Protection Working Party: Opinion 12/2011 on smart metering. Article 29 Data Protection Working Party, 2011

[Depa09]   Department of Industry, Radiocommunication Act: Notice No. SMSE-010-09 – New issue of SRSP-301.7. Canada Gazette Notice, 2009

[Cavo10]   Cavoukian, Ann: Privacy by Design: Achieving the Gold Standard in Data Protection for the Smart Grid. Office of the Information and Privacy Commissioner of Ontario, 2010.

How to have the cake and eat it, too: Protecting Privacy and Energy Efficiency in the Smart Grid

Klaus Kursawe

Institute for Computing and Information Science,
Radboud University Nijmegen
P.O. Box 9010, NL-6500 GL Nijmegen, The Netherlands
kursawe@cs.ru.nl

Abstract

The ongoing introduction of the Smart Grid is making huge promises in terms of energy efficiency and cost savings, but at the risk of consumer privacy. This risk has shown to have a significant impact, and in some countries, privacy concerns have already caused a pushback that has significantly delayed smart grid deployment as well as increased deployment costs. In this paper we describe how much of the privacy risk can be mitigated, without hampering the business case or causing significant extra costs. By using modern Privacy Enhancing Technologies, it is possible to create a win-win situation, where both the business use case and the privacy protection profit at the same time.

1 Introduction

By adding more intelligence and measurements to the electricity distribution network, the Smart Grid promises vast energy savings due to a better alignment of demand and supply. Furthermore, the increasing use of weather depended green energy sources such as photovoltaic and wind energy, and the potential addition of electronic vehicles to the distribution network, a more sophisticated system is unavoidable. One important component in the future Smart Grid will be measurements and control in the consumers homes due to Smart Meters. Those meters will continuously monitor and report energy consumption, and potentially takes some degree of control on the attached devices. To enable this technology, the European Commission wants 80% of all European households to be equipped with a Smart Meter by 2020. Simultaneously, the continuous measurement is a substantial privacy risk, as it allows deriving a large amount of personal data of the consumer. Due to this risk, the Dutch government in 2010 halted a law for compulsory smart meter installation on the ground of privacy issues, causing a huge delay in the installation and significant economical damage.

In this report, we show that privacy protection does not need to contradict energy savings and business goals. Instead, we show that by using modern privacy enhancing technologies, privacy protection can turn from a zero-sum game to a positive sum game, leading to both better privacy and higher quality measurements and thus better energy efficiency. This is possible by performing all computations on privacy critical data under encryption, where the electricity provider

N. Pohlmann, H. Reimer, W. Schneider (Editors): Securing Electronic Business Processes, Vieweg (2011), 164-173

only obtains the result of the computation, but does not learn anything about the input data. This way, it is possible to use much more fine-grained measurements, e.g., measure in smaller intervals or report the energy consumption of different device types independently.

2 A short primer on the Smart Grid

This has become especially important with the increasing switch to renewable energy sources. While classical energy generation is largely predictable and under tight control of the operators, renewable sources such as wind or solar power can be highly variable, and generate both a sudden surplus of energy and a sudden shortfall. The promise of the Smart Grid is to match the unpredictability in the supply by more control over the demand. This is done by more precise measurements of the demand to allow for a better forecast, but also by actively controlling the demand side. To this end, energy prices will be highly dynamic and flexible, and some energy intensive appliances – such as electric heaters and climate controls – may be directly controlled by the grid provider. Especially important here is 'peak shaving', i.e., reducing the maximum spikes in power consumption.

While the Smart Grid encompasses many components, the part that is most interesting from a privacy point of view s the smart metering architecture. To this end, electricity meters in consumers' homes will get some computation power, as well as the ability to communicate with the backend, with other meters in the same household (e.g., gas- and water meters), and potentially with household appliances like the HVAC system. The goal is to provide the grid operator with detailed information on the power consumption, control flexible appliances either directly or through dynamic pricing, and to help a consumer to optimize their consumption pattern.

The projections on energy and cost savings of the smart grid are immense. In 2008 study, the Electric Power Research Institute estimated savings of up to 3.7 billion kWh due to peak demand reduction alone, and a total of \$35 billion in electricity costs for the United States [EPRI2008]. In addition to the economic value, the smart grid is also seen as an important contributor to CO_2 savings, which has prompted major regulators to speed up its deployment. In the EU, the goal is to have 80% of all households equipped with smart meters by 2020, while the US is substantially subsidizing the deployment due to the Energy Independence and Security Act of 2007.

3 Privacy Risks

While the major part of the smart grid does not deal with consumer data at all, one important component – the smart meter – will be in the consumers home, and measure and report data that allows deep insights into the consumer behavior. This ranges from obvious ones such as vacation time and sleeping patterns to information about health (e.g., sleep disorders), social behavior, or even religion. Furthermore, there is no good way for a consumer to temporarily opt out – while a mobile phone can be left at home when a consumer does not want to be traced, the meter will always be active (there are some proposals to include batteries in consumers' homes to allow them to mask some sensitive data, though the practicality of this approach can be questioned). In theory, the measurement at the meter allows for even greater detail – prototypes have already shown that it is possible to determine relatively precisely which appliances are turned on at any given time, and to some extend even the activity on those appliances.

This privacy risk is not only a problem for end consumers, but has already proven to be a substantial business risk. In the Netherlands, the parliament has passed a law to speed up the smart meter rollout by making the deployment of a smart meter compulsory. While the grid operators where preparing for roll-out and making substantial investments, the Dutch Senate blocked the law on the ground that it violated the European Convention of Human Rights because of privacy reasons. This unforeseen issue stopped the roll-out completely, and cost the companies involved millions of Euros. Privacy is since playing an important role in regulatory guidelines, both in North America [NIST10] and Europe [EC11].

3.1 The Limits of Anonymisation

As a reaction to the increased privacy worries, a number of proposals have been made on how to add better privacy to the Smart Grid. The traditional way towards more privacy is to separate data that can directly identify users from the actual measurement data, and only associate the measurement with a pseudo-anonymous device identifier. However, with this approach, the data is still there, and the only protection is that the link between device identifier and the identifying data is not directly available; protecting this link is a tedious, expensive and risky task, as various data breaches in the past have show. An additional risk is that it is not entirely clear anymore what kind of data is actually personally identifiable, which has been identified as a generic limit to the anonymisazion approach [Ohm09]. As smart metering data may reveal a lot about the circumstances and the habits of a person, it cannot be excluded that a re-identification is possible based purely on the measurement data, when seemingly harmless data does contribute towards identifiable data once collected in sufficient amounts and cross linked to other, public data sources. That this kind of re-identification is possible has been shown in past studies, e.g., on Netflix move preference data [NaSh08]. In all those cases, data that was anonymised (such as movie preferences, or anonymised health data) could be de-anonymised with a surprising efficiency. It is therefore no longer possible to cleanly separate between personal identifiable data and harmless data, as each additional data item makes identification a little bit easier. Due to the wealth of data that can be derived in smart grid readings, there is a clear indication that the approach of simply separating identifiable and anonymous data is a good start, but has limited efficiency both in terms of data protection and business opportunity compared to modern privacy enhancing technologies such as the ones presented here.

As a more concrete example, grid data may reveal that a person always stays up late when a particular TV show is on, which in return may give some demographic data. It also can be linked with some semi-public data (e.g., people who 'like' this show on social networks) to assist in the de-anonymisation. Additional data mining may give information about my occupation, holiday schedule, religious preference, etc, which all narrow down the anonymity.

In addition to the possibility of re-identification, another risk- and cost factor is the secure storage of critical data. As we have seen in numerous data leaks in the recent past, preventing data leakage is hard, even for well funded and reasonably competent organizations. This shows that collecting data and then attempting to protect it from unauthorized access is risky, expensive, and in many cases inefficient. We therefore argue that the best protection from such events is if the data is not there in the first place.

4 Privacy by Design

The *Privacy by Design* principle has been developed the privacy commissioner of Ontario, and is rapidly becoming a standard in the deployment of privacy sensitive systems; for the smartgrid, the concept has been adopted by the Ontario smart grid deployment, and is recommended to be applied for European smart girds by the European Commission [EC11]. The basic concept builds on seven relatively abstract principles [Cavo11], namely, respect for users, lifecycle protection, proactive/preventive rather than reactive privacy, visibility and transparency, embedded privacy in the system design, privacy by default, and positive sum privacy. A concrete analysis and guidance on the how these principles can be used in a practical setting can be found in [GuTD11].

An important aspect to make privacy happen in real systems is the aim for 'positive sum' technologies. This means, that a privacy technology is designed with the business case in mind, and optimized to not inhibit the business case – rather, if done right, it can even be supportive and allow for better quality data and cheaper deployment costs. This contradicts the common view on privacy as being opposed to business goals, and being in the way of allowing companies to make money.

The second of the principles we will focus on in the rest of this paper is the concept data minimization; once this is deployed properly, many of the others (e.g., embedded privacy) follow implicitly. The basic idea to this end is that data cannot only be minimized by not collecting it; it can also be minimized by making only processed data visible to the grid operator, while hiding the unprocessed data items.

The concept of data minimization is a useful tool where the concept of removing personally identifiable information hits its natural limits. Rather than trying to separate personally identifiable data from the rest, the idea here is to determine which data is really needed to perform the task given, and then deploy technologies that assure that only that data is used.

Concretely, for the smart grid operator, the main usage of smart grid related data is demand-control, i.e., getting a detailed overview on the nature of the current electricity command, and regulate it by means of price changes or direct communication with heavy electricity consumers, such as HVACs and electric vehicles.

For this business-case, the grid operator does not need to know any individual consumption data – it is enough for them to have the aggregate of the consumption of all appliances in a particular area. The primary reason why individual information is collected is that grid operators do not know how to derive the aggregates directly, and thus they collect privacy critical data they actually do not need.

More precisely, the smart grid operator needs to see only data that is aggregated over a sufficiently large set of customers, and never needs to see any of the individual data items. This aggregated data is enough for all use cases we found with the two exceptions. The first one is billing, which can be done in a much more coarse resolution, and the second one consumer awareness - for which the data can be directly transferred to the consumer or a third party acting on behalf of the consumer, without any need of the grid operator to ever see that data. There also are privacy preserving protocols that allow computations on masked data of an individual meter [RiDa10,JaJK11], which build on a similar principle as the aggregation protocols but are out of scope here.

For the other published usecases [EPRI2008] especially for the most promising ones in terms of energy savings (performing demand/response and peak shaving functionality), aggregated data is fully sufficient. Thus, with a privacy preserving aggregation protocol, most of the energy- and cost saving benefits of the Smart Grid are preserved, while largely eliminating the privacy issues.

Once such protocols are deployed, they open additional opportunities for the grid operator. For example, it is of great interest to what extend the consumption would be reduced if the electricity price changes. This is difficult to see from the normal measurements, as the energy could be consumed by a device that can react quickly on price change (e.g., a fridge or an electric heater, which can easily be tuned down) or one that cannot (e.g., a computer). As the privacy issue is critical enough on overall consumption data, there is not even a debate on making such more detailed data available to the grid operator. By aggregating data over several households without revealing the individual input data, this is suddenly no longer an issue – the grid operator can see what all fridges in a neighborhood consume together, but does not see the consumption of individual fridges. Similarly, it is no longer a problem to have a higher measurement frequency (e.g., one measurement per minute), as no privacy relevant data is transmitted anymore.

This way, the grid operator gets more detailed data where it is relevant for them, because they do not see data where they do not need it.

In the next section, we will describe how the aggregation is done concretely. Our approach does not need any additional trusted hardware; all necessary operations can be done on the meter and the backend, using existing hardware for computation and communication.

4.1 Computing under Encryption

It is known since quite some time that it is possible to allow certain computations to be performed on encrypted data without the need of decryption – that is, an untrusted party can perform the computation on encrypted input, and return the encrypted output, while never learning the concrete values. A variant of such a scheme has for example been deployed to help with double auctions for Danish farming industry [BCDG+08]. So far, this technology has mostly been seen as too expensive to use in embedded systems, and thus few applications have been tested in the real world. An excellent demonstration is shown in, Balasch et al. , where the authors have build a prototype that can use this approach for privacy friendly road tolling [BRTG+10], and have implemented their protocol on a device of comparable computation resources as real on board units for road tolling.

Thus, the data never needs to leave the meter in unprotected form – each individual data item is protected, while the grid operator can derive the results of some computations derived from the data.

Due to the high costs already associated with a smart meter rollout, it is vital that the privacy technology does nod add a substantial new cost factor. The most critical factor in there are the meters - given the large number of meters that will be deployed, every cent of extra costs will translate into millions of additional costs for the grid providers. Thus, it is vital to keep the extra code to be executed on the meter small enough to fit into existing memory, and fast enough to run on the current processors without causing a visible slowdown. Furthermore, the communication bandwidth of the meters is quite restricted, as a large number of smart meters may share a single, noisy powerline channel for communication with the backend. Finally, communication standards have already been developed (e.g., the DLMS/COSEM), and additional protocols need to fit into the framework of those standards

For our protocols, this means that meter functionality has to be absolute minimal in terms of computation (on the meter side), and the meters – once initialized - should only need to send one single (short) message, without requiring any further interaction with the backend or with other meters. The latter is a challenge few comparable systems need to meet, and where our work differs from related protocols in the literature such as [GaJa10].

Furthermore, we have to consider that the bandwidth available to an individual meter may be very limited; there can be a large number of meters attached to a noisy powerline communication channel, which does exclude communication heavy protocols. In addition, in some legislations it is not allowed that meters of different households communicate with each other, as that is seen as a potential vector for meter based malware. Ideally, after the system setup, meters would only unicast messages to the backend, and not be involved in any further computation.

4.2 The Data Aggregation protocols DiPA and LoPA

In this section, we outline two concrete protocols for privacy protecting data aggregation. For the scope of this work, we only give an intuition on the protocol mechanism and a basic outline; the more detailed protocols as well as the protocols for efficient key initialization can be found in [KDK11].

The first protocol, DiPA (Diffie-Hellman based Private Aggregation) is a simple cryptographic protocol based on the Diffie-Hellman public key scheme. The main mechanism here is a *homomorphic commitment* scheme, which can be implemented very efficiently using Diffie-Hellman on elliptic curves.

A commitment scheme is a simpler tool than an encryption scheme. It allows a user to fix some secret (*commit* to it), and to later reveal the secret and prove that this was the value she committed to. As opposed to an encryption, a commitment scheme is easier to implement, and it does not need a secret decryption key, which means that there is less key management required.

As visualization, one can think of the original value as a Lego-car, the commitment scheme as a rubber hammer, and the commitment as a heap of Lego-bricks. Committing to a value (car) means to smash it with the hammer, and showing the heap of stones to the verifier. It is now computationally hard for the verifier to reconstruct the car from the heap, while it is easy to verify that a given car corresponds to the given heap.

The special property of *homomorphic commitments* is that it is possible to perform computations on the commitments, which then correspond to computations on the original plaintext, i.e.,

$$\text{Commit}(A+B) = \text{Commit}(A) * \text{Commit}(B)$$

In our visualization, this means that two Lego cars can be added up to a transformer (which is the addition on the original value side). Similarly, if one adds the heaps generated by the two individual cars, one gets the heap generated by the transformer, so the addition on the original values has an equivalent operation on the commitments.

These commitments form is the basis of the aggregation protocol. Because of the homomorphism, we can sum up commitments various parties to a commitment of the aggregate.

Public parameters:

G: Group of prime order p

H: $\{0,1\}^* \rightarrow$ G : Hash function (Random Oracle)

Private Meter Keys

$r_i \in$ G : random values

Aggregator Key(s)

$r_A = \Sigma\, r_i$

Meter side:

For measurement m_{ik} iwith index k, meter i :

computes g=H(j)

sends $g^{r_i + m_{ik}}$ to the aggregator

Aggregator:

Compute $\Pi g^{r_i + m_{ik}} = g^{\Sigma(r_i + m_{ik})} = g^{\Sigma r_i} g^{\Sigma m_k}$

Using knowledge of $\Sigma\, r_i$, compute $g^{\Sigma m_{ik}}$

Compare if this fits with the expected measurement

Fig. 1: DiPA (Diffie Hellman Private Aggregation) Protocol

While this protocol only allows us to compare values we already know, it is easy to transform into a protocol that computes actual aggregates. To this end, we simply perform the standard aggregation protocol on individual bytes, and then brute force those on the backend server (given the small domain of measurement values, this should not be more than a few hundred tests, which a modern PC can easily handle).

A main advantage of this protocol is that it allows for different sets of meters to be aggregated on, without requiring any change to the meter configuration. Instead, the aggregator needs to know the sum of the corresponding masking values. This would allow, for example, to separately aggregate over all meters in one particular district, as well as over all meters of consumers that also generate energy.

The LoPA (Low overhead Private Aggregation protocol) is even simpler, but does sacrifice some flexibility for this simplicity. In this protocol, the group of meters whose measurements are aggregated is fixed, and all meters in one group know of each other. Each two meters in one aggregation group share a common secret x (i.e., in a group of ten meters, each meter needs to keep nine such secrets). When a measurement is to be protected, one meter adds its corresponding x for all its peers to its output value, while the other one subtracts it. Thus, the overall effect of the secrets cancels out completely, and an aggregator summing up all values gets the exact sum of all measurements. However, if only one measurement is missing, not all the secrets cancel out, and the reading is unreadable. To protect privacy over several readings, the secrets need to be changed after each reading; this can easily be done without any interaction and little computational overhead by applying a hash function such as SHA-256.

Public parameters:

    H: $\{0,1\}^* \rightarrow \{0,1\}^*$: Hash function

Private Meter Keys

    r_{ij} : Pairwise shared key between meters i and j

Aggregator Key(s)

    --

Meter side:

For measurement with index k and value m_{ki} in meter i :

    computes $R_{ki} = \Sigma\ s(i,j) * H(k,r_{ij})$, where s(i,j) = -1 if i<j, 1 otherwise

    send $R_{ki} + m_{ki}$ to the aggregator

Aggregator:

    Compute $\Sigma\ R_{ki} + m_{ki} = \Sigma\ m_{ki}$

Fig. 2: LoPA (Low overhead Private Aggregation) protocol

One major advantage of this approach is that there is no public key cryptography involved once the system is initialized, and all operations are simple additions as well as a hash function. This not only reduces the computation overhead to the absolute minimum, but also allows the message size to stay exactly the same – a masked 32-bit value still is a 32-bit value, as opposed to the homomorphic commitment based protocol, where it needs to be long enough to be cryptographically secure. Thus, this protocol integrates very neatly into the existing DLMS/COSEM standard, and no changes have to be made to the message format.

The price is a somewhat a smaller flexibility – in this protocol the aggregation group is fixed by the keys the meters have, and it is not possible to aggregate over different sets of meters simultaneously. Also, a meter does need enough memory to store all the shared keys with its peers. This does not have a large impact in practice, however, as the sets of meters should be kept small anyhow for stability reasons.

5 Implementation & Practical Issues

To validate the concept, both protocols presented above have been prototyped by Elster SG on their production meters, together with the billing protocol presented in [RiDa10], and the application scenarios have been discussed intensively with a Dutch grid operator. The low overhead protocol has been fully integrated into the existing protocol stack. In the end, the meters could successfully report masked measurements to a fourth meter, which was used to compute the aggregate. The cryptographic protocol has been implemented to verify the performance impact, but not yet integrated into the communication stack due to the change in the message formats this would have required. For both protocols, the computation overhead for the masking was essentially instant (i.e., far below one second), and thus easily within the scope of 15 minute measurement intervals.

One additional issue that comes in the nature of the aggregation protocols is that it is impossible to compute a sensible aggregate if a single measurement is missing. This is unavoidable – if it were possible to compute such an aggregate, the aggregator could easily compute the difference of an aggregate with all meters and with all meters bar one, and then derive the measurement of that meter by comparing the aggregates. In practice, however, that means that a single failed meter brings down its entire aggregation group.

For some use cases, this is entirely tolerable. For example, if the protocols are used for fraud detection, the failure of a meter is exactly the event we want to detect, and the protocols will detect it. For load balancing and demand response, however, this is a different issue.

The most practical solution for this problem is to group meters in small groups of ca 20 meters, and then computes the larger aggregate by summing up the aggregates of those groups. A single failed meter will still bring down 19 of its peers – however, on the larger scale of a demand response system, the loss of 20 meters is still tolerable (one should also note that meters are not overly likely to fail) as long as it is detected and the output is not used in further computations. This approach also makes it easier to accommodate the more efficient low overhead protocol – once there are only small groups of meters, the limited scalability of this protocol is no longer an issue.

6 Conclusions

In this paper, we have shown a privacy technology for data aggregation in a smart metering setting, which allows a grid provider (or any other authorized party) to compute aggregates of measurement data without needing access to the individual – privacy critical - measurements themselves.

The main message is twofold. Firstly, modern privacy enhancing technologies have reached a level of practicability that does allow them to work in a real system – and while larger scale tests still have to be done before a real deployment is possible, the implementation already demonstrates that an integration into existing architectures and hardware is feasible. Secondly, we show a practical example of 'positive-sum' privacy, i.e., a privacy technology that has been developed together with the businesses, and that does fit into the overall business model and its requirements. In doing so, the technology even can generate positive value for the business – not only by helping to comply to regulation and saving costs on otherwise needed technology, but by allowing to have more privacy *and* actually use more data.

References

[BRTG+10] Josep Balasch, Alfredo Rial, Carmela Troncoso, Christophe Geuens, Bart Preneel and Ingrid Verbauwhede. PrETP: Privacy-Preserving Electronic Toll pricing. In 19th USENIX Security Symposium, pp 63-78, 2010.

[Cavo11]:   Cavouican, Ann: Privacy by Design: The 7 foundational principles, 2011

[BDDG+08]: Peter Bogetoft, Dan Lund Christensen{, Ivan Damgard,Martin Geislerz, Thomas Jakobsen,Mikkel Kroigaard, Janus Dam Nielsen, Jesper Buus Nielsen,, Kurt Nielsen,, Jakob Pagter, Michael Schwartzbach, and Tomas Toft: Secure Multiparty Computation Goes Live, 2008

[EC11]   Smart Grids: From innovation to deployment. Communication from the Commission, 2011

[EPRI08]: The Green Grid: Energy Savings and Carbon Emissions Reduction Enabled by a Smart Grid. EPRI Report no 1016905, 2008.

[GaJa1]   Flavio Garcia, and Bart Jacobs: Privacy Friendly Energy Metering via Homomorphic Encryption. Workshop on Security and Trust Management (STM 2010)Lecture Notes in Computer Science, Vol. 6710, pp 226-238, 2011

[GoJu04]   Phillipe Golle, Ari Jules: Dining Cryptographers Revisited. Eurocrypt 2004 ,pp 456-473, 2004.

[GuTD11]   Seda Gürses, Carmella Troncoso, and Claudia Diaz: *Engineering Privacy by Design*. In Conference on Computers, Privacy & Data Protection (CPDP), 2011.

[JaJK11]   Marek Jawurek, Martin Johns, Florian Kerschbaum: Plug-in privacy for Smart Metering Billing. Privacy Enhancing Technologies Symposium (PETs),pp 192-210, 2011.

[KDK11]   Klaus Kursawe, George Danezis and Markulf Kohlweis: *Privacy Friendly Aggregation for the Smart Grid*. Privacy Enhancing Technologies Symposium (PETs 2011), pp 175-191, 2011

[NaSh08]   Arvind Narayana, Vitaly Shmatikov: Robust De-anonymisation of Large Sparse Datasets. IEEE Symposium on Security and Privacy,Oakland, 2008

[NIST10]   NISTir 7628: Guidelines for Smart Grid Cyber Security, 2010

[Ohm09]   Paul Ohm: Broken Promises of Privacy: Responding to the Surprising Failure of Anonymizaion. 57 UCLA Law Review, pp. 1701 – 1778, 2010

[RiDa10]   Alfredo Rial & George Danezis: Privacy-friendly smart metering.. Microsoft Research Technical Report MSR-TR-2010-150, 2010.

Security of Wireless Embedded Devices in the Real World

Timo Kasper · David Oswald · Christof Paar

Chair for Embedded Security
HGI, Ruhr-University Bochum
Universitaetsstrasse 150
44801 Bochum, Germany
{timo.kasper | david.oswald | christof.paar}@rub.de

Abstract

In the past years, wireless embedded devices have become omnipresent. Portable tokens communicating via an RF (Radio Frequency) interface are employed in contactless applications such as access control, identification, and payments. The survey presented in this paper focuses on those devices that employ cryptographic mechanisms as a protection against ill-intended usage or unauthorizedly accessing secured data. By analyzing different commercial products, i.e., electronic passports, the remote keyless entry system KeeLoq, a Mifare Classic based contactless payment system, and a public transport system relying on Mifare DESfire cards we demonstrate that it is feasible to recover the secret cryptographic keys from various cryptographic tokens. At hand of the real-world examples, the implications of a key extraction for the security of the respective contactless application are illustrated.

1 Introduction

Wireless tokens have become ubiquitous in our everyday life. RFID (Radio Frequency Identification) technology is used in the supply chain as a barcode replacement, in the medical sector (pace makers, patient wristbands), as a countermeasure against product piracy, or helps to prevent car theft in the form of car immobilizers. Contactless cards, representing the most powerful variant of RFIDs, enable amongst others comfortable ticketing, contactless payments and secure access control. Active, battery-powered remote controls possess their own transmitter enabling greater operating ranges. They are often used in Remote Keyless Entry (RKE) systems that have already replaced the conventional mechanical keys for accessing the majority of modern cars and buildings.

Wireless communication implies new, additional threats as compared to contact-based systems: a transponder residing in a pocket or wallet could be read out or modified without the owner taking note of it and the transmission of data via the RF field can be monitored or relayed from a distance. Hence, many wireless applications require protecting the over-the-air interface: a private phone call must not be monitored by a neighbour, a door must not be opened by an intruder, and it must be made impossible for a customer to charge his contactless payment card except at a dedicated charging terminal by paying money into the system. To realize security mechanisms that prevent from fraud and unauthorized access, or to establish confidentiality and data protec-

N. Pohlmann, H. Reimer, W. Schneider (Editors): Securing Electronic Business Processes, Vieweg (2011), 174–189

tion, cryptography in distinct flavours is widespread in today's wireless tokens. Encryption or authentication schemes incorporating secret cryptographic keys shall guarantee security, data integrity, and ensure the intended functionality of the wireless systems in general.

1.1 Pervasive Wireless Technology

The huge variety of wireless applications implies that the products differ amongst others in the dimensions, operating frequency, the maximum achievable range for a query, and their computational power [Fin03]. Some examples of wireless tokens are illustrated next.

1.1.1 Passive Wireless Devices (RFID)

Passive RFIDs as exemplified in the top of Figure 1 are generally restricted with respect to their energy consumption, i.e., the amount of switching transistors during their operation [LSR06], since their energy is supplied wirelessly by the RF field of a base station or reader. This limitation has a direct impact on the cryptographic capabilities of RFID devices — implementing state-of-the-art cryptography is sometimes infeasible [RCT06].

The cost-efficient transponders at the low end are used for applications in which no security is required, e.g., in the supply chain Electronic Product Code (EPC) Gen 2 tags [EPC10] enable the wireless identification of tagged objects from a distance and without a line-of-sight ("auto-ID"). Other applications of non-cryptographic RFID transponders include baggage handling at airports, automated toll collection (eToll), and the identification of animals, e.g., tracking cattle and tagging pets. Besides, RFIDs are used to tag humans: wristbands identify patients in hospitals to avoid mixing them up and (unsecured) RFID interfaces integrated in pace makers [HHBR+08] enable to (re)program their operating parameters through the human tissue.

More advanced RFID devices providing simple encryption schemes are integrated into car keys for anti-theft systems, i.e., immobilizers, and are used in medium-security applications for access control purposes. Cryptographic transponders can also help to prevent product forgery: RFID chips are integrated into spare parts, such as batteries of mobile phones, ink cartridges of printers, and (mechanical or electrical) components of cars. The protected devices operate only if genuine parts are identified by means of their transponders and otherwise report fraud or malfunction, e.g., a printer will not work if a forged ink cartridge is inserted.

Contactless smartcards as standardized in ISO/IEC 14443 [Int01] are basically smartcards or memory cards, augmented with a wireless interface. They are used worldwide in a wide range of security-sensitive applications, e.g., for identification, access control, and payment purposes. They (optionally) offer a wide range of security features, including cryptographic co-processors for encryption. Various multi-purpose applications have emerged that rely on contactless smartcards, e.g., the OpenCard in Prague (Czech Republic) combines micro-payments, ticketing for public transport, and services of the public library.

1.1.2 Active Wireless Devices

Battery-powered, active tokens illustrated in the bottom of Figure 1 enable operating ranges in the order of tens or hundreds of meters and can provide strong cryptography. They often serve as remote controls for RKE systems, e.g., for opening cars. Simple one-button key fobs operate unidirectionally without encryption or other security measures. More advanced devices possess a bidirectional RF interface and implement protection schemes, e.g., authentication by challenge-response schemes before access to a secured area is granted.

Semi-active devices combine passive communication interfaces with battery-powered technology, e.g., sensors for monitoring and recording environmental conditions [Sav10]. The advanced transponders are mainly used in the supply chain for tagging containers with large assets, e.g., for the transportation of medical supplies, food and other goods.

1.1.1 Comparison of Wireless Devices

However, the computational power and the corresponding achievable level of security differ largely in each of the two groups: while read-only RFIDs and fixed-code tokens for the purpose of simple object identification and tracking provide no security, memory cards such as Mifare Classic and unidirectional (transmit-only) rolling-code devices such as KeeLoq remote controls employ some type of encryption mechanism. Contactless smartcards, e.g., Mifare DESFire, can execute modern, secure ciphers and hence enable secure challenge-response schemes, as also implemented in corresponding active, bidirectional keyfobs.

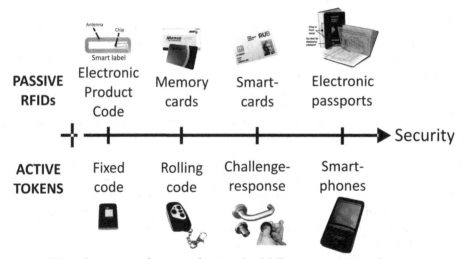

Fig. 1: Computational power and security level differ amongst active and passive tokens.

The most powerful passive device is probably the electronic passport [BSI]: it enables computationally demanding cryptographic schemes including public-key ciphers, and in addition features a protection against Man-In-The-Middle (MITM) attacks. Smartphones on the active side contain even more powerful microcontrollers. They can basically perform any desired type of cryptography and provide various communication channels, such as Wi-Fi, Global System for Mobile Communications (GSM), Universal Mobile Telecommunications System (UMTS), and Bluetooth. Some phones possess a Near Field Communication (NFC) interface [ECM] that is compatible to contactless smartcards and hence constitutes a link between active tokens and passive RFID devices — smartphones equipped with NFC can connect passive devices to the cloud.

1.1.3 Security Considerations

Embedded systems are generally prone to security risks, since they are often in the possession of potential adversaries in large amounts. In the context of wireless technology some special threats evolve or are of particular importance. For example, copying a mechanical key premises physical access to the key or at least to the door lock. In contrast, circumventing a contactless system may be possible from a distance and without leaving any physical traces.

The limited energy supply of RFID tags and the cost sensitivity of high-volume applications often tempts manufacturers to minimize the production costs at the expense of the quality, e.g., by using outdated but "cheap" cryptographic components. As a consequence, cryptography and other security measures may be very lightweight or not employed at all, even when security or privacy issues are relevant.

1.2 Focus and Organization of the Paper

The scope of this paper is narrowed to certain wireless embedded devices that are analyzed by a low-skilled adversary, as detailed in the following. Next, an outline of the paper is given.

1.2.1 Analyzed Wireless Devices

Simple low-end devices, such as read-only RFID transponders and active fixed-code systems, provide no effective security measures — the corresponding threats are obvious and hence no in-depth analysis is required. Smartphones are also excluded from the investigations, since they can be regarded as portable computers and hence different attack vectors apply: for extracting secrets, in most cases computer-related threats such as trojan horses, root kits, and computer viruses play a more important role, compared to physical or cryptanalytical attacks. This survey instead focuses on the remaining portable devices with high security demands and limited computational power, i.e., the most widespread contactless smartcards and active keyfobs that employ cryptography. Applications relying on weak, proprietary cryptographic schemes (Mifare Classic cards and KeeLoq remote controls) are considered as well as those incorporating publicly known, highly secure ciphers (Mifare DESFire cards and electronic passports).

1.2.2 The Attacker

Ross Anderson and Markus Kuhn [AK98] and a paper by IBM [ADDS91] give a good classification of adversaries according to their funding and skills. The authors distinguish between three types of adversaries, i.e., clever outsiders, knowledgeable insiders, and funded organizations. This paper focuses on those attacks that are realistic for an adversary with a limited budget, i.e., attacks that can be performed by clever outsiders or knowledgeable insiders.

The cryptographic algorithm itself is assumed to be known to the attacker (no security only by obscurity!). Still, the specific implementation of the device to be attacked and other confidential information, e.g., the source code or an open sample device, is assumed to be not available to the attacker. The adversary has access to equipment such as oscilloscopes etc. that can be found in university labs. The auxiliary tools for physical and protocol attacks, as introduced in Section 5, are hence low-cost devices and often self-built from off-the-shelf components, with their design typically being publicly available.

1.2.3 Outline of the Paper

Tools for security analyses are introduced in Section 2. Next, the evolving real-world attacks are illustrated by analyzing commercial wireless products: as an example for a weak key derivation scheme enabling a recovery of the secret keys by means of brute-force, the approach of decrypting the communication of electronic passports is detailed in Section 3. The impacts of extracting the keys of a KeeLoq remote keyless entry system by means of power analysis are covered in Section 4. A flawed contactless payment system relying on Mifare Classic cards is attacked in Section 6 by exploiting a weak implementation on the card and mathematical vulnerabilities of the cipher. Finally, Section 7 illustrates that side-channel analysis can also be applied to contactless smartcards by recovering the keys of Mifare DESfire cards employing 3DES. Our attack is exemplified by decrypting the content of "Opencards" used in Prague for public transport and other purposes.

2 Tools for Security Analysis

In order to conduct physical attacks, (customized) hardware for performing the security analyses, the communication with the different targets, and assisting the data acquisition need to be developed. In [KOP10] a unified framework for advanced implementation attacks is introduced that allows for conducting automated side-channel analysis, fault injection, and other physical attacks. It enables analyzing all kinds of (wireless) embedded cryptographic devices including RFIDs. The developed cost-effective and freely programmable devices comprise a multi-function RFID reader and a card emulator for contactless smartcards. The low-cost framework disproves the common belief that highly sophisticated and expensive equipment is required to conduct physical attacks. All further details about the realization of the customized RFID hardware are described in [Kas06, KCP, KOPvM11].

2.1 Customized RFID Reader

For the security analyses and practical attacks in the field the freely programmable RFID reader developed in [KCP] is used. In contrast to commercially available products, the customized device enables to fully control the communication and inject faults by manipulating the RF field with a high timing accuracy of approximately 75 ns, which is a key advantage in the context of key-recovery from Mifare Classic cards (see Section 8). The multi-purpose reader device is equipped with an Atmel ATmega32 microcontroller; an RF interface for 13.56 MHz, as required for implementing the ISO 14443 protocol for smartcards; and some components for signal processing. All relevant protocols for communicating with electronic passports, Mifare Classic, Mifare DESfire, and many other contactless cards are implemented.

2.2 Chameleon

A custom-built hardware for emulating contactless smartcards compliant to ISO 14443, that can cooperate with the customized reader, has been developed in [KOPvM11]. The device, termed Chameleon, is based on an Atmel XMega microcontroller and can support basically all relevant (cryptographic) protocols used by contactless smartcards today, e.g., those based on AES or Triple-DES (3DES). The versatile device, which is open-source and can be built for less than 20 €, can technically appear as any modern contactless smartcard.

As a proof of concept, a full emulation of Mifare Classic cards on the basis of a highly optimized implementation of the stream cipher Crypto1 has been implemented. The device enables the creation of exact clones of such cards, including their Unique Identifier (UID). Further implementations realize the first emulation of DESfire and DESfire EV1 cards in the literature. The capabilities of the emulator are practically demonstrated by spoofing several real-world systems, e.g., doors secured by a widespread access control system based on identifying the UID of Mifare Classic cards are unauthorizedly opened. In Section 8, the Chameleon emulates a contactless payment card, which allows an attacker to set the stored credit balance as desired and hence make an infinite amount of payments.

2.3 Data Acquisition

A controlling PC and a USB oscilloscope form the basis of the data acquisition system, as used for the side-channel attacks in this article. The acquired data can be side-channel information (e.g., current, voltage, EM emanation or timing information), or communication data such as bitstreams in any format which then later can be evaluated by a PC.

The Picoscope 5204 dual-channel storage USB2.0-oscilloscope [Pic08] is used for digitizing physical observables during the attacks, e.g., information leakage in the context of a side-channel analysis (SCA). It costs approximately 2000 € and features a maximum sample rate of 1 GHz, an 8-bit Analog to Digital Converter (ADC) with a huge 128 MSamples waveform memory. The input bandwidth is 250 MHz, with a minimum input range of ±100 mV.

Various types of probes for acquiring side-channel leakage and other information can be connected to the oscilloscope. The MI 145 passive high impedance probes that are supplied with the Picoscope have a bandwidth of B = 250 MHz at a 1:10 attenuation ratio (corresponding to B = 10 MHz for a 1 : 1 ratio). They are typically sufficient for measuring the power consumption of a device via the voltage drop at a resistor inserted into the supply path of the targeted device. For measurements of electromagnetic (EM) emanations, near-field probes manufactured by Langer EMV[1] are utilized, e.g., an RF-U 5-2 probe is used for the EM analysis of Mifare DESfire cards in Section 9. The captured signal is preamplified with the PA-303 amplifier [Lan] to meet the dynamic range of the oscilloscope.

2.4 COPACOBANA

This paragraph briefly introduces a customized, reconfigurable hardware platform termed cost-efficient parallel code breaker and analyzer (COPACOBANA). The architecture of the high-performance, low-cost cluster that can be realized for less than US$ 10,000 has been publicized in 2006 [KPP+06]. COPACOBANA appears to be the only reconfigurable parallel Field Programmable Gate Array (FPGA) machine optimized for code breaking tasks reported in the open literature. Depending on the actual algorithm, the parallel hardware architecture can outperform conventional computers by several orders of magnitude [GKN+08].

Since cryptanalytical applications demand for plenty of computing power, a total of 120 low-cost Xilinx6 Spartan3-XC3S1000 devices are installed on the COPACOBANA cluster[2]. The top level

---

1   www.langer-emv.de
2   see http://www.copacobana.org for all details

entity of COPACOBANA is a host-PC which is used to initialize and control the FPGAs, as well as for the accumulation of results. Data transfer between the FPGAs and the host-PC is accomplished by a dedicated control interface that connects COPACOBANA to a computer either via USB or Ethernet.

The hardware is optimized for computational problems which are parallelizable onto independent nodes with low communication and memory requirements, e.g., exhaustive key search. Note, that more than one COPACOBANA device can be attached to a single host-PC in order to further increase the performance. The next chapter employs COPACOBANA for extracting the secret keys used for the encryption of electronic passports.

3 Extracting Keys of Electronic Passports

This section tackles the security of the probably most secure wireless system based on passive RFID technology: the e-Pass (electronic passport), as specified by the International Civil Aviation Organization (ICAO) is deployed in many countries all over the world. To ensure interoperability between different countries, all e-Passports comply with the ISO/IEC 14443 standard. Technical specifications published by the European Commission [Eur06] are binding for the Schengen agreement countries. All e-Passports issued in the EU contain an embedded contactless chip that holds at least the same information that is printed on the identity information page of the passport, e.g., the name of the holder, date of birth, and a facial image. Optionally, an e-Passport can contain biometric identifiers, e.g., a fingerprint or an iris scan of the holder of the passport. The passports provide sophisticated cryptographic mechanisms to protect the private (biometric) data stored on it, including both public-key and symmetric cryptography [FOfIS]. The correctness of the private data is proven by a certificate of the issuing country and the digital photograph stored in the passport is optimized for automatic face recognition [JMV07].

The security of the first generation of passports is questionable, as detailed in this section. The key-search attacks presented in [LKLRP07] tackle the implementation of a security mechanism in the electronic passport as issued in Germany since November 2005 and are applicable to electronic passports of various other countries. After publicizing our findings as summarized in this section, a new version of the German electronic passport (additionally containing two fingerprints of the passport holder) was released in November 2007 with an improved variant of the here attacked key derivation scheme.

3.1 Related Work on Electronic Passports

The security and privacy threats have been widely discussed, e.g., in [JMW05, KK05, HHJ+06, JMV07, CLRPS], and have provoked public debates. In 2010, an attack for tracking the movements of a particular passport without having to break the passport's cryptographic key has been proposed in [CS10]. The authors show that the duration of computing a MAC during the authentification is key-dependent and hence enables identifying individual passports without decrypting the communication. While this attack requires actively interrogating the passport from a maximal range of some centimetres, the findings presented in this section allow tracking of individuals from a distance of several meters by means of eavesdropping.

3.2 Basic Access Control

The Basic Access Control (BAC) provides a means of mutual authentication and encrypting the data exchanged between the e-Passport and an RFID reader. Current realizations of the BAC, that shall prevent unauthorized access to the data stored on electronic passports, deploy symmetric cryptography based on SHA-1 and Triple-DES. The secret keys for the BAC are derived from the Machine Readable Zone (MRZ) printed on the document which contains data such as the passport number, date of birth and expiration date. The mechanism also serves as a protection against relay attacks.

Deriving the encryption and authentication keys for the BAC from the MRZ data is the cause for a security flaw: as we have shown in [LKLRP07], low entropy of the derived BAC keys enables straightforward attacks with a relatively small complexity compared to an exhaustive key search attack on Triple-DES. Instead of filling the digits of the MRZ with random alphanumerical values (which would result in sufficient entropy to prevent from a key recovery) the keys are generated from predictable personal information and other data with low entropy (such as dates).

3.3 Recovering the Secret Keys

Using the code-breaker COPACOBANA introduced in Section 3, in realistic scenarios the key for the BAC can be recovered almost in real-time, i.e., the time needed for a person to pass an inspection system at the border control: the achieved throughput of the implemented brute-force attack is 240 million, i.e., approx 2^{28} BAC keys per second. Testing 2^{35} key candidates, corresponding to a realistic scenario in which some personal data of the victim is known to the attacker, requires 2 minutes and 23 seconds on one COPACOBANA.

This enables to extract the keys from eavesdropped communication with an electronic passport and decrypt the intercepted private data. Two approaches for the key recovery are presented: one requires monitoring both directions of the communication, while for the second attack eavesdropping on the far-ranging requests of the reader is sufficient. Despite the secure cryptographic primitives being employed, the private data interchanged during the BAC is hence at risk of getting into the hands of unauthorized persons or organizations.

Such information is exploitable by criminals. Ari Juels et al. [JMW05] point out problems that are imposed on e-passport holders such as identity theft, tracking, and hotlisting. In the worst case scenario, an attacker may devise an RFID enabled bomb that is keyed to explode when reading a particular individual's RF identifier [JMW05]. The main cause for the found security vulnerabilities is the flawed key derivation from the MRZ.

4 A Remote Keyless Entry System: KeeLoq

Compared to passive RFID devices, active, battery-powered systems possess much more resources and are capable of performing basically any type of cryptographic operation. "Do real-world wireless systems relying on actively powered components accordingly provide a higher level of security?" To answer the question, the potency of power analysis when applied to active wireless tokens and the corresponding receivers is demonstrated at hand of the security analysis of Kee-Loq Rolling Code systems in [vTJ11, KKMP09, EKM+08, MK09, NK09], as summarized next.

4.1 The KeeLoq Cipher and Rolling Code Scheme

The KeeLoq block cipher is widely used for security relevant applications, e.g., RKE and alarm systems for securing the access to a car or a building, as well as passive RFID transponders for car immobilizers [Mic]. The cipher was developed in the 1980s in South Africa and licensed by Microchip Technology Inc. in the 1990s. Since then, it has been integrated in many products incorporating their secure authentication product family. The cipher had been kept confidential for about two decades.

KeeLoq did not receive much attention until 2006, when the algorithm got known to the public and moved into the focus of the international cryptographic research community. Shortly after the first cryptanalysis of the cipher [Bog07], more analytical attacks were proposed [CBW08, IKD+08], revealing mathematical weaknesses of the cipher. Despite the impressive contribution to the cryptanalysis of the cipher, the real-world impacts of the existing attacks are limited, as described in more detail in [EKM+08].

In the most widespread "rolling-code" mode of KeeLoq, the unidirectional remote controls generate dynamic codes based on encrypting a counter with the device key of the remote control. The individual device keys are derived from the (known) serial number of the remote control by a (cryptographic) function involving a manufacturer key. Knowing the latter hence implies knowledge of all device keys in a KeeLoq system.

4.2 Power Analysis of KeeLoq

The developed highly efficient SCA attacks based on Simple Power Analysis (SPA) and Correlation Power Analysis (CPA) techniques enable to break the wireless access control system with minimal efforts. The attacks efficiently reveal both the secret key of a hardware implementation in the remote control and the manufacturer key stored in a software implementation in the receiver. As a result, a practical key recovery of a remote control, e.g., in order to clone it, is feasible in few minutes from only ten power traces. For a full key-recovery of the 64 bit manufacturer key of commercial products by SPA, one single measurement of a fraction of a KeeLoq decryption is sufficient, without the prior knowledge of neither a plaintext nor a ciphertext.

4.3 Cloning Remote Controls by Eavesdropping

After the one-time extraction of the manufacturer key as a prerequisite, recovering the secret key of a remote control and replicating it from a distance, just by eavesdropping on at most two transmitted messages, is demonstrated. This cloning approach without physical access to the remote control has serious real-world security implications, as the eavesdropping attack can be conducted by an unskilled adversary, while the technically challenging part (i.e., the SCA attack) can be outsourced to specialists. Furthermore, a denial-of-service attack can be mounted. An instantiation of an exhaustive key-search on COPACOBANA, to evaluate the security of other (seed-based) key-derivation schemes for KeeLoq, is detailed in [NK09]. All the described attacks have been verified on several commercial KeeLoq products.

The single point-of-failure in the key distribution in the system, i.e., deriving the keys of the remote controls from their serial number via a manufacturer key, enables dramatic attacks once the manufacturer key has been recovered. Even a low-skilled intruder can spoof a KeeLoq receiver with technical equipment for less than 40 € and take over control of an RKE system, or deactivate an alarm system, leaving no physical traces.

The case of KeeLoq illustrates how widespread commercial applications, claiming to be highly secure, can be practically broken with modest cost and efforts using SCA. Thus, physical attacks must not be considered to be only relevant to the smartcard industry or to be a mere academic exercise. Rather, effective countermeasures need to be implemented not only in high-value systems such as smartcards, but also in wireless security applications.

5 Pitfalls of a Mifare Classic-based Payment System

Mifare Classic cards [NXP08b, NXP08a] have made their way into many public transportation systems such as the Octopus card in Hong Kong [Oct97], the Oyster card in London [Tra03], the OV-Chipkaart in the Netherlands [OV-05] and the CharlieCard in Boston [Mas06]. The cards are widely used for access control and are also employed for payment applications, e.g., in the contactless payment system analyzed in [KSP], as summarized next.

5.1 Mifare Classic

Mifare Classic cards comply with ISO/IEC 14443 and are basically memory cards, i.e., information can be stored in the internal EEPROM with an integrated digital control unit to handle the communication with a reader. Authentication and encryption with the integrated proprietary Crypto1 stream cipher shall prevent replay attacks, cloning and eavesdropping.

Soon after the reverse-engineering of the Crypto1 cipher and the Random Number Generator (RNG) on the Mifare Classic cards [NESP08], security vulnerabilities were found: a random nonce generated by the card is only dependent on the time elapsed between the power-up of the card and the issuing of the authentication command by the reader. Hence, by controlling the timing, the same nonce can be reproduced with a certain probability. This weakness has been first exploited by a key-stream recovery attack requiring to eavesdrop on genuine authentications [dKGHG08]. A secret key can then be derived from two eavesdropped authentications between a card and a genuine reader [GdKGM+08]. Later, the first card-only attacks emerged [GvRVS09, Cou09] that enable a key extraction from any Mifare Classic card utilizing a customized RFID reader.

5.2 Analyzing a Contactless Payment System

We have combined the existing card-only attacks and implemented the most efficient key-recovery attack to date on the low-cost RFID reader introduced in Section 3.1. The developed reader enables precise control of the communication and the RF field such that the RNG is completely bypassed and, exploiting properties of the weak Crypto1 cipher, an efficient key-recovery becomes possible. Using this implementation to extract the secret keys from payment cards and employing the Chameleon introduced in Section 3.2 we investigated a large commercial contactless payment application based on Mifare Classic cards [KSP].

During the analysis it turned out that the commercial payment cards store the credit balance (up to 150 €) autonomously and no effective countermeasures against fraud are implemented in the back end. With our hardware set-up it takes less than 2 minutes to recover the relevant secret keys from the used payment card (less than 30 seconds per sector key). Once the keys of one card are compromised, the security of the whole system collapses instantaneously, as all contactless payment cards turn out to have *identical secret keys* and no additional cryptographic mechanisms or obvious other checks are implemented on the system level.

An adversary can, in 40 ms and imperceptibly for the victim, read out a card or write to it, increase or decrease its credit balance, clone his card and impersonate the victim. Furthermore, a criminal can sell counterfeit cards or program the Chameleon to emulate a new random card, and hence permit an unlimited amount of payments. Another fatal flaw on the organizational level enables converting fraudulently increased virtual money to real cash. Most attacks, including the key recovery, can be carried out by an unskilled adversary using an RFID reader and open-source software for extracting the keys and modifying the cards.

The key-recovery is feasible due to a weak RNG and the usage of an outdated cipher in Mifare Classic cards. The analyzed system amplifies the evolving risks by the lack of a key distribution. While basic measures improving the security of such a flawed system, such as individual keys for each card and consistency checks in the back end are commonly known, they have been fully ignored by the system integrator, enabling straightforward fraud. The obvious idea of solving the security problems of the analyzed contactless payment system just by upgrading to a more sophisticated class of cryptographic contactless cards, e.g., Mifare DESfire, is not promising, as illustrated in the next section.

6   EM Side-Channel Attacks on Mifare DESfire

Mifare DESfire (MF3ICD40) cards [NXP04a] are employed in several large payment and public transport systems around the world, e.g., the Clippercard employed in San Francisco or the OpenCard deployed in Prague. The contactless smartcards employ a mathematically secure cipher, i.e., 3DES. Hence, mathematical cryptanalysis and attacks on the protocol level are not promising and another class of implementation attacks, i.e., side-channel analysis, is required for a key extraction. Again, the customized reader introduced in Section 3.1 serves as the basis for performing the first non-invasive side-channel attacks on commercial cryptographic RFIDs in the literature [KOP09], that rely on extracting and processing the information leakage contained in the EM emanations.

6.1   Related Work

Oren and Shamir [OS07] presented a successful side-channel attack against Class 1 EPC tags operating in the UHF frequency range which can be disabled remotely by sending a secret "kill password". Small fluctuations in the reader field during the communication with the tag allow to consecutively deduce to the correct password bits. However, the very limited type of RFID tag does not offer any cryptography.

At the CHES 2007, Hutter et al. [HMF07] performed an EM attack on their own AES implementations on a standard 8-Bit microcontroller and an AES co-processor in an RFID-like setting. The antenna and analogue frontend are separated from the digital circuitry, while on a real RFID tag these components are intrinsically tied together. In contrast to their work, we face the real-world situation, i.e., we have no knowledge about the implementation details of the unmodified contactless smartcard to be attacked. We analyze a black-box device with all RFID and cryptographic circuitry closely packed on one silicon die and get no help like artificial triggering for the alignment.

6.2 Key Extraction via the EM Side Channel

For the side-channel analysis, an EM probe (see Section 3.3) is placed close to the antenna of the contactless card. Then, known plaintexts are sent to the device. Its energy consumption during the encryption with 3DES is digitized and then processed with a PC. By correlating the measured information leakage with the modelled power consumption, details about the data processed by the card can be deduced. In [KOP09], we illustrate new techniques for facilitating a key recovery by means of Correlation Power Analysis (CPA) in the presence of the field of an RFID reader. We develop special analogue circuitry and evaluations methods, tailored to the analysis of contactless smartcards, that aim at isolating the information leakage contained in the EM emanations and that are generally applicable for analyzing all kinds of cryptographic RFIDs.

The effectiveness of the developed methods is practically verified by analyzing the security of Mifare DESfire cards. We investigate the leakage model applicable for the data bus, locate the time window of the encryption, and describe a CPA on the 3DES hardware implementation running on the contactless smartcard. The analysis pinpoints weaknesses in the protocol, reveals a vulnerability towards side-channel attacks (despite of integrated countermeasures), and results in the first successful key-recovery of the secret 112-bit keys of the cryptographic smartcard [KOP10]. The extraction of one 3DES key requires approximately 250,000 traces, which can be recorded in 7 hours with our current measurement setup. After that, all necessary evaluation steps can be carried out offline, without further physical access to the card, in approximately 12 hours using a standard PC.

6.3 Extracting the Secret Keys of Opencards

A Mifare DESFire MF3ICD40 offers 4 kByte of storage that can be assigned to up to 28 separate applications. 14 possible keys per application plus one master key amount to a maximum of 393 secret keys that can be used for protecting the card. For extracting each key, a separate side-channel attack is required. In practice, however, usually only a few keys are actively used, so most attacks can be carried out within a reasonable timespan. To verify the efforts required for extracting all keys of a commercial system, we analyzed the Opencard system deployed in Prague. In the multi-purpose Opencard application, Mifare DESfire cards enable amongst others ticketing in the public transport, usage of the public library, and payments for parking in the city centre.

The access to the application list of an Opencard is not restricted (it could also be secured by a key), i.e., this information can be read without any authentication. We found three applications: from our experiments we deduce that very likely one is dedicated to public transport, another one to payments, and the last application contains general information such as the expiry date of the card. With our attack we extracted the secret keys of all applications as used by the Opencard system and read out the (decrypted) content of several Opencards. We found that the master key for altering various security parameters of the cards seems to be identical for all cards. Likewise, the key for the application storing general information on the cards, containing three files, is the same for all analyzed cards. The application for public transport containing one large file (480 bytes) and the application for payments containing three files are both secured with diversified keys that seem to be individually derived for each card. We were able to reveal personal data such as the date of birth from personalized cards, and intend to continue the analysis of the system.

6.4 Consequences of the Key-Recovery Attack

This section demonstrates that the mathematical security of a cipher is not sufficient to guarantee the desired protection in a real-world product: implementation attacks such as side-channel analysis pose a real threat and allow for extracting secret keys even from implementations of secure ciphers, if physical access to the device is given. Appropriate countermeasures against power-analysis attacks are also required for RFIDs: the strong noise induced by the EM field of the reader does not hinder extracting cryptographic keys, as demonstrated at the example of Mifare DESfire MF3ICD40 cards[3] used for the commercial Opencard system. Knowing all keys, an attacker can arbitrarily access the content and functionality of a Mifare DESfire card. The non-invasive key-recovery attack requires no modification of the card and leaves no physical traces.

7 Conclusion

A cost-effective toolset that is optimized for physical and protocol attacks on the security of wireless devices was presented, which can be extended to analyze virtually any type of cryptographic device. By analyzing real-world wireless systems with this toolset, various significant security vulnerabilities were pinpointed that can be exploited by a malicious opponent.

A brute-force attack implemented on the code-breaker COPACOBANA targets the basic access control scheme securing electronic passports: in practical scenarios the cryptographic keys protecting the private data are revealed in seconds. Further, the most efficient practical key-recovery attack on Mifare Classic cards known to date has been implemented. It enables to extract one sector key of a payment card in approximately 30 seconds. Since identical keys are used in all payment cards of the system, the key-recovery enables straightforward fraud.

Powerful side-channel attacks on commercial products were demonstrated in practice: the cryptographic keys of KeeLoq remote controls and the corresponding receivers of the remote keyless entry system can be extracted from approximately 10 power measurements and one single power measurement, respectively. Side-channel analysis of the electromagnetic field emanated by Mifare DESfire cards reveals the 112-bit secret keys used by their 3DES engine, however, with comparatively large efforts.

The developed tools and techniques set new lower bounds for the cost and efforts required for extracting keys with power analysis and other practical attacks. We demonstrate that many real-world systems are fully assailable and should be secured with modern cryptographic measures.

---

3 NXPs follow-up product Mifare DESFire EV1 [NXP08c] promises a higher security level, including a protection against side-channel analysis, and is not (yet) broken.

References

[CBW08]   Nicolas T. Courtois, Gregory V. Bard, and David Wagner. Algebraic and Slide Attacks on KeeL-
           oq. In FSE 2008, volume 5086 of Lecture Notes in ComputerScience, pages 97–115. Springer,
           2008.

[CLRPS]   Dario Carluccio, Kerstin Lemke-Rust, Christof Paar, and Ahmad-Reza Sadeghi. E-Passport: The
           Global Traceability or How to Feel Like an UPS Package. InWorkshop on Information Security
           Applications (WISA 2006), volume 4298 of Lecture Notes in Computer Science, pages 391–404.
           Springer.

[Cou09]   Nicolas Courtois. The Dark Side of Security by Obscurity - and Cloning MiFare Classic Rail and
           Building Passes, Anywhere, Anytime. In SECRYPT, pages 331–338. INSTICC, 2009.

[CS10]   Tom Chothia and Vitaliy Smirnov. A traceability attack against e-passports. In Financial Cryp-
           tography and Data Security, volume 6052 of Lecture Notes in Computer Science, pages 20–34.
           Springer, 2010.

[dKGHG08] Gerhard de Koning Gans, Jaap-Henk Hoepman, and Flavio D. Garcia. A Practical Attack on
           the MIFARE Classic. In CARDIS, volume 5189 of Lecture Notes in Computer Science, pages
           267–282. Springer, 2008.

[ECM]   Standards ECMA-340 and ECMA-352 for the Near Field Communication Interface and Proto-
           col. http://www.ecma-international.org.

[EKM+08]   Thomas Eisenbarth, Timo Kasper, Amir Moradi, Christof Paar, Mahmoud Salmasizadeh, and
           Mohammad T. Manzuri Shalmani. On the Power of Power Analysis in the Real World: A Com-
           plete Break of the KeeLoq Code Hopping Scheme. In CRYPTO 2008, volume 5157 of Lecture
           Notes in Computer Science, pages 203–220. Springer, 2008.

[EPC10]   EPCGlobal GS1. EPC Tag Data Standard 1.5, August 2010. http://www.gs1. org/gsmp/kc/
           epcglobal/tds.

[Eur06]   European Commission. EU - Passport Specification. http://ec.europa.eu/justice_home/doc_
           centre/freetravel/documents/doc/c_2006_ 909_en.pdf , June 2006.

[Fin03]   Klaus Finkenzeller. RFID Handbook: Fundamentals and Applications in Con- tactless Smart
           Cards and Identification. John Wiley and Sons, 2nd edition, 2003.

[FOfIS]   Germany Federal Office for Information Security. Advanced Security Mechanisms for Machine
           Readable Travel Documents – Extended Access Control. http://www.bsi.de/fachthem/epass/
           EACTR03110_v110.pdf .

[GdKGM+08] Flavio D. Garcia, Gerhard de Koning Gans, Ruben Muijrers, Peter van Rossum, Roel Verdult,
           Ronny Wichers Schreur, and Bart Jacobs. Dismantling MIFARE Classic. In ESORICS, volume
           5283 of Lecture Notes in Computer Science, pages 97–114. Springer, 2008.

[GKN+08]   Tim Güneysu, Timo Kasper, Martin Novotný, Christof Paar, and Andy Rupp. Cryptanalysis with
           COPACOBANA. IEEE Transactions on Computers, 57(11): 1498–1513, 2008.

[GvRVS09] Flavio D. Garcia, Peter van Rossum, Roel Verdult, and Ronny Wichers Schreur. Wirelessly Pick-
           pocketing a Mifare Classic Card. In IEEE Symposium on Security and Privacy, pages 3–15.
           IEEE, 2009.

[HHBR+08] Daniel Halperin, Thomas S. Heydt-Benjamin, Benjamin Ransford, Shane S. Clark, Benessa
           Defend, Will Morgan, Kevin Fu, Tadayoshi Kohno, and William H. Maisel. Pacemakers and
           Implantable Cardiac Defibrillators: Software Radio Attacks and Zero-Power Defenses. In Pro-
           ceedings of the 2008 IEEE Symposium on Security and Privacy, pages 129–142. IEEE Computer
           Society, 2008.

[HHJ+06]   Jaap-Henk Hoepman, Engelbert Hubbers, Bart Jacobs, Martijn Oostdijk, and Ronny Wichers
           Schreur. Crossing Borders: Security and Privacy Issues of the European e-Passport. In Hiroshi
           Yoshiura, Kouichi Sakurai, Kai Rannenberg, Yuko Murayama, and Shin ichi Kawamura, editors,

First International Workshop in Security (IWSEC 2006), volume 4266 of Lecture Notes in Computer Science, pages 152–167. Springer, 2006.

[HMF07]   Michael Hutter, Stefan Mangard, and Martin Feldhofer. Power and EM Attacks on Passive 13.56 MHz RFID Devices. In Pascal Paillier and Ingrid Verbauwhede, editors, Cryptographic Hardware and Embedded Systems - CHES 2007, LNCS 4727, pages 320 – 330. Springer, 2007.

[IKD+08] Sebastiaan Indesteege, Nathan Keller, Orr Dunkelman, Eli Biham, and Bart Preneel. A Practical Attack on KeeLoq. In EUROCRYPT 2008, volume 4965 of Lecture Notes in Computer Science, pages 1–18. Springer, 2008.

[Int01]   International Organization for Standardization (ISO). ISO/IEC 14443: Identification Cards - Contactless Integrated Circuit(s) Cards - Proximity Cards, Part 1-4, 2001. www.iso.ch.

[JMV07]   S. Vaudenay J. Monnerat and M. Vuagnoux. About Machine-Readable TravelDocuments. In Workshop on RFID Security (RFIDSec'07), pages 15–28, 2007.

[JMW05]   Ari Juels, David Molnar, and David Wagner. Security and privacy issues in e-passports. In Security and Privacy for Emerging Areas in Communications Networks, 2005. SecureComm 2005., pages 74–88. IEEE, September 2005.

[Kas06]   Timo Kasper. Embedded Security Analysis of RFID Devices. Master's thesis, Ruhr Universität Bochum, July 2006. http://www.emsec.rub.de/media/crypto/attachments/files/2010/04/timo_kasper___embedded_security_analysis_of_rfid_devices.pdf .

[KCP]   Timo Kasper, Dario Carluccio, and Christof Paar. An Embedded System for Practical Security Analysis of Contactless Smartcards. In Workshop in Informa- tion Security Theory and Practice, WISTP 2007, volume 4462 of Lecture Notes in Computer Science, pages 150–160. Springer.

[KK05]   G.S. Kc and P.A. Karger. Security and Privacy Issues in Machine ReadableTravel Documents (MRTDs). RC 23575, IBM T. J. Watson Research Labs, April 2005.

[KKMP09] Markus Kasper, Timo Kasper, Amir Moradi, and Christof Paar. Breaking KeeLoq in a Flash: On Extracting Keys at Lightning Speed. In Progress in Cryptology - AFRICACRYPT 2009, volume 5580 of Lecture Notes in Computer Science, pages 403–420. Springer, 2009.

[KOP09]   Timo Kasper, David Oswald, and Christof Paar. EM Side-Channel Attacks on Commercial Contactless Smartcards using Low-Cost Equipment. In WISA 2009, volume 5932 of Lecture Notes in Computer Science, pages 79–93. Springer, 2009.

[KOP10]   Timo Kasper, David Oswald, and Christof Paar. A Versatile Framework for Implementation Attacks on Cryptographic RFIDs and Embedded Devices. Volume 10 of Lecture Notes in Computer Science, pages 100–130. Springer, 2010.

[KOPvM11] Timo Kasper, David Oswald, Christof Paar, and Ingo von Maurich. Chameleon: A versatile emulator for contactless smartcards. In ICISC 2010, Seoul, Korea, Lecture Notes in Computer Science. Springer, 2011.

[KPP+06] Sandeep Kumar, Christof Paar, Jan Pelzl, Gerd Pfeiffer, and Manfred Schimmler. Breaking Ciphers with COPACOBANA - A Cost-Optimized Parallel Code Breaker. In Louis Goubin and Mitsuru Matsui, editors, Cryptographic Hardware and Embedded Systems (CHES 2006), volume 4249 of Lecture Notes in Computer Science, pages 101–118. Springer, 2006.

[KSP]   Timo Kasper, Michael Silbermann, and Christof Paar. All You Can Eat or Breaking a Real-World Contactless Payment System. In Financial Cryptography 2010, volume 6052 of Lecture Notes in Computer Science, pages 343–350. Springer.

[Lan]   Langer EMV-Technik. Details of Near Field Probe Set RF 2. www.langer-emv.de

[LKLRP07] Y. Liu, T. Kasper, K. Lemke-Rust, and C. Paar. E-Passport: Cracking Basic Access Control Keys. In Proceedings of OTM'07, Part II, volume 4804 of Lecture Notes in Computer Science, pages 1531–1547. Springer, 2007.

[LSR06]   Tobias Lohmann, Matthias Schneider, and Christoph Ruland. Analysis of power constraints for cryptographic algorithms in mid-cost RFID tags. In Josep Domingo-Ferrer, Joachim Posegga, and Daniel Schreckling, editors, Smart Card Research and Advanced Applications, volume 3928 of Lecture Notes in Computer Science, pages 278–288. Springer, 2006.

[Mas06]   Massachusetts Bay Transportation Authorit. The Charlie Card Reusable Ticket System. http://www.mbta.com/fares_and_passes/charlie, 2006.

[Mic]   Microchip. HCS410/WM, KeeLoq Crypto Read/Write Transponder Module. http://ww1.microchip.com/downloads/en/DeviceDoc/41116b.pdf.

[MK09]   Amir Moradi and Timo Kasper. A New Remote Keyless Entry System Resistant to Power Analysis Attacks. In 7th International Conference on Information, Communications and Signal Processing (ICICS), pages 1062–1067. IEEE Press, 2009.

[NESP08]   Karsten Nohl, David Evans, Starbug, and Henryk Plötz. Reverse-Engineering a Cryptographic RFID Tag. In Paul C. van Oorschot, editor, USENIX Security Symposium, pages 185–194, 2008.

[NK09]   Martin Novotný and Timo Kasper. Cryptanalysis of KeeLoq with COPACOBANA. In Workshop on Special Purpose Hardware for Attacking Cryptographic Systems (SHARCS'09), 2009.

[NXP95]   NXP. Mifare Classic. http://www.nxp.com, 1995.

[NXP04a]   NXP. Mifare DESFire Short Form Specification MF3 IC D40, 2004. http://www.nxp.com/acrobat_download/other/identification/SFS075530.pdf .

[NXP08a]   NXP. Mifare Classic 1K MF1 IC S50 Functional Specification. http://www.nxp.com/acrobat_download/other/identification/M001053_MF1ICS50_rev5_3.pdf , 2008.

[NXP08b]   NXP. Mifare Classic 4K MF1 IC S70 Functional Specification. NXP, 2008. http://www.nxp.com/acrobat/other/identification/M043541_MF1ICS70_ Fspec_rev4_1.pdf .

[NXP08c]   NXP. Short Data Sheet Mifare DESFire EV1 MF3 IC D41. http://www.nxp.com/acrobat_download/datasheets/MF3ICD21_41_81_SDS_2.pdf , 2008.

[Oct97]   Octopus. Octopus Card in Hong Kong. http://www.octopuscards.com/consumer/products/en/index.jsp, 1997.

[OS]   Yossi Oren and Adi Shamir. Power Analysis of RFID Tags. http://www.wisdom.weizmann.ac.il/~yossio/rfid/.

[OS07]   Yossef Oren and Adi Shamir. Remote Password Extraction from RFID Tags. Volume 56, pages 1292–1296, Washington, DC, USA, 2007. IEEE Computer Society. http://iss.oy.ne.ro/RemotePowerAnalysisOfRFIDTags .

[OV-05]   OV-chipkaart. All about the OV-chipcard. http://www.ov-chipkaart.nl/allesoverdeov-chipkaart, 2005.

[Pic08]   Pico Technology. PicoScope 5200 USB PC Oscilloscopes, 2008.

[RCT06]   Melanie R. Rieback, Bruno Crispo, and Andrew S. Tanenbaum. The Evolution of RFID Security. volume 5, pages 62–69, Jan-Mar 2006.

[Rob]   Harko Robroch. ePassport Privacy Attack, Presentation at Cards Asia Singapore, April 26,2006. http://www.riscure.com.

[Sav10]   Savi Technology, Inc. Data Sheets of Savi ST-6XX Active RFID Tags, 2010. http://www.savi.com.

[Tex]   Texas Intruments. Texas Instruments to deliver RFID solution for Master- Card PayPass. http://www.ti.com/rfid/docs/news/news_releases/2005/rel01-17-05a.shtml .

[Tra03]   Transport for London. What is Oyster? http://www.tfl.gov.uk/tickets/oysteronline/2732.aspx, 2003.

[Ver]   R. Verdult. Proof of Concept, Cloning the OV-Chip Card. http://www.sos.cs.ru.nl/applications/rfid/2008-concept.pdf.

[vTJ11]   Henk C. A. van Tilborg and Sushil Jajodia, editors. Encyclopedia of Cryptography and Security 2. Springer, September 2011. to appear.

Leveraging Strong Credentials and Government Standards to secure the Mobility Cloud

Philip Hoyer

Director Strategic Solutions
ActivIdentity (UK)
117 Waterloo Road, London SE1 8UL
phoyer@actividentity.com

Abstract

There is a continuing trend of deperimeterization of networks via proliferation of mobile and mobile-based devices accessing more and more sensitive resources. This problem is both compounded and accelerated by the consumerization of the mobile devices, since it is more difficult to secure devices which are effectively not owned by the enterprise. Even if strong credentials are deployed at an organization, mobile access to sensitive resources and email is often a security exception. Fundamentally, strongly securing messaging and access to resources from the mobility cloud is imperative to maintain a high level of security in these often security-compromised times.

This paper will highlight the importance of leveraging existing investment into strong credentials with proven government standards to secure the mobility cloud.

1 Introduction

One does not need to be a fan of Apple to start agreeing with Steve Jobs' statement that 'We live in the post-PC era'. Consumption of services, personal and enterprise is driven by an increasingly mobile workforce that requires access from multiple devices depending on the user convenience of the moment. Currently this is embodied by the smart phone and the tablet, undoubtedly more and potentially hybrid form factors will come. What is clear though is that these form factors are built around mobile technologies and often are not given to the employee as traditionally the laptop was, but are potentially an asset of the individual used 'also' to work and with that to access sensitive enterprise resources. Compound that with an unprecedented speed of change in platforms with relatively low maturity but high appeal and adoption and one has indeed a security battlefield in the post-PC era that is as different as the real battlefield was between the first (trench static warfare) and second (high mobility speed of movement) world wars.

1.1 Current observed trends in mobility threats and what we need to protect against

In June 2011 for the first time Mobile application consumption surpasses web consumption in the US. [FLU11]. Also Web traffic and service usage increasingly originates from mobile phones, matter of fact as part of its key predictions for IT organizations and users in 2010 and beyond, Gartner Research [GAR10] has predicted that mobile Web access will surpass traditional PC access by 2013.

Mobile platforms are becoming the new attack ground. Mobile ecosystem is becoming the same malware ridden security sieve we are used to on the PC. To counter that, major players are pushing mobile endpoint security (e.g. Symantec). On the other hand there have been sophisticated coordinated attacks on both Mobile and PC (ZEUS + mobile spyware to get to out of band OTP) [EWK10] specifically designed to target Mobile Banking.

The increasing reports about Advanced Persistent Threats (APT) used as an attack doctrine give us every reason to anticipate APT will soon aggressively exploit mobile devices. APT target specific enterprises, typically using social media to identify specific employees, then deploy customized malware to evade antivirus applications, followed by stealing credentials to steal data.

Mobile platform being increasingly used for new category of devices (tablets), especially iOS, Android but recently also webOS and soon WinMobile 7. Tablets are being used increasingly to access sensitive enterprise resources especially by middle and upper management and an increasingly mobile workforce. Tablets are also being pushed as the new thin client (Citrix, etc)

If one considers that as we have seen from previous big shifts in computing history new platforms focus mainly on functionality, often overlooking security considerations, there is a perfect breeding ground for malware and potential attacks.

On the other hand the convenience of the mobile platforms and their appeal cannot be reasoned away and their adoption often comes from directly from people in the boardroom demanding the CIO and CISO to support their use.

Let's see then from an Enterprise perspective what use cases Enterprise personnel want to perform with their mobile devices and hence what needs to be protected.

1.2   A look and classification of the most required use cases that need to be protected

The following table is a classification of use cases Enterprise users want to perform from mobile devices that need to be protected in order of importance that ActivIdentity has found in the current marketplace:

Table 1: Use cases to secure in Mobility.

Category	Use case
Secure Messaging	email on phone / tablet
	Messages (IM, SMS, etc)
Secure Enterprise Access (e.g. Browser 2 factor portal access, mobile VPN, Application Specific tunnel back into the Enterprise)	from phone / tablet using local security (e.g. local secure element)
	from phone using existing Secure Element e.g. CAC/PIV smart card)
	from tablet using existing phone with Secure Element capability (e.g. Bluetooth connected)
	from tablet (using local Secure Element)
Physical Access	phone
SaaS Access	Salesforce.com secure 2fa access from phone / tablet

Interestingly there does not seem to be a great difference in terms of importance between industry verticals (Government, Enterprise, etc). What rather seems to be a crucial factor is the relevance and importance of intellectual property within the organization and what kind of impact a breach could have.

1.3 Leveraging existing government standards for resource classification and strong credentials

It is hence most pertinent to leverage work done in government standards to help in assessing what an organization has in terms of critical resources and what the potential impact on the organization would be in case of breach.

1.3.1 Resource classification based on Levels of access

Challenge: how do I protect what I have got and with what if I do not control it?

Since most likely the mobile device is owned by the individual and not by the Enterprise, the security context is less controlled. An Enterprise will have several categories of resources to protect.

To help with this there is an emerging consensus of a model of classification of resources, which originates from the government in form of the "E-Authentication Guidance for Federal Agencies" published as a memorandum of the Office of Management and Budget M-04-04 [OMB0404]. This proposed resource classification is based on a risk model and potential impact of breach defining 4 levels of Impact Profiles in terms of access to resources:

Potential Impact Categories for Authentication Errors	Assurance Level Impact Profiles			
	1	2	3	4
Inconvenience, distress or damage to standing or reputation	Low	Mod	Mod	High
Financial loss or agency liability	Low	Mod	Mod	High
Harm to agency programs or public interests	N/A	Low	Mod	High
Unauthorized release of sensitive information	N/A	Low	Mod	High
Personal Safety	N/A	N/A	Low	Mod High
Civil or criminal violations	N/A	Low	Mod	High

Fig. 1: OMB M04-04 Assurance Levels

Once an Enterprise has classified some of the resources and as mentioned before we are moving to a world where most global Enterprises have considerable resources at level 3 and high IP Enterprises (e.g. Pharmaceuticals, Gas & Oil etc) substantial resources at level 4 a new challenge presents itself:

Challenge: Once I know what I need to protect, how do I establish Identity and based on what?

As the figure above shows the potential impact is with errors of authentication, meaning erroneously assuring the identity of one user against the attacker. So what authentication technology shall an Enterprise employ? Again an Enterprise can leverage work done in the federal government as NIST SP 800-63-1 "Electronic Authentication Guideline" Dec 2008, which defines a recommendation based on industry best practice of potential threats against use of specific authentication technologies

Especially interesting is the analysis of effective protection when multiple authentication factors are combined:

	Memorized Secret Token	Pre-registered Knowledge Token	Look-up Secret Token	Out of Band Token	SF OTP Device	SF Cryptographic Device	MF Software Cryptographic Token	MF OTP Device	MF Cryptographic Device
Memorized Secret Token	Level 2	Level 2	Level 3	Level 3	Level 3	Level 3	Level 3	Level 4	Level 4
Pre-registered Knowledge Token	X	Level 2	Level 3	Level 3	Level 3	Level 3	Level 3	Level 4	Level 4
Look-up Secret Token	X	X	Level 2	Level 2	Level 2	Level 2	Level 3	Level 4	Level 4
Out of Band Token	X	X	X	Level 2	Level 2	Level 2	Level 3	Level 4	Level 4
SF OTP Device	X	X	X	X	Level 2	Level 2	Level 3	Level 4	Level 4
SF Cryptographic Device	X	X	X	X	X	Level 2	Level 3	Level 4	Level 4
MF Software Cryptographic Token	X	X	X	X	X	X	Level 3	Level 4	Level 4
MF OTP Device	X	X	X	X	X	X	X	Level 4	Level 4
MF Cryptographic Device	X	X	X	X	X	X	X	X	Level 4

Fig. 2: NIST SP800-63-1 mapping of authentication technologies to Levels of Access

As one can see for Level 4 resources the choice is limited and the preferred option is to use a MultiFactor cryptographic device. Effectively a strong credential which use is protected by multiple factors such as 'what the user knows' and 'what the user has' (proof of possession).

So let's look at how and what we can leverage to have strong credentialing on mobile devices.

2 Strong credentialing and availability of secure key storage on mobile platforms

Established ways to perform identity assurance are based on the concept of strong credentials. A credential is a way that allows the proof or assurance of the identity in the context of the use case that the identity is about to perform.

Often strong credentials are based on concepts of multi factor authentication.

Factors like proof of possession leverage cryptography and keys to prove that the identity assured (the user) is in possession of that key in that specific moment.

This implies that for Strong Credentialing there must be a secure and strong container for keys that can be leveraged.

As mentioned previously the mobile platforms can be new and evolve rapidly so for secure transactions like payment or access to highly sensitive resources the mobile platform itself (OS capabilities) is deemed too insecure to protect the keys.

The alternative is to leverage a secure key storage within what is called a Secure Element (SE), basically a form of smartcard chip that includes a vetted (certified) secure execution environment that has secure application and key storage and cryptography.

On a mobile platform one currently can find three distinct flavours of Secure Elements:

1. The SIM or UICC issued and controlled by the Mobile Network Operator (MNO)
2. An embedded Secure Element (chip on the handset circuit board) issued and mostly controlled by the handset manufacturer
3. A smart removable Secure Element such as a smart MicroSD – carrier independent and potentially issued by the service provider (the Enterprise that needs to protect its resources for example)

The most prominent flavour of secure element in the mobile space is a GlobalPlatform Javacard that can run multiple secure applications or applets.

So how can we exploit the presence of a Secure Element to secure the use cases and ultimately the sensitive Enterprise Resources?

2.1 Stack elements required to secure the mobility cloud

To be able to support a secure use case there are several layers of components on the handset that need to be present to ultimately leverage strong credentialing provided by the Secure Element:

1. The **handset application** that the user uses and is enabled for strong credentialing (for example supports PIN entry to 'unlock' the usage of a key for authentication or email signing
2. The middleware – that exposes to the application the crypto functionality needed by the handset application (e.g. sign, encrypt, decrypt, check PIN, etc)
3. The Secure Element (SE) driver – that exposes to the middleware the low level (APDU) access to the secure element (SIM. Embedded SE, Smart MicroSD, etc)
4. The Secure applet that protects and manages the keys and provides crypto services
5. The Secure Element (SE) – (SIM, Embedded, Smart MicroSD, etc)

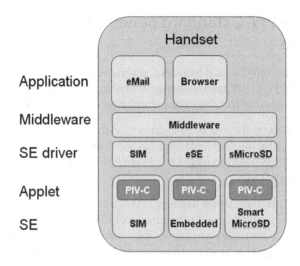

Fig. 3: Secure Credentialing Mobile stack leveraging Secure Elements

2.2 How to leverage PIV the de-facto standard for strong credentialing in the Mobility Cloud

As mentioned previously government standards help to classify the resources and indentify what authentication technology (strong credentialing) is needed, there is also a government standard that can be leveraged to provide strong credentialing and it is called PIV.

PIV was born out of post 9/11 mandated by the Homeland Security Presidential Directive 12 to create a standard for identifying and credentialing federal employees and contractors. It is Smart Card based, PKI + biometrics issued following a standard process and card interface specified in FIPS201 [FISP201].

The main use cases supported are:
- Logical access
- Email signing and encryption
- File signing/encryption
- Network VPN access
- Can be used for Physical Access - see NIST publication 800-116 [NSP800-116]
- Mandated to be used for Physical Access - see OMB-11-11 [OMB1111]

As one can immediately notice these cover the required use cases that must be secured from mobile devices.

Because of the clout and purchasing power of the US government, several vendors supply the different components needed and there is a mature list of approved and certified infrastructure components: Middleware, Card Applets, Secure Elements.

But how does this fit and how can one leverage this on a mobile device? Especially in an Enterprise whose employees are not employees of the US federal government?

2.3 Leveraging PIV-C standard penetration into the mobile eco system

As the PIV standard can only be used by federal government employees two additional flavours of PIV have surfaced: PIV-I (PIV interoperable, for people that interact with the US federal government) and in the context of this discussion more interestingly PIV-C (PIV compatible).

PIV - C (PIV-compatible) is defined as an identity card that meets the PIV technical specifications so that PIV infrastructure elements such as card readers are capable of working with the card, but the card itself has not been issued in a manner that assures it is trustworthy by Federal government relying parties.

This means that if an Enterprise where to adopt PIV-C it can leverage the mass market economy of the existing PIV market and rely on the mature list of PIV components out there, with trusted interoperability. Not only are these components approved but to be approved by the government they had to undergo stringent security certifications such as FIPS and common criteria.

Even if the PIV-C is defined in the context of a smart card effectively its components (Applet, Drivers, etc) can be used within the context of the mobile ecosystem. Matter of fact a PIV-C certified applet can be loaded into all three Secure Elements of the handset (SIM, Embedded and smart MicroSD).

Matter of fact the support for the PIV standard in terms of PIV-C in the mobile stack elements is already present so it is possible to find:

1. **Strong credential enabled handset applications** that are enabled e.g. supports PIN entry to 'unlock' the usage of a key for authentication or email signing leveraging middleware
2. **PIV-C compatible middleware** – exposing to the application the crypto functionality (e.g. sign, encrypt, decrypt, check PIN, etc)
3. **The Secure Element (SE) driver** – that exposes to the middleware the low level (APDU) access to the secure element (SIM. Embedded SE, Smart MicroSD, etc)
4. **PIV-C certified and approved applets** that protects and manages the keys and provides crypto services
5. **The Secure Element (SE)** – (SIM, Embedded, Smart MicroSD, etc) capable of harbouring and receiving the PIV-C applet.

No other strong credentialing standard is currently embedded or found in any comparable implementation in the mobile ecosystem.

So by leveraging PIV-C in the mobile ecosystem it allows an Enterprise:

- Leverage existing best practice of Strong Credential Issuance based on FIPS 201
- Leverage the support for PIV-C in the existing Mobile Ecosystem
- Leverage strong credentialing with keys managed in a PIV-C applet to protect resources up to Level of Access 4 (highest)
- Leverage PIV-C support to secure all required use cases: Secure messaging (sign, encrypt/ decrypt), secure enterprise access (authentication using PIV-C authentication certificate with 2 factor PIN)
- Leverage PIV-C standard making security stronger and more affordable
- Reduce risk of security solution because standard based and more interoperable

2.4 Surf the NFC wave to secure the Enterprise

As explained above the main security anchor to provide strong identity assurance from the mobile devices to the Enterprise is based on storing credentials required for the use cases within a PIV-C applet in a Secure Element.

Depending on the Secure Element the issuance of the credentials is more or less complex.

It is definitely possible to issue a Smart MicroSD with the PIV-C applets and then load the required credentials on them (personalising the applet).

This still requires the issuance of the Smart MicroSD with its related operational cost.

Another way is to leverage an existing embedded Secure Element in the handset. One of the drivers for Secure Elements to be in the phone with the capability to separately have management (loading) of the required PIV-C applet is to store secure Near Field Communication Services such as contactless payments (e.g. Visa Paywave) and transit applications.

This wave of technology will sweep the mobile ecosystem and within the next 2-3 years the main mobile devices that will be used to access the enterprise resources will have NFC and an embedded Secure Element or NFC capable SIM on board.

What this means is that to secure the mobility cloud from an enterprise perspective it is possible to surf the NFC wave or leverage the existence of the Secure Elements in the phone to load the PIV-C application as the container for the strong credentials without physically issuing the secure element. This will dramatically lower deployment cost of secure credentials to mobile devices. This opens the technology used by governments to secure Level of Access 4 resources based on PIV-C to the masses.

3 Conclusion

Enterprises face a new security battle with a fast moving battlefield with the increasing usage of non enterprise issued mobile devices used to consume enterprise services and to access sensitive enterprise resources.

Enterprises can leverage existing government standards to classify their resources (OMB-M04-04) and to understand how to protect the access to the resources and services (NIST-SP800-63-1).

Enterprises that require protecting resources of the highest sensitivity (classified as Level of Access 4) can leverage PIV-C prevalence in the mobile ecosystem to secure the following use cases:
- Secure Messaging (e.g. email sign, encrypt / decrypt)
- Secure Enterprise Access (e.g. Browser 2 factor portal access, mobile VPN, Application Specific tunnel back into the Enterprise)
- Physical Access
- SaaS Access

Enterprises can leverage best practice PIV issuance of keys to a Secure Element to provide the security anchor required in a current threat infested mobile ecosystem:

- Via issuance of an Enterprise controlled Smart MicroSD
- Leveraging NFC service delivery capability to embedded Secure Elements and or SIM

With innovative solutions based on PIV-C Enterprises can secure their mobility cloud now!

References

[GAR10]   Gartner: "Key predictions for IT organizations and users in 2010 and beyond", In: www.gartner. com 2007.

[FLU11]   comScore, Alexa, Flurry Analytics, "u.s. Mobile Apps vs Web Consumption, Minutes per Day",June 2011.

[EWK10]   eWeek Europe, "Zeus Malware targets European Mobile Banking", http://www.eweekeurope. co.uk/news/news-security/zeus-malware-targets-european-mobile-banking-10148

[OMB0404] Office of Management and Budget Memorandum M-04-04 "E-Authentication Guidance for Federal Agencies",2003

[NSP800-63-1] NIST SP 800-63-1 "Electronic Authentication Guideline" Dec 2008

[FIPS201] FIPS PUB 201-1,"Personal Identity Verification (PIV) of Federal Employees and Contractors", http://csrc.nist.gov/publications/fips/fips201-1/FIPS-201-1-chng1.pdf

[NSP800-116] NIST SP 800-116 "A Recommendation for the Use of PIV Credentials in Physical Access Control Systems (PACS)" Nov 2008

[OMB1111] Office of Management and Budget Memorandum M11-11 "Continued Implementation of Homeland Security Presidential Directive (HSPD) 12– Policy for a Common Identification Standard for Federal Employees and Contractors", Feb 2011

Security Management, Identity & Access Management

Security Architecture in a Collaborative De-Perimeterised Environment: Factors of Success

Yulia Cherdantseva[1] · Omer Rana[1] · Jeremy Hilton[2]

[1]Cardiff University
{y.v.cherdantseva | o.f.rana}@cs.cardiff.ac.uk

[2]Cranfield University
j.c.hilton@cranfield.ac.uk

Abstract

Security Architecture (SA) is concerned with such tasks as design, development and management of secure business information systems. These tasks are inherently complex and become several orders of magnitude more sophisticated in a Collaborative De-Perimeterised Environment (CDePE). Although significant research exists about the technical solutions that may be used in a CDePE, we believe there is an important gap in current literature in addressing the specifics of collaboration and de-perimeterisation at the stages of design and management of a SA. This paper discusses how a CDePE is addressed in the ISO/IEC 27000 series of standards and identifies ten factors, besides technical ones, that are important for the success of a SA. This paper emerged as a result of an analysis of the current state of the information security discipline and of the modern trends in the discipline.

1 Introduction

Many disciplines have adopted the term *Architecture* from the science of designing and erecting buildings. The term is widely used in computer and information sciences; the field of information security is not an exception. As town building architecture defines rules for the construction of buildings, Security Architecture (SA) is concerned with the design and development of secure business information systems, i.e. systems that are free from danger and damage, reliable and resistant to failures and attacks [ShCL05: p.2].

The main aim of a SA is overall business security. A SA generally provides a framework for enabling security controls of different layers to operate coherently together and depends on three aspects [ShCL05: pp.19-24]:
- The business goals of an organisation implementing it;
- The environment in which an organisation operates;
- The technical capabilities available at the current phase of Information and Communications Technologies (ICT) evolution.

N. Pohlmann, H. Reimer, W. Schneider (Editors): Securing Electronic Business Processes, Vieweg (2011), 201-213

A SA is often investigated purely from a technical viewpoint, whereas the impact of the business goals and the environment on a SA is ignored. We believe that the environment in which an organisation operates is very important and should be taken into account while developing and maintaining a SA. The tasks of SA as a science are inherently complex and become several orders of magnitude more sophisticated in the present environment, which we refer to as a Collaborative De-Perimeterised Environment (CDePE) and describe below.

The term *De-Perimeterisation* was coined by the Jericho Forum (JF), an international association of organisations that concentrates on the issues of secure business in a networked environment. The term refers to the erosion of an organisation's hard perimeter in response to the evolution of ICT and consequent change of business needs. Formally, the JF describes De-Perimeterisation as "the concept of architecting security for the extended business boundary and not an arbitrary IT boundary" [OGJF07].

Thus, a CDePE is an environment where third parties gain access to data and services hosted by the organisation internally and, similarly, the organisation accesses data and services hosted by other organisations. Previously, the distinction was clear: there were people inside the perimeter (staff) who were fully trusted and people outside the perimeter (non-staff) who were not trusted. At present, organisations need to allow access to data not only to its staff - remote and mobile, but also to service providers, collaborators, authorities and customers. Any organisation, to a greater or lesser degree, participates in collaboration and information sharing, works in a distributed environment and has started to exploit Cloud computing capability (mostly for remote data storage, but also, in some instances, for outsourcing high throughput computation) in order to reduce costs and to increase efficiency and commercial profit. As a result, in a CDePE perimeters of organisations erode and "closed" systems no longer exist.

We do not consider a de-perimeterised environment as an equivalent of a distributed environment. A distributed environment may also have a hard perimeter, whereas de-perimeterisation accentuates a need even for a distributed environment to soften its boundaries. Nor do we consider Cloud computing to be the only idiosyncratic feature of the stated environment. Cloud computing is only one many aspects of a CDePE and we discuss it in Section 3.8. A CDePE reflects the complexity that emanates from a plethora of activities, including collaborative information sharing, Cloud computing, remote and mobile working and from the cascading impact of the intensive linkages between them.

An open architecture of an organisation with a softened perimeter provides business opportunities, but, at the same time, makes information security a greater challenge. With the unprecedented level of interconnectivity available today, previously used strategies of perimeter security are unsustainable. An approach to information security is required that allows an organisation to operate within a soft perimeter and to protect information outside of the organisation's perimeter as well as inside it. This new approach is based on multi-layered security and accumulates protection capabilities of technologies, organisational measures, human factors and legislation.

Currently, within de-perimeterisation research a strong emphasis is placed on technologies [OGJF07]. However, de-perimeterisation is a socio-technical phenomenon worthy of detailed research not only from the standpoint of technical network specialists, but also from the standpoint of managers, system and security architects. Although significant research exists about technical solutions that may be used in the CDePE, there is an important gap in the current literature in addressing peculiarities of this environment at the stages of design, development and management of a SA. Therefore, to cover this gap, we attempt to summarise and debate information security issues relevant to managers, system and security architects. Our aim is not a development of a new framework for a SA, but rather an identification of factors that are essential for the success of a SA in addition to any existing framework.

The remainder of this paper is structured as follows: Section 2 discusses how a CDePE is addressed in the ISO/IEC 27000 family of standards that provides a widely used framework for a SA. Section 3 outlines the factors that deserve to be taken into account while designing, implementing and managing a SA. Section 4 draws conclusions from the preceding discussion.

2 How the ISO/IEC 27000 Series of Standards Addresses a CDePE

The ISO/IEC 27000 series of standards is published jointly by the International Organization for Standardization (ISO) and the International Electrotechnical Commission (IEC), and reserved for information security matters. ISO/IEC 27001:2005 emulates the success of its predecessor BS7799 and sets the trend for this growing family of standards. It specifies the requirements towards an Information Security Management System (ISMS) and covers a wide range of issues, such as risk assessment; management responsibilities and commitment; resource management and provision; training, awareness and competence. Another constituent of the series is ISO/IEC 27002:2005 that contains a code of practice for information security management.

Both ISO/IEC 27001 and ISO/IEC 27002 were developed at the time when the business world was not so considerably affected by de-perimeterisation. Although the ISO/IEC 27000 family provides some basic recommendations that are applicable in a CDePE, these recommendations should be significantly extended and updated by an organisation wishing to make use of them in the present environment. Below we consider how a CDePE is addressed in ISO/IEC 27001 and ISO/IEC 27002, as well as we discuss any omissions in the standards. We start our analysis with ISO/IEC 27001:2005, where Section 4.2.1 a) suggests that an organisation shall

> *"Define the scope and boundaries of the ISMS in terms of the characteristics of the business, the organization, its location, assets and technology, and including details of and justification for any exclusions from the scope."*

In the case of a "closed" system, it is easy to assume that the boundaries of the ISMS are equal to the boundaries of an organisation, whereas the task of defining the boundaries and the scope of the ISMS in the de-perimeterised environment is more complicated. According to the definition, the ISMS is a "part of the overall management system, based on a business risk approach, to establish, implement, operate, monitor, review, maintain and improve information security" and as such it "includes organisational structure, policies, planning activities, responsibilities, practices, procedures, processes and resources" [BSIS05]. In the CDePE practices, procedures and policies may spread over multiple organisations that work together in order to achieve a common goal. Therefore, to define the boundaries of the ISMS an organisation should decide whether it should include service providers, collaborators and customers in the scope and to what extent they should be included. Neither ISO/IEC 27001, nor ISO/IEC 27002 provides any further details about establishing the scope and boundaries of the ISMS.

Section 4.2.3 f) of ISO/IEC 27001:2005 states the need to "undertake a management review of the ISMS on a regular basis to ensure that the scope remains adequate". Section 7.3 of the same document further explains that the modification of the ISMS may be done in response to internal and external events, including changes to contractual obligations and legal requirements. The above, should be translated into the requirement to conduct a revision of the ISMS boundaries with every change in collaboration or information exchange agreements, as well as with any change within an external party that affects common business processes or policies.

> *"4.2.4 c) communicate the actions and improvements to all interested parties with a level of detail appropriate to the circumstances and, as relevant, agree how to proceed."*

In a CDePE information security of one organisation may strongly depend on the reliability of the ISMS of other organisations. Thus, a change or an improvement in the ISMS, that affects cross-organisational business policies must be pre-agreed between the involved parties and, where possible, must be developed in co-operation. The collaborating parties should be adequately prepared and relevant security controls should be put in place before such a change goes live.

Section 4.3.2 of ISO/IEC 27001:2005 suggests the need to protect and control documents required by the ISMS and, more specifically, to establish a procedure to define the management actions needed to ensure identification of documents of external origin. In a CDePE, in addition to identification of an external document, it is also needed to recognise the level of its confidentiality and to implement pertinent controls and procedures in order to process, store and transmit a document in accordance with the author's security requirements. The document may have a certain level of access in the original information system, but when transferred to another system the privilege rights may be ignored or wrongly interpreted. The procedures and policies related to the processing, storage and transmission of the external documents should be agreed between the parties involved. ISO/IEC 27002:2005 in Section 7.2.2 declares that one of the possibilities to achieve appropriate security of external documents is through the ability "to interpret the classification labels from other organisations." In fact, consistent cross-system document level security may be reached through the integration of information systems of collaborating parties. More efficient approaches to secure processing of external documents may include agreed-upon document classification schema and integrated authentication system [Simm04].

Delving deeper into this question, Sections A.7.2.1 and A 7.2.2 require classification of information within the organisation, its labelling and appropriate handling. In a CDePE, an organisation should not only recognise and treat external documents in accordance with the author's security guidelines, but also protect its own information assets outside of its perimeter. An organisation should ensure that its information is treated in conformance with the organisation's security requirements outside the organisation's perimeter. One of the modern concepts for user-friendly communication of security needs and controls on inter-organisational level is the icon-based labelling scheme known as Protective Commons [HiTa08]. Protective Commons emulate Creative Commons retaining a focus on document protection.

Information security associated with outsourcing is perfunctorily covered by Section A.6.2 of ISO/IEC 27001:2005 that defines the requirement to identify risks related to the involvement of external parties and by Section A.10.2 that defines the requirements to monitor the conformance of the services provided by third parties to the agreements. Corresponding security controls are outlined in Sections 6.2 and 10.2 of ISO/IEC 27002:2005. The above sections consider neither the risk management perspective of outsourcing [Isec11b], nor the requirements towards out-sourcing agreements. In the environment where an organisation significantly depends on the services provided by third parties, financial penalties should be established for information secu-rity breaches occurring due to the fault of service providers as well as for failures to provide the service (i.e. meet particular Quality of Service requirements). This measure identifies the under-lying financial intensives that encourage service providers to pay more attention to customers' information security [Ande01].

Section 12.1 of ISO/IEC 27002:2005 defines the need for security requirements to be established at the early stages of the information system development process. Hence, security requirements for multi-organisational business processes and integrated information systems should also be defined at the initial stage of system requirements formulation and extended at the stage of sys-tem modelling and design. There is a significant gap in the research and practice in this area, although some attempts to model security aspects in the Business Process Modelling Notation (BPMN) collaboration diagram exist [RFMP07].

Both ISO/IEC 27001 and ISO/IEC 27002 address information security issues within a single organisation. However, with emerging interest in e-commerce, supply chain and joint product development, where complex business processes spread over multiple organisations, the overall control and consistency of procedures across organisations are essential. In 2011, in order to ad-dress this evolving area of inter-organisational processes the Object Management Group (OMG) introduced into the BPMN 2.0 the concept of choreography, the essence of which is the coordina-tion of communications between organisations or processes without an overarching process in charge of such coordination [OMG11]. Addressing information security in choreography process is a critical challenge in virtue of the fact that security in these processes could only be achieved if business processes of all parties involved and communications between them are secure.

While collaboration and information sharing leverage new business opportunities, it is important to prevent exposure of strategic organisational knowledge. The ISO/IEC 27000 is focused on data and information assets and does not actually distinguish knowledge as a valuable asset. This, consequently, leads to a failure to address threats to this critical asset caused by collaboration and de-perimeterisation [AlSa10]. The importance of distinguishing knowledge assets as well as assessing its business value is derived from a necessity to retain strategic advantage in a highly competitive world.

The analysis of the ISO 27000 series of standards leads to a conclusion that although the series provides strong basis for information security, it does not comprehensively reflect the complexity of a CDePE. The series is actively growing in response to a rapidly changing environment. Thus, several new standards in this series, that will more coherently address the modern environment, are expected to emerge within the next 2-3 years. The release of ISO/IEC 27036 - *IT Security - Security techniques - Information security for supplier relationships*, a multi-part standard ad-dressing risks to information related to the external parties, is expected in 2012. The standard is anticipated to provide a solid basis for security of outsourcing and, potentially, for Cloud comput-ing as a form of outsourcing [Isec11b]. ISO/IEC 27010 - *Information Technology - Security tech-niques - Information security management for inter-sector and inter-organizational communica-tions*, another emerging standard of the series, is a supplement to ISO/IEC 27001:2005 and ISO/IEC 27002:2005. It considers in more detail the inter-organisational information security issues and information exchange between organisations that are only briefly addressed by other existing standards [BSIS11]. A committee draft of the standard (that is currently available for review) still does not address all the issues discussed above. The draft expires on 31 August 2011 and hopefully the final version will cover issues relevant to a CDePE more exhaustively.

Thus, the requirements and controls outlined in ISO/IEC 27001 and ISO/IEC 27002 do not comprehensively cover the issues of information security that arise in a CDePE from managerial and system architects' perspectives. In the next section we list and analyse the issues that should be taken into account by managers, system and security architects in addition to the security requirements defined in published standards of the ISO/IEC 27000 series.

3 Factors of Success

3.1 Comprehensive and Systematic Approach

Any organisation that aims to increase commercial profit, gain trust of partners and effectively and efficiently use new technologies in a CDePE should protect information in a comprehensive and systematic manner. Comprehensive protection refers to the exploitation of countermeasures of different layers in order to achieve "complete" security. Countermeasures could include, but are not limited to an organisation's strategy, policies and procedures; business processes; training and educational programs; technical security controls; and legal measures. Reliance on any single layer of defence does not often provide adequate security. Security controls of different layers should support information security concurrently. If any of the controls fail, the others should be sufficient to provide an adequate level of information security until the functionality of the failed control is restored. With regards to the comprehensiveness of information protection, a SA helps to avoid a piecemeal approach to information security: rather than applying security countermeasures in an ad-hoc manner, a SA creates a holistic enterprise-wide picture and allows to structure inter-relationships between the various measures being considered. The additional task of a SA in a CDePE is to provide a comprehensive approach to inter-organisational business processes and accompanying information sharing.

A systematic approach refers to addressing information security at every stage of a system lifecycle, including such stages as requirements analysis, system design, implementation and maintenance. Hence, security requirements in multi-organisational projects should be agreed at the initial stage of system requirements formulation and at the stage of system design. At present, information security at cross-organisational business processes is very rarely addressed at the design level. Information security is often left for the computer specialists to sort out as an a posteriori task.

The above implies that a CDePE, that significantly affects a SA, should also be addressed at every protection layer and at every stage of a system development lifecycle. We believe that a comprehensive and systematic approach to information security and, consequently, to the specifics of the environment in which the system (and therefore the SA) should operate is the most important and unconditionally required factor of a successful implementation of a SA.

3.2 Adjusted Security Framework

It is often mentioned that a good security framework should serve as a road map for information security. An organisation should carefully consider and choose a security framework to follow, since the belated change of a framework may lead to unnecessary additional work and costs. Despite a plethora of existing security frameworks promising high standards of information protection, an organisation should not entirely rely on any of them. There are two underlying reasons for this. First, existing standards and best practices fail to address the effects of changing environment and newly emerging threats in a timely way. As alluded to in Section 2 of this paper, commenting on the ISO/IEC 27000 series of standards, it takes several years to adjust the series to the new environment. Second, neither bodies that develop security standards and frameworks, nor certification organisations are financially or in any other way accountable for the security failures in organisations that follow the standards and practices. In fact, information security strongly depends on economic motives, but in this case such motives are absent [Ande01].

Thus, it is always up to an organisation to fine-tune a framework for the current environment as well as to adjust it to a particular business context. The challenge for a contemporary security framework is to find an optimum balance between information sharing and information protection staying within legal and compliance regulations.

3.3 Senior Management Role

Section 6.1.1 h) of ISO/IEC 27001 states that management should "ensure that the implementation of information security controls is co-ordinated across the organization." In the present landscape, in addition to co-ordinating the implementation of security controls within the organisation, senior management should be involved in agreeing security controls with collaborating parties and other members of the information exchange. Security aspects of inter-organisational information exchange require attention at the level of senior management because only such individuals (and stakeholders) have the required level of understanding of business needs to be able to answer questions such as:

- Who are the prospective strategic partners?
- To what degree does a company want to share or segregate its information?
- How much does the company trust a partner or a third party?
- What is the liability for information misuse by partners and third parties?

Consequently, in a CDePE the following responsibilities should be included into the scope of managers in addition to those declared in ISO/IEC 27001:2005:

- Within the organisation's security strategy define the level of trust for each external party;
- Collaborate with the third parties' management in order to agree cross-organisational security strategy, policies and controls;
- Ensure cross-organisational consistency of security strategies, policies and controls within the collaborating community;
- Ensure adequate protection of the organisation's information and knowledge assets outside of the organisation's perimeter.

3.4 Responsibilities Allocation and Required Qualities of Information security Personnel

A CDePE stems new responsibilities not only for managers as discussed above, but also for information security personnel. Some newly emerging responsibilities may be as follows:

- Communicate with external parties in order to develop consistent cross-organisational security policies and procedures;
- Develop and implement procedures for informing relevant external parties about changes in organisation's security strategies, policies and procedures;
- Address security concerns in relationships with customers.

Furthermore, information security personnel should co-ordinate all activities that aim to protect information in order to prevent omissions that may arise due to a granular approach. In many cases information sharing needs are defined at the business level, some security controls are realised to protect information at the technical level, liability for information misuse is defined in agreements by legal personnel – all these measures contribute to information security and, therefore, require overarching administration. ISO/IEC 27002:2005 requires clear definition and allocation of information security responsibilities. Thus, the importance of the activities mentioned above should be recognised by an organisation and responsibilities for them appropriately allocated.

In addition to clearly defined responsibilities, information security personnel should have up-to-date technical knowledge, understanding of business and economics, and good communication skills. However, the most important quality of information security personnel in the current rapidly altering environment is open-mindedness. At present, there is no commonly agreed definition of information security and the set of security goals is variable within security standards: some standards limit the realm of information security to confidentiality, integrity and availability [CNSS10, ISACA08]; others include non-repudiation, accountability, reliability and authenticity [ISO09]. The limitation of the scope of information security and, consequently, of personnel responsibilities to the certain goals may lead to the overlooking of new threats and vulnerabilities that are constantly emerging in the ever-changing world of ICT. Therefore, staff responsible for information security should perceive an overall protection of information as their major goal, rather than the achievement of goals predefined in standards. Moreover, personnel should be ready to protect information from both known and unknown threats and quickly adapt to the new environment. We refer to this important quality of information security personnel as open-mindedness.

3.5 Up-to-date Security Policies and Procedures

The organisation's security policies and procedures should be constantly revised and improved in order to be adequate for a rapidly changing environment. They should cover continually emerging technologies in a timely manner. Therefore, the process for the introduction of improvements should be predefined and established. In a CDePE, this process apart from development and implementation of an improvement should include the agreement of an improvement with external parties, raising awareness among internal and external personnel, and analysis of external parties' feedback regarding an improvement introduced.

Most recently the policies and procedures that address threats emerging from mobile communications and social networking are the focus of security specialists. If use of mobile devices is a business necessity for an organisation, then mobility should be appropriately addressed by security policies. The policies may be, for instance, as follows:

- Access to a mobile device must be protected by a password of a certain strength;
- In case of the loss of a mobile device an organisation retains the right to destroy all the data on the device;
- The same security policies should be applied to the mobile device independent whether it is within an organisation's network or outside it.

With the rapid growth of the social networking industry the risk of data leakage through social networks becomes more significant. In 2010, 20% of companies encountered data loss via social networking sites [Good10]. To address this threat, security policies should clearly define which information may and may not be exposed at social networking sites, blogs and professional communities.

3.6 Involvement of Interested Parties

ISO/IEC 27001:2005 states that security actions and improvements should be communicated to all interested parties where interested parties are implicitly limited to the employees and stakeholders of an organisation. There are two extensions required to the above statement in the CDePE. First, the scope of the interested parties becomes broader: apart from interests of internal parties, interests of employees and stakeholders of external organisations involved should be taken into account while taking decisions about security actions. This is due to the fact that while the most of the security changes done by the organisation affect the organisation's personnel productivity, some of the changes may affect productivity of the personnel of other organisations that use services or data provided by the organisation. Therefore, it is preferable to reach a consensus not only between security people and internal users, but also between security people and external users in order to prevent security improvements being banned as reducing productivity.

Second, a more in-depth involvement of external parties is required. It should not be limited to the communication of security policies to external parties. Security policies and procedures should be planned, designed and implemented in close rapport with interested parties. The level of involvement of a party in the above processes may vary depending on the status of the party: service provider, collaborator, authority or customer. Section 5.1.1 of ISO/IEC 27002:2005, for example, declares the requirements towards an Information Security Policy Document (ISPD), which is considered in the standards as a purely internal document that only is some cases communicated to the external parties. In the CDePE, the ISPD should equally address protection of information within and outside an organisation's perimeter and, as such, parts of the document that cover security of collaborative information sharing should be developed with the close cooperation of the parties involved.

3.7 Information Security Training and Awareness

Training and awareness programs require regular revisions and updates in order to remain adequate for a rapidly changing environment. The programs should instruct employees in a clear form about how to do business securely using new technologies and make them aware in a timely way about emerging threats. The areas that at present are rarely or poorly addressed by training and awareness programs and require more attention are social networking, mobile communications and social engineering.

Furthermore, the reasoning behind information security countermeasure should be made clear to personnel in order to overstep rote compliance [BoJe02]. Rote compliance is only sufficient until a situation that is not covered by any of the existing policies or procedures occurs. At present, hardly any organisation, in terms of its security policies and procedures, will be able to keep pace with the fast evolution of technologies. Therefore, to solve this problem any security training or awareness program should pursue two major aims. Firstly, to teach system users to exploit common sense when using progressive technologies or working in unforeseen circumstances. Secondly, to educate users to perceive information security as everyone's personal responsibility, rather than something that has nothing to do with their day-to-day activities. As any information security measure - technical or organisational - could be disregarded by simple carelessness, an understanding of the reasoning behind security measures and an appreciation of personal responsibility may help to improve information security with minimal cost.

3.8 Approach to Outsourcing

Many organisations outsource IT functions: the reason is obvious - outsourced services may cost several times less than maintaining in-house IT. Cloud computing, a modern form of outsourcing, significantly reduces business costs. The problem that arises with outsourcing is that organisations often ignore such in-house activity as development of information security strategy and inconsiderately rely on outsourcing companies in terms of security, forgetting that security is not a feature that outsourcing companies provide by default. Security measures supplied should meet requirements of the organisation's information security strategy and policies, should be carefully negotiated and stated in contracts as well as financial penalties for the information security breaches occurred by fault of service provider. For Cloud computing the contract should, for example, prevent access of the cloud provider's personnel to confidential data, prevent data sharing with unauthorized third parties, require destruction of data after termination of the contract as well as state the liability for data misuse. The new member of the ISO/IEC 27000 family – ISO/IEC 27036 - *IT Security - Security techniques - Information security for supplier relationships* – promises to address information security issues in outsourcing in detail. The standard is currently in preparation.

Whereas development security strategy by an organisation itself is preferred, outsourcing strategy development is also possible, but should be done with the active involvement of an organisation's management, which is accountable and is the only party that has an in-depth understanding of the business needs.

Finally, it is not a question of what is more secure - in-house or outsourced IT. It is a question of a SA to be adjusted to a preferred way of operation [ShCL05: p.146].

3.9 Security Return on Investment

Security Return on Investment (ROI) is a very popular topic. There are different approaches to economics of security. Some authors argue that security should be evaluated in a similar way to other business projects in terms of ROI. Others, on the contrary, claim that information security does not have an ROI. Third argue that security is more similar to insurance as it reduces risks to business and prevents possible losses.

In fact, cost and benefits calculations based on risk analysis are needed as they serve as a bridge between managers and security specialists. They help to translate security concerns through probability arithmetic into monetary terms that are familiar to management and allow estimation of security projects [KoDK00]. Security projects *per se* are different from most business projects, although they have some similarity with PR and advertising projects in a sense that it is very hard to measure benefits, whereas costs are obvious. As a result, the standard way of ROI calculations is not always sufficient for security projects. It is possible to quantify the financial benefits and measure the effectiveness of information security, but adequate calculations and analysis are quite complex and time-consuming. Sherwood et al., for example, propose a method for security ROI calculations based on a set of 85 attributes, each with suggested metrics and measurements [ShCL05: pp.79-110].

Despite the difficulty of adequate calculations, a demonstration of ROI significantly increases popularity and, more importantly, the budget of a security project. Management quite often actively supports a security project at the initial stage, but loses interest in the project at further stages if they cannot see a positive ROI. Thus, to maintain management's support, financial benefits of information security measures should be quantified and clearly articulated to stakeholders and other interested parties at every stage of a security project.

The importance of the economic side of information security is lately recognised by ISO/IEC, which is currently in preparation of ISO/IEC TR 27016 - *IT Security - Security techniques - Information security management - Organisational economics*. The standard, which is expected to be released in 2013, will cover financial perspectives of information security [Isec11a].

3.10 Business Continuity

Any system may fail to some extent at a certain point. Therefore, the aim of a SA is not only to prevent security failures, but also to allow a system to fail in a "good" way, i.e. with minimum destruction and negative consequences to the business. In a CDePE, managers and security experts should be concerned with two questions with regards to business continuity. Firstly, how failure on the side of collaborators, service providers or other external parties involved may injure an organisation and what an organisation should do in a case of such a failure. Secondly, how a security failure on the organisation's side will affect external parties and what should be done to reduce or prevent a negative effect.

Section 14 of ISO/IEC 27002:2005, that describes information security aspects of business continuity management, does not comprehensively address issues relevant to involvement of external parties. In terms of the impact of external parties on an organisation the ISO/IEC 27000 series and, in particular ISO/IEC 27031:2011 - *Information technology - Security techniques - Guidelines for information and communication technology readiness for business continuity*, concentrates on ICT-related risks and does not consider risks of system failures that may crop up from business interdependencies [SKHA08].

A SA should be built to avoid the complete dependence of a system on external parties. If, for instance, important business data resides in the Cloud, additional remote backups could guarantee data availability, in case of the failure of a cloud service provider. Thus, the responsibility to develop a SA that will support business continuity in the interdependent environment resides with system and security architects, and should take appropriate place among their other duties.

4 Conclusion

The evolution of ICT recently resulted in a noticeable phenomenon referred to as *de-perimeterisation*. The significance of this complex socio-technical phenomenon is still underestimated. This implies that the specifics of the present environment, affected by collaboration and de-perimeterisation, are often overlooked or ignored at the level of business strategy, system design and in a SA in general. To cover this gap, the paper presented an overview of the factors that are important to be taken into consideration while developing and managing a SA in a CDePE. The factors described in the study are necessary, but not sufficient conditions for a successful SA. Nevertheless, addressing the factors covered in this paper will significantly increase the chances of an organisation to build a successful SA.

This work emerged as a result of an analysis of the modern trends and the hot topics of the information security discipline. The value of the paper is also in sketching a contemporary picture of a successful SA adapted to the interconnected landscape and in outlining areas worthy of attention and subsequent research. Hence, it may be of interest to managers, system architects, information security professionals and young researchers.

References

[AlSa10]   Aljafari, R., Sarnikar, S.: A Risk Assessment Framework for Inter-Organizational Knowledge Sharing. Sprouts: Working Papers on Information, 2010 [online]. Available at: http://sprouts. aisnet.org/880/1/KMDSS_Sprouts.pdf [Accessed: 10 July 2011]

[Ande01]   Anderson R.: Why Information Security is Hard – An Economic Perspective. Computer Security Applications Conference, 2001. ACSAC 2001. Proceedings 17th Annual, pp. 358-365

[BoJe02]   Boyce J., Jennings D.: Information Assurance: Managing Organizational IT Security Risks. Butterworth-Heinemann (Elsevier Science), 2002, p.13

[BSIS05]   BS ISO/IEC 27001:2005 - Information technology - Security techniques - Information security management systems - Requirements. 2005, p.2, def. 3.7, 3.8

[BSIS11]   Draft BS ISO/IEC 27010 Information Technology - Security techniques - Information security management for inter-sector and inter-organizational communications. Reference number of document: ISO/IEC FCD 27010, 2011

[CNSS10]   Committee on National Security Systems: National Information Assurance (IA) Glossary, CNSS Instruction No. 4009, 26 April 2010, p.37

[Good10]   Goodchild J.: Survey: Fear of data loss, security risks via social media sites on the upswing, 2010 [online]. Available at: http://www.csoonline.com/article/616218/survey-fear-of-data-loss-security-risks-via-social-media-sites-on-the-upswing [Accessed: 10 July 2011]

[HiTa08]   Hilton J., Tawileh A.: Sustained Control of Critical Corporate Information. 5th Middle East Chief Information Officer Conference & IT Exhibition, ME CIO 2008. Summit, Nov. 25, 26 & 27, 2008, Bahrain [online]. Available at http://www.jeremy-hilton.com/node/1 [Accessed: 30 July 2011]

[ISACA08] Information Systems Audit and Control Association: ISACA Glossary of Terms, 2008 [online]. Available at: http://www.isaca.org/Knowledge-Center/Documents/Glossary/glossary.pdf [Accessed: 10 July 2011]

[Isec11a] IsecT Ltd.: ISO/IEC TR 27016 - IT Security - Security techniques - Information security management – Organizational economics (DRAFT) [online]. Available at: http://www.iso27001security.com/html/27016.html [Accessed: 10 July 2011]

[Isec11b] IsecT Ltd.: SO/IEC 27036 - IT Security - Security techniques - Information security for supplier relationships (DRAFT) [online]. Available at: http://www.iso27001security.com/html/27036.html [Accessed: 10 July 2011]

[ISO09] ISO/IEC 27000:2009 (E) Information technology - Security techniques - Information security management systems - Overview and vocabulary, def. 2.19

[KoDK00] Kokolakis S., Demopoulos A., Kiountouzis E.: The use of business process modelling in information systems security analysis and design. Information Management & Computer Security, 2000, Vol. 8 Iss: 3, p.108

[OGJF07] The Open Group, Jericho Forum: Business rationale for de-perimeterisation, 2007 [online]. Available at: https://www.opengroup.org/jericho/Business_Case_for_DP_v1.0.pdf [Accessed: 10 July 2011]

[OMG11] The Object Management Group: Business Process Model and Notation, Version 2.0, 2011 [online]. Available at: http://www.omg.org/spec/BPMN/2.0/PDF/ [Accessed: 10 July 2011]

[RFMP07] Rodríguez A., Fernández-Medina E., Piattini M.: A BPMN Extension for the Modeling of Security Requirements in Business Processes. EICE - Transactions on Information and Systems, 2007, Volume E90-D Iss. 4, pp. 745-752

[ShCL05] Sherwood J., Clark A., Lynas D.: Enterprise Security Architecture: A Business-Driven Approach. CMP Books, 2005

[Simm04] Simmonds P.: De-perimeterisation – this decades security challenge, presentation, 2004 [online]. Available at: http://www.blackhat.com/presentations/bh-usa-04/bh-us-04-simmonds.pdf [Accessed: 10 July 2011]

[SKHA08] Sutton S., Khazanchi D., Hampton C., Arnold V.: Risk Analysis in Extended Enterprise Environments: Identification of Critical Risk Factors in B2B E-Commerce Relationships. Journal of the Association for Information Systems, Vol. 9, Nos. 3-4, pp. 151-174, 2008

El Metodo –
Managing Risks in Value Chains

Maarten Hoeve · Rieks Joosten · Edwin Matthijssen ·
Caroline van der Weerdt · Reinder Wolthuis

TNO
Netherlands Organization for Applied Research
www.tno.nl
{maarten.hoeve | rieks.joosten | caroline.vanderweerdt | edwin.matthijssen |
reinder.wolthuis}@tno.nl

Abstract

The ability to organize resource-allocation on the basis of actual need allows a business to become highly flexible, cost efficient and robust against crises. Doing so requires that functionalities and the associated responsibilities are properly defined, delegated to other parties where needed, and checked to ensure that the risks involved remain at an acceptable level. A framework called 'El Metodo' is presented that helps organizations do just that. Also, a simple use-case illustrates how 'El Metodo' supports the construction of an early-warning system that signals risks that become unacceptably high due to causes elsewhere in the resource chain. Finally, we present an overview of what businesses have to say about this method.

1 Introduction

Even though there is a lot of guidance with respect to (IT) risk management (e.g. [STGF02], [ISO31000], [ISF11]), its practice is generally still cumbersome. First, a comprehensive overview of (shackles in) value chains within an organization is rare as businesses become more service-oriented and hence complex. Consequently, it is difficult to determine what should be agreed upon in service level agreements (SLA's) between services adjacent in a value chain. When things turn sour, this can easily lead to finger-pointing. Secondly, risk management usually receives management attention when major incidents have occurred, but this attention wanes when the incident has been solved. Also, organizations may spend so much time continuously recovering from smaller incidents, that setting up risk management in a structured fashion doesn't seem to be an option. Finally, even when risks may be managed 'locally', solutions may not be optimal if the risks that adjacent shackles run (or manage) are not properly communicated.

Main features of the economy are the specialization and the division of work (e.g. [Sabe82], [PiSa90]). This is usually done by dividing companies into business units, departments or teams, each with their own responsibility. It also requires close cooperation and coordination. A well-known example is a production chain, where several companies or departments contribute until the product is complete. Another example is the supply chain that results in electrical energy being delivered to a wall outlet. Risk management across such value chains requires a clear delineation of the responsibilities between the shackles of value chains, so that risks (and the mitigation

N. Pohlmann, H. Reimer, W. Schneider (Editors): Securing Electronic Business Processes, Vieweg (2011), 214-223

thereof) can be explicitly assigned. Also, it requires a clear understanding of how the various shackles interoperate and cooperate to produce the final product, so that risks related to misunderstandings between shackles can be pinpointed.

El Metodo is a framework that helps to sort out the shackles, to assign responsibilities in case of disagreement, and to provide a clear understanding of how shackles interact with one another. Also, it provides managers with a means to do risk management within a shackle and relate that to the risks (and the management thereof) of 'adjacent' shackles. When multiple shackles decide to share risk information, El Metodo provides the basis for an early warning system that allows managers to be informed as risks start to 'line up', which may result in a catastrophe if not treated immediately.

This article is built up as follows. First, we introduce the basic concepts of El Metodo and illustrate them with examples. Then, using the same examples, we show how risk management is done both within functionalities and in value chains. using the same examples. This is followed by a discussion of the method, a specification of work to be done and conclusions.

2 El Metodo - the Method

To get a grasp on the division of work, El Metodo defines a functionality (a shackle in a value chain) as a coherent set of obligations, and a manager[1] that is responsible for fulfilling them. Functionalities come in many kinds: a company, a business unit or department, an information process, an IT system (or application), or even a project. Functionalities should be properly scoped, meaning that they should be distinct, and manageable.

The latter is important as managers, like all humans, have physiological limitations that make them err more as the scope grows [Mille56]. Therefore, functionalities with a scope whose size exceeds that what is humanly manageable, should be decomposed, resulting in (subsidiary) functionalities, each with its own obligations and its own manager. 'Outsourcing' these functionalities to their respective managers makes the scope of the outsourcing functionality smaller. Splitting of subsidiary functionalities should continue until the remaining scope has become manageable for its manager.

2.1 Designing Functionalities

Consider a functionality that provides IP-connectivity between various locations. Its manager defines the functionality by creating a list of its obligation, i.e. criteria or rules for the fulfillment of which he is responsible to some other functionality. Examples:
  • IP-connectivity is provided for at least 99.9% of the time.
  • IP-connectivity services comply with the Data Protection Act.
  • Annual revenue of IP-connectivity is at least € R and annual costs are at most € C.

A manager can only meet his obligations if he can rely on some expectations to be fulfilled, either within his own scope of control (internal expectations) or by some other functionality (external expectations). The method requires that for every obligation of importance, the manager makes every expectation explicit that need to be fulfilled in order for him to fulfill the obligation. As an

---

1 We use the term ‚manager' to also include a management team.

example, the manager of the IP-connectivity functionality may associate the following expecta-
tions to the obligation that IP-connectivity is provided for at least 99.9% of the time:
- Every router has an availability of > 99.95%.
- At any time, every router is either powered by Energy Co, or by its UPS
- Routers X and Y are connected with two glassfiber networks (the A-net and B-net)
- At any time, either the A-net or the B-net is operational (or both).

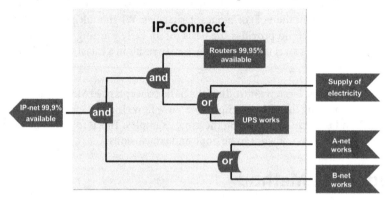

Fig. 1: Linking Expectations and Obligations

From the overview that the manager gets by linking expectations and obligations, he can judge
whether or not he can fulfill his obligations.

Besides managing single functionalities, the method also helps to get a grip on the value chain by
linking obligations and expectations of *different* functionalities. Every expectation of one functionality to another must correspond with an obligation of that other functionality to the expect-
ing one. Signaling any lack of such correspondence allows the managers to take appropriate action and align their functionalities. Thus, there is no confusion later on about who is responsible
for what.

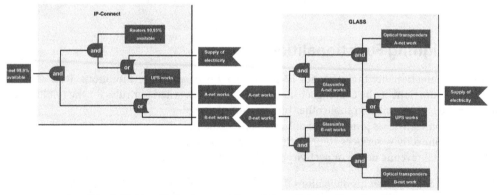

Fig. 2: Linking Obligations and Expectations Between Functionalities

Figure 2 illustrates the linking of expectations of the functionality 'IP-connect' with obligations of the functionality 'Glass'. Not only does this provide insight in functional dependencies, it also helps to (partly) automate risk management, as we shall see in the next section.

2.2 Managing Risk in Functionalities

Within organizations, risk management may take different forms, depending on the subject (financial, information, environment, health and safety, continuity), or the time horizon (long-term, medium term and short term) or hierarchical levels (e.g. organization, business unit and division). Many standard process models or frameworks provide guidance, such as ISO31000, MoR, ISO27001, BS25999 etc.

Roughly speaking, traditional risk management consists of determining the scope within which to manage risks and make an inventory of the (most important) risks within that scope. This is done by identifying threats, estimating the probability of occurrence and computing the risk using "Risk = Probability x Impact" (R=PxI). Then, the nature of these risks is assessed upon which it is decided to either accept them or choose and implement controls to mitigate them[2]. As this modifies the threats, probabilities and thus risks, the cycle starts again, until all remaining risks are accepted.

El Metodo equates functionalities with risk management scopes. Thus, every manager of a functionality runs his own risk management process. The idea behind this is that risks are limited to this scope, and the manager has the best knowledge for this.

Once the expectations, obligations and their interdependencies have been identified, they can be used to identify risks. Failure to fulfill a particular obligation constitutes a threat to a scope. For example, failure to fulfill "compliance with the Data Protection Act" is a threat as it may cause the government to impose a fine. Also, any expectation that is not fulfilled constitutes a threat to every obligation to which it is important. Thus, the charted obligations and expectations allows managers to estimate the probability of non-fulfillment, and associate a risk to each of them using the traditional formula R=PxI. Completeness of the risk assessment depends on completeness of the lists of obligations, expectations and their dependencies.

Changes in environmental conditions, customer numbers, laws and regulations all may cause changes in the list of obligations, expectations and dependencies. Therefore, it is necessary to update such lists every once in a while, which is readily complemented with an update of the estimates of likelihoods and risks.

Once obligations, expectations and dependencies are charted, risks can be computed using the traditional formula R=PxI. Determining probabilities and impacts is different for obligations and expectations.

The probability associated with an expectation of a manager is an estimate of the expectation not being fulfilled. For an internal expectation this is the probability something is wrong within the scope itself and should be readily assessable by the manager. For an external expectation, we may assume that there is an obligation of another functionality that corresponds with the expectation. Then, the probability associated with the expectation equals the probability of the other

---

2   Strictly speaking there are 2 other options, but they are not relevant for our purpose.

functionality not fulfilling its (corresponding) obligation. Ideally, this probability would be communicated so that the probability of the external expectation going sour is 'automatic'. However, if the manager of the other functionality is reluctant to share this information, the manager can estimate the likelihood himself basing it on trust, past experience, performance reports and/or audits.

The probability associated with an obligation of a manager is an estimate of the obligation not being fulfilled. When the dependencies between obligations and expectations are well-charted, the probability of not fulfilling an obligation can be derived using the probabilities of the expectations of which it depends, using dependency functions resembling those of Fault Tree Analysis.

The impact of an obligation is a measure of the maximum severity of the consequences of non-compliance with that obligation (disregarding any implementation knowledge). Managers assess the impact themselves; they may relate this e.g. to penalties as specified by law, penalties agreed in SLA's with customers, or morale. The impact of an expectation is an indicator of the importance of the expectation to the scope as it is derived from the impacts of all obligations to which the expectation is relevant.

Risks for every obligation and expectation can be computed based on their respective impacts and probabilities. Note that for management, qualitative measures such as Low/Medium/High, or number ranges (as done by the ISF) are useable. However, we also envisage that quantitative measures can be used in conjunction with qualitative assessments. After all, every scope will be able to produce a mapping between quantitative and qualitative measures as this mapping is, and remains, particular to that scope. We will use the characters L, M and H to denote Low, Medium and High respectively as we proceed with an example.

3 Putting El Metodo to Use - an Example

Looking back to the IP department of which the expectations and obligations have been linked, we see that failure of the "99.9% availability" obligation would have major consequences. Thus, the manager estimates the impact of this obligation as 'H'. The manager knows that the routers and UPS are very reliable, and hence sets the corresponding probabilities to 'L'. Since power is know to fail sometimes, he sets the probability to 'M'. Finally, the department 'Glass', which provides the physical connection between the routers, provides probabilities for all expectations towards that department. This results in the following overview:

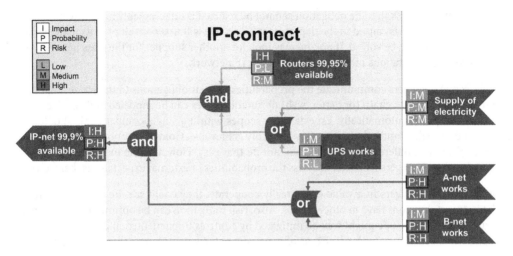

Fig 3: Computation of probability associated with an obligation

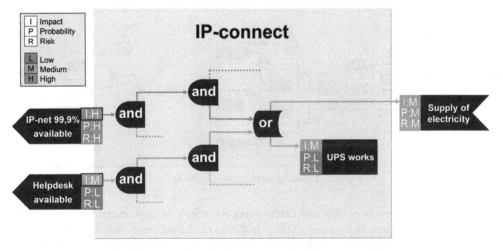

Fig 4: Computation of an impact associated to an expectation.

When a manager has computed the risks and finds one or more unacceptably high, he must take measures. If a risk associated with an external expectation is too high, he may decide to find a second supplier, a replacement supplier, or voice additional expectations to the supplier that will enhance its trust in the expectation being met. If a risk is associated with an internal expectation, the manager must reorganize the work within its own scope of control. If the risk associated with an obligation is too high, he may either search for causes - to be found in the set of expectations of which the obligation depends - adding or modifying this set until the risk becomes acceptable. Alternatively, he may do some 'expectations management' with the parties to which he has the obligation. The manager is free to choose between all of these options, as that is what his job consists of: taking responsibility for compliance with its obligations. Also, it helps to structure the negotiations between (managers of) different scopes.

In the example, the risk that the obligation can not be realized is unacceptably high. The manager sees that the problem is caused in the department 'Glass'. He will first consult with its manager to see if the problem can be solved. If not, he may look for another supplier for the glass network, or he manage the expectations of the customers of the IP network.

Ideally, scope managers communicate the probabilities of their obligations to the scopes that depend on them. Then, a chain (or better: web) of functionalities can be modeled and corresponding risks computed automatically. Especially for scopes within a single company this should be feasible because the required transparency is readily achievable. Communication of probabilities between scopes in different companies may not be that easy. However, the method still works, although scope managers will need to assess the probabilities of external expectations themselves.

Note that if all managers in a value chain really cooperate, they could see the effects that their risk treatment decisions have in other scopes. Also, risk mitigation can be optimized as risks that are run in a specific scope might well be mitigated by controls implemented in another scope. El Metodo itself is oblivious to the decisions of managers to the extent they wish to cooperate.

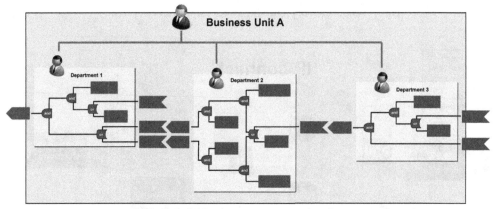

Fig 5: Risk Management across a value chain

By repeating the process over time and determining the effects of implemented measures and environmental conditions, an overview of the actual risks can be obtained relatively easy. Also, in the event that the implementation of an action takes a long time (long-term project), the progress of the project and its effects on reducing the risk have to be monitored.

4 Discussion

Starting to use the method requires organizations to change the way they do risk management. Rather than having a small group of risk managers responsible for managing all risks in an organization, this responsibility should be transferred to the people that already bear the responsibility of the business functionality from which the risk stems: line managers, product managers, project managers, as well as owners of processes, applications, systems, networks etc. After all, they should be running the risks, so that they decide which risks to mitigate, how to invest their resources and, if necessary, what additional resourcing to request for from higher management. Currently, and despite various efforts to quantify risks, such decisions are still often based on gut feeling rather than on knowledge of causes and consequences. The method aims to have a risk management process in every scope and sets out to provide results of sufficient value to their managers that they will actually use it. This is very much in line with the list of practices from [FrAn11].

The method only works if the scope managers see the purpose of systematically identifying and assessing risks. They should be structural and honest with respect to filling in their part of the obligations and expectations. After all, it is in their own interest, because they will face the consequences of not living up to their obligations. But for many managers it may feel like an extra responsibility and extra bureaucracy. Moreover, it can be very confronting for a manager to make its obligations explicit.

It will take time and resources to implement the method. Scope managers must learn how the method works and obtain skills in keeping obligations and expectations. Also, after everything is set up, maintenance of the overview, even if it is only their own scope, will take effort.

If the method is used, it has a great advantage: risks are assessed by people who do this the best, namely the scope managers. The method ensures that the entire organization becomes aware of the risks and be responsible for managing those risks.

The method gives scope managers the tools to manage their own risks. They will identify and assess risks systematically, and will see the consequences of their choices. Also: the more complete the list of obligations and expectations, the more complete the overview of risks will be. They can compute probabilities, risks and impacts in a relatively straightforward way, and tooling that automates this process is readily thinkable. Also, they may confer with their colleague managers using a common risk language. Thus the method helps managers make decisions and better cooperate with one another.

The work of risk managers is simplified by the method. By using the method, an overview of value chains is created (and maintained) by the participants of that chain; risk managers only need to look for signals such as unaccepted risks, or expectations that are not matched with obligations, which is easy when the method is used with a supporting system. Every signal relates to a task that managers of the associated scopes need to do.

We have talked to the security officers (which also bear risk management responsibility) of a number of Dutch corporations to verify the ideas of our methodology. They recognize the problems that are sketched in section one. All security officers have to deal with a struggle for management attention, the companies do have to deal with risks stemming from their suppliers and they do not have a coherent overview of current risks. They appreciate our methodology to provide a structured manner to deal with risks. Although they do not consider the presented method to be a completely new way of thinking, they do see the usefulness of method, in which several useful elements are combined into one comprehensive and structural approach.

Currently, we are developing a tool for risk managers and scope managers so that they can get a quick overview of obligations, expectations, their dependencies and the associated impacts, probabilities and risks. For now, it will only provide them with a better understanding of where risks come from. In the future, this tool may automatically generate a risk register that keeps track of risks as they dynamically change.

5 A Look into the Future

At this moment the method provides a uniform manner at the operational level for understanding risks. This is useful for individual scope managers, as they get insight in their own scope and in the relations with other scopes, in terms of obligations and expectations. Managers also get insight in risks, what their impact is and what the probability is, since there is one for every obligation and expectation.

Supporting such managers with a single tool would be beneficial for them, as they could then simply write down or remove any obligation or expectation as and when necessary, and see the effects as they do so. We believe that this could be a valuable asset not only to managers, but also to others, e.g. marketeers or SLA managers.

Also, we think that (drawing) techniques used in e.g. fault tree analysis could be useful for having managers specify the functions that compute the probability of obligations not being met from the corresponding probabilities of the expectations on which such obligation depend.

A supporting system would even be more beneficial if multiple scopes started using the same system. This would not imply that everyone has access to everyone else's information, but it could mean that managers that trust each other's information, in particular the probability estimates, will be relieved of tasks that can be computed from such shared information. For example, if a manager trusts the probabilities computed in another scope, and such probabilities are shared, then the probability of every expectation to that scope can be computed from the probability of the corresponding obligation in that other scope.

Such cooperation on risk issues in a value chain would facilitate the propagation of risk estimates through a value chain. Consequently, if risks 'line up', i.e. if selected risks from various shackles in a chain become so high that delivery of the final product of the chain becomes risky, this will automatically be signalled provided each manager signals his own risk dynamically. Eventually, a system might even provide advice with respect to measures to be taken in order to prevent catastrophes taking place.

What should be further investigated is the added value of the method for chains with scopes in different organizations. The feeling is that this method offers advantages, but this depends largely on whether the organizations are willing to share information and what information it is.

6 Conclusion

In this article we presented a new way of treating risk in value chains. The method combines several existing elements into a new and structured method. This method can be automated very easily. The method does not use standard threat lists, but takes obligations of organizations and their expectations put upon themselves or others (e.g. suppliers) as a basis. In the method, completeness of the risk assessment depends on completeness of the lists of obligations, expectations and their dependencies.

An advantage of the method is that it brings risk assessment to the 'floor'. Rather than having a small group of risk managers (often on staff level) responsible for managing all risks in an organization, this responsibility can be transferred to the people that already bear the responsibility of the business functionality from which the risk stems: line managers, product managers, project managers, as well as owners of processes, applications, systems, networks etc.

The method offers clear advantages for scopes within an organization. The idea is that this method also offers advantages to cross organization risk assessment (in value chains), but this depends largely on whether organizations are willing to share information. Even if organizations are not willing to share information, the method can still be used by estimating the necessary parameters based on trust, past experience, performance reports and/or audits. We will continue to perform research in this area.

We have checked the method with a number of Dutch corporations and they do see the advantages of this method and have indicated they want to be involved in or informed about the future development of the method.

References

[FrAn11] Frigo, M.L, Anderson, R.J.: Strategic Risk Management: A Foundation for Improving Enterprise Risk Management and Governance. Journal of Corporate Accounting & Finance, Volume 22, Issue 3, pages 81–88, March/April 2011.

[ISF11] International Security Forum: The 2011 Standard of Good Practice for Information Security. ISF, June 2011.

[ISO31000] ISO 31000:2009: Risk management -- Principles and guidelines, November 2009.

[Mille56] Miller, George A.: The Magical Number Seven, Plus or Minus Two: Some Limits on Our Capacity for Processing Information. In: The Psychological Review. 1956, vol. 63, p. 81-97.

[PiSa90] Piore, M.J, Sabel, C.F: Second Industrial Divide: Possibilities for Prosperity. Basic Books, 1990.

[Sabe82] Sabel, C.F: Work and politics: the division of labor in industry. Cambridge University Press, 1982.

[StGF02] Stoneburner, G, Goguen, A and Feringa, A: Risk Management Guide for Information Technology Systems. NIST Special Publication 800-30. National Institute of Standards and Technology, July 2002.

A Systematic Approach to Legal Identity Management – Best Practice Austria

Herbert Leitold[1] · Arne Tauber[2]

[1] Secure Information Technology Center - Austria, A-SIT
Herbert.Leitold@a-sit.at

[2] Graz University of Technology, E-Government Innovation Center, EGIZ
Arne.Tauber@egiz.gv.at

Abstract

Electronic identity (eID) initiatives have in many cases started with state-issued credentials for secure authentication of natural persons. While citizen eID is a major leap, e-business and e-government processes are in many cases carried out by legal persons or professional representatives. Comprehensive mandate systems that seamlessly integrate with the national identity management (IDM) system are still rare.

Austria is one example where electronic representation has been part of the citizen card concept from the beginning. In this paper we present the Austrian system as a case study. The system has been established about a decade ago. Experience made with the system led to adaptation and improvements. We describe the original approach of storing a mandate record asserting representation on the citizen card. This initial approach was comparable to attaching an excerpt of the constitutive register to an application in the paper world. Issuance of the electronic mandate had to be applied for by the representative upfront. With the emergence of improved services and technological progress and incorporating experience with the original system, the approach has recently been amended to so-called "online mandates" where the assertion of a representation is created just in time (JIT) when it is needed by the application. This gives fresh assertions, improves usability and better fits an increasing demand for mobility. The paper describes the Austrian system for electronic representation and how it emerged over time. Examples where the system is used are given.

1 Introduction

Electronic identity (eID) is on top of the agenda of states' e-government initiatives for a while. eID can take various forms. Examples are smartcards, mobile eID, soft certificates, or national authentication gateways. Meanwhile, most states have implemented some form of eID. For Europe, a 2009 European Commission study on eID interoperability on Pan-European eGovernment Services [Comm09] reported that 13 out of 32 surveyed states issue smartcard eID and 13 issue non-card tokens (some states issuing both smartcard eID and non-card tokens).

The same study however also reported on electronic representation that: "[...] a systematic approach to mandate management and authorisation functionality – i.e. the ability to allocate, retract or verify specific permissions of a specific entity - in the examined eIDM systems was still altogether rare. 22 countries out of 32 (69%) have no form of mandate/authorisation management, other than *the allocation of certificates or credentials to the representatives of a specific legal entity. 8 countries out of 32 (25%) have implemented an ad hoc form of mandate/authorisation management covering specific applications or service types; and only two countries have implemented systems of mandate/ authorisation management which can be characterised as systematic: in Austria, an open approach to mandates based on signed XML records was adopted, and Belgium is currently implementing a systematic approach to managing authorisations.*" [Comm09].

The situation of lacking representation and mandates in national IDM systems creates a challenge. This is due to many contacts with administration being initiated by companies, organisations, or professional representatives. These cases are in particular interesting, as they may have frequent contacts – thus the applicant gains most from any increase in efficiency that electronic processes offer. Awareness for the need of representation and legal entity IDM is broadly given. This is for instance manifested by the Digital Agenda for Europe (DAe) [Comm10], which not only takes citizens' benefits into account, but focuses on competitiveness and mobility of businesses, particularly small and medium-sized enterprises (SME). Moreover a follow-up to the eID Large Scale Pilot STORK[1] is supposed to address the issue on a pan-European scale, as the Call for Proposals defining its scope asks to "*[…] also test the interoperability of the different approaches, at national and EU level, for persons and legal entities, including the facility to 'mandate' between them.*". This project is expected to commence in 2012 and to run for three years.

While the need of eID and mandates is evident on the European level, no generally applicable solution seems to be given yet. In such a situation solutions that have proven themselves in operation can serve as best practice. Such a solution is the Austrian system that is described in this paper, i.e. one of the two countries that have been highlighted as having implemented a systematic approach in the [Comm09] study.

The remainder of this paper is structured, as follows: In section 2 some general considerations on electronic representation are given. This will describe the complexity that comes with a comprehensive mandate system. The Austrian citizen card and its mandate concept are introduced in section 3. The implementation of the system is described in section 4. The original mandate system that went operational in 2005 is described. This first approach was storing static mandate records. The experience made with it are discussed, that led to migrating to dynamic just-in-time creation of mandates. Dynamic creation is referred to as "online mandates". In section 5 a few examples are described where the system is used in practice. Finally, conclusions are drawn.

2 Initial Thoughts on Electronic Representation

At first sight, one might consider electronic representation a not too complex task. Work has been done on delegation in role-based access control (RBAC) by [KaCr06] or with a permission-based delegation model (PBDM) in RBAC by [ZhOS03]. Such systems however rather link delegation to intra-organisation IDM, whereas mandating in national IDM asks for open systems serving a heterogeneous landscape of legacy systems. An alternative approach seen in literature is linking the mandate to a PKI by using attribute certificates [FaHT10]. Attribute certificates can e.g. assert the function of a person holding a X.509 certificate. Legal representation is however not limited to the role of a person, think e.g. of mandating an agent for one single action, such as licensing a car.

---

1 http://www.eid-stork.eu

Representations have been categorised by [Röss09] into (1) *bilateral representations* (also referred to as "direct mandates" between a mandator and a proxy), (2) *substitution* (an indirect representation where the mandator empowers an intermediary that delegates to the proxy), and (3) *delegation* (a direct representation initiated by an intermediary).

In the various scenarios, empowerment can be based on:
- a constitutive register (Commercial Register, Register of Associations, …),
- a competent authority (asserting a profession, e.g. tax accountant or lawyer), or
- a wilful act (mandate established by a person).

A systematic representation system needs to be flexible enough to cover the various scenarios. I.e., the system shall allow an elderly person to mandate a relative to act on her behalf, shall be able to assert the statutory representatives of a company, or allow a representative to delegate specific powers to staff.

3 The Austrian eID and Mandate System

In this section we sketch the Austrian citizen card system. For brevity, we limit the discussion to key aspects needed for understanding the mandate system. For a detailed description the reader is referred to [LeHP02] or the citizen card Website[2].

The Austrian citizen card concept can be characterized by two key aspects, (1) technology neutrality and (2) using sector-specific identifiers: Technology neutrality refers to an approach where various different public-sector-issued or private-sector-issued tokens can serve as eID. To date, health insurance cards, bank cards, professions' service cards or mobile phones are issued as citizen cards. The common requirement is that the token needs to be capable of qualified electronic signatures, i.e. is a Secure Signature-Creation Device (SSCD) as defined by the EU Signature Directive [EU99]. To integrate the various tokens, a high-level interface has been defined which is implemented by a middleware referred to as citizen card environment (CCE).

The second key aspect of the citizen card concept is its sector specific personal identification numbers (ssPIN) approach. The IDM system is based on a persistent unique citizen identifier that is cryptographically derived from the Central Register of Residents (CRR). This identifier is referred to as source personal identification number (sourcePIN) and is only stored on the citizen card. The sourcePIN is stored in a data structure referred to as "Identity Link" and is controlled by the citizen. For data protection reasons, the sourcePIN may not be directly used in applications. By using one-way hash functions, ssPINs are created for each sector of state activity (health, tax, education, etc.), created specifically for private sector organisations, respectively.

The legal basis for the citizen card has been established in 2004 by the E-Government Act [Aust10]. This Acts also defines electronic representation: *"Where the citizen card is to be used for submissions by a representative, a reference to the permissibility of the representation must be entered in the Citizen Card of the representative. This occurs where the sourcePIN Register Authority, having been presented with proof of an existing authority to represent or in cases of statutory representation, enters in the citizen card of the representative, upon application by the representative, the sourcePIN of the data subject and a reference to the existence of an authority to represent, including*

---

2 http://www.buergerkarte.at/index.en.php

any relevant material or temporal limitations. [...]". In a nutshell, to create ssPINs of the manda-tor, her sourcePIN is stored in the citizen card of the representative (where the technical concept "citizen card" is a logical unit that comprises both the actual token and software components the middleware "CCE").

To implement the electronic mandate, a general XML-structure has been developed. The struc-ture is illustrated in figure 1 and consists of: Identity data of the representative and the mandatory (name, date of birth and sourcePIN for natural persons; name and registration number of legal persons), the MandateContent and constraints scoping what the representative is empowered to, and a link to a mandate revocation service. The structure is digitally signed by the SourcPIN Authority which is the authotity in charge of issuing sourcePINs for citizen cards.

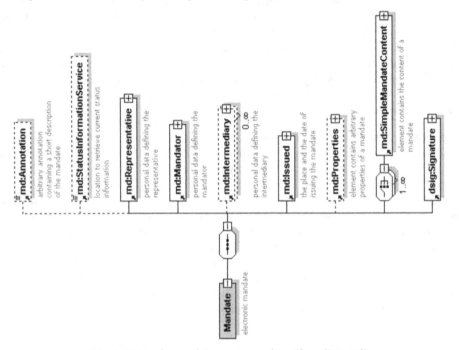

Fig. 1: XML schema of electronic mandates (from [Röss09])

For the basic understanding of the system, a more detailed technical description is deemed not necessary. Thus, optional data shown in figure 1, such as the identifiers of intermediaries or the mandate annotations are not described for brevity. We refer the reader interested in such details to [TaRö09] and [Röss09].

4 Practical Implementation of the Mandate System

This section discusses how the Austrian mandate system evolved over time. In sub-section 4.1 the original system is discussed. It used static mandate records that have been issued solely upon request of the mandator. Out of lessons learned and with the emergence of constitutive registers making information available online – mainly a Business Service Register – the approach emerged to so-called online mandates. These are discussed in sub-section 4.2.

4.1 Original System – Mandates as Static Info-Boxes

In the first Austrian mandate system electronic mandates were stored within so-called info-boxes, special data storage on the citizen card. The process for storing a mandate on the citizen card required several steps with manual intervention. First, the representative had to make an electronic application with her citizen card by declaring all necessary data, e.g. company name and number, residence, etc. This application was electronically signed by the representative and filed in the back office. An official in charge then manually checked by consulting the constituent registers (Company Register, Central Register of Associations, etc.) whether the applicant was a legitimate representative of the legal person. If so, the electronic mandate was created and the applicant was informed that she can store the mandate on her citizen card. In case of a local CCE the electronic mandate was stored as encrypted XML file on the hard disk since data storage on smart-cards is limited and thus may hold only a few mandates per card. In case of the mobile CCE mandates were stored as encrypted data structure within the citizen card account database in the mobile CCE environment.

The approach of storing electronic mandates on the citizen card had several drawbacks: First, citizens have to apply in advance for storing an electronic mandate on their citizen card even though the empowerment information is already available from constitutive registers by electronic means. Second, the mandate information is not "fresh" and mandates must be manually revoked in case e.g. a business manager leaves a company. Third, even if there are several software producers in the market that offer CCEs, only one has implemented mandate management in its CCE. Moreover, in the last few years new CCE minimal footprint technologies without the need for a local middleware have emerged [OrCB10]. This kind of CCE runs as Java Applet within the web browser and has no provision for storing any info-box data like electronic mandates. Last not least, mandates are bound to a specific eID token. Austrian citizens may have multiple eID tokens (smart-card, mobile phone, etc.) and thus mandates must be stored on each of their tokens. This and the fact that mandates are not directly stored on the eID, but in the software used to access the eID, may limit citizens' mobility.

We have learned from five years of experience and adapted the concept of electronic mandates towards an online, systematic and token-independent approach enabling legal identity management on the basis of the citizen card and "live" information from constitutive registers. The next section discusses in detail the architecture and process flows of our online, systematic and token-independent approach.

4.2 Online-Mandates – Dynamic JIT Generation

Figure 2 illustrates the architecture and basic working principle of the JIT generation of online mandates from both the representative's and mandator's perspective. As a precondition the power of representation must be evident from a constitutive register. This could be a register for representations between natural persons (bilateral mandates) or a public register of legal persons, like the Company Register, or the Central Register of Associations. The concept of online mandates involves the following entities, which are illustrated in figure 2.

APP. This is the (e-government) application, at which the representative authenticates and acts on behalf of the mandator.

MOA-ID is an open source identity provider middleware of the Austrian e-government initiative, which bundles several authentication and identification functionalities for the Austrian citizen card.

The **Mandate Issuing Service (MIS)** is the core component, which handles the communication with all involved entities and generates online mandates on demand. The MIS is operated by the SourcePIN Register Authority (SPRA) a subdivision of the Austrian Data Protection Commission.

The **SourcePIN Register** (SPR) is the interface between the MIS and the Central Residents Register (CRR) and the Supplementary Register. It is used by the MIS to request a mandator's sourcePIN on demand.

Bilateral. The SPRA hosts a central constitutive register for the mandate management between natural persons. Mandators can access the service with their citizen card and enter a power of representation for any other natural person, e.g. a postal mandate to retrieve certified electronic mail on one's own behalf. Besides the management GUI for citizens, the service provides a web service interface for the retrieval of empowerment data by the MIS.

The **Business Service Portal** (BSP) acts as a hub for several constitutive registers of legal entities. In this way the MIS has to implement only two interfaces to constitutive registers. One for mandates between natural persons and one for the representation of legal persons.

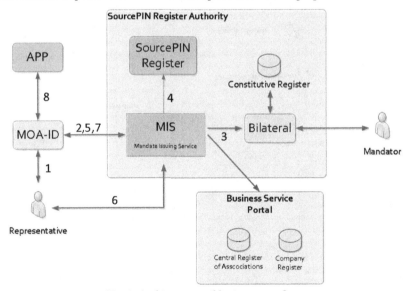

Fig. 2: Architecture and basic process flows

On the basis of this architectural model, the process flow of the JIT generation of online mandates is as illustrated in figure 2 (numberings) and Figure 3 (detailed process steps).

1. The representative accesses the protected APP resource and gets redirected to MOA-ID. She confirms to act on someone else's behalf by ticking a particular checkbox on the authentication GUI.

2. MOA-ID sends a first request to the MIS using a simple object access protocol (SOAP) web services interface. The request contains the following elements:

   a. **IdentityLink** of the representative. By means of these data the representative can be uniquely identified to search for empowerment data in the constitutive registers.

   b. **Signature certificate**. This element is optional and if present is used to identify professional representatives, which have a particular object identifier attribute in the qualified signature certificate of their citizen card [TaRö09].

   c. **A Redirect-URL** denotes the location where the MIS should redirect the representative after successful selection of a mandate.

   d. **Filters** can be passed to limit the scope of empowerment, e.g. to allow only postal mandates.

3. The MIS searches both registers (Bilateral, BSP) for empowerment data belonging to the representative. The representative is identified by her ssPIN. MOA-ID search filters are directly passed through to the registers.

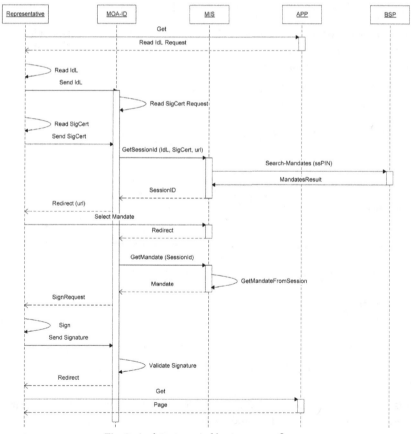

Fig. 3: Architecture and basic process flows

1. For each found data set the MIS generates an electronic mandate stub holding the corresponding data. If the mandator is a natural person, the MIS contacts the SPR for the mandator's sourcePIN.

2. The MIS creates a temporary session, which is valid for a limited period (e.g., 5 minutes) and binds the generated electronic mandates stubs to this session. The session ID is returned to MOA-ID.

3. MOA-ID redirects the representative to the MIS GUI where she can select a mandate from the result set in step 3. After successful selection (or abort) the GUI redirects the representative back to the MOA-ID Redirect-URL set in step 2c.

4. MOA-ID contacts the MIS a second time and submits the assigned session ID. The MIS subsequently electronically signs the selected mandate stub and returns the electronic mandate back to MOA-ID.

5. MOA-ID may check the selected mandate and continues the representative's authentication and identification process. Finally it forwards the authentication information as security assertion markup language (SAML) assertion to the APP.

Online mandates can only be used once. Each newly generated mandate is assigned a unique ID, which is persistently stored by the MIS and applications may thus automatically check whether this ID has been used already before. One major benefit of the new online mandate management system is its downwards-compatibility. Applications just have to upgrade the identity provider middleware MOA-ID. The structure of online mandates is identical to local mandates stored in the CCE. Applications, which have processed local electronic mandates before, thus now seamlessly work with online mandates as well.

5 Mandates in Operation

A typical use case for empowerment is the postal mandate. A general manager, authorized officer or other employees may have a postal mandate to be allowed to accept mail items for a company or other legal person. Postal mandates are also a helpful instrument when taking in charge certified mail items on behalf of another physical person.

With the Document Delivery System (DDS), Austria is operating an electronic certified mail system for the secure, reliable and evidential document exchange between citizens, businesses and administrations [Taub11]. One key feature of this system is the empowerment through electronic mandates.

To illustrate how the original mandate system worked, Figure 4 shows the login process at one of the Austrian certified electronic mail providers [3] by using MOA-ID and the former local mandates.

1. In this example a local CCE is chosen (Screenshot 1, top left of figure 4).

2. As soon as MOA-ID has retrieved the IdentityLink, the CCE shows a popup dialog where the representative can choose her postal mandate (Screenshot 2, top right).

---

3   https://www.meinbrief.at

3. The representative creates a proof of receipt by signing the acceptance of any incoming mail items with her citizen card. An additional text part manifests the act of empowerment (Screenshot 3, bottom right of figure 4).

4. Finally, the representative sees the mailbox of the legal person (company name "Testfirma" – Screenshot 4, bottom left).

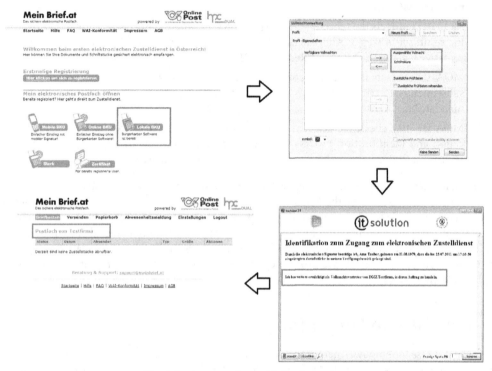

Fig. 4: Login screenshots with local mandates

The login process with the new online mandates system is illustrated in Figure 5. In this case the Java Applet-based online CCE is shown:

1. To start the process, the representative has to tick a checkbox to explicitly express the intention of acting on someone else's behalf (this is shown in Screenshot 1, top-left of figure 5).

2. MOA-ID then retrieves the IdentityLink holding the representative's SourcePIN and then redirects the representative to the MIS GUI where she can choose her postal mandate (Screenshot 2, top-right). In that example case, the representative has just one mandate. The representative selects this mandate and is redirected back to MOA-ID.

3. The citizen has to sign a proof of receipt with her citizen card, thus accepting any incoming delivery. To indicate the representation, an additional text part manifests the act of empowerment (highlighted in Screenshot 3, bottom right in figure 5).

4. Finally, the representative sees the mailbox of the legal person (company name "Testfirma" – Screenshot 4 bottom left).

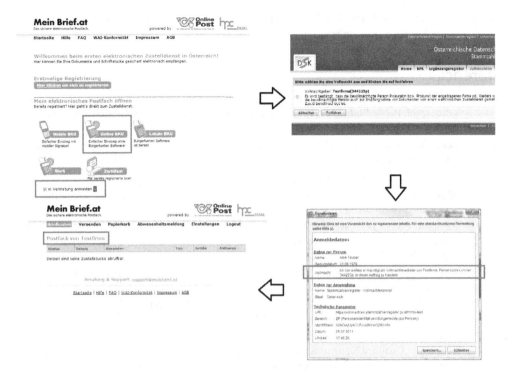

Fig. 5: Login screenshots with online mandates

Besides certified electronic mail, the Data Processing Register of the Austrian Data Protection Commission is a second application supporting online mandates. It registers all applications processing personal data. The registration may be conducted by application providers online with the help of the citizen card and, if desired, as representative using online mandates.

6 Conclusion

The paper has discussed the Austrian electronic mandate and representation system. Austria defined electronic representation as part of the citizen card system from its beginning. The legal basis has been established with the E-Government Act in 2004 and the technical implementation went operational in 2005 – shortly after the mass-roll outs of citizen cards have started. The original approach was to store electronic mandates as static XML records on the citizen card of the representative. This basically mimicked the paper world where the mandatory or a constitutive register issues a paper mandate that is handed in by the representative.

A five year experience with the original approach has shown some drawbacks. A major one was low usability of explicitly applying for an electronic mandate, while many legal representations anyhow are kept in electronic databases. Moreover storing mandates on the citizen card faces limited memory of smartcards or limited portability of the mandate. This led to shifting to so-called online mandates. The basic idea is that the representative is presented all active representations she is empowered to. These representations are derived from either a mandate database for bilateral mandates, or from constitutive registers such as a Company Register. The online mandate system has been implemented in 2011.

References

[Aust10] The Austrian E-Government Act: Federal Act on Provisions Facilitating Electronic Communications with Public Bodies. In: Austrian Federal Law Gazette, part I, Nr. 10/2004; last amended part I, Nr. 111/2010

[Comm09] European Commission: Study on eID Interoperability for PEGS: Update of Country Profiles. IDABC Programme, 2009

[Comm10] European Commission: A Digital Agenda for Europe, COM(2010) 245, 2010

[KaCr06] Khambhammettu, Hemanth; Crampton, Jason: Delegation in Role-Based Access Control, In: Proceedings of ESORICS'2006. p.174-191

[EU99] European Union: Directive 1999/93/EC of the European Parliament and of the Council of 13 December 1999 on a Community framework for electronic signatures, Official Journal L 013 , 19/01/2000 P. 0012 – 0020.

[FaHT10] Farrell, Stephen; Housley, Russ; Turner, Sean: An Internet Attribute Certificate Profile for Authorization. IETF RFC 5755, 2010

[LeHP02] Leitold, Herbert; Hollosi, Arno; Posch, Reinhard: Security Architecture of the Austrian Citizen Card Concept, In: Proceedings of ACSAC'2002, p. 391-400

[OrCB10] Orthacker, Clemens; Centner, Martin; Bauer, Wolfgang: Minimal-Footprint Middleware for the Creation of Qualified Signatures. In: Proceedings of the 6th International Conference on Web Information Systems and Technologies, 2010, p. 64-69

[Röss09] Rössler, Thomas: Empowerment through Electronic Mandate – Best Practice Austria. In: Proceedings of 9th IFIP WG 6.1 Conference on e-Business, e-Services and e-Society, I3E 2009, Editor: Springer, IFIP Advances in Information and Communication Technology, 2009, Volume 305/2009, p. 148-160.

[TaRö09] Tauber, Arne; Rössler, Thomas: Professional Representation in Austrian EGovernment. In: Proceedings of the 8th International Conference EGOV 2009. Editor: Springer LNCS, Volume 5693/2009, p. 388-398.

[Taub11] Tauber, Arne: A survey of certified mail systems provided on the Internet. In: Computers & Security, 2011, in press.

[ZhOS03] Zhang, Xinwen; Oh, Sejong; Sandhu, Ravi: PBDM: A Flexible Delegation Model in RBAC. In: Proceedings of the eighth ACM symposium on Access control models and technologies SACMAT 2003, p. 149-157

Provisioning without APIs:
The Challenge to Integrate IT-Systems without Interfaces into an IAM System and a Compliant Solution from the Finance Industry

Michael Groß

Siemens Enterprise Communications GmbH & Co KG
SEN SER ISS CNS IAM
gross.michael@siemens-enterprise.com

Abstract

In optimizing their processes, businesses and other organizations pursue three main goals: lower costs, increased security and compliance with legal and internal requirements. An elegant way of supporting all these goals at once is to use a comprehensive Identity and Access Management System (IAM) – an indispensable cornerstone of every modern IT security infrastructure.

Introducing an IAM system can become a comprehensive task for an organization because of the wide range of functionality offered by today's Identity Management Systems. IAM's basic functionality is the automated user (de-)provisioning in all connected IT systems, and its value is proportional to the number of connected systems.

These systems are typically connected to the central IAM system using published technical interfaces like software APIs, file import or web services. However, in today's organizations this technical integration is often either not possible or not cost-effective.

This paper presents an innovative approach to implement a cost-effective solution to this challenge developed as an extension to an existing IAM system. The solution is currently in use in a large German financial organization and relies on a combination of a process orientated approach, supporting IAM approval methods and continuous, thorough validation of the connected IT systems without technical interfaces. These systems are categorized depending on the type of (non-)connectivity, and connected using one of three different approaches based on predefined templates.

1 Introduction to Identity Management

Whenever access to sensitive customer or personnel data is necessary employees within organizations more and more depend on business processes which are supported by IT systems, because they have to fulfill these processes efficiently, verifiably and securely. In order to fulfill the tasks of a certain business process everyone involved in the process needs to have access to a variety of different IT systems.

N. Pohlmann, H. Reimer, W. Schneider (Editors): Securing Electronic Business Processes, Vieweg (2011), 235-245

The number of IT-Systems on the one hand and the complexity of administrative processes for identity information on the other hand demand the usage of an Identity Management System. Based on the definition in [Itut10] Identity Management offers:

> *"A set of functions and capabilities used for assurance of identity information supporting business and security applications".*

The number of functions and capabilities can be widespread but there are several services which are essential to an Identity Management System.

- **Integration of different identity sources:** An Identity Management System must be able to support different identity sources. Depending on the structure of an organization there may be different Human Resource Systems for internal employee data. Additionally identity information of external employees, business partners and even customers has to be integrated. Combining these different identity sources in to a single consolidated Identity Store is an important service. All other services of the Identity Management System rely on these consolidated and actual data.
- **Integration of business information:** Structural information like legal entities, organizational units, cost centers, locations, etc. is necessary to describe identity data within the actual working context. Like identity data, organizational data is stored in different systems. An Identity Management System integrates these data with the identities stored.
- **Management of rules and roles:** With the combined information about identities and their organizational relationships rules and roles can be integrated in the Identity Management System. The goal of storing rules and roles in an Identity Management System is to establish a logical layer for the modeling and management of entitlement information that is generic enough to cover many of the relevant IT system's authorization/access control methods.
- **Enforcement of entitlements to IT-Systems:** The IT system's access decisions are typically based on locally stored user and access information. An Identity Management System helps to combine local access information of a specific IT system with the centrally stored information. The access decisions based on the rules, roles and business information are enforced on the specific IT systems.

To summarize this, one of the main tasks of an Identity Management System is to provide a process-oriented framework for managing identities and organizational information on the one hand and role and rules for access and privilege management on the other hand.

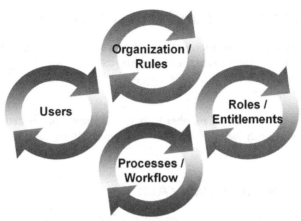

Fig 1: Process oriented framework for Identity Management

The introduction of an Identity Management System within an organization is not to be done with a single project. In fact it is necessary to establish an Identity Management Program which constantly evolves. The following steps are reasonable:

- **Step 1**: Set up an Identity Management Pilot:
  - Start with a well-defined functional scope
  - Integration of a fixed amount of IT systems
- **Step 2**: Increase the Integration Density
  - Extend the Identity Management System through the integration of additional IT systems.
- **Step 3**: Increase the Functional Scope
  - Extend the functional scope of the Identity Management System

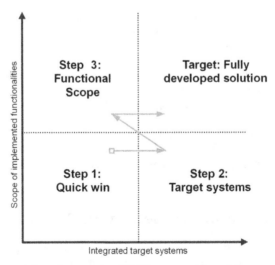

Fig 2: Introduction of an IAM-Program with useful strategy

2 Compliance for User and Entitlement Management

Granting access to corporate information not only covers aspects of given processes within an organization or technical requirements of the IT infrastructure in place. Today access to sensitive information like customer, financial or engineering data more and more becomes a major legal issue for any organization.

This becomes obvious at the growing number of laws and regulations issued by governments around the world dealing with the question how to ensure confidentiality, integrity and availability of sensitive data.

2.1 Example – Sarbanes Oxley Act:

According to the Sarbanes Oxley Act the management of an organization is responsible "for establishing and maintaining an adequate internal control structure and procedures for financial reporting" [Tugp02].

Two overall security goals are covered by the Sarbanes Oxley Act.
- *Integrity:* The information given in the financial reports must not be manipulated.
- *Availability:* The financial reports have to be available on a clearly defined regular basis.

As mentioned in [A10n05] Section 404 is the most critical for Information Technology (IT) professions. *"Section 404 of the Act focuses heavily on the effectiveness of the internal controls used to govern the accuracy of information reported in financial reports and emphasizes the importance of ethical conduct and reliable information."*

2.2 Example - Basel II:

With the introduction of Basel II, financial institutions are asked to implement an enterprise-wide risk management with a new focus on operational risks [Kpmg03]. According to [Bcob04] operational risk is defined as:

> *"Operational risk is defined as the risk of loss resulting from inadequate or failed internal processes, people and systems or from external events. This definition includes legal risk, but excludes strategic and reputational risk."*

For organizations, like financial institutions, which rely heavily on the use of IT systems, having appropriate controls in place, which increases the security level is essential to cut down operational risks. Granting access rights to IT systems in accordance with audit requirements hereby is a key requirement.

2.3 Example – Certification based on ISO 27001

Compliance with the BSI basic protection catalogues[1] is necessary for organizations which apply for an ISO 27001 certificate. The BSI basic protection catalogue specifies different safeguards which are related to Identity and Access Management. Some examples are [Bsi05]:

---

1   Issued by Federal Offices for Security in the Information Technology (BSI) (http://www.bsi.de)

- *S 2.8 Granting of (application/data) access authorizations:* "The person responsible in each given case must arrange for, and document, the assignment of, and changes in, access privileges." Access privileges have to be assigned on a "Need-To-Know" principle.
- *S 2.30 Provisions governing the configuration of users and of user groups:* "The appropriate assignment of access rights and assurance of orderly and controlled operations are only possible if procedures governing the designation of users and user groups have been defined."
- *S 2.220 Guidelines for access control:* Restrictive allocation of rights: "Where extensive rights are granted to employees (e.g. to administrators) this should be as restrictive as possible."

In order to fulfill these standards and regulations an organization has to prove evidence about the fact: Who has been granted access to which data at a given time. The services introduced with an Identity and Access Management Program typically helps an organization to give answers to these questions. Compared to the effort necessary, to collect access data without the structured information generated by an Identity Management System, the usage of an IAM system helps to get the job done faster and more cost effective, whenever a certain security issues arises or an audit report has to be assembled.

But not only laws and regulations lead to the understanding that an Identity and Access Management Program is an important building block within an overall IT architecture. Also best practice approaches to IT governance indicate the necessity of an IAM program.

The COBIT[2] framework for example defines necessary processes with four domains. Within the Domain **"Delivery and Support"** the following control objectives are defined as part of the process definition DS5 **"Ensure System Security"**:

- **DS5.3 Identity Management** [Itgi07]: Ensure that all users (internal, external and temporary) and their activity on IT systems (business application, IT environment, system operations, development and maintenance) are uniquely identifiable. Enable user identities via authentication mechanisms. Confirm that user access rights to systems and data are in line with defined and documented business needs and that job requirements are attached to user identities. Ensure that user access rights are requested by user management, approved by system owners and implemented by the security-responsible person. Maintain user identities and access rights in a central repository. Deploy cost-effective technical and procedural measures, and keep them current to establish user identification, implement authentication and enforce access rights.
- **DS5.4 User Account Management** [Itgi07]: Address requesting, establishing, issuing, suspending, modifying and closing user accounts and related user privileges with a set of user account management procedures. Include an approval procedure outlining the data or system owner granting the access privileges. These procedures should apply for all users, including administrators (privileged users) and internal and external users, for normal and emergency cases. Rights and obligations relative to access to enterprise systems and information should be contractually arranged for all types of users. Perform regular management review of all accounts and related privileges.

---

2 Control Objectives for Information and related Technology (COBIT) published by the IT Governance Institute

3 Increasing the Integration Density

Following the rules and regulations mentioned in the previous chapter one of the essential goals concerning the verifiability of access rights is completeness. This means that a complete overview of all access rights of a user is desirable.

To achieve a consistent security level for the access and rights management across all IT applications, in order to gain compliance for user and entitlement management, there are some challenges organizations have to cope with.

- **Different processes:** To manage identity information for different groups of people organizations often use different processes, and on top of that the information is typically stored in different places. For internal employees an onboarding process exists within the Human Resources (HR) department. For external employees a second process might be in place in order to register the identity information. If it comes to partners or customers often a variety of processes is used, because the relationship to these people is managed by different departments within the organization.
- **Amount of applications:** There is not just one application which is used by the employees in order to do their daily business. In fact there are a lot of them, each supporting the requirements of a specific business process. While introducing new applications, normally the first thing to do is to look at the use cases and features, which are available within the application and how these features can help to better support a business process. Often the question, how to set up the access rights for that application and the user management process is one of the last tasks handled whenever a new application is integrated into the IT infrastructure.
- **Distributed user information:** According to the different identity processes and the variety of application the information about identities and their access rights is widely spreads across the databases available within the IT infrastructure of an organization.

In larger organizations these challenges tend to get even worse as there might not be just one HR process. Because of reorganizations, mergers and acquisitions a constant change of the processes in place and the available IT systems is normal.

An Identity Management System helps to better meet these challenges, because the services offered are focused on the following aspects.

- **Identity Life Cycle:** The central component of an Identity Management System is a repository for identities, the identity store. Every person, which is managed by the Identity Management System is stored as an identity object. John Doe is stored only once together with all attributes necessary to support his life cycle process within the organization (surname, given name, communication data, organizational context information, information about his "lifetime" within the organization, etc.) This object is the reference for all other related identity objects within other IT systems. Typically a global identifier (GID) is introduced for every identity object.
- **Integration of Identity Sources:** Identity objects are added to the identity store either manually or automated through the integration of their respective source system (e.g. synchronization with the HR system).

- **Support of RBAC[3]:** In order to simplify the assignment of privileges to a user in terms of reducing the complexity and increasing the transparency, mechanisms for role management and rule management should be supported by the Identity Management System. Roles are used to consolidate fragmented and technically oriented permissions to human readable roles which are driven by the organization and the function a user has within an organization. Rules are used to automatically assign roles to users based on their organizational context information.
- **Focus on Entitlement:** The process of managing accounts for IT applications not only consists of granting access rights. Resource management (e.g. assignment of mailboxes, creating home drives, file share, etc.) is also an important part of the IT administration. An Identity Management System can also support this processes. But in order to focus on security the main task of the Identity Management system lies on the process of access management and enforcement of the privileges onto the IT systems.

As already mentioned, an essential aspect of gaining compliance is the number of IT systems, which are connected to the Identity Management System. Unfortunately, the integration of IT applications within an Identity Management Systems is not always easy to accomplish, for different reasons. Some of them are:

- **Availability of a Provisioning Interface:** Today most of the IT systems in place still use their own repository to store user and access information. This information is necessary to decide whether the execution of a particular function or access to specific data is to be granted at runtime. Enforcing the decisions, made within the Identity Management System to these applications requires a technical interface, which allows information about access rights to be transfered to the application. Unfortunately there are still applications which do not provide such an interface.
- **Integration Costs:** If a provisioning interface to an IT system is not available as a standard feature, there may be a chance to implement a provisioning interface as an extension. An Identity Management System typically offers a framework to set up a specific connector to an application which is capable of doing the provisioning job. This increases the integration costs as the interface has to be specifically developed.
- **Amount of Users:** There are applications which are only used by a small amount of users. The integration of such systems with an automated provision interface might not be cost effective.
- **Process Boundaries:** IT systems and services are quite often provided by an outsourced service partner. The maintenance tasks to run the application and to update the access management information within the application (adding new users, assigning privileges) lies within the responsibility of the service provider. The business issues change requests to the service provider, to update the identity and access information. Quite often the process defined to issue change requests include media disruptions, which cumber automatic provisioning or even makes it impossible. Adapting the established processes between the organization and the service provider is often time-consuming and expensive, or simply not possible.

The process based approach to integrate such IT systems, described in the next chapter, shows a cost-effective way, without loosing the possibility to provide a holistic view of a user's access rights for the IT systems used by him.

---

3   Role-Based Access Control defined by NIST, National Institute of Standards and Technology

4 Process based System Integration

Whenever physical integration of a specific target system is not possible, the integration with a process based approach is a reasonable alternative, as some important security and compliance aspects are covered.

This chapter describes the different steps of the approach on a process level. Aspects of the technological integration details depend on the specific Identity Management System used for the implementation of an Identity Management Program.

The following figure shows the different steps of the Process based System Integration.

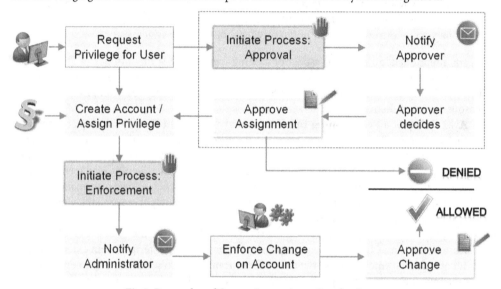

Fig 3: Process based System Integration – Step-by-Step

1. **Request Privilege:** In order to grant access to a specific system or a privilege to a user the responsible person requests a privilege assignment. The responsible person for an internal employee is typically the manager; the responsible person for an external employee is typically the internal employee the external employee works for. If the Identity Management System support mechanisms for delegated administration, the privilege to issue a request might have been delegated (e.g. a specific team within the department).

2. **Approve Privilege Assignment (optional):** According to the scope of the privilege requested, it might be necessary to secure the assignment by means of a specific approval process. Business requirements might demand a 4-eye-principle. To validate the assignment different persons in the company for each user and privilege have to accept the assignment: the relevant manager of the employee and the manager (owner) of the privilege.

   a. **Initiate Approval Process:** If the approval step is necessary, the Identity Management System calculates the necessary approvers, depending on to the specific approval process, decides in which order the approvals are performed.

   b. **Notify Approver:** Each approver is notified individually, reminding him that an approval task has to be carried out by him.

c. **Decision**: Each approver makes a decision about the specific request, considering the relevant business and compliance rules.

d. **Approve Assignment**: To carry out the approval, the approver uses the services delivered by the Identity Management System. The decisions made are stored by the Audit Service and thus are available for subsequent analysis operations. If necessary the approval steps can be secured by the usage of a digital signature. According to the decisions made by the necessary approvers, the Identity Management System either accepts or rejects the privilege request. If the privilege request is rejected, the access for the user is denied.

3. **Create Account / Assign Privilege**: For the creation of a system account or a privilege assignment there are different starting points.

a. **Assignment Request**: An assignment request directly leads to the creation of the privilege, if a specific approval is not necessary.

b. **Result of the Approval Process**: An accepted approval for a specific assignment request.

c. **Rule based Assignment**: Besides the assignment request, access to the system privileges may also be the result of business rules managed by the services of the Identity Management System (e.g. all employees of a specific department are granted access the department's file share; all members of a project team are granted access to the project workspace within the project management system.) To decide upon these rules the relevant business information has to be available within the Identity Management System as mentioned in chapter 1.

4. **Initiate Enforcement Process**: After the creation of the privilege assignment within the Identity Management System, the assignment has to be enforced upon the specific target system (e.g. creation of an account for the network operating system; assignment of a role within the ERP-System[4]). For systems directly connected to the Identity Management System the enforcement is carried out by the provisioning service. As mentioned in chapter 3 there are several reasons why a provisioning service might not be available to enforce the privilege assignment. For these systems the Identity Management System offers an approval based enforcement process.

5. **Notify Administrator**: As for the privilege approval process the responsible administrators are notified about a new change request for the systems they are responsible for. Each of the following change requests might be the result of the preceding processes.

a. Create a new account

b. Deactivate an existing account

c. Delete an existing account

d. Set up a new group/role membership

e. Delete an existing group/role membership

6. **Enforce Change**: In order to carry out the change request the administrator uses the services delivered by the Identity Management System. Thus all relevant identity information is available (e.g. the correct spelling of given name and surname; the correct name of the system account which has been calculated within the Identity Management System by the naming rule for that system).

---

4 Enterprise Resource Planning System

7. **Approve Change:** After having accomplished the changes in the target system the administrator finishes the change request by an approval step. With this he certifies the fulfillment of the change request. This approval step is stored by the Audit Service and thus is available for subsequent analysis operations.

The process-based integration of the administrators, or responsible persons of an IT system, which is not ready for automatic provisioning closes the gap between automated and manual Identity Management, and provides an overall seamless view about a user's access rights. Compared to an automated provisioning (systems integrated with APIs) the steps of the process-based integration mostly carried out manually by an administrator. However, through the tight integration into the entitlement process, the just-in-time information of the administrator, what has to be done for whom (account and group management) errors are minimized. In addition, the fact that the administrator has to document or even certify what he has done helps that all actions are carried out with the utmost accuracy, especially as the certification is audited and will be validated on a regular basis.

5 Conclusion

The complete information about users and their access rights including all IT systems used within an organization is an essential aspect for organizations gaining compliance with today's laws and regulations. In order to compile this information the relevant processes have to be clearly defined and have to follow organizational and security relevant requirements. Herby it is necessary for organization to focus on the following goals:
- **Completeness:** All information about an user's access rights in every IT application should be included.
- **Readiness for audit**: Access rights of a user have to be comprehensible at any time – even backdated to a specific point in time.
- **Efficiency**: The processes to be implemented have to demand as little resources as possible to be cost efficient.
- **Clarity:** Privilege structures have to be composed in a clear structure to gain transparency.
- **Execution:** The process to enforce decisions about privilege assignments has to be focused on a short processing time.

The process based approach, described in this paper, helps to achieve these goals for IT systems, which cannot be integrated to an existing Identity Management System with a direct provisioning approach. This concerns applications, which need to be integrated for security reasons but do not provide a provisioning interface, or the development of an individual interface is expensive or time-consuming. Nevertheless these systems need to be integrated in order to get a complete view of the IT resources an employee has in use for audit purposes.

The solution covers the whole process from authorization request, approval steps up to the execution of the request within the IT system. Using this solution, the audit and compliance requirements for an organization could be met in an easy, cost-effective way, even for specialized legacy systems which were used by few users.

The solution is currently in use at a large german financial organization. So far, the solution has met its targets and has been extended to more IT systems by the customer himself, based on the template-based approach. This reduces the need to rely on external expertise, while integrating additional IT systems, thus reducing external costs and speeding up the integration process.

References

[A10n05]   A10 Networks, Whitepaper – Identity Management and Sarbanes-Oxley Compliance, (http://www.a10networks.com), 2005, p 4

[Bcob04]   Basel Committee on Banking Supervision, International Convergence of Capital Measurement and Capital Standards – A Revised Framework, Bank for International Settlements, ISBN print: 92-9131-669-5, 2004, p 137

[Bsi05]   BSI, IT-Grundschutz Catalogues - Safeguards, Federal Offices for Security in the Information Technology (BSI) http://www.bsi.de, 2005

[Itut10]   ITU-T, Recommendation ITU-T X.1252 - Baseline identity management terms and definitions, http://www.itu.int, 2010

[Itgi07]   IT Governance Institute, CobiT 4.1, IT Governance Institute (http://ww.isaca.org/cobit), 2007, p 118

[Kpmg03]   KPMG, Basel II: A Worldwide Challenge for Banking Business, Financial Services, KPMG International, 2003, p 1, p 4

[Tugp02]   The U.S Government Printing Office (GPO), Public Law 107 - 204 - Sarbanes-Oxley Act of 2002, http://www.gpo.gov/fdsys/pkg/PLAW-107publ204/content-detail.html, 2002

A Structured Approach to the Design of Viable Security Systems

Jan Zibuschka · Heiko Roßnagel

Fraunhofer IAO
Nobelstr. 12, 70569 Stuttgart
{jan.zibuschka | heiko.rossnagel}@iao.fraunhofer.de

Abstract

This paper argues that the widely lamented failure of many security solutions in the market is due to an overly technology- and complexity-driven design approach. We argue that it is the responsibility of the system designers to make sure that their designs lead to an increased security when implemented in practice, including both adoption and usability aspects. We build on earlier approaches and findings from IT security and related disciplines, but integrate them in a larger paradigmatic framework targeting specifically the security domain. To achieve a viable security solution, designers have to make sure that their solution provides an effective security improvement and is compliant with market demands. We present several methods that can be applied to assess market compliance already in the early stages of the design process.

1 Introduction

Technological solutions that address issues like security, privacy and reliability have been developed by companies and in research projects. However, they often appear disconnected from markets, user needs and economic contexts. As a result several security and privacy technologies have become market failures in recent years, like for example advanced electronic signatures [Roßn06] or web anonymity services [Feig02]. Economic issues are often neglected by technology developers. Instead security solutions continue to be designed with technological factors in mind, valuing increases in security guarantees and even technical complexity over practical relevance. The underlying assumption is that these technologies will become a market success, based on their technological sophistication and the elegance of their design. The resulting business models are usually poorly designed and fail to address important success factors appropriately. Costs and benefits of security solutions are often not distributed fairly, leading to a lack of incentive for users to adopt. Also, vendors of security technology often fail to consider the users' willingness to pay when creating their price models, which results in overprizing and eventually a lack of market success. In addition, these technologies often fail to address user requirements, such as usability and accessibility by individuals and organizations [Gree04]. We argue that a viable security system needs to satisfy the requirements of all involved stakeholders to be accepted. We also argue that it is the responsibility of the system designers to make sure that their design leads to an increased security when implemented in practice. This leads to a new paradigm that designers of secure systems and security solutions need to make sure that their system has good chances of diffusion, and that it actually increases security when deployed in the field. We present several methods that can be applied to assess market compliance already in the early stages of the design process. This requires a paradigm shift in security research as a whole, focusing on security

N. Pohlmann, H. Reimer, W. Schneider (Editors): Securing Electronic Business Processes, Vieweg (2011), 246-255

outcomes rather than technological complexity. Solving this problem with technologies such as the ones that have been presented as paradigms in e.g. [Bish08] seems highly unlikely. We build on earlier approaches and findings from IT security and related disciplines, but integrate them in a larger paradigmatic framework targeting specifically the security domain.

The rest of the paper is structured as follows. We will first consider related work in section 2, before we present our viable security paradigm in section 3. Our approach requires designer to consider aspects of market compliance during the early stages of the design process. Therefore, we present several methods that can be applied to achieve this goal in section 4, before we summarize our results.

2 Related Work

Hevner et al [Hevn04] have recently proposed a Design Science approach, where IT artifacts are developed and then evaluated using behavioral methods, as a promising vector for research that contributes both to the scientific knowledge base (the research is rigorous) and to practice (it is also relevant). While this approach brought the Information Systems (IS) domain closer to the subjects classically addressed in computer science, we propose a paradigm shift that would bring the IT security domain closer to IS. A similar approach has been proposed by Fenton et al [Fent94] in the Software Engineering domain, arguing that in this domain, a lot of new technologies are developed which claim to lower development effort needed and make software e.g. more readily adaptable or maintainable, without ever giving any evaluation of such systems beyond the demonstration that effort might be lowered in very specific scenarios envisioned by the designers of the solution. This strategy has a following in the software engineering domain even though it has long been realized that properties of software development projects are often counter-intuitive, e.g. adding more manpower to a late project may increase its delay [Broo95]. Glass, one of the co-authors, even hypothesized that this attitude might lead to a serious crisis in software design, where a lot of projects fail [Glas94]. A detailed overview of the research streams influencing our approach can be found in Figure 1.

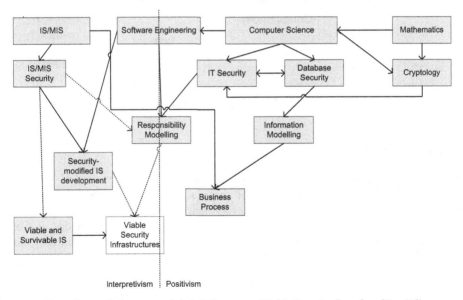

Fig. 1: Research Streams and their Influence on Viable Security (based on [Sipo05])

3 Viable Security

In this section we present a model of the factors that need to be addressed to achieve viable security solutions. We define a viable security solution as a solution that is successful on the market and provides a security improvement when deployed in practice. To achieve a viable security solution, designers have to make sure that their solution provides an effective security improvement and is compliant with market demands. If one of these requirements is not addressed, improved security will not be achieved in practice. A solution that provides effective security but fails in the marketplace will not provide security improvements, because it will not be used. Similarly, a solution that is a market success but does not provide effective security when deployed in practice will not lead to a security improvement either. This is commonly referred to as 'snake oil' [Mich03]. Figure 2 illustrates our viable security model, identifying those two dimensions and the main factors influencing them.

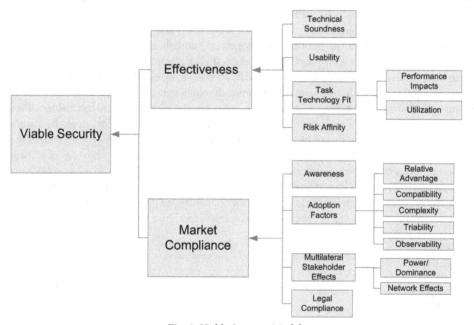

Fig. 2: Viable Security Model

3.1 Effectiveness

The factors influencing the effectiveness of a security solution comprise technical soundness, usability, task-technology-fit and risk affinity. All these factors have to be addressed by system designers. If possible a solution should be an improvement over the state of the art in all four areas. Optimizing one factor at the cost of downgrading other factors is not a good idea, as overall security outcomes might suffer. There are numerous security solutions that are technically sound but do not achieve effective security improvements in practice [Whit99].

3.1.1 Technical Soundness

To achieve effective security, solutions have to be technically sound. This is a natural requirement but by far not the only one. This requirement has been well recognized in IT-security research and may have been overemphasized in the past in comparison to other requirements, which are mentioned in some works, but mostly ignored by IT security researchers. This focus on technical soundness over other requirements (in particular usability) has been recognized by several authors as one of the largest roadblocks standing in the way of increased computer security. For example Adams and Sasse [Adam99a] point out that *"insufficient communication with users produces a lack of user-centered design in security mechanisms"*.

3.1.2 Usability

If the solution is technically sound but users are not able to understand and use it in its supposed way, effective security will not be achieved [Whit99]. This has been recognized in the past by several researchers [Whit04] and considerable work has been done in this area. But as [Smet02] point out, *"improving the usability of security technology is only one part of the problem"* and that it is necessary to *"design usable and useful systems that provide security to end-users in terms of the applications that they use and the tasks they want to achieve."*

3.1.3 Task Technology Fit

Information technology in general is more likely to have a positive impact on individual performance and be used if the capabilities of the IT match the tasks that the user must perform [Good95]. Goodhue and Thompson argue that in order to have a *"positive effect on individual performance, technology (1) must be utilized and (2) must be a good fit with the task it supports"*.

To be utilized a security solution has to be accepted by the different stakeholders of the system [Gree04]. If stakeholders do not accept the solution they will start to find ways to circumvent it [Adam99a]. One example is the enforcement of password policies. If users are forced to remember randomly generated passwords, they tend to write them down, if they are forced to change them regularly, they go through great lengths to be able to use identical or similar passwords [Smit02]. Stakeholder acceptance can be influenced by usability, but it is not the only influence. Just because a solution is easy to use does not mean that it will be automatically accepted by stakeholders. It has also to be perceived as useful and not too burdening [Herl09]. This factor is more relevant than usability in most settings [Davi89]. Providing a perceived usefulness to the different stakeholders of the system is a factor that is often neglected when security solutions are designed. Instead designers wrongly assume that providing security is by itself a sufficient benefit, and justifies any amount of inconvenience for users, leading to solutions that are not accepted by some of the stakeholders and therefore ineffective [Herl09] [Beau09]. Even worse, some security solutions require changes to be made to existing business processes and therefore unduly inhibit business operation. Instead they should support existing business processes or act as enablers for new business. Utilization of security technology alone does not improve security outcomes if the technology is a bad fit for the task it is supposed to support.

3.1.4 Risk Affinity

Risk affinity has been identified as a relevant factor in the diffusion of security solutions, and can be seen as part of the explanation why organizations and especially governments are more willing to invest in security than individuals, and even more willing to invest than a rational economic analysis would suggest [Adam99b]. It has also been identified as one of the factors undermining large scale security deployments and standards, which will naturally gravitate towards the solution preferred by less risk-averse stakeholders [Deke99]. Another factor that is often neglected is that the usage of security solutions might affect the behavior of the person using it. A perceived increase in security might lead a higher willingness to take risks [Asna08].

3.2 Market Compliance

In the information systems literature, a variety of theoretical perspectives have been advanced to provide an understanding of the determinants of usage. An important line of research has examined the adoption and usage of information technology from a diffusion of innovation perspective [Roge03]. This research examines a variety of factors, and has been applied to explain the adoption and diffusion of a great variety of innovations ranging from new methods of agriculture to modern communication technology.

3.2.1 Awareness

Awareness of the security risks is required to perceive a relative advantage of adopting and using the security solution. If such awareness does not exist, the solution will not be adopted. Such a lack of awareness or underestimation of security risks can be further reinforced by the tendency of users to assume that negative events are less likely to happen to them than to others and that positive events are more likely to happen to them than others [Rhee05]. Even if the individual is aware of the risks, he or she also has to know about the existence of security technology in order to adopt. If this knowledge about existing technology is obtained, the user enters a persuasion phase, in which an opinion is formed on the usefulness of the technology in addressing the needs of the adopter.

3.2.2 Adoption Factors

In his seminal work [Roge03] Rogers defines five attributes of innovations, as perceived by the members of the social system that determine the rate of adoption: Relative Advantage, Compatibility, Complexity, Triability and Observability. The most influential attribute is the perceived relative advantage, which is the degree to which an innovation is perceived as better than the idea it supersedes. It is not so important if the innovation has an objective advantage, but rather if the individual perceives the innovation as advantageous. Security solutions usually are preventive innovations, which are ideas that are adopted by an individual at one point in time in order to lower the probability that some future unwanted event (i.e. attack) will occur [Roge03]. Preventive innovations usually have a very slow rate of adoption, because the unwanted event might not happen even without the adoption of the innovation (i.e. no attack occurs despite not using security solutions). Therefore, the relative advantage often is not very clear cut. Furthermore, costs and benefits of security solutions are often not distributed fairly, leading to a lack of incentive for users to adopt. Costs can be monetary cost, but can also be incurred in form of performance costs (i.e. slow data transfer when using anonymity services), search costs (i.e. for finding and installing the right technology) or other intangibles. Only if the potential benefits of using security technologies outweigh the associated costs, a positive adoption decision will be formed by the individual. A lack of (social) compatibility with the existing values, past experience, and needs of potential adopters can also be a key inhibitor for the adoption success of security solutions. Security solutions that require massive changes to common work practices often fail in the marketplace. The same is experienced with solutions not meeting social expectations. Complexity, which is the degree to which an innovation is perceived as difficult to understand and use, is highly influenced by the usability of the solution. If the users have the impression that the system is difficult to use or to obtain, they are unlikely to adopt unless the perceived relative advantage significantly outweighs these hindrances. For enterprises that want to adopt a security solution, a major factor influencing the perceived complexity will be how easily the system can be adapted to and integrated in existing business processes. If major adjustments to existing processes have to be made, the complexity of adopting the innovation increases significantly and the costs of adoption will increase with it as well. Signalling quality is a common problem for security solutions [Back05]. It's hard to understand and to see the differences in the applied security is not easy for normal users. This asymmetric information about the reliability of the used technology could lead to a lemons market as defined in [Aker70]. In this seminal article the author argues that information asymmetry and uncertainty about the product quality will lead to a market failure, unless appropriate counteracting mechanisms are undertaken. In a market that contains good and bad (lemons) security solutions, imperfect information about the quality causes the user to average the quality and price of the service used. The information gap enables the opportunistic behaviour of the owner of a lemon to sell it at average price. As a result, the better quality service will not be used since the price it deserves can not be obtained. The consequence of such practice will lead to a continuous fall of both quality and value of services and eventually to a market failure. Tendencies towards such a market failure have been observed for the PKI market [Back06] and the market for privacy solutions [Roßn10].

3.2.3 Multilateral Stakeholder Effects

The usefulness of many security solutions is diminished if they do not have a significant user base. Examples include SSL [Ozme06] and anonymization services [Ding05]. A critical mass of individuals has to adopt the innovation before it is of use for the average member of the system [Mahl99]. The individuals who have adopted an innovation form a network and with each new member the overall value of the network increases [Mahl99]. This fundamental phenomenon is usually referred to as 'network effects'. Another aspect of network externalities is that it is often possible for stakeholders to externalize costs incurred due to the system deployment to other entities that do not benefit from the security deployment. One example for this is the German eID concept, where users have to bear the costs of systems that are mainly beneficial for government and enterprises [Roßn06]. In value-networks dominant stakeholders exist that can act as a champion for the technology influencing other stakeholders to adopt the same technology more rapidly [Roge03]. Those stakeholders' requirements may be more relevant for the actual adoption of systems. All in all, if different stakeholders are involved in the system, their interests have to be balanced in order to achieve adoption. This leads to complex situations where the needs of all stakeholders have to be considered and even quantifiable requirements can't be trivially offset against each other.

3.2.4 Legal compliance

Legislation and regulation can have huge impacts on the market success of technologies in general and security and privacy technologies in particular. Policy makers can decide to stimulate the adoption of certain security or privacy solutions using different methods ranging from information provisioning campaigns, informing users about the risks and available security solutions, to enforcing mandatory adoption by issuing fines for noncompliance [Ozme06]. Furthermore states can decide to roll out security solutions to all their citizens. Laws and regulations can also indirectly affect the market success of security solutions, by creating a need for companies to invest in security and privacy solutions in order to be compliant with regulations. For example privacy disclosure laws require organisations to notify affected individuals if personal data under their control is believed to have been acquired by an unauthorised person. These laws could create incentives for companies to invest in better security measures [Ande08]. However other results raise major doubts about the effectiveness of the privacy breach disclosure legislation [Munt09]. This shows that the economic effects of such regulations in regard to security and privacy solutions are another area where a lot of research is necessary.

4 Methods to Assess Market Compliance

We will now present several methods that can be applied to assess market compliance in the early stages of the design process.

4.1 Stakeholder Analysis

IT security researchers often focus on security or privacy guarantees offered to the user, without giving equal thought to the security needs of other stakeholders. One example is the area of privacy-enhancing identity management, which focuses on the interest of the user to keep his private information confidential or at least have a certain transparency of how it is used [Clau01]. However, there are also examples of the reverse effect, e.g. in the area of government smart card infrastructures, which are mainly driven by involved governmental agencies and enterprises, leading to scenarios where the user has to bear the costs, but does not gain any tangible benefits [Adam99a]. In any case, interests of some stakeholders are commonly ignored even by advocates of "multilateral security" or similar paradigms. However, a credible analysis [Vidy08] of all involved parties and their interests would certainly benefit the security solutions' success in the market. Stakeholder analysis is an established method for this, integrating ethical as well as tangible and intangible business requirements [Vidy08]. Different possible methods can be employed for stakeholder analysis in practice, e.g. focus groups, interviews, use cases, or observation [Whit04]. In regard to security solutions this approach has been successfully applied e.g. in the case of privacy friendly location based services [Zibu07]. A detailed description on how to apply this approach can be found in [Vidy08].

4.2 Ex-ante Evaluation using Diffusion of Innovations Theory

The adoption and diffusion of information technology has been well researched in the economics and information systems domains. This has led to the development of widely accepted and used theories such as the diffusion of innovations theory [Roge03] and the technology acceptance model [Davi89]. However, the adoption of security technology has not enjoyed similar attention. Instead, IT security technologies continue to be designed with technological factors in mind. We propose using Rogers' five attributes that determine the diffusion of innovations to structure ex-ante evaluations of IT security technology, specifically in the phase of system design. This is especially helpful in the context of security, as it directly addresses several fields where security solutions have had problems, such as usability/complexity [Dham08] or observability [Ande01]. In addition to the perceived attributes of innovations, innovation process and interactiveness of the innovation can also be considered to make decisions about initiatives, as for example [Ding05] consider network effects in the context of anonymization. While this approach is not meant to discover new empirical evidence of a system's chances of success, it may be used by system designers to structure the knowledge available to them from different sources, such as IT security-related surveys performed by consultancies or public bodies, or academic sources. It can be used by designers of IT security systems to assess the market compliance of their systems, identify non-security-related factors that may impact the success of the system, and adapt the high-level design of the system accordingly. System designers do not need the specific numbers that form the basis for empirical analyses but rather need business requirements they can consider in their designs, while marketing often is not aware of technological affordances. This structured method of analysis has been successfully applied to electronic signatures [Roßn06], web anonymizers [Roßn10], and federated identity management [Hühn10]. A comprehensive description on how to apply this method can be found in [Roßn11].

4.3 Measuring Willingness to Pay

User preferences are central to the success of new products. In operational research and marketing, models have been developed for selecting optimal products and determining profit-maximizing pricing strategies. Many of these models use estimates of consumer preferences and willingness to pay (WTP), which is the price point at which a consumer becomes indifferent as to the choice between purchasing or not purchasing a product. One approach to measure this WTP is Choice-Based-Conjoint analysis. By focusing on WTP different designs can be easily compared and the prospective users' preferences can be expressed in a single dimension. Using this quantitative approach a choice experiment has to be conducted by presenting different choice sets including a no-purchase option to prospective customers. This method has been successfully applied to several security solutions such as electronic signatures [Roßn07] and federated identity management [Muel06]. A detailed description on how to apply this method can be found in [Gens10].

5 Conclusion

In this paper we have argued that the widely lamented failure of many security solutions in the market is due to an overly technology- and complexity-driven design approach. We took the viewpoint that it is the responsibility of the system designers to make sure that their designs leads to an increased security when implemented in practice, including both adoption and usability aspects. We've build on earlier approaches and findings from IT security and related disciplines, but integrate them in a larger paradigmatic framework targeting specifically the security domain. To achieve a viable security solution, designers have to make sure that their solution provides an effective security improvement and is compliant with market demands. We have presented several methods that can be applied to assess market compliance already in the early stages of the design process.

References

[Adam99a] Adams, A., Sasse, M.A.: Users are not the enemy. Commun. ACM. 42, 12, 40-46 (1999).

[Adam99b] Adams, J.: Cars, Cholera, and Cows: The Management of Risk and Uncertainty. Policy Analysis. (1999).

[Aker70] Akerlof, G.A.: The Market for „Lemons": Quality Uncertainty and the Market Mechanism. The Quarterly Journal of Economics. 84, 3, 488-500 (1970).

[Ande08] Anderson, R. u. a.: Security economics and the internal market. ENISA. (2008).

[Ande01] Anderson, R.: Why Information Security is Hard - An Economic Perspective. Computer Security Applications Conference. S. 358-365 , Las Vegas (2001).

[Asna08] Asnar, Y., Zannone, N.: Perceived risk assessment. Proceedings of the 4th ACM workshop on Quality of protection. S. 59-64 ACM, Alexandria, Virginia, USA (2008).

[Back06] Backhouse, J. u. a.: Spotting lemons in the PKI market: engendering trust by signalling quality. Electronic Commerce and the Digital Economy. (2006).

[Back05] Backhouse, J. u. a.: A question of trust. Commun. ACM. 48, 9, 87-91 (2005).

[Beau09] Beautement, A., Sasse, A.: The economics of user effort in information security. Computer Fraud & Security. 2009, 10, 8-12 (2009).

[Bish08] Bishop, M. u. a.: We have met the enemy and he is us. Proceedings of the 2008 workshop on New security paradigms. S. 1-12 ACM, Lake Tahoe, California, USA (2008).

[Broo95] Brooks, F.: The Mythical Man-Month: Essays on Software Engineering. Anniversary Edition Addison- Wesley, Reading, MA (1995).

[Clau01] Clauß, S., Köhntopp, M.: Identity management and its support of multilateral security. Computer Networks. 37, 2, 205-219 (2001).

[Davi89] Davis, F.D.: Perceived Usefulness, Perceived Ease of Use, and User Acceptance of Information Technology. MIS Quarterly. 13, 3, 319-340 (1989).

[Deke99] Dekel, E., Scotchmer, S.: On the Evolution of Attitudes towards Risk in Winner-Take-All Games. Journal of Economic Theory. 87, 1, 125-143 (1999).

[Dham08] Dhamija, R., Dusseault, L.: The Seven Flaws of Identity Management: Usability and Security Challenges. IEEE Secur. Privacy Mag. 6, 2, 24-29 (2008).

[Ding05] Dingledine, R., Mathewson, N.: Anonymity loves company: Usability and the network effect. Designing Security Systems That People Can Use. O'Reilly Media. (2005).

[Feig02] Feigenbaum, J. u. a.: Economic barriers to the deployment of existing privacy technologies (position paper). Proceedings of the Workshop on Economics of Information Security. (2002).

[Fent94] Fenton, N. u. a.: Science and substance: a challenge to software engineers. Software, IEEE. 11, 4, 86-95 (1994).

[Gens10] Gensler S u.a.: Willingness to Pay Estimation with Choice-Based Conjoint Analysis. Working Paper, Goethe-University of Frankfurt (2010).

[Glas94] Glass, R.L.: The Software-Research Crisis. IEEE Softw. 11, 6, 42-47 (1994).

[Good95] Goodhue, D.L., Thompson, R.L.: Task-Technology Fit and Individual Performance. MIS Quarterly. 19, 2, 213-236 (1995).

[Gree04] Greenwald, S.J. u. a.: The user non-acceptance paradigm: INFOSEC's dirty little secret. Proceedings of the 2004 workshop on New security paradigms. S. 35-43 ACM, Nova Scotia, Canada (2004).

[Herl09] Herley, C.: So long, and no thanks for the externalities: the rational rejection of security advice by users. Proceedings of the 2009 workshop on New security paradigms workshop. S. 133-144 ACM, Oxford, United Kingdom (2009).

[Hevn04]   Hevner, A.R. u. a.: Design Science in Information Systems Research. MIS Quarterly. 28, 1, 75-105 (2004).

[Hühn10]   Hühnlein, D. u. a.: Diffusion of Federated Identity Management. SICHERHEIT 2010. GI, Berlin (2010).

[Mahl99]   Mahler, A., Rogers, E.M.: The diffusion of interactive communication innovations and the critical mass: the adoption of telecommunications services by German banks. Telecommunications Policy. 23, 10-11, 719-740 (1999).

[Mich03]   Michener, J.R. u. a.: "SNAKE-OIL SECURITY CLAIMS" THE SYSTEMATIC MISREPRESENTATION OF PRODUCT SECURITY IN THE E-COMMERCE ARENA. Michigan Telecommunications and Technology Law Review. 9, 211 (2003).

[Muel06]   Mueller ML, Park Y, Lee J and Kim T: Digital identity: How users value the attributes of online identifiers. Information Economics and Policy 18(4), S. 405-422 (2006).

[Munt09]   Muntermann, J., Roßnagel, H.: On the Effectiveness of Privacy Breach Disclosure Legislation in Europe: Empirical Evidence from the US Stock Market. Identity and Privacy in the Internet Age. S. 1-14 (2009).

[Ozme06]   Ozment, A., Schechter, S.E.: Bootstrapping the adoption of Internet security protocols. Fifth Workshop on the Economics of Information Security. , Cambridge, UK (2006).

[Rhee05]   Rhee, H.-S. u. a.: I am fine but you are not: Optimistic bias and illusion of control on information security. ICIS 2005 Proceedings. (2005).

[Roge03]   Rogers, E.M.: Diffusion of Innovations, 5th Edition. Free Press (2003).

[Roßn06]   Roßnagel, H.: On Diffusion and Confusion – Why Electronic Signatures Have Failed. Trust and Privacy in Digital Business. S. 71-80 (2006).

[Roßn07]   Roßnagel H und Hinz O: Zahlungsbereitschaft für elektronische Signaturen. In Wirtschaftsinformatik 2007, S. 163-180, Universitätsverlag, Karlsruhe (2007)

[Roßn10]   Roßnagel, H.: The Market Failure of Anonymity Services. Information Security Theory and Practices. Security and Privacy of Pervasive Systems and Smart Devices (WISTP 2010). S. 340-354 (2010).

[Roßn11]   Roßnagel H und Zibuschka J: Assessing Market Compliance of IT Security Solutions: A Structured Approach Using Diffusion of Innovations Theory. In: Strategic and Practical Approaches for Information Security Governance: Technologies and Applied Solutions IGI Global, im Erscheinen (2011).

[Sipo05]   Siponen, M. T. (2005) Analysis of modern IS security development approaches: towards the next generation of social and adaptable ISS methods, Information and Organization, 15, 339–375.

[Smet02]   Smetters, D. K., and R. E. Grinter: Moving from the design of usable security technologies to the design of useful secure applications. In Proceedings of the 2002 workshop on New security paradigms, 82-89. Virginia Beach, Virginia: ACM (2002).

[Smit02]   Smith, R.E.: The Strong Password Dilemma. Computer. 18, 2, (2002).

[Vidy08]   Vidyaraman, S., M. Chandrasekaran, and S. Upadhyaya: Position: the user is the enemy. In: Proceedings of the 2007 Workshop on New Security Paradigms, 75-80. New Hampshire: ACM (2008).

[Whit04]   Whitten, A.: Making Security Usable. School of Computer Science, Carnegie Mellon University (2004).

[Zibu07]   Zibuschka, J. u. a.: PRIVACY-FRIENDLY LBS: A PROTOTYPE-SUPPORTED CASE STUDY. Proceedings of the 13th Americas Conference on Systems (AMCIS 2007). , Keystone, Colorado, USA (2007).

Fighting CNP fraud – a Case Study

Marc Sel

PwC
marc.sel@pwc.be

Abstract

This article discusses fraud and fraud fighting techniques, particularly in an Internet-based CNP (Card Not Present) context. This scenario continues to be increasingly popular. We will illustrate it with a case study for an airline. As non-cash payments increase with our mobile life-style, so does the use of credit card payments over the Internet. Such use is referred to as CNP (Card Not Present), since the Merchant accepting the card has no contact with the cardholder except for the electronic transaction that is carried out. As there are many parties involved (merchant, service provider for IT services and website, payment providers, acquiring and issuing banks, switch, etc), determining liability in case of fraud is often not trivial. We will describe a real-world case, where the merchant experienced a fraud rate of more than 4% on his Internet payments. We will discuss the technical and legal safeguards that were implemented to fight the various frauds that were taking place. These safeguards concentrated on the implementation of 3D Secure for the CNP transactions, legal action, and an improvement of logical access controls for the airline reservation platform.

1 Context

Fraud and fraud-fighting will most likely continue to go hand-in-hand. In the context of our client, Airline Z999 (real name withheld), fraud had gradually been ramping up over some years to reach an unacceptable level.

There were two major components of the fraud. One component consisted of what could be referred to as "value chain" fraud, where employees engaged in fraudulent transactions such as selling tickets for a high price, delivering lower value tickets and pocketing the difference. Most of this fraud was addressed though improvement of logical access controls and complementary safeguards. This is not addressed here.

The other component consisted of "CNP (Card Not Present)" fraud with credit card sales over the internet. This is addressed further in this article. As the statistics of e.g. the European Central Bank and Eurostat show, card payments are increasing and will most likely continue to increase. For this reason, many different and complementary initiatives have been undertaken to fight card fraud. Credit cards are issued by an entity such as a bank. The issuer may outsource some of the activities to a service bureau. Issuance is governed by a scheme (e.g. VISA or MasterCard for credit cards). Regulation known as KYC (Know Your Customer) was enforced to make sure banks are reasonably sure who they serve or issue credit cards to.

N. Pohlmann, H. Reimer, W. Schneider (Editors): Securing Electronic Business Processes, Vieweg (2011), 256-263

Obvious, while significant attention has been paid to establishing and operating schemes, this should be seen in the light of the basic challenges that apply to identity management. This includes approaches that diverge widely across the globe with regard to issuing identity cards. However such cards are used as a bootstrap security measure by the issuers. While in Europe, the European Commission in the context of the Digital Agenda announced plans to issue an eAuthentication directive, it is clear that the practical consequences of it are still a long way ahead.

Equally important are the different implementation speeds with regard to EMV's "pin & chip" [EMVCO], leaving a window of opportunity for fraudsters that deploy skimming techniques (copying the magstripe information of a credit card, which may be combined with capturing the PIN e.g. using a tiny camera).

Furthermore for many years we witnessed the roll-out of the guidelines of the Payment Cards Industry forum [PCIDSS]. Their "Data Security Standard" aims at the protection of cardholder data, used in transaction, settlement, reconciliation, chargeback, loyalty rewards, marketing, etc. A company acting in payment transactions is expected to comply with these guidelines. An important technique is the limitation of the Cardholder Data Environment (CDE), where it is suggested to use the credit card in transaction, but once authorised, sent the cardholder data to a "secure vault" and replace it either by an encrypted version, or a random unique number ("tokenization"). However, bear in mind that the PCI guidelines mainly protect the others from potential mistakes that you as a merchant could make, not the other way around. That such measures make sense has been demonstrated for example by the well-known Hannaford case in the United States, where data of approximately 4.2 million cards was stolen in 2008.

2 Problem and analysis

2.1 A short description of the problem

Airline Z999 was experiencing a cumulated 4,5+% fraud on ticket sales with regard to one particular African country. The main reason for this was a high amount of "chargebacks", i.e. cases where the cardholder denies having placed the order and requesting to reverse the transaction. The set-up was such that no liability was taken by any party in the chain such as issuer, processor, acquirer, etc. As a consequence the merchant (Airline Z999) was taking the losses. When cardholders claimed they did not authorise a particular transaction, they were refunded at the merchant's expense.

The overall set-up can be depicted as follows:

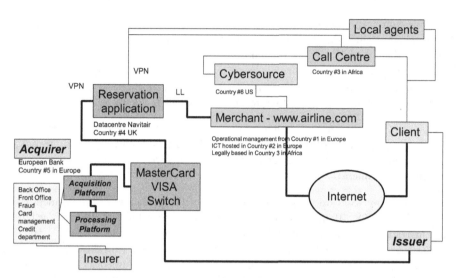

Fig. 1: Major actors involved in selling airline tickets

A client typically approaches the airline via its merchant website. Alternatively, he could contact local agents or the call centre, however the latter are not involved in the CNP fraud scenarios we discuss.

The merchant website offers a wide range of tickets and promotions, as well as opportunities for combining the plane ticket e.g. with hotel reservation or car rental, and insurance. This is a website with a content which is updated frequently, to reflect the commercial strategy of the airline.

Once a potential customer made up his mind and configured his order, the reservation application allows him to check availability and offers him the possibility to make a reservation.

Part of this reservation is requesting authorisation for credit card payment. This is requested by the reservation application to the acquirer, i.e. the merchant's bank. The acquisition platform, operated by the acquirer, will request the issuer for authorisation, i.e. whether the cardholder is valid and agrees to the transaction. Upon obtaining such authorisation, the reservation is made and the ticket will be made available to the customer.

It is important to notice that for airlines on the Africa-EU routes, it is not uncommon that the person paying for the ticket is different from the person travelling. As such, the potential control of challenging the traveller to demonstrate the credit card's presence at check-in time, is not commercially viable.

2.2 Sales process on merchant website

The airline's website is an important commercial channel. As expected, it offers a range of tickets, allowing clients the choice to book well in advance as well as « last minute ». It was based on state-of-the-art technology, but given its commercial role it did not address authentication of the customer. Such authentication is less relevant, what matters to the merchant is that the ticket is paid for, and that the traveller complies with air travel regulation. While the former is addressed through the acquiring process, the latter is addressed through the traditional channels (e.g. at the airport).

Airline Z999 was already making use of a Cybersource plug-in on its website. This plugin routes information captured during the commercial offering to a rules engine. There this information is interpreted, and used to block potentially fraudulent transactions up-front. Only those transactions that are not blocked by the rule engine make it to the actual reservation process. Rules contain elements such as black-listed IP and email addresses used by fraudsters in the past.

2.3 Reservation and payment authentication

Once the customer configured her order and made it past the anti-fraud rule engine, the airline will request authorisation from its bank to charge her credit card. The airline's bank is referred to as the acquiring bank, since it will be acquiring the transaction and later hopefully the money. The payment instruments used are governed by law, and are implemented in the schemes from e.g. VISA. The protocol that governs the communication between merchant and scheme is described in rulebooks, such as e.g. the document « Rules for VISA merchants – Cards acceptance and Chargeback management guidelines ».

In a normal case, authorisation is granted, and the transaction passes later into the subsequent states of captured and settled. However, in the case of fraud where e.g. skimmed or counterfeit cards have been used, the genuine cardholder will discover the fraudulent transaction on his statement. He will then request to reverse the transaction via his issuer, resulting in a chargeback situation that escalates to the acquirer and further on to the merchant.

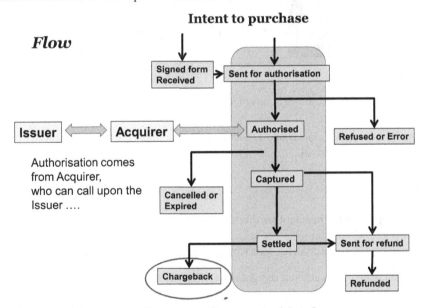

Fig. 2: Different states of a payment and their flow

To avoid such situations, at least two different payment authentication protocols have been proposed, SET (not discussed here) and 3-D Secure.

3-D Secure got his name from the fact that it structures the actors in a payment transactions in three domains. For a detailed description see [3DS]. It is also known under the brand names 'Verified By VISA', or MasterCard's 'SecureCode'. 3-D Secure's objective is payment authentication, which is the process of verifying cardholder account ownership during a purchase transaction in an online commerce environment.

The 3-D Secure model divides payment systems as follows:
- Issuer Domain—Systems and functions of the issuer and its customers (cardholders);
- Acquirer Domain—Systems and functions of the acquirer and its customers (merchants);
- Interoperability Domain—Systems, functions, and messages that allow Issuer Domain systems and Acquirer Domain systems to interoperate globally.

This can be depicted as:

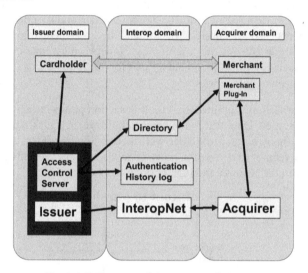

Fig. 3: 3-D Secure model – conceptual overview

For a critique of the security aspects of 3-D Secure, see for example the article by Steven Murdoch and Ross Anderson [MurAnd10].

2.4 Analysis

A merchant accepts diverse payment methods through his acquirer contract(s). The terms and conditions that the scheme imposes are reflected in the merchant/acquirer contract. Note that there is no merchant/scheme contract, everything passes through the acquirer.

3-D Secure was created as an attempt to fight a.o. CNP fraud. The idea is to shift liability towards the issuer – however implementation is complex and acceptance is slow. When an acquirer is enrolled in 3-D Secure, accepts a card, and requests authorisation of the issuer via the 3-D Secure protocol, liability shifts towards to issuer. The onus is now on the issuer to use his 3-D Secure implementation to let the card holder authenticate himself against the issuer. This should demonstrate that both card and cardholder are involved in the transaction.

However, achieving this liability shift in practise is not trivial. Scheme holders do not disclose their responsibilities and liability fully to the public or merchants. The public document *"Visa International - Operating Regulations - Volume I — General Rules - 15 November 2008"* contains the following illustrative statement in the section "About the Operating Regulations":

> *"In order to safeguard the security of our cardholders and merchants and the integrity of the Visa system, we have omitted certain proprietary and competitive information from this manual. As such, a reader of this manual may observe non-sequential section numbering, and information that may seem out of context or incomplete regarding the subject addressed. Visa makes no representations or warranties as to the accuracy or completeness of the text contained in this manual."*

The actual responsibilities and liabilities are described in the contracts between acquirer and scheme holder, and the merchant does not necessarily have a direct link to the scheme holder. In our case there certainly was not. As such the merchant is in a weak position and may end up being liable. In the case of our client, the acquiring bank was reluctant to explain to the merchant that such liability shift was possible and preferred to claim that as per French law, an Internet sale classified as a "remote sales" and the merchant was liable in case of chargeback. The bank's representatives argued that an end-customer who disputes a payment is by default always right, and the charge back becomes a matter of discussion between merchant and customer. It is not up to the bank to get involved, it is up to the merchant to prove that the customer is wrong. Obviously, in an Internet CNP transaction such a course is unrealistic from a merchant perspective.

3 Solution

The solution consisted of a combination of legal and technical measures. First it was paramount to enforce the liability shift towards the issuer from a legal perspective. As the merchant/acquirer contract was governed by French law, and internet sales are classified as a "remote sales" ("ventes à distance") the contractual arrangements merchant/acquirer had to be amended to reflect the specific condition of credit card sales over the Internet.

Second, but in practise in parallel, the technical implementation of 3-D Secure took place. This implied that a merchant 3-D Secure plug-in was installed (referred to as the MPI – Merchant Plug-In). This MPI will route the cardholder authentication parts of the 3-D protocol to the ACS (Access Control Server) of the Issuer. This authentication can be simply password based, or alternatively it can make use of a token. Upon the protocol exchange between cardholder and issuer's Access Control Server, the issuer can conclude that has sufficient evidence to assume the genuine cardholder is participating in the protocol. In practise, the handling of the 3-D protocol is often handled by a payment service provider (PSP).

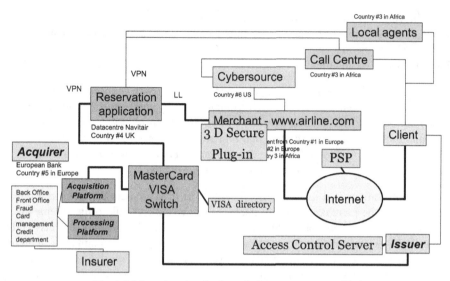

Fig. 4: Major actors involved – solution components added

4 Conclusion

Scheme holders go to great lengths to design and roll-out schemes such as 3-D Secure. While these can be critised in many ways for offering only a partial solution, it is obvious that at least they have the merit of trying to improve the situation.

Nevertheless it can be expected that a more effective and reliable solution will come from an end-to-end payment authentication created by a means under control of the cardholder.

Furthermore, it is obvious that legal alignment needs to be in place as well.

Finally it is obvious that the 3-D Secure approach did not have respect for privacy as a design criteria. This is illustrated by the fact that the transaction information gets forwarded from merchant (who does need to know the details in order to make the reservation) to acquirer (who only needs to know that the card holder is good for credit, nothing more) to the issuer (who only needs to know that his card holder wants to spent money). While cash is anonymous, when paying by credit card my bank gets all the transaction details. To make things worse, most banks outsource the handling of the 3-D protocol to a PSP, who has access to even more data because he handles transactions from multiple banks.

While Airline Z999 was happy with the results obtained, it is obvious that there remains significant room for improvement.

References

[PCIDSS]   Payment Card Industry – Data Security Standard, https://www.pcisecuritystandards.org/security_standards/.

[3DS]   3-D Secure system overview, https://partnernetwork.visa.com/vpn/global/ retrieve_document. do?documentRetrievalId=119

[EMVCO]   www.emvco.com

[MurAnd10] Verified by Visa and MasterCard SecureCode or, How Not to Design Authentication, Steven J. Murdoch and Ross Anderson, Financial Cryptography and Data Security, 2010, 25-28 January 2010, Tenerife.

eID &
eGovernment

ETSI STF 402 – Standardizing the pan-European Infrastructure for Registered Electronic Mail and e-Delivery

Juan Carlos Cruellas[1] · Jörg Apitzsch[2] · Luca Boldrin[3] ·
Andrea Caccia[4] · Santino Foti[5] · Paloma Llaneza[6] · Gregory Sun[7]

[1]Universidad Politécnica de Cataluña
cruellas@ac.upc.edu

[2]bremen online services
ja@bos-bremen.de

[3]InfoCert
luca.boldrin@infocert.it

[4]UNINFO
andrea.caccia@studiocaccia.com

[5]Critical Path
Santino.Foti@criticalpath.net

[6]Llaneza & Asociados
pll@palomallaneza.com

[7]Macau Post eSign Trust Certification Authority
gregsun@seps.macaupost.gov.mo

Abstract

This paper outlines the main achievements of the ETSI STF-402 in the area of Registered Electronic Mail (REM henceforth), related to the provision of means for achieving interoperability between solutions that make use of S/MIME for structuring messages and SMTP as transport and some identified solutions using SOAP on HTTP respectively for the same purposes.

The paper provides details of 2 new technical specifications defining means for allowing exchange of messages between REM providers using SMIME on SMTP and systems that are compliant with Universal Postal Union (UPU henceforth) S52-1 specifications, as well as with implementations of Business Document Exchange Network (BUSDOX henceforth). It also provides details of a binding profile specifying how providers may exchange REM Messages and evidence as XML messages within SOAP structures transported over HTTP. SPOCS LSP and STF-402 have very closely cooperated in its generation, following a model that both

N. Pohlmann, H. Reimer, W. Schneider (Editors): Securing Electronic Business Processes, Vieweg (2011), 267-278

entities firmly believe could be exportable in the future within the EU context for speeding up the production of EU standards tuned to actual needs of the market.

The paper also provides hints on a report documenting test suites for supporting REM interoperability tests and the new version of ETSI TS 102 640 on REM.

1 Background

Early in 2006, ETSI identified an increasing need across Europe for a trustable electronic mail system, suitable to exchange electronic messages with a similar reliability to paper Registered Mail, i.e. systems able to generate trusted electronic evidence attesting that certain events had taken place (submission by a sender of a message to a recipient, delivery of the message to the recipient, etc). By that time, there were already implementations at national level within a number of European countries (like Posta Elettronica Certificata –PEC- in Italy, Electronic Court and Administration Post Office (EGVP) in Germany, IncaMail in Switzerland), and even legislation providing legal value to the evidence set generated by such kind of systems. Those systems also address end to end security issues (authentication, confidentiality, and electronic signatures of messages). They, however, were designed as "closed circuits" and not able to interoperate, so it was not possible to provide evidence on the transmission and/or delivery of one e-mail to senders and recipients subscribed to different systems.

ETSI Specialist Task Force 318 (STF 318 henceforth), a project funded directly by the ETSI membership formalized the concept of Registered Electronic Mail (REM henceforth) and delivered in January 2010 the ETSI Technical Specification (TS) 102 640 on "Registered Electronic Mail (REM)", a document to enable implementations of REM systems issuance of reliable evidence endorsed by relevant legislation, which was structured in the following five parts:
- Part 1: "Architecture" – specifying the architectural elements of Registered E-Mail.
- Part 2: "Data requirements, Formats and Signatures for REM" – specifying data requirements and syntax for the different types of REM messages, evidence and signatures.
- Part 3: "Information Security Policy Requirements for REM Management Domains" - specifying requirements on the security of a Provider of Registered E-Mail (REM Management Domain –REM-MD henceforth).
- Part 4: "REM-MD Conformance Profiles" specifying requirements that any provider claiming REM services provision must accomplish.
- Part 5: "REM-MD Interoperability Profiles" specifying requirements allowing interoperability among different REM service providers.

When the STF-318 was near of finalizing its work, it ascertained that an ever increasing number of Registered E-Mail (REM) and REM-like systems based on SMTP were already operational under development or in the design phase throughout the EU and the EEA (in Italy, Switzerland, France, Belgium, Germany, Spain), and this meant that it could be assessed that over 50% of the EU population already had or shortly would have SMTP based REM like systems available.

At the same time, the Universal Postal Union (UPU) was also developing a SOAP-based mailing system, and the European Commission was supporting and funding a number of very relevant Large Scale European Projects, which had to deal in one way or the other, with the reliable exchange of electronic documents between different parties in different contexts: PEPPOL (Pan-European Public eProcurement On-Line), SPOCS (Simple Procedures Online for Cross-border

Services) and STORK (Secure identity across borders linked) being the most relevant ones at that time. All of them had already decided to use SOAP on HTTP as the technical means for implementing such an exchange, which lead to conclude that SOAP based systems will in the future likely affect most of the EU Member State Public Administrations and, in a time lapse that is still difficult to foresee, possibly nearly all the postal authorities at the global level.

ETSI identified the real risks of a lack of interoperability between those systems based on different protocols. Indeed, if no mechanism suitable to allow mails exchange "across the technical borders" were commonly developed, two possible alternative situations might have occurred:

1. each EU Member State (or group of EU Member States) independently would have developed a mechanism of this type;
2. in those EU Member States where this did not occur, SMTP based and SOAP based mailing systems would not interoperate.

In the first case the consequence would be a multiplication of efforts and disbursement. In the second case there would be a strong penalisation of users, in particular of citizens and SMEs that would need to resort to a duplicated application to interface both systems, yet without even achieving full operations between the two mechanisms.

If, instead, it was decided to develop one EU solution, this interface would allow both "worlds" to take benefit from it with far lower costs.

In the view of the former considerations, ETSI got funding from the European Commission for setting up in March 2010 the Specialist Task Force 402, in charge of developing technical specifications for solving the interoperability between REM solutions based on different transport protocols. The present paper:

- Reviews the fundamental concepts formalized by STF-318 in the ETSI TS 102 640 specification.
- Provides an overview of the major goals of the STF-402
- Provides details of the specifications produced by the STF 402.

2 Review of Registered Electronic Mail fundaments as per STF-318

The ETSI TS 102 640 developed by the STF-318 specified an architecture encompassing the functional model shown in Figure 1.

The core entities in such model are the REM service providers. For them, the STF-318 coined the term Registered Electronic Mail Management Domain (REM-MD henceforth), adopting "Management Domain" term from X.400 specifications. This figure shows two REM-MD systems interacting and one REM-MD system interacting with Standard (i.e. conventional not registered) Electronic Mail providers (SEM-MD).

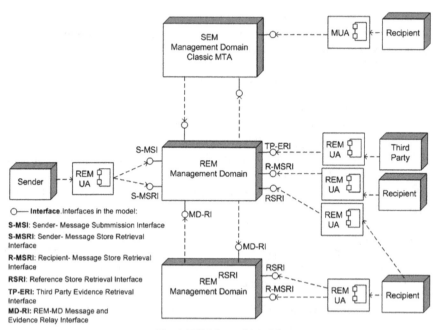

Fig. 1: REM Logical Model

The added value provided by a REM-MD resides in the issuance of a set of evidence eligible to have legal value when supported by suitable legal instruments, which may be used even in court as attestations of the occurrence of certain events. ETSI TS 102 640 specifies a set of evidence. Below follow a list of the mandatory ones:

1. Evidence attesting acceptance of submission. This evidence proves that the REM-MD accepted to take charge of a message submitted in a specific time, and addressed to a certain recipient(s), by a subscriber to that service (sender), authenticated by some specific means. The evidence attesting non acceptance by the REM-MD of that message is also mandatory.

2. Evidence attesting delivery of the message (attesting also its integrity and authenticity) to the recipient's (or recipient's delegate) mailbox, or attesting download of the message by these users when the message is downloaded from a REM-MD repository. The evidence attesting that the message has not been delivered to or downloaded by the purported recipient(s) or delegate(s) after a certain period of time is also mandatory.

The set of evidence also includes optional evidence, like the evidence attesting successful retrieval of message by the recipient; successful (or unsuccessful) forwarding of messages and/or evidence between the REM-MDs serving sender and recipient(s); the evidence attesting successful (or unsuccessful) submission towards SEM systems, and the evidence attesting reception of a message from a SEM system.

TS 102 640 fully defines the semantics and contents of each evidence (among which appear the evidence type, the event that triggers the generation of the evidence, the event time, the details of the sender, and the details of the recipient). It also specifies XML, PDF (as XFA forms), and ASN.1 formats for them. Specifications are also given for the signatures to be applied on them (evidence may be individually or collectively signed by the REM-MD).

In its part 2, TS 102 640 also specified a format for the so-called REM-MD Envelope, an S/MIME construct able to encapsulate the whole original message (including headers, body and attachments), any set of evidence generated by the REM-MD, any notification generated by the REM-MD, and the corresponding electronic signatures generated by the REM-MD, securing the whole package and ensuring authenticity and integrity. Figure 2 shows its structure.

REM-MD Envelope					
	Headers	MIME message headers profiled for a **multipart/signed** MIME message			
	Body (signed data)	Headers	MIME part headers profiled for a **multipart/mixed** message		
		Body	REM-MD Introduction MIME section 0..1	Headers	MIME part headers profiled for a text/plain or a **multipart/alternative** MIME content
				Body	In the case of **text/plain** the body contains a message created by the REM-MD, which is intended to be displayed automatically upon display of the REM-MD Message/REM Dispatch. Text may contain URIs
					In the case of **multipart/alternative** the body contains: • a part headers profiled for an inline body content. The present document contains a message created by the REM-MD, which is intended to be displayed automatically upon display of the REM-MD Message/REM Dispatch. Text may contain URIs • a part profiled for **message/external-body** (RFC 2046). The present document contains an URI for automatic processing of access by reference to a message in a REM-MD Repository
			Original Message MIME section 0..1	Headers	MIME part headers profiled for an enveloped **message/rfc822** message
				Body	Optional full, self-contained RFC-822 message as submitted by the sender. (the Original Message). Only present in REM Dispatch
			REM-MD Evidence MIME section 0..N	Headers	MIME part headers profiled for an **application/octet-stream, application/xml** or **application/pdf**
				Body	Optional REM-MD Evidence as required by the specific content-type
	REM-MD Signature	Headers	MIME part headers profiled to S/MIME **application/pkcs7-signature** signature on the whole REM-MD Message/REM Dispatch		
		Body	S/MIME Signature generated by the Sender's REM-MD covering the whole structure		

Fig. 2: REM-MD Envelope structure

TS 102 640 distinguish two styles of operation for REM-MDs, namely:

1. **Store & Forward** (S&F henceforth). In this style the original message submitted by the sender is directly conveyed to the recipient(s). The message may be packaged with the suitable set of evidence.

2. **Store & Notify** (S&N henceforth). In this style the REM-MD stores the original message in one repository under its control and submits a secure notification to the recipient(s), including the required details for downloading such a message and the suitable set of evidence.

3 STF-402 goals

The major goals of the STF-402, according to its Terms of Reference, are summarized below:

1. To produce technical specifications that allow interoperability between REM solutions based on different formats and transport protocols. These technical specifications will eventually be integrated as a new part of the former ETSI TS 102 640, with three sub-parts.

2. To produce an ETSI Technical Report specifying a test suite for future REM interoperability tests, aiming at overcoming the interoperability hindrance between both, implementations using the same transport protocols and also between SMTP and SOAP based implementations.

3. To take advantage of the opportunity that this action would imply to obtain feedback from UPU, PEPPOL, SPOCS, STORK and other implementers, providers and owners of REM solutions and to let them raise comments to the ETSI TS 102 640, Parts 1 to 5 so that the STF might assess them and eventually incorporate those improvements that makes this TS more tuned with market needs.

4. Organize an international workshop on Registered Electronic Mail and e-Delivery as the optimal way for the STF to present the roadmap of its ongoing work and for getting feedback to the work done so far.

4 New Technical Specifications: TS 102 640 Part 6

The STF-402 produced the new Part 6 of ETSI TS 102 640: "Interoperability between REM- Solutions based on different transport protocols". This document includes three sub-parts, which are briefly presented in the following sub-sections.

4.1 TS 102 640 Part 6-1

ETSI TS 102 640 Part 6-1: "REM-MD UPU Interoperability Profile" specifies requirements for achieving interoperability between REM-MDs that are compliant with ETSI TS 102 640 Parts 1 to 5, and service providers that are compliant with UPU S52-1: "UPU Postal Registered electronic Mail functional specification" (PReM henceforth). Such service providers are called Designated Operators within UPU/PReM specifications (UPU/PReM DO henceforth). For developing this document the STF very closely co-operated with UPU.

The technical approach selected by this document was to specify a set of requirements for setting up the technical components, policies and processes that are able to provide a gateway service between a REM-MD and a UPU/PReM DO, i.e., that are able to forward messages and evidence sets from subscribers in one provider to subscribers in the other provider without loss of trust in the evidence set provided in each side and with preservation of integrity and authenticity of the original message.

As a consequence of this, this document profiles how REM-MD Envelopes originated within the REM domain have to be packaged within SOAP messages and forwarded to the UPU/PReM domain, and the other way around, how REM-MD Envelopes must be extracted from SOAP messages generated within the UPU/PReM domain and be forwarded to the REM domain.

The document also identifies which Web Service operations, from the whole set of operations specified by UPU/PReM, must be implemented by the gateway. Additionally, this document defines a profile of each of these operations, specifying requirements on each of the operations' component data elements.

Finally, the specification deals with the details of mutual recognition achievement between providers at two levels:
- Between different UPU/PReM DOs. This specifications recommends to build up through the utilization of ETSI Trust-Service Status Lists (TSL henceforth), which lists those UPU/PReM DO recognized within the PReM Policy Domain. For this, the document specifies a TSL profile that is tuned to the requirements and needs expressed by UPU.
- Between REM-MDs and UPU/PReM DOs, assuming that also REM-MDs trust building relies on listing the REM-MDs and their statuses within a TSL. In that way, technical means would exist for a REM-MD to check whether a UPU/PReM DO is recognized within UPU Policy Domain and vice versa. At the European level, it is foreseen that the existing REM-MDs can be supervised and/or voluntarily accredited within the corresponding EU Member State and, in consequence listed within the national Trusted List (TL henceforth) issued by such Member State, which is based on the ETSI TSL. The List of Lists, issued, maintained and published by the European Commission, also based on ETSI TSL and which points to all and each EU national TLs, would allow to any UPU/PReM DO to check the status of a specific REM-MD within Europe.

4.2 TS 102 640 Part 6-2

ETSI TS 102 640 Part 6-2: "REM-MD BUSDOX Interoperability Profile" specifies requirements for achieving interoperability between REM-MDs that are compliant with ETSI TS 102 640 Parts 1 to 5, and service providers that are compliant with Business Document Exchange Network (BUSDOX henceforth) set of specifications. Such service providers are called BUSDOX Access Points within BUSDOX specifications (BUSDOX AP henceforth). For developing this document the STF very closely co-operated with PEPPOL (Pan-European Public Procurement Online) LSP WP8 representatives.

The technical approach selected by this document was to specify a set of requirements for setting up the technical components, policies, and processes that are able to provide a gateway service between a REM-MD and a BUSDOX AP. This document covers two different scenarios. In the first one a user subscribed to a REM-MD wants to send a message to a recipient that is registered to a certain BUSDOX network instance, through the REM-MD she is subscribed with. In the second scenario a sender subscribed in a BUSDOX network instance wants to send a message to a recipient who is registered to a certain REM-MD.

In order to completely fulfil the gateway function, this document specifies:
- A new scheme for REM-MD participant identifiers, which allows identifying REM-MDs as participant in the BUSDOX networks.
- A new scheme for REM document identifiers, which allows signalling a certain document exchanged within the BUSDOX network as coming from a REM-MD.
- A profile for the MIME messages submitted by the sender subscribed to the REM-MD when addressed to a recipient subscribed in BUSDOX, which incorporate, within some extra headers, the required details for its transit within the BUSDOX network.
- A profile of the Service Metadata Locator (SML henceforth) and the Service Metadata Publishing (SMP henceforth) services, for allowing the gateway components to retrieve the published metadata of the purported recipient within the BUSDOX network.
- A profile for the MIME message that the gateway components will compose when receiving a SOAP message from the BUSDOX network.
- A profile of the Service Metadata Locator (SML henceforth) and the Service Metadata Publishing (SMP henceforth) services, for allowing the gateway components to retrieve the published metadata of the REM-MD that is serving the purported recipient of a BUSDOX message.

4.3 TS 102 640 Part 6-3

ETSI TS 102 640 Part 6-3: "REM-MD SOAP Binding Profile" defines a binding profile that specifies how a REM-MD may exchange REM Messages and Evidence as XML messages within SOAP structures transported over HTTP. This document actually complements TS 102 640-2 where it is specified how REM-MDs may exchange REM Messages and Evidence as S/MIME structures transported over SMTP.

This document was produced in a very close cooperation with SPOCS (Simple Procedures Online for Cross- Border Services) Large Scale Project, who found itself facing a situation where almost each EU Member State had specified its own Single Point Of Contact portal (in application of Directive 2006/123/EC, Art. 8) including e-Delivery services which were completely unable to interoperate with analogous services within the EU.

In order to overcome this lack of interoperability. , especially in the exchange of reliable electronic evidence, SPOCS defined an interoperability architecture based on national gateways. At the core of the architecture lies a standardized "lingua franca" for gateway-to-gateway communication. The STF 402 and SPOCS agreed to specify this lingua franca as a SOAP on HTTP binding for the exchange of REM-MD Envelope contents, suitably specified in XML for their inclusion within SOAP messages.

This document specifies the XML Schema of two XML messages:
1. The REMDispatch, which incorporates the original message as submitted by the sender, certain metadata (including information on the sender, the recipients and further constraints on the delivery), an optional list of evidence, a XAdES signature and an optional construct, NormalizedMsg, which is a "normalized" form of the original message that

may be produced by the sender's REM-MD, intended to disburden REM-MDs from the need to have knowledge of syntax and semantics of all foreign REM-MD message formats. Figure 3 shows a high level view of this message.

2. The REMMDMessage, which mostly incorporates the evidence list as generated by the REM-MD, for serving to those scenarios where the evidence are not packaged within the same message than the original message.

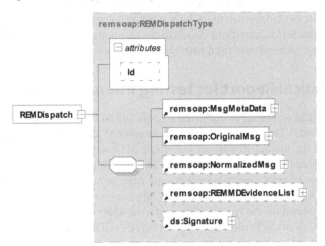

Fig. 3: REMDispatch message structure

This document fully defines the format of the whole SOAP message enclosing the aforementioned messages, specifying the set of standard WS-* bricks to be used as well as their profiling.

In line with the REM concept of maintaining a strict coupling between the original messages and its related evidence, it was chosen to transport REMDispatch/REMMDMessage as a whole in the body of the SOAP message.

Finally, the document fully specifies the whole set of Web Service operations the REM-MDs must support, namely: AcceptREMDispachOperation, invoked by the sender's REM-MD on a recipient's REM-MD in order to send a REMDispatch to a given destination; and AcceptREM-MDMEssageOperation, normally invoked by the recipient's REM-MD on the sender's REM-MD in order to provide some evidence related to events on a REMDispatch which has been previously exchanged.

5 Additional products of STF-402

In addition to the new technical specifications outlined above, the STF-402 has also produced:
- A reviewed version of the TS 102 640 Parts 1 to 5.
- The ETSI Technical Report (TR henceforth): "Test suite for future REM interoperability test events".

Sub-sections below provide additional details.

5.1 New revision of TS 102 640 Parts 1 to 5

The most relevant changes to the previous version of these parts of the aforementioned Technical Specification are:
- The specification of a profile for the Service Information Section of the ETSI TSL for publishing the information of a REM-MD in this kind of lists, which, as it has been mentioned before will play a critical role in building trust between providers across the EU.
- A change in the Evidence structure, which, while keeping backwards compatibility, explicitly incorporates SAML assertions details in the component devoted to include the details of the authentication method used with the user of the service.

5.2 ETSI Technical Report for testing interoperability

The STF-402 has produced the ETSI Technical Report 103 071: "Test suite for future REM interoperability test events". This document defines a number of test suites for supporting interoperability tests within the field of Registered Electronic Mail as specified in ETSI TS 102 640. It adopts a layering approach for the definition of the aforementioned test suites:
- First a number of tests cases on evidence are defined so that entities testing interoperability may concentrate in identifying potential problems caused only by evidence. These tests do not depend on the type of format and transport binding expected. Test cases are specified for each of the Evidence defined within ETSI TS 102 640 Part 2, each one testing a relevant part of the Evidence structure.
- Secondly, a number of tests cases are defined for testing interoperability regarding the REM-MD Envelope format and contents. Tests are defined for testing interoperability when the REM-MD Envelope is including only one section or several combinations of different sections. Different suites are defined for the REM-MDs using SMIME on SMTP and for the REM-MDs using SOAP on HTTP.
- Thirdly, a number of test cases for testing interoperability among the electronic signatures generated by the REM-MD on both the REM-MD Envelope and the individual Evidence are also defined.
- Fourthly, a number of tests cases are defined on complete flows of REM Objects between REM-MDs compliant with ETSI TS 102 640 specifications, so that entities testing interoperability may check several complete flows, including successful and unsuccessful (by well defined reasons) cycles. Test suites for three scenarios are defined:

1. Sender and recipient subscribed to the same REM-MD. Here again, a test suite is specified for REM-MD operating on the Store & Forward style of operation; and one test suite is specified for REM-MD operating on the Store & Notify style of operation.

2. Sender and recipient are subscribed to different REM-MDs. This test suite covers three different scenarios: both REM-MDs operate under Store & Forward style of operation; sender's REM-MD operates under Store & Notify style of operation; recipient's REM-MD operates under Store & Notify style of operation.

3. Finally, a number of tests cases are defined for testing REM-MD/PReM gateway as specified in ETSI TS 102 640 Part 1 Sub-part 1: "REM-MD UPU PReM Interoperability Profile".

6 Conclusions

The present paper summarizes the main achievements of the ETSI STF-402 in the area of Registered Electronic Mail, more specifically in relationship with the provision of means for achieving interoperability between solutions that make use of different set of protocols for formatting the information and for transporting it, namely between those ones that use S/MIME on SMTP and some identified solutions using SOAP on HTTP (UPU/PReM solution and BUSDOX solution).

Additionally, the Part 6-3 complements the original ETSI TS 102 640 as it provides an alternative to the usage of S/MIME structures for packaging messages and evidence, transported on SMTP, by specifying a SOAP message structure also able to package messages and evidence, and by fully defining a Web Service for the exchange of such information using HTTP as transport protocol.

The publication of the Technical Report containing test suites may be considered as the foundations for organizing interoperability tests events, which have proved in the context of other ETSI specifications, to be extraordinarily useful tools for speeding up interoperable implementations and for improving and tuning the specifications themselves.

Finally, is worth to mention the benefits of the close co-operation with UPU, PEPPOL and SPOCS for the production of the different profiles. Special mention deserves the case of SPOCS, as in this case, the technical solution proposed and implemented for solving a problem identified within that LSP, was, simultaneously being standardized in the form of an ETSI TS. This was facilitated by the fact that some of the members of the STF-402 team were also members of the SPOCS project. This lead that by the time that this document was approved by the Technical Committee in charge within ETSI there existed one real implementation deployed for the piloting phase of the project.

The STF-402 firmly believes that this model of joint development of technical solutions and their standardized specification, by the joint work of the EU projects members directly working in the definition and implementation of a certain technical solution, and the experts in the related standardization area, is a perfectly exportable model in the future within the EU context, which would speed up the production of European standards really tuned to the actual needs of the market.

7 References

This list restricts to some core concepts and specifications referenced by TS 102 604. Referenced documents which are not found to be publicly available in the expected location might be found at http://docbox.etsi.org/Reference.

The new version of ETSI TS 102 640: "Electronic Signatures and Infrastructures (ESI); Registered Electronic Mail (REM) is not published yet; initial version is available at: http://www.etsi.org/deliver/etsi_ts/102600_102699/10264001/ thru ...10264005

[1]   ETSI TS 102 640-1: "Electronic Signatures and Infrastructures (ESI); Registered Electronic Mail (REM)"; composed of

   • Part 1: Architecture

   • Part 2: Data requirements, Formats and Signatures for REM

   • Part 3: Information Security Policy Requirements for REM Management Domains

   • Part 4: REM-MD Conformance Profiles

- Part 5: REM-MD Interoperability Profiles (based on SMTP/MIME)
- Part 6.1: REM-MD UPU PReM Interoperability Profile
- Part 6.2: REM-MD BUSDOX Interoperability Profile
- Part 6.3: REM-MD SOAP Binding Profile

[2]   IETF RFC 5322: "Internet Message Format".

[3]   ETSI TS 102 231, v3.1.2, Electronic Signatures and Infrastructures (ESI); Provision of harmonized Trust-service status information; http://www.etsi.org/deliver/etsi_ts/102200_102299/102231/03.01.02_60/ts_102231v030102p.pdf

[4]   ISO/IEC 27001:2005: "Information technology - Security techniques - Information security management systems - Requirements".

[5]   IETF RFC 3851: "Secure/Multipurpose Internet Mail Extensions (S/MIME) Version 3.1 Message Specification".

[6]   W3C Recommendation Web Services Addressing 1.0; http://www.w3.org/TR/ws-addr-core/.

[7]   OASIS Standard WS-Security; http://www.oasis-open.org/specs/index.php#wssv1.1.

[8]   SOAP Version 1.2 Part 1: Messaging Framework (Second Edition), W3C Recommendation 27 April 2007, http://www.w3.org/TR/soap12-part1/

[9]   SPOCS Project, latest corrigenda of D3.2 Specifications for interoperable access to eDelivery and eSafe systems, http://www.eu-spocs.eu/index.php?option=com_processes&task=showProcess&id=18&Itemid=61

[10]   PEPPOL BusDox v. 1.0 specifications, http://www.peppol.eu/work_in_progress/wp8-Solutions%20architecture %2C%20design%20and%20validation/specifications/v1-0-specifications.

[11]   UPU S52-1: "Functional specification for postal registered electronic mail", http://www.upu.int/nc/en/activities/standards/standards-documents.html?download=catalogueStandardsCatalogueOfUpuStandardsEn.pdf&did=367

About ETSI:

ETSI produces globally-applicable standards for Information and Communications Technologies (ICT), including fixed, mobile, radio, converged, broadcast and internet technologies and is officially recognized by the European Commission as a European Standards Organization. ETSI is a not-for-profit organization whose 700 ETSI member organizations benefit from direct participation and are drawn from 60 countries worldwide. For more information, please visit: www.etsi.org

About ETSI Specialist Task Forces (STF):

STFs are teams of highly-skilled experts working together over a pre-defined period to draft an ETSI standard under the technical guidance of an ETSI Technical Body and with the support of the ETSI Secretariat. The task of the STFs is to accelerate the standardization process in areas of strategic importance and in response to urgent market needs. For more information, please visit: http://portal.etsi.org/stfs/process/home.asp

The work carried out here is co-financed by the EC/EFTA in response to the EC's ICT Standardisation Work Programme

CEN/ETSI Rationalised Framework for Electronic Signature Standardisation

Nick Pope[1] · Olivier Delos[2] · Juan Carlos[3] · Marjo Geers[4] ·
Peter Lipp[5] · Paloma Llaneza Gonzales[6] · Béatrice Peirani[7] ·
Antoine de Lavernette[7] · Stefan Santesson[8]

[1](Editor) Thales e-Security
nick.pope@thales-esecurity.com

[2](STF lead) Sealed
olivier.delos@sealed.be

[3]UPC

[4]Collis

[5]IAIK

[6]Llaneza A+A

[7]Gemalto

[8]3xA Security AB

Abstract

Electronic signatures have been adopted in a number of nations as means of assuring the authenticity of electronic documents. As of today the electronic signatures standardization landscape is rather complex and does not offer a clear mapping with the requirements of Directive 1999/93/EC on a community framework for electronic signatures. The current multiplicity of standardisation deliverables together with the lack of usage guidelines, the difficulty in identifying the appropriate standards and lack of business orientation are detrimental to the interoperability of electronic signatures.

This paper describes a framework developed by CEN and ETSI, funded by the European Commission, for rationalising the current electronic signature standards and to provide a basis for any future standards in this area. This paper discusses the impediments caused by the current plethora of standards in this area and the needs for rationalisation, describes the systematic approach proposed for rationalising these standards and outlines the approach proposed to guide users from the business needs to easy selection of the most appropriate standards and options.

This paper is based on the draft CEN ETSI Rationalised Framework [ESig11] drafted by CEN ETSI joint STF 425 funded by European Commission under Mandate 460. This draft has been sent out for public review and comment and the full text is available via the STF web page at: http://portal.etsi.org/stfs/STF_HomePages/ STF425/STF425.asp

Note the Rationalised Framework, and the ideas presented in this paper are subject to revision. The final text will also be available through the same web page and the ETSI document download page.

N. Pohlmann, H. Reimer, W. Schneider (Editors): Securing Electronic Business Processes, Vieweg (2011), 279-289

1 Current Electronic Signature Standards Scene

As a response to the adoption of Directive 1999/93/EC [EUDi99] on a Community framework for electronic signatures in 1999, and in order to facilitate the use and the interoperability of eSignature based solution, the European Electronic Signature Standardization Initiative (EESSI) was set up to coordinate the European standardization organisations CEN and ETSI in developing a number of standards for eSignature products. This initiative produced a number of specifications building on the work of internationally recognised standards for PKI and digital signatures.

As of today the electronic signatures standardization landscape is rather complex and does not offer a clear mapping with the requirements of Directive 1999/93/EC [EUDi99] on a community framework for electronic signatures. The current multiplicity of standardisation deliverables together with the lack of usage guidelines, the difficulty in identifying the appropriate standards and lack of business orientation is detrimental to the interoperability of electronic signatures. It has resulted in a lack of truly interoperable e-signature applications and in a lack of trust in the existing framework. We particularly face problems with the mutual recognition and cross-border interoperability of electronic signatures.

The figure below identifies the most relevant specifications produced under EESSI, as well as their types and interrelationships. It clearly shows that its structure is very complex, the interrelationships and dependencies between specifications are very difficult to be clearly understood, there is a lack of business orientation in its inception, as well as lack of documents devoted to guide stakeholders interested in implementing electronic signatures in their daily operation. Finally, the type of specifications produced was not European Norms, and more than that, some of them, by its own nature, have expired.

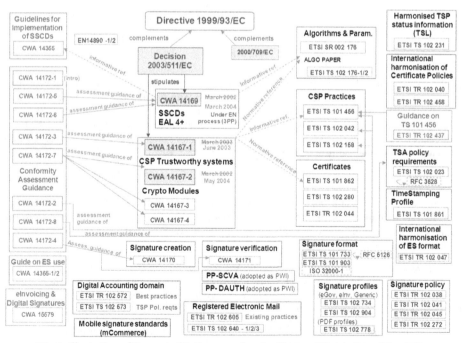

Fig. 1: Illustration of Current of E-Signature Standardisation (Update from [Pipe07])

2 Objectives of the Rationalised Framework

The objectives of the rationalisation of the structure and the presentation of the European Electronic Signature standardisation documents are:

- To allow business stakeholders to more easily implement and use products and services based on electronic signatures. A radical business driven and guidance approach will underlie the rationalisation exercise of the eSignature standardisation framework. Business driven guidance will be provided for maximising successful implementation of eSignatures based products, services and applications by guiding the stakeholders through the definition and parameterisation of the different elements or components of eSignatures and/or eSignature based services/applications and guiding them consequently through the selection of the appropriate standards and their implementation.
- To facilitate mutual recognition and cross-border interoperability of eSignatures.
- To simplify standards, tune them to business needs, reduce unnecessary options and avoid diverging interpretations of the standards
- To target a clear status of European Norm for standardisation deliverables whenever this is applicable
- To facilitate a global presentation of the eSignature standardisation landscape, as well as the availability and access to the standards.

3 Classification Scheme

3.1 Introduction

In order to help business stakeholders implementing electronic signatures and to help them to identify the most relevant standards for their business needs, the proposed rationalised framework of standards is organized around three main aspects, namely:

- Functional areas. The framework is primarily structured in functional areas whose documents exclusively deal with that area. Further, a number of sub-areas are defined for some of them.
- Document types. The framework does not incorporate Technical Specifications only, but different types of documents aiming at providing guidance as well as tools that help stakeholders implementing electronic signatures in their business.
- Rationalized identification scheme of the documents. Finally, the framework proposes a normalized approach to the identification (i.e. numbering) of each single document within the framework, which is tightly related to the *area*, *sub-area* and *type of document-*structure.

The sub-section below provides details of each aspect.

3.2 Functional Areas

The 6 areas for standardisation of eSignatures are:

1) **Signature Creation and Validation:** This area focuses on standards related to the creation and validation of electronic signatures, covering:

    i. the expression of rules and procedures to be followed at creation, verification and for preservation of eSignatures for long term,

    ii. signature formats, packaging of signatures and signed documents, and

    iii. protection profiles for signature creation/verification applications.

2) **Signature Creation Device**: This area will focus on standards related to Secure Signature Creation Devices as defined in the eSignature Directive 1999/93/EC [EUDi99], on signature creation devices used by Trust Service Providers as well as on other types of signature creation devices.

3) **Cryptographic Suites**: This area covers standardisation aspects related to the use of signature cryptographic suites, i.e. the suite of eSignature related algorithms including key generation algorithms, signature algorithms including their parameters and padding method, verification algorithms, and hash functions.

4) **Trust Service Providers (TSPs) supporting eSignatures:** This includes TSPs issuing qualified certificates, TSPs issuing public key certificates other than qualified certificates, Time-Stamping Services Providers, TSPs offering signature validation services, TSPs offering remote signature creation services (also called signing server). The current list covers those services supporting electronic signature which exist to date; other Trust Services may be identified at a future date.

    NOTE: Trust Service Providers supporting eSignatures is closely related to Certification Service Provider as defined in the eSignature Directive 1999/93/EC.

5) **Trust Application Service Providers:** This covers Trust Service Providers offering value added services applying electronic signatures that rely on the generation/verification of electronic signatures in normal operation. This includes namely registered mail and other e-delivery services, as well as long term archiving services. This list may be extended as further services applying electronic signatures are identified.

6) **Trust Service Status Lists Provider**: This area covers the standardisation related to the provision of trust service status lists.

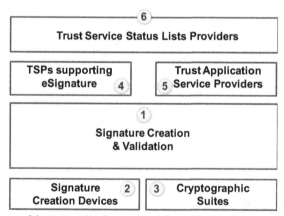

Fig. 2: Overview of the Rationalised Framework for electronic signature standardisation

3.3 Document Types

The documents required for standardisation of each of the above electronic signature functional areas have been organised around the following five types of documents:

1. **Guidance**: This type of documents does not include any normative requirements but provide business driven guidance on addressing the eSignature (functional) area, on the selection of applicable standards and their options for a particular business implementation context and associated business requirements, on the implementation of a standard (or a series of standards), on the assessment of a business implementation against a standard (or a series of standards), etc.

2. **Policy & Security Requirements**: This type of document specifies policy and security requirements for services and systems, including protection profiles. This brings together use of other technical standards and the security, physical, procedural and personnel requirements for systems implementing those technical standards.

3. **Technical Specifications**: This type of document specifies technical requirements on systems. This includes but is not restricted to technical architectures (describing standardised elements for a system and their interrelationships), formats, protocols, algorithms, APIs, profiles of specific standards, protection profiles, etc.

4. **Conformance Assessment**: This type of document addresses requirements for assessing the conformance of a system claiming conformance to a specific set of technical specifications, policy or security requirements (including protection profiles when applicable). This primarily includes conformance assessment rules (e.g. common criteria evaluation of products or assessment of systems and services).

5. **Testing Compliance & Interoperability**: This type of document addresses requirements and specifications for setting-up interoperability tests or testing systems or for setting-up test or testing systems that will provide automated checks of compliance of products, services or systems with specific set(s) of technical specifications.

Fig. 3: Illustration of Document Types in the Rationalised Framework

3.4 Rationalised Framework with Sub-Areas

This rationalisation of the structure for eSignature standardisation framework for some area can be broken down into further sub-area as illustrated in Fig. 4 below. This identifies the primary sub-areas within the six eSignature (functional) areas as described here above. For each area, a common set of up to 5 types of document will address aspects applicable to all sub-areas, and per sub-area additional documents address aspects specific to each sub-area.

So far sub-areas have been identified in areas 1, 2, 4, and 5.

In the Signature Creation and Validation area 1, we have identified sub-areas focusing on the specific standardised Advanced Electronic Signature formats, respectively CAdES, XAdES and PAdES, as well as the Advanced Signature Container (ASiC) format of containers that bind to-gether a number of signed data objects with Advanced Electronic Signatures applied to them or time-stamp tokens computed on them.

In area 2, Signature Creation Devices, three sub-areas have been identified to group documents with regards to the type of signature creation device, namely Secure Signature Creation Devices (SSCDs), signature creation devices used by Trust Services Providers (TSPs) and other signature creation devices.

Area 4, TSPs supporting eSignatures, has been divided in sub-areas focusing on the different types of such TSPs, namely Trust Service Providers issuing Qualified Certificates (TSP$_{QC}$), Trust Service Providers issuing public key certificates which are not qualified (TSP$_{PKC}$), Time-Stamping Service Providers (TSSPs), Signature Generation Service Providers (SGSPs) and Signature Vali-dation Service Providers (SVSPs).

Area 5, Trust Application Service Providers, contains two sub-areas, respectively the one dedi-cated to Registered Electronic Mail (REM) and Registered Electronic Delivery (RED) services provisioning, and the one dedicated to Information Preservation Service Providers (IPSP).

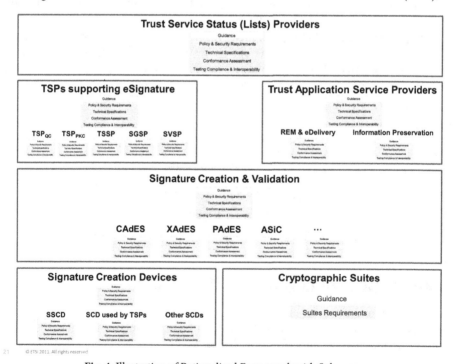

Fig. 4: Illustration of Rationalised Framework with Sub-areas

3.5 Numbering Scheme

As mentioned before, the framework proposes a numbering scheme of each single document, which depends on the area, the sub-area and its type. This will avoid an arbitrary allocation of numbers, completely unrelated to actual contents. It will instead consolidate a framework where similarities in numbers will be a clear signal of close relationship between specifications.

The framework proposes the following numbering scheme: **DD L 66xxx-z-w Vm.a.b**

Below follows a short explanation of the components of this scheme:
- **DD** indicates in letters the type of deliverable in the standardization process (TS –Technical Specification-, EN –European Norm-, etc).
- **L** is a digit also identifying the type of deliverable in the standardization process.
- **66** groups the whole set of documents within the Rationalised Framework or Electronic Signatures under one series: the **66000** series.
- The three digits **xxx** after 66 indicate the serial number of the document, as follows:
  - The first digit ("Xxx") following **66** is a code indicating the area (0-generic; 1-signature creation and validation; 2-signature creation devices; 3-cryptographic suites; 4-Trust Service Providers supporting eSignatures; 5-Trust Application Service Providers; 6-Trust Service Status (Lists) Providers).
  - The second digit ("xXx") is a code for the specific sub-area where the document is actually located.
  - The third digit ("xxX") is a code for the type of document (0-Guidance; 1-Policy and Security Requirements; 2-Technical Specifications; 3-Conformance Assessment; 4-Testing Compliance and Interoperability)-

Finally, in **Vm.a.b**, **Vm** indicates the major version number, **a** indicates the technical version number and **b** the editorial version number.

For example the number EN 366 122 denotes that this EN in the 66 series for area 1 (signature creation and validation), sub area 2 (CAdES) and is a technical specification (last digit 2).

4 Application of Classification Scheme

The application of the classification scheme to signature creation and validation is described below to illustrate how the scheme works.

The documents for electronic signature standardisation for signature creation and validation are summarised in the following table with further details provided below. The table also shows a proposal for the numbering of each document following the scheme outlined in section 3.5:

Table 1: Standards for Signature Creation and Validation

						Signature Creation and Validation
						Sub-areas
						Guidance
TR	1	66	1	0	0	Business Driven Guidance for Signature Creation and Validation
						Policy & Security Requirements
EN	3	66	1	0	1	Policy & Security Requirements for Signature Creation and Validation
EN	3	66	1	1	1	Protection Profiles for Signature Creation & Validation Applications
						Technical Specifications
EN	3	66	1	1	2	Procedures for Signature Creation and Validation
EN	3	66	1	2	2	CAdES - CMS Advanced Electronic Signature Formats
EN	3	66	1	3	2	XAdES - XML Advanced Electronic Signature Formats
EN	3	66	1	4	2	PAdES - PDF Advanced Electronic Signature Formats
EN	3	66	1	5	2	ASiC - Associated Signature Containers
EN	3	66	1	6	2	Signature Policies
						Conformance Assessment
EN	3	66	1	1	3	Conformance Assessment for Signature Creation & Validation Applications (& Procedures)
						Testing Compliance & Interoperability
TS	1	66	1	0	4	General requirements on Testing Compliance & Interoperability of SC&V
TS	1	66	1	2	4	CAdES Testing Compliance & Interoperability
TS	1	66	1	3	4	XAdES Testing Compliance & Interoperability
TS	1	66	1	4	4	PAdES Testing Compliance & Interoperability
TS	1	66	1	5	4	ASiC Testing Compliance & Interoperability
TS	1	66	1	6	4	Testing Compliance & Interoperability of Signature Policies

On the top of the whole set there is a generic **guidance document** (TR 166 100), which targets at stakeholders willing to introduce and implement eSignatures in a business electronic process. This document will provide business guidance for electronic signature standardisation from the viewpoint of signature creation and validation (section 4 of the present paper outlines intial trends of expected guidance).

Following the guidance document there are documents providing requirements for policies for environments applying signature creation and verification (EN 366 101), as well as documents on the security requirements of systems and products for signature creation and verification (EN 366 111). Then the technical specification specify formats and protocols for electronic signatures. Under conformance assessment is general documentation on how signature creation and verification can be assess to be secure and in line with specified policies. Finally, specifications define tests that may be carried out to test compliance with particular technical specifications.

The rationalised framework provides details for all the areas of standardisation based aound the same classification scheme. For details see [Esig11].

5 Guidance

5.1 Introduction

An essential aspect of implementing the CEN/ETSI Rationalised Framework is ensuring that businesses employing electronic signature standards can quickly and easily identify the relevant standard and select the appropriate options. To this end guidance document is required for each area. Depending on the perspective a business user is likely to start in one area but may be lead into the guidance for other areas for further details on the relevant choices. For business users concerned with signature creation and verification may start with guidance on signature creation and validation and then move on to guidance in other areas (e.g. in selecting specifics relating to TSPs supporting eSignatures) as illustrated in the figure below.

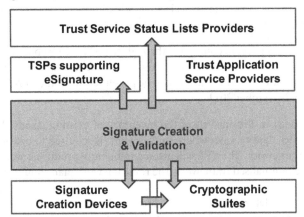

Fig. 5: Signature Creation & validation viewpoint of Rationalised Framework

5.2 The Guidance Approach

It is recognised that guidance is needed to assist in the selection of standards for electronic signature and their implementation in an electronic business process. In order to assist the stakeholder (users, suppliers, regulators, etc.) once he conducted his analysis on the business requirements for the use for eSignatures, the guidance first identifies eSignature business factors that are important when implementing electronic signatures and commonly should be considered in selecting the appropriate solution. Having identified the business factors applicable to the business context (e.g. through a business analysis), the guidance will assist the stakeholder in mapping the applicable business factors into the selection of the appropriate standards and the technical rules for their implementation (potentially including initialisation and parameter configuration of those standards and their options).

Some initial proposals for the factors to be taken into account when selecting standards are given in an annex to the Rationalised Framework. These include:
- factors relating to the application requiring signatures such as: the type of data to be signed and workflow requirements;
- factors mainly influenced by legal provisions associated to the business context in which the business process takes place such as the signature level (e.g. qualified) and requirements for the durability resulting for requirements for retention of signed document;
- factors related to the actor applying an electronic signature such as the type of actor (e.g. physical person, legal person such as a company), and the level of assurance required in that identity;
- requirements to apply other parameters to the signature such as the time and location of signing.

6 Next Steps

The publication of the draft special report on the Rationalised Framework for Electronic Signature Standardisation is the first major milestone of the STF 425 work. This includes the detailed presentation of the draft rationalised framework and a separate annex (available for download either in document form or as an spreadsheet) containing an inventory of existing standardisation at the International, European and national / sector level.

Stakeholders are invited to provide comments through the STF 425 webpage (http://portal.etsi. org/stfs/STF_HomePages/STF425/STF425.asp). Those comments will then be integrated in an updated version of the Rationalised Framework to be presented at a joint CEN/ETSI workshop to be held in Paris end of November 2011.

The next step will consist in the analysis of the inventory of existing standards against the rationalised framework to identify areas where further work is required to provide standards and guidelines to fit the framework. The STF will also consequently produce a work plan for implementing the complete rationalised framework The resulting work plan should at least include the following activities:

- development of guidelines for each of the areas of the rationalised framework,
- supporting the progression of the e-signature specifications through to European Norms (EN),
- further activities needed to complete the rationalised framework ,
- procedures and practices for conformance assessment and interoperability testing of signature creation and verification systems as well as certification service providers,
- preparation of interoperability tests events (both remote and face to face) of signature creation and verification systems, including the necessary infrastructure.

7 Conclusions

As of today the electronic signatures standardization landscape is rather complex and does not offer a clear mapping with the requirements of Directive 1999/93/EC on a community framework for electronic signatures. The current multiplicity of standardization deliverables together with the lack of usage guidelines, the difficulty in identifying the appropriate standards and lack of business orientation is detrimental to the interoperability of electronic signatures. Also due to the fact that many of the documents have yet to be progressed to full European Norms (ENs), their status may be considered to be uncertain.

It has resulted in a lack of truly interoperable e-signature applications and in a lack of trust in the existing framework. We particularly face problems with the mutual recognition and cross-border interoperability of electronic signatures.

The definition of a rationalised framework for electronic signature standards will allow business stakeholders to easily implement and use products and services based on electronic signatures. It will allow a harmonized use of electronic signatures in line with Directive 1999/93/EC and its future revision and will favour the take up of electronic signature standards by the industry. This will result in a simplified access of enterprises and citizens to cross-border electronic public services.

About CEN:
The European Committee for Standardization (CEN) is a major provider of European Standards and technical specifications. It is the only recognized European organization according to Directive 98/34/EC for the planning, drafting and adoption of European Standards in all areas of economic activity with the exception of electrotechnology (CENELEC) and telecommunication (ETSI). CEN's 31 National Members work together to develop voluntary European Standards (ENs). These standards have a unique status since they also are national standards in each of its 31 Member countries. More than 60.000 technical experts as well as business federations, consumer and other societal interest organizations are involved in the CEN network that reaches over 480 million people. For more information, please visit : http://www.cen.eu/cen/pages/default.aspx

About ETSI:
ETSI produces globally-applicable standards for Information and Communications Technologies (ICT), including fixed, mobile, radio, converged, broadcast and internet technologies and is officially recognized by the European Commission as a European Standards Organization. ETSI is a not-for-profit organization whose 700 ETSI member organizations benefit from direct participation and are drawn from 60 countries worldwide. For more information, please visit: www.etsi.org

The European Committee for Standardization (CEN) is a major provider of European Standards and technical specifications. It is the only recognized European organization according to Directive 98/34/EC for the planning, drafting and adoption of European Standards in all areas of economic activity with the exception of electrotechnology (CENELEC) and telecommunication (ETSI). CEN's 31 National Members work together to develop voluntary European Standards (ENs). These standards have a unique status since they also are national standards in each of its 31 Member countries. More than 60.000 technical experts as well as business federations, consumer and other societal interest organizations are involved in the CEN network that reaches over 480 million people. For more information, please visit : http://www.cen.eu/cen/pages/default.aspx

About ETSI / CEN Specialist Task Force 425 (STF 425):
STFs are teams of highly-skilled experts working together over a pre-defined period to draft an ETSI standard under the technical guidance of an ETSI Technical Body and with the support of the ETSI Secretariat. The task of the STFs is to accelerate the standardization process in areas of strategic importance and in response to urgent market needs. CEN ETSI joint STF 425 funded by European Commission under Mandate 460 aims to define a rationalised structure for e-signature standardisation and provide a detailed work programme for subsequent phases to bring current standardisation in line with the rationalised framework. For more information, please visit: http://portal.etsi.org/stfs/STF_HomePages/STF425/STF425.asp

References

[ESig11]   Rationalised Framework for Electronic Signature Standardisation – Joint CEN / ETSI special report to be published. http://portal.etsi.org/stfs/STF_HomePages/STF425/STF425.asp

[EUDi99]   Directive 1999/93/EC of the European Parliament and of the Council of 13 December 1999 on a Community framework for electronic signatures. http://eur-lex.europa.eu/LexUriServ/LexUriServ.do?uri=CELEX:31999L0093:EN:NOT

[Pipe07]   Study on the standardisation aspects of e-signatures, SEALED, DLA Piper et al, 2007. http://ec.europa.eu/information_society/policy/esignature/eu_legislation/standardisation/index_en.htm

Integrating Components from the CIP ICT PSP LSP Projects with a National eGovernment Infrastructure – a Concept Study

Jon Ølnes

Difi - Agency for Public Management and eGovernment
P.O.Box 8115 Dep, N-0032 Oslo, Norway
jon.olnes@difi.no

Abstract

eGovernment services today mainly serve users in a home country. There is a clear need to extend services to cross-border operation to serve even foreign users. Enhancing existing, national eGovernment infrastructures to meet the challenge is a better approach than changing each and every individual service. Cross-border eGovernment services are the topic of the Large Scale Pilots (LSP) conducted under the EU's CIP ICT PSP programme. This paper shows at a conceptual level how components developed by the LSPs can be integrated with a national eGovernment infrastructure (Norway) to enable existing and future services to handle foreign users. There is no plan to implement the concept although implementation should be entirely achievable.

1 Introduction

The topic of cross-border eGovernment services has high attention in the EU; see e.g. documents such as the eGovernment Action Plan [EC-1] and the Digital Agenda for Europe [EC-2]. The EU's internal market is also at stake, e.g. public procurement and service provisioning across borders. eGovernment service use is still mainly national but the need for cross-border services will inevitably increase due to increased mobility of people and services.

This paper is a concept study showing how results from the CIP ICT PSP Large Scale Pilots (hereafter "LSP") [CIP-ICT] might be combined with components of the Norwegian eGovernment ICT infrastructure into a comprehensive system working cross-border. The study targets a real, operational environment, using the Altinn portal [Altinn] as the service platform.

Implementation of the concept has never been planned but some of the LSPs show demonstrators along the lines of this paper. A full implementation is in principle entirely achievable (in the view of the author) since most components are available, and implementation would to a large extent consist of integration activities. If implemented, both quality and sustainability (continued support after termination of the LSP) of components must be carefully considered.

N. Pohlmann, H. Reimer, W. Schneider (Editors): Securing Electronic Business Processes, Vieweg (2011), 290-306

In the absence of an implementation plan, the purpose of the study is only to show at an architectural level how different pieces may fit together in a "jigsaw puzzle" of components to achieve cross-border interoperability. The paper assumes that eGovernment services are provided at a national (state, region, municipality) level. Cross-border services are achieved by enabling the national services to serve actors from other countries, focussing in particular on users from other EU/EEA member states.

An eGovernment service will build on its national eGovernment infrastructure. All LSPs require some national infrastructure to be in place; establishing this is outside of the scope of the LSPs. Cross-border components to enhance a national infrastructure can be instantiated either as distributed components that constitute parts of the national infrastructures or as more or less centralised, "international" components. Required functionality not present in a national infrastructure must be built into the individual eGovernment services of that country.

Chapter 2 briefly presents the LSPs and chapter 3 gives short descriptions of the relevant components provided by them. Chapter 4 describes the relevant components and services of the Norwegian eGovernment infrastructure in the same way. Chapter 5 describes process steps and use of the components to grant a foreign user access to a service in Altinn, exemplified by the PSC (Point of Single Contact) for the Services Directive. Chapter 6 presents conclusions.

Disclaimer: The author's opinions are expressed in this paper, not the opinions of Difi.

2 CIP ICP PSP Large Scale Pilot (LSP) Projects

A part of EU's Competitiveness and Innovation Programme (CIP) is the ICT Policy Support Programme (PSP) [CIP-ICT] to support EU ICT policy decisions. An important part of the ICT PSP is the Large Scale Pilot (LSP) projects for interoperability of eGovernment services across Europe.

The note brings in elements from all existing LSPs except epSOS [epSOS] and e-CODEX [e-CODEX]. epSOS includes activities in identity management that could be relevant but in this paper is out of scope. Results from e-CODEX have not been considered as this project is fairly new. The other LSPs are briefly introduced below. Co-ordination activities aim to reuse results and reduce overlap and inconsistencies in the approaches taken by the different LSPs. Informal co-ordination is also achieved by the fact that there is considerable overlap in participants of the different LSPs.

Norway (Difi) leads the PEPPOL project and is involved in most activities of this LSP. Norway (Norwegian Directorate of Health) participates in epSOS and Norway has an observatory role (the Brønnøysund Register Centre) in SPOCS. Norway does not participate in STORK and e-CODEX; thus no STORK components exist in Norway and these would have to be instantiated to realise the concept described in this paper.

2.1 STORK

STORK [STORK] is more generic in nature than the other LSPs. STORK shall enable use of national eIDs for access to government services in other European countries. Focus is primarily on authentication and provision of identity attributes for access to on-line services.

STORK establishes a pan-European authentication system (see 3.1) and runs several demonstrators on use of this system showing also delivery of identity attributes. Demonstrators run until the end of STORK, end of 2011. In the context of this paper, the demonstrator on delivery of electronic documents (see 3.3.1) is of particular relevance together with similar activities in PEPPOL (the transport infrastructure) and SPOCS.

A follow-up project to STORK is expected to start beginning of 2012.

2.2 PEPPOL

PEPPOL [PEPPOL] is an LSP to support cross-border public procurement in the EU's internal market. From the start, PEPPOL focussed mainly on the post-award phase of public procurement (after entering of an agreement) and system-to-system exchange of structured (XML in this case) procurement messages such as orders and invoices. Later, the pre-award (tendering) phase has also been focussed; in this case most documents will today be non-structured or partly structured information meant to be read by humans. PEPPOL's solutions are used for pilots that run until end of April 2012 (end of the project).

PEPPOL has established a reliable and secure transport (messaging) infrastructure that can be used across Europe (see 3.3.2). Although targeted at support for procurement processes and messages, this component could be adapted to be reusable for other purposes. The infrastructure is based on Web Services, i.e. a middleware type messaging infrastructure.

Since procurement documents can be signed (a requirement for tenders in most countries), PEPPOL has established a pan-European eID and e-signature validation system (see 3.2) This component is generic and open for reuse in other contexts, as described by this paper.

Another area of interest is the specification and eventually instantiation of a European system for issuing and validation of VCD (Virtual Company Dossier) [PEPPOL-D2.2], enabling pan-European exchange of qualification documents for public tenders, mapping national requirements for documentation in one country into the required documents to be submitted by an actor in another country, and attesting to the authenticity of the submitted documents. The VCD idea has been extended by SPOCS, see below.

2.3 SPOCS

SPOCS [SPOCS] is the LSP in support of the EU Services Directive. SPOCS will enhance completion of electronic procedures for businesses that have an interest in cross-border activities. The Point of Single Contact (PSC) defined by the Services Directive will be used. Through the PSC a business shall be able to meet all administrative obligations by electronic procedures and electronic documents.

SPOCS requires secure and reliable document transfer across Europe, including use of signed documents. In this respect, SPOCS provides excellent cases for reuse of infrastructure components provided by other LSPs, inspiring the scenarios described in this paper. SPOCS pilots three professions (travel agent, real estate agent) as examples of service establishment. Pilots run until end April 2012 (end of project).

Reuse of the STORK authentication system and the PEPPOL eID and e-signature validation system has been decided by SPOCS. However, due to requirements that differ from PEPPOL, SPOCS has specified its own interoperability solution including eDelivery and eSafe (see 3.3.3). SPOCS has extended the PEPPOL VCD into a concept termed OCP (Omnifarious Container for eDocuments) [SPOCS-D2.2]. This paper does not detail use of VCD or OCP type services and trusted issuers but mentions this as a potential future step.

3 Components Used from the LSPs

A component from an LSP may be in the form of:
- A service (one or several instantiations);
- Software code for building a service or for integrating to a service;
- A specification, ultimately a standard;
- Legal measures like agreement frameworks;
- Guidelines, best practices etc. – encompassing also policy and other areas.

For software code or specifications, instantiation into a service is necessary for an operational environment. In the cases where the LSPs provide software or services, status may vary from production quality code/services to prototypes instantiated only to be able to run a few trials. Quality must be carefully considered when components are relied upon in an operational environment; unless quality (and security) is sufficient, no critical services can be supported.

3.1 STORK Authentication and Identity Attribute System

STORK has specified and established a pan-European system for authentication and exchange of identity attributes. The main approach builds on one PEPS (Pan-European Proxy Service) in each participating country; extending this to several PEPSes per country or one PEPS serving several countries does not influence the discussions of this paper. The "middleware" approach taken by a few countries is not described here as it has little relevance to Norway.

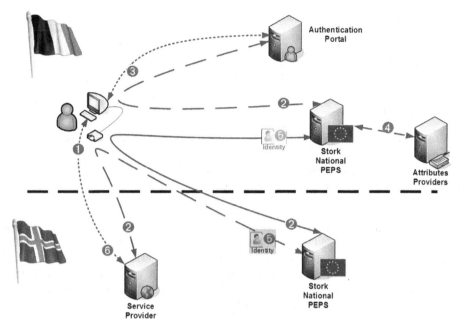

Fig. 1: STORK authentication system

The system is shown in the figure above and the process is briefly described as follows with reference to the figure:

1. A user in Belgium (upper part of the figure) accesses a service in Iceland.

2. The Icelandic service sees a foreign user and redirects the user to the Icelandic PEPS, which is the only PEPS it needs to know. The Icelandic PEPS asks the user for country of origin and redirects further to the Belgian PEPS (all PEPSes are known to one another). The Belgian PEPS redirects to an authentication portal in Belgium.

3. The user authenticates using any mechanism supported by the portal, i.e. the Belgian user is authenticated in the user's home country. Usually, the authentication portal will issue a SAML assertion for the user. The user is redirected back to the Belgian PEPS.

4. Optionally, the Icelandic service may request attributes containing further information about the user (name, address, age etc.). Such requests can be answered by involving attribute providers in the user's home country. An attribute request may be mandatory, meaning that authentication shall fail if the attribute is not available, or optional, meaning that the attribute shall be returned if available.

5. The Belgian PEPS issues a SAML assertion containing the user's identity and requested available attributes and redirects to the Icelandic PEPS.

6. The Icelandic PEPS translates the SAML assertion into the Icelandic SAML format (or other type of assertion) and finally redirects the user to the service.

The STORK system is operational, although the service and security level of PEPS installations and thus the whole system may be questioned. A new CIP ICT PSP LSP will start beginning of 2012 to follow up on STORK results. This project, and other measures taken by the EU Commission, shall ensure continued existence and enhancement of the infrastructure.

3.2 PEPPOL eID and e-Signature Validation Service

PEPPOL has specified and established [PEPPOL-D1.3] an operational service infrastructure for eID validation, primarily to be used in conjunction with e-signatures.

The figure below shows the architecture of the PEPPOL validation service (VS) infrastructure. A document is signed by an actor in country 1, using an eID selected independently by this actor. The document is received by an actor in country 2. Regardless of the eID used, the VS trusted by the receiver is called over a Web Service interface specified in [PEPPOL-D1.3]. The VS returns not only an answer on validity but also on quality and (national) approval status of the eID and e-signature, thus required quality can be assessed by the receiver.

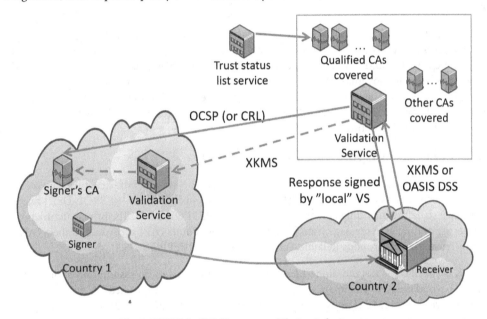

Fig. 2: PEPPOL eID/eSignature validation infrastructure

The VS may import the Trust Status Lists of qualified CAs (Certificate Authority – eID issuer) published by all EU/EEA member states [EU-TSL] and may add additional, non-qualified CAs. If a CA is not directly covered by the VS, the VS may chain the request to another (e.g. national) VS covering the CA in question. The goal is coverage of all qualified CAs in the EU/EEA area and additionally as many other qualified or non-qualified CAs as possible (within or outside of Europe).

In Norway, Difi has signed a contract for VS provisioning with the Polish service provider Unizeto. Unizeto provides a PEPPOL compliant version of their WebNotarius service [WebNotarius], covering more than 400 different CAs in the EU/EEA area and other countries, notably Eastern Europe. The service is available to Norwegian eGovernment services and to any actor involved in PEPPOL pilots for the duration of PEPPOL. The service offers a very high quality and security level and will continue to exist after the end of the PEPPOL project.

3.3 Cross-Border Reliable and Secure Messaging

3.3.1 Email-Based and Middleware-Based Messaging

There are essentially two approaches at reliable messaging in use: middleware based and email based. For email based messaging, the REM (Registered Electronic Mail) specifications of ETSI [ETSI-102-640] can be used. Such systems are deployed in some countries, e.g. Italy and Slovenia. Systems based on middleware (Web Services, possibly also ebXML) are also in use, notably in Austria and Germany. Work on standardisation of "middleware based REM" is in progress in ETSI. Both the PEPPOL transport infrastructure (see 3.3.2) and the SPOCS interconnecting infrastructure (see 3.3.3) are middleware based. See [SPOCS-D3.1] for a survey of existing solutions.

STORK's pilot on eDelivery [STORK-D6.4.3] consists mainly of use of STORK authentication to enable access for users to a "mailbox" in another country. However, STORK also has a limited pilot between Austria and Slovenia on delivery of documents from Austria's middleware based messaging system to Slovenia's email based system and vice versa. In this, a Delivery Gateway supporting a Delivery Gateway Protocol has been specified and developed [STORK-D6.4.1] to bridge the different technologies. This is used as a starting point for parts of SPOCS' work on an interconnecting infrastructure (see 3.3.3).

3.3.2 PEPPOL Transport Infrastructure, BusDox

The PEPPOL transport infrastructure is shown in the figure below. The infrastructure consists of technical specifications termed BusDoX (Business Document Exchange) [PEPPOL-D8.2] and a governance structure including agreements framework [PEPPOL-D8.3]. The infrastructure provides secure and reliable message transfer between Access Points (AP) according to the START (Secure Trusted Asynchronous Reliable Transport) protocol [PEPPOL-D8.2].

BusDoX is specified as a stand-alone messaging system that makes no assumption about functionality beyond the APs. The interface offered to access an AP is not specified, except for a direct user interface called LIME (Lightweight Message Exchange) [PEPPOL-D8.2] that users may use to log on to upload or retrieve messages.

BusDoX is primarily targeted at system-system integration and exchange of structured (XML in the PEPPOL case) documents by automated processes. The specifications are however agnostic to document format and content and thus may also support human readable documents.

An AP may be integrated into other systems, e.g. procurement systems, or it may be a separate component or service. In neither of these cases is there any requirement for secure and reliable messaging outside of the infrastructure itself; i.e. end-to-end security and reliability is not in scope of the BusDoX specifications.

Each actor implementing an AP must enter into the appropriate agreements, and the AP will in turn receive a certificate issued by a CA internal to the PEPPOL infrastructure. The certificate is used to authenticate, sign and encrypt messages exchanged over the infrastructure and vouches for the authorisation of the AP to be part of the infrastructure. This governance structure is designed to survive after the end of PEPPOL but responsibilities need to be settled.

The infrastructure has one central Service Metadata Locator (SML – essentially a DNS type service) for addressing. When sending a message, the sender's AP queries the SML for the AP to use for the receiver for this particular purpose (e.g. e-invoicing in the case of PEPPOL) and for the related Service Metadata Publisher (SMP). The SMP publishes further addressing information and information about business protocols and formats supported. Since an actor may use different APs for different purposes, the business protocol in question is explicitly stated in BusDoX.

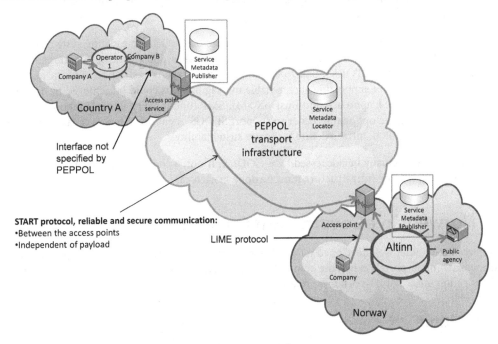

Fig. 3: PEPPOL transport infrastructure

3.3.3   SPOCS Reliable Messaging

Unlike PEPPOL, the requirement of SPOCS [SPOCS-D3.2] is to interconnect existing (national) reliable messaging systems to achieve end-to-end reliable and secure messaging. SPOCS adds: mapping of different message formats and transport protocols (partly based on STORK work, see 3.3.1), cross-solution addressing and routing, trust establishment (based on use of a "SPOCS TSL" (Trust Status List) identifying the approved messaging systems), and authentication and authorisation across systems.

SPOCS addresses primarily exchange of documents in (at least partly) manual processes, where documents are intended for human readers (e.g. PDF format).

SPOCS [SPOCS-D3.2] also specifies the concept of eSafe for secure document storage for actors. There are a few working eSafe solutions, mainly focussed on a national context.

Only messaging systems providing a sufficient quality of service can connect to the SPOCS interconnect infrastructure; thus SPOCS provides end-to-end reliability and security. Note that a messaging system may be just a central mailbox system (e.g. an "eSafe"); no network or distributed functionality needs to be in place at a national level.

Future governance of the infrastructure, after end of SPOCS, is not settled.

3.3.4 Converging the Approaches

As stated above, PEPPOL and SPOCS have different requirements for reliable messaging. Unfortunately, this has led to two different specifications and pilot infrastructures. PEPPOL's need to connect systems directly leads to functionality that is not needed by SPOCS, and BusDoX' lack of end-to-end guarantees does not fulfil SPOCS' needs.

In the opinion of the author, convergence should be possible. Reliable messaging systems could connect to the PEPPOL infrastructure through dedicated APs implementing functionality as specified by SPOCS (and STORK). BusDoX would have to guarantee restriction of traffic to prohibit sending to APs not supporting such reliable messaging. This could be achieved by a combination of SPOCS' TSL approach and BusDoX SML/SMP functionality. Excess functionality in BusDoX must be made optional in order to support SPOCS' scenarios. The governance system specified for the PEPPOL infrastructure facilitates sustainability.

Convergence may actually be addressed by e-CODEX. If not, a choice between BusDoX or the SPOCS interconnecting infrastructure must be done in each case.

4 Norwegian eGovernment Components

Norway has a rather well developed national eGovernment infrastructure. In this paper, the Altinn portal (other portals exist), the comprehensive register infrastructure, and the common authentication service of ID-porten are referred to.

4.1 Altinn

The Altinn portal [Altinn] was established as a single point of access for all reporting obligations from businesses to the Norwegian public sector. The scope of Altinn is increasing, encompassing also services to individual citizens such as tax reporting. Altinn is integrated to the Norwegian register infrastructure and in particular to business registers. Altinn is a service platform where services from various government agencies are defined and configured. Eventually the resulting information is transferred to the IT-systems of the agency in charge.

With respect to reporting from businesses, about 80 % of the reports are received by system integration (Web Services) between Altinn and business systems (e.g. internal accounting systems or systems of accounting agencies). The rest, and most reporting from individuals, is received by online form filling.

Altinn has an extensive logging system coined as a "TTP log" to support evidence in case of disputes. In this, Altinn is considered as a third party separate from the public agency responsible for the actual service accessed. This system is among other things used to implement "simple" electronic signatures of type "click to consent". Most eGovernment services in Norway need only this type of "signature" and Altinn provides the necessary platform.

4.2 Point of Single Contact (PSC)

The Norwegian PSC according to the Services Directive is operated by the Brønnøysund Register Centre as a service in Altinn. At present, the PSC is only a collection of links. The first version of a real, online service is planned to be in place late 2011.

4.3 Messaging Infrastructure

Each actor (business, public agency, individual user) on Altinn has a message box containing a copy of documents submitted and received. One may evaluate if this solution meets the requirements of a SPOCS eSafe solution (see 3.3.3). Altinn forwards messages to the systems of the public agencies by means of Web Services using point-to-point integration separately to each system.

Similar but separate solutions are found in other portals for communication between the public and the private sector, e.g. municipality portals, but altogether no consolidated, reliable messaging infrastructure exists in Norway (except internally in the health sector where a messaging system based on ebXML is in use).

A decision has been taken to make e-invoicing mandatory for suppliers to the Norwegian government. The invoicing system will be based on PEPPOL specifications and invoice services will be provided by commercial actors. To enable interoperability, these actors will be required to establish APs to the PEPPOL transport infrastructure, which will then be used also as a national messaging infrastructure for this purpose.

4.4 The Register of Business Enterprises

Norway has a well-developed register infrastructure that eGovernment services rely upon. The most important registers are the Population Register (see below), the Property Register, and the Register of Business Enterprises. The latter is the responsibility of the Brønnøysund Register Centre, which also runs several other registers.

The Register of Business Enterprises lists information about all enterprises registered in Norway, including identification of persons holding designated roles. Persons are identified by Personal Identifier or D-number (see below).

4.5 The Population Register, Personal Identifier

Norway has a central Population Register under the responsibility of the Norwegian Tax Administration covering the entire population and providing some core attributes of personal information. A programme for modernisation of the register has been launched.

All permanent residents are assigned an 11 digit Personal Identifier (fødselsnummer, English: birth number) of which 6 digits represent the date of birth. From the remaining 5 digits, the person's gender can be derived. The Personal Identifier is used as a common identifier across most eGovernment services as well as for some other purposes, e.g. for banks since banks need to report information to the tax administration. Non-permanent residents and other persons requiring identification (e.g. a person living outside of Norway but with an assigned role in the Register of Business Enterprises) are also registered in the Population Register and are assigned a so-called D-number, which is also a personal identifier. The D-number (the origin of the letter D is long since forgotten) is syntactically similar to the Personal Identifier and can be used equally to this for most purposes.

4.6 ID-porten – "the ID-portal"

ID-porten [ID-porten] is the common identity provider for the Norwegian public sector. When a user (person) needs to log on to a public service, the user is redirected to ID-porten, which presents a menu of authentication mechanisms (eIDs). The user selects mechanism to authenticate. ID-porten then issues a SAML assertion containing the user's Personal Identifier or D-number (the only identifier supported at present) and the quality level of the mechanism. The user is redirected back to the service and the SAML token is transferred as proof of identity.

Several hundred services from more than 100 public agencies, including many municipalities, use ID-porten. Starting mid-2011, Altinn uses ID-porten for authentication.

5 Access to Service in Altinn, Scenario Steps

5.1 Overview, and Connection to Messaging Infrastructure

This chapter shows how the components described above may be combined to support a business process in Altinn, exemplified by a procedure from a foreign user towards the Norwegian PSC in support of the Services Directive. In this aspect, the scenario is similar to SPOCS use cases; however since the integration is done in a generic way in Altinn, all Altinn services may be supported in the same way.

The steps are described as follows:

1. A foreign user registers as an Altinn user (STORK).
2. The foreign user logs on to Altinn (ID-porten and STORK).
3. The foreign user submits documents for an application (document upload, messaging infrastructure, possibly PEPPOL VCD or SPOCS OCD).
4. The documents are verified (PEPPOL eID/e-signature validation service).
5. The result of the application is sent back to the user (STORK login to message box in Altinn or use of messaging infrastructure).
6. The user and the enterprise are entered in Norwegian registers (the Population Register and the Register of Business Enterprises).

For messaging, a simple approach is to use the message box system in Altinn and STORK authentication to access this from abroad. However it would be fairly easy to integrate Altinn to a reliable messaging infrastructure, e.g. by implementing a PEPPOL AP in Altinn. In this case, documents may be submitted to and from Altinn using this infrastructure.

Integrating to the PEPPOL infrastructure is particularly tempting given the fact that 80 % of the reporting to Altinn from enterprises is done by system to system integration. Enabling use of the PEPPOL infrastructure for message transport between systems in the enterprises and Altinn may be beneficial.

5.2 Registering a foreign User in Altinn, Naming

Today, Altinn has a rudimentary "self-registration" to provide a minimum of services to foreign users. The user creates a user profile, supplies basic information (that is not verified) and selects username and password. Referring to STORK assurance levels, this is at best level 1.

This can be enhanced by use of the STORK infrastructure using an authentication procedure as described in the next section to register the user. For this initial authentication, Altinn may request attributes to be returned from the user's home country according to STORK's specifications. A user profile is created, possibly pre-filled by the attributes returned through the STORK infrastructure. Such procedures are extensively used in STORK's demonstrators.

Note that registration is in Altinn as a whole, not for a particular service like the PSC. Thus, the user obtains access to all Altinn services capable of handling a foreign user.

If Altinn is connected to a pan-European messaging infrastructure, the user should be allowed to register an address for delivery of documents, e.g. a REM mailbox in the user's home country. Altinn may submit documents to this address. SPOCS TSL may be used to ensure that the address registered belongs to a messaging system with sufficient capabilities.

A problem that is addressed, but not solved, by STORK is unique and persistent identification (naming) of persons across borders. Preferably, authentication via the STORK infrastructure should return the same persistent identifier (one attribute uniquely identifying the person) each time the person accesses the same service and independent from the authentication mechanism used. Alternatively, a set of several attributes with persistent values may together provide such identification. The identifier or set of attributes may be "universal" (same for all services and all contexts), sectoral (services in a particular context) or even service specific.

For some countries, e.g. Norway, this is achievable. If Norway integrates to the STORK infrastructure (not in place today) the Norwegian PEPS will redirect to ID-porten for authentication. ID-porten authenticates the person by the Norwegian Personal Identifier or D-number regardless of authentication method. The Personal Identifier may in turn be translated into other identifiers for foreign services, either by ID-porten itself, by the Norwegian PEPS, by the Population Register (see 5.7) containing several identifiers, or otherwise.

For some countries, either naming/identification of the user will depend on the authentication method (different names for different mechanisms), and/or the name will change over time; e.g. when a certificate expires a new certificate is issued with different naming attributes.

Naming and identification is not further discussed in this paper. It is assumed that a registered user in Altinn is recognised each time the user authenticates by identifier or attributes; possibly this requires that the same authentication mechanism (in the user's home country) is used every time.

5.3 Logging on to Altinn Using ID-porten and STORK

Two alternatives can be seen for authentication of foreign users in Altinn:

1. Altinn is agnostic to the origin of the user and always redirects to ID-porten for authentication. ID-porten must separate between Norwegian and foreign users and will redirect the latter to the Norwegian PEPS.

2. Altinn itself separates between Norwegian and foreign users. Norwegian users are direct-ed to ID-porten while foreign users are directed to the Norwegian PEPS. This is simpler to implement in the short term but leaves more complexity to Altinn. Also, other future services in need of STORK functions will need both integrations.

Alternative 1 is preferred and the process flow is shown in the figure below. The advantage is that Altinn (and other eGovernment services in Norway) even in the future will need only integration to ID-porten for authentication. Only ID-porten, not individual services, needs to integrate to the Norwegian PEPS. This will require adaptation of the existing ID-porten interface, including the SAML token format for the Norwegian public sector:

- The SAML token returned from ID-porten must be adapted to use identification from the user's country of origin as alternative to Norwegian Personal Identifier.
- The redirection from Altinn to ID-porten should be extended to allow request for attrib-utes as defined by STORK.
- If the previous point is implemented, the SAML token returned from ID-porten must be able to mediate relevant attributes as defined by STORK.

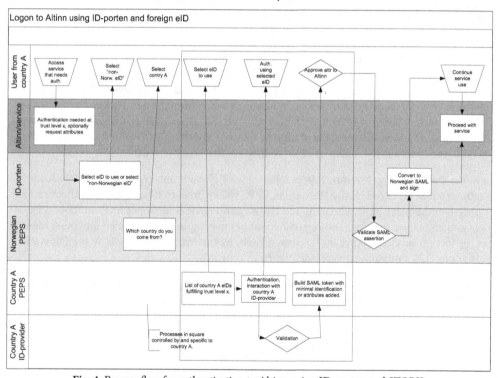

Fig. 4: Process flow for authentication to Altinn using ID-porten and STORK

5.4 Submitting Documents to the Service in Altinn

After registering in Altinn and logging in to Altinn, the user is ready to access the service, e.g. the PSC for the Services Directive. Access may consist of form filling in Altinn and/or submission of documents needed to support the service use.

Document submission may be done in various ways:

- Documents are uploaded by use of the Altinn user interface.
- If Altinn is connected to a pan-European messaging infrastructure such as the PEPPOL infrastructure or the SPOCS system, documents may be submitted through the user's national messaging system addressing the service in Altinn as receiver.
- In the future, a document package like the PEPPOL VCD or SPOCS OCD may be defined for the particular operation, e.g. applying to a competent authority in Norway through the PSC to obtain permission to offer a specific service.

For some services, e.g. the PSC, documents will typically be signed by the user, or by other representatives of the enterprise submitting the application, or by other actors such as the issuer of a certificate or attestation needed to support the application.

Following submission, a receipt shall be given to the user by Altinn. In the simplest case, this may be display of a confirmation web page to the user, preferably with functionality that allows storing of a printable version of the page. Alternatively, or additionally, a receipt may be submitted to the user's message box in Altinn and/or submitted via the PEPPOL (or SPOCS) infrastructure to the user's home messaging system.

A submitted receipt should be signed by Altinn. In Norway a corporate, non-personal signature would be recommended; this uses neither a qualified signature nor a qualified certificate since such a certificate can only be issued to a natural person in Norway.

5.5 Validating Signed Documents, Using the PEPPOL VS

When documents are finally submitted to the PSC in Altinn, two tasks must be performed:

1. Verify signatures on all documents and ensure that they formally fulfil necessary requirements for quality and approval status (e.g. qualified signature or advanced signature using a qualified certificate).
2. Verify that all documents needed have been submitted and that the documents are authentic and trustworthy. This is not detailed further in this paper, apart from the observation that verification may be done either in Altinn or at the competent authority, and that use of a VCD/OCD approach will simplify automated verification of documents.

The current service offered by a PEPPOL VS handles only eID certificates. Signature processing must be done in Altinn. [PEPPOL-D1.3] defines a service interface allowing entire documents to be submitted and verified (all signatures on the document) but this interface is not implemented. Following successful signature verification in Altinn, considering signature format and related requirements, the certificate(s) that supports the signature(s) is submitted to the Unizeto service by Web Service.

The response from the VS assesses both validity and quality of the certificate according to the quality rating system defined in [PEPPOL-D1.3]. Certificates/signatures that are valid but not according to quality (signature policy) requirements may be discarded.

Following successful signature verification, documents are sent on to the competent authority, which need not bother to check signatures again (signatures may even be removed if desired). Altinn must however perform some post-processing, at a minimum logging the response(s) from the VS and possibly building XAdES/CAdES/PAdES structure(s) suitable for archival. Documents are stored in the Altinn message boxes of both the user and the competent authority. Note that archival is the responsibility of the competent authority; Altinn only provides the option of a "copy archive" together with the TTP log.

5.6 Sending Answer back to the User

Following processing by the competent authority, a document containing the answer (grant or denial) shall be delivered to the user. The document should be signed by the competent authority using either a personal signature from the responsible person (in Norway this can be expected to be an advanced but not qualified signature supported by a qualified certificate) or a corporate signature representing the authority as such (neither signature nor certificate will be qualified).

Two alternatives can be envisaged for delivery; both as depicted by STORK's pilot on message delivery and message delivery scenarios in SPOCS:

- The user is asked to log on (via ID-porten and STORK) to the "message box" in Altinn to collect the document. When the user downloads the document, the event is logged in Altinn as receipt confirmation.
- The document is sent from Altinn via the reliable messaging infrastructure (PEPPOL or SPOCS) to the user's account in the home country messaging system.

In the latter case, the user should verify signatures upon receiving the document; e.g. the home country messaging system may integrate to a PEPPOL VS service for this purpose.

The messaging system of the user shall ensure that a receipt confirmation is returned to Altinn. If supported, the confirmation may be signed by the user; however this is not likely to be required by a service in Norway. If the confirmation is signed, the signature is checked by the PEPPOL VS when arriving in Altinn.

5.7 Entering User and Enterprise in Norwegian Registers

Upon receiving a permission to offer a service or other business activity in Norway, the enterprise may be registered in the Norwegian Register of Business Enterprises.

This registration includes naming of persons that are authorised for certain roles related to the enterprise, e.g. managing director, board member, accountant, and auditor. At present, all persons are identified by the Norwegian Personal Identifier (D-number allowed). This is a common situation in Norway as well as other countries: national identifiers are used as "user names" in eGovernment systems.

A suggested solution is to enrol foreign persons on demand in the Norwegian Population Register and assign D-numbers to them. Following an authentication and attribute exchange procedure via ID-porten and STORK, the persistent identification of the person from the home country is registered in the Population Register and a D-number is created and linked to this identification. The Population Register will thus hold a mapping from the foreign identifier/name to the Norwegian D-number.

Enrolment of a person in the Population Register may need to be done at various steps of a process depending on the ability of the service in question to handle users without a Norwegian identifier. In some cases enrolment can be done after request processing and only if the user actually obtains some rights or obligations in Norway; in other cases enrolment may have to be done before even entering the service. The latter may call for the possibility of transient entries in the Population Register, to be deleted if the user does not obtain anything.

The user will not need to obtain a Norwegian eID. Following authentication through ID-porten and STORK, ID-porten may check with the Population Register whether a mapping to D-number exists. Alternatively, the mapping from foreign identification to D-number may be recorded somewhere else, e.g. in ID-porten, instead of in the Population Register.

A programme for modernisation of the Population Register is in progress and should consider the necessary measures to enable enrolment based upon an authenticated identity from another country, provided that naming is sufficient (see 5.2) and that identification and authentication are sufficiently reliable. An assurance level may be assigned to the register entry to show the quality of the identification/authentication.

5.8 Norwegian Attributes, STORK, ID-porten, Pop. Register

The scenarios above do not cover the situation of a Norwegian user requesting access to a service in another country. As usual for STORK, the result would be a redirection to the Norwegian PEPS, which in turn would redirect to ID-porten for authentication. Presumably, the Norwegian PEPS and ID-porten should be co-located. After authentication, the user is redirected back from ID-porten to the Norwegian PEPS and on to the service.

The existence of the central Norwegian Population Register gives an excellent opportunity to support attribute requests according to STORK. If ID-porten is integrated with the Population Register, most attribute requests can be answered by register lookups. Note that even if the user must approve attribute delivery to the service in question according to standard STORK procedures, further checks may be necessary to ensure that delivery is legally permitted according to Norwegian legislation.

User approval of attribute delivery is a PEPS functionality in STORK; however in Norway this should be a function of ID-porten, allowing similar attribute delivery also in the national case where the PEPS is not involved.

6 Conclusion

This paper shows at a conceptual/architectural level how components from the CIP ICT PSP Large Scale Pilots (LSP) can be used to enhance a national (Norway in this case) eGovernment infrastructure to provide generic support for cross-border services. No implementation of the solution is planned although this could be entirely achievable.

The LSP components used are: the STORK authentication and attribute exchange system, PEPPOL's eID and e-signature validation service, and cross-border reliable messaging infrastructure as specified by both PEPPOL and SPOCS. The VCD/OCD concept developed by PEPPOL and SPOCS is also referred to.

The national infrastructure components used are: the Altinn portal as service platform and national messaging system, ID-porten as a common authentication service, and the Norwegian register infrastructure represented by the Population Register and the Register of Business Enterprises. All services instantiated in Altinn can build on the combined infrastructure consisting of national and LSP components. Enabling services for cross-border operation is used at an infrastructure level and not at a per service level.

References

[Altinn]   Altinn portal, information in English. https://www.altinn.no/en Altinn is run by the Brønnøysund Register Centre. http://www.brreg.no/english

[CIP-ICT]   Competitiveness and Innovation framework Programme, ICT Policy Support Programme. http://ec.europa.eu/information_society/activities/ict_psp/index_en.htm

[EC-1]   European Commission. The European eGovernment Action Plan 2011-2015 – Harnessing ICT to Promote Smart, Sustainable & Innovative Government. Communication from the Commission to the Council, the European Parliament, the European Economic and Social Committee and the European Committee of the Regions, December 2010.

[EC-2]   European Commission. A Digital Agenda for Europe. Communication from the Commission to the Council, the European Parliament, the European Economic and Social Committee and the European Committee of the Regions, August 2010.

[e-CODEX]   e-CODEX – eJustice Communication via Online Data Exchange. http://www.ecodex.eu

[epSOS]   epSOS – European Patients, Smart Open Systems. http://www.epsos.eu

[ETSI-102-640] Electronic Signatures and Infrastructures (ESI); Registered Electronic Mail (REM); Architecture, Formats and Policies – Parts 1-2. ETSI TS 102 640, 2010.

[EU-TSL]   EU-level Trust Status List (TSL) pointing at national lists issued by competent authorities in the EU/EEA Member States. Human readable (PDF) and machine readable (XML) lists. https://ec.europa.eu/information_society/policy/esignature/trusted-list/tl-hr.pdf https://ec.europa.eu/information_society/policy/esignature/trusted-list/tl-mp.xml

[ID-porten] ID-porten (the ID-portal), the common identity provider for the Norwegian public sector, some information in English. http://www.difi.no/elektronisk-id/frequently-asked-questions-about-electronic-id ID-porten is run by Difi. http://www.difi.no/artikkel/2009/11/about-difi

[PEPPOL]   PEPPOL – Pan-European Public Procurement On-Line. http://www.peppol.eu

[PEPPOL-D1.3] Demonstrator and Functional Specifications for Cross-Border Use of eSignatures in Public Procurement. PEPPOL Deliverable D1.3, 2011.

[PEPPOL-D2.2] Specification of Architecture and Components Enabling Cross-Border VCD. PEPPOL Deliverable D2.2, 2010.

[PEPPOL-D8.2] Version 1.0 of the PEPPOL Transport Infrastructure. PEPPOL Deliverable D8.2, 2010.

[PEPPOL-D8.3] Transport Infrastructure - PEPPOL EIA (Enterprise Interoperability Architecture). PEPPOL Deliverable D8.3, 2011.

[SPOCS]   SPOCS – Simple procedures Online for Cross-border Services. http://www.eu-spocs.eu

[SPOCS-D2.2] Standard Document and Validation Common Specifications. SPOCS Deliverable D2.2, 2010.

[SPOCS-D3.1] Assessment of Existing eDelivery Systems & Specifications Required for Interoperability. SPOCS Deliverable D3.1, 2010.

[SPOCS-D3.2] Specifications for Interoperable Access to eDelivery and eSafe Systems – Functional Specification, Architecture and Trust Model. SPOCS Deliverable D3.2, version 1.1, 2011.

[STORK]   STORK – Secure Identity Across Borders Linked. https://www.eid-stork.eu

[STORK-D6.4.1] eDelivery – Functional Specification. STORK Deliverable D6.4.1, 2009.

[STORK-D6.4.3] eDelivery – Detailed Planning. STORK Deliverable D6.4.3, 2010.

[WebNotarius] Unizeto WebNotarius validation service. https://www.webnotarius.eu

On Secure SOA Based e/m-Government Systems

Milan Marković

Banca Intesa ad Beograd, Bulevar Milutina Milankovića 1c, Belgrade, Serbia
milan.z.markovic@bancaintesabeograd.com

Abstract

In this paper, a possible model of secure e/m-government system based on secure desktop or JAVA mobile application and SOA-Based e/m-government platform is described. The proposed model consists also of additional external entities/servers, such as: PKI, XKMS, STS, UDDI and Time Stamping Authority. An example of the secure e/m-government online services is particularly emphasized: sending e/m-residence certificate request and obtaining the e/m-residence electronic document (e/m-residence certificate) as a municipality's response. This scenario example could also serve as a model for any e/m-government online services consisting of sending some requests to the e/m-government platforms and obtaining responses as corresponding governmental electronic documents.

1 Introduction

This work is related to the consideration of some possible SOA-based secure e/m-government online systems, i.e. about secure communication between citizens and companies with the small and medium governmental organizations, such as municipalities, or other governmental organizations and/or agencies.

We have considered a general model of such systems consisting of three main parts:

- Secure JAVA mobile client application and/or JAVA desktop application,
- SOA-Based e/m-government platform, and
- External entities: PKI (Public Key Infrastructure), STS (Security Token Service), XKMS (XML Key Management Service), TSA (Time Stamping Authority), and UDDI (Universal Description Discovery and Integration).

Although the generic e/m-government model is proposed and considered, and although the model supports the usage of desktop JAVA web service application too, a main emphasis and contribution of the paper is the Secure JAVA Mobile Web Service application communicating with the Web Service of the proposed m-government platform. Thus, in a sequel, we will use only a term m-government system and consider only secure JAVA Mobile application for simplicity. In a process of developing the secure JAVA Mobile Application we have used the J2ME development environment [KoVi04].

The work presented and examples described are included in the general framework of the EU IST FP6 SWEB project (Secure, interoperable cross border m-services contributing towards a trustful

N. Pohlmann, H. Reimer, W. Schneider (Editors): Securing Electronic Business Processes, Vieweg (2011), 307-316

European cooperation with the non-EU member Western Balkan countries, SWEB) [MaDj10], [MaDj11], [PKPM08], [CGH+08].

The paper is organized as follows. A consideration of security in mobile communication is given in Chapter 2 while description of the possible m-Governmental architecture is given in Chapter 3. Chapters 4 is dedicated to possible m-residence certificate scenario. Chapter 5 is dedicated to the consideration about secure JAVA mobile Web Service application while SOA-based Web service platform is described in Chapter 6. Conclusion is given in Chapter 7.

2 Security in Mobile Communication

This paper mainly identifies the need for security in mobile communications, such as mentioned in [MaDj10], [MaDj11], and presents a secure mobile framework that is based on widely used XML-based standards and technologies such as XML-Security (XML-Signature, and XML-Encryption) and Web Services Security (WS-Security).

Besides security aspects of the XML communication, a possible Federation ID system based on security token service is considered too. In this work, SAML (Security Assertion Markup Language) tokens/assertions have a role of security tokens. Communication between JAVA mobile application, or the SOA-Based platform itself, and STS server is realized by using WS-Secured SOAP communication.

We have also used XKMS protocol [MaDj10], [MaDj11] in the proposed m-government system. It enables the integration of keys and certificates into mobile applications as well as the implementation of PKI X.509v3 digital certificate registration, revocation, validation and update mechanisms.

Besides STS and XKMS, the client applications and the platform used also the time stamping functionalities in order to create timely valid electronic documents with digital signatures of long-term validities. In this sense, a suitable TSA also represents an important part of the proposed model.

Regarding security needs in m-government online systems, the proposed model addresses main security functionalities (business security needs) in a following way:

- **User authentication** – the Secure JAVA Mobile application needs the user password based authentication to launch the application itself. This prevents accessing the application from non-authorized persons. In fact, there is a two-step user authentication procedure since the user needs to present another password (passphrase) to enable application access to its asymmetric private key stored in the JAVA key store inside the application for the functions that needs the user's electronic signature.
- **User identity** – as reliable electronic identities of different users and entities in the proposed system, PKI X.509v3 electronic certificates are used issued by corresponding Certification Authorities (CA).
- **Federation Identity** – in the proposed model, we used SAML token as the federation ID. SAML token is issued to users, government civil servants or platforms itselves after proper entity's authentication to the STS server. The STS server issues the SAML token to the users after successful entity's authentication based on the entity's electronic certificate.

- **User authorization to the proposed platform** – a process of the user authorization to the platform is based on the obtained SAML token carrying the user's role which is presented to the m-government platform together with the signed m-governmental service request. The SAML token could also serve as the Federation ID to access any other Web service-based governmental platform without a need for the user to be authenticated again.
- **Authenticity, Integrity and Non-repudiation of transactions** – the user applies digital signature (XML Signature) on each request sending to different entities (STS server, m-government platform) based on RSA algorithm.
- **Confidentiality** – in the proposed model, the WS-Security mechanism (WS-Encryption) is used to encrypt all communication between the Secure JAVA Mobile application and STS server and/or m-government platform. This request-response application protocol is much more suitable for the mobile communication system compared to session-based SSL/TLS protocols, proposed in [LeLS07], since it does not need much more expensive session establishment between the user and the server side.
- **Electronic signature verification on the user's side** – Secure JAVA mobile application has functions of electronic signature verification of transactions (Web service responses from different entities) including electronic certificate validation function. The latter function is implemented by applying communication with XKMS server which is more natural solution to SOAP based request-response Web service systems than using CRL (Certificate Revocation List) validation or other techniques described in [LeLS07].
- **Long-term validity of transactions** – in order to justify reliable time of creating m-government requests and documents, we used time stamping in order to include reliable and signed time stamps both to the user's requests and governmental responses (m-government documents). This enables a more reliable proof of time when requests/documents are created as well as a fact if that signer's electronic certificates were valid in the moment of signing. Besides, implemented time stamping functionality enables possibility to realize functions of long-term validity of stored requests/documents.

3 Possible e/m-Government Architecture

The proposed m-government model is presented on Fig. 1 [MaDj10], [MaDj11], [PKPM08], [CGH+08] and consists of:

- Mobile users (citizen, companies) who send some Web Services requests to m-government platform for a purpose of receiving some governmental documents (e.g. residence certificate, birth or marriage certificates, etc.). These users use secure JAVA mobile Web Service application for such a purpose.
- Fixed/Desktop users connecting to the proposed Web Service governmental platform through some desktop secure Web Service application (could be JAVA-based too).
- Web Service endpoint implementation on the platform's side that implements a complete set of security features. Well processed requests with all security features positively verified, the Web Service platform's application proceeds to other application parts of the proposed SOA-Based platform, including the governmental Legacy system for issuing actual governmental certificates requested. In fact, the proposed platform could change completely the application platform of some governmental organization or could serve as the Web Service „add-on" to the existing Legacy system implementation. In the latter case, the Legacy system will not be touched and only a corresponding Web Service interface should

be developped in order to interconnect the proposed SOA-Based platform and the Legacy governmental system.

- External entities, such as: PKI server with XKMS server as a front end, STS, UDDI and TSA.

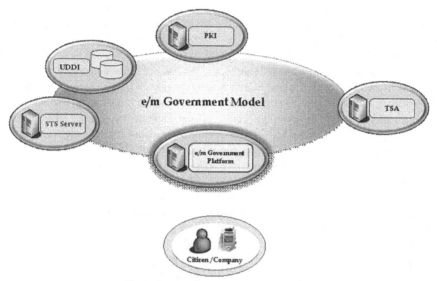

Fig. 1: Proposed e/m-government model

Functions of the proposed external entities are following:

- **STS server** – is responsible for strong user authentication and authorization based on PKI X.509v3 electronic certificate issued to users and other entities in the proposed model. Communication between STS server and the user's JAVA mobile application is SOAP-based and secured by using WS-Security features. After the succesful user authentication and authorization, the STS server issues a SAML token to the user which will be subsequently used for the user authentication and authorization to the Web Service of the proposed m-government platform. The SAML token is signed by the STS server and could consist of the user role for platform's user authentication and authorization.

- **UDDI server** – is a platform-independent, XML based registry for businesses worldwide to list themselves on the Internet. In this paper, UDDI server is used to store information about SWEB-enabled municipal organizations including WSDLs and URLs defining a way to access these m-governmental platforms.

- **PKI server** - is responsible for issuing PKI X.509v3 electronic certificates for all users/entities in the proposed m-governmental model (users, civil servants, administrators, servers, platforms, etc.). Since some certificate processing functions could be too heavy for mobile users, the PKI services are exposed by the XKMS server which could register users, as well as locate or validate certificates on behalf of the mobile user. This is of particular interests in all processes that request signature verification on mobile user side.

- **TSA server** - is responsible for issuing time stamps for user's requests as well as for platform's responses (signed m-documents).

4 Possible m-Residence Certificate Scenario

In this Section, we will describe a local m-Residence scenario where the citizen requests a governmental document from his original municipality of residence.

A citizen of city A needs a certification for his principal residence in city A. He will contact the municipality of city A for that. In this process, he sends a request to this municipality first. The municipality creates his mRCertificate. He gets a final notification message and can pick up his mRCertificate afterwards.

In a more detailed view, there are three system objects belonging to the municipality. It is the platform, the local IT Infrastructure (Legacy system) and the civil servant as the human actor. The citizen sends his request to the platform, which in return first sends a notification back about the incoming request and then forwards the request to the Civil servant for approval. After this, the request is sent to the legacy system, where the mRCertificate is created. After that, the Civil servant has to approve this mRCertificate. Furthermore, there is a final notification sent to the mobile to inform the citizen that he can pick up his mRCertificate. Finally, the mRCertificate needs to be retrieved by the citizen using the document retrieval service (see Fig. 2).

In order for a mobile user to request a specific m-government service, following all the steps described on Fig.2, he/she must successfully complete the previously described steps:

- To successfully install the secure stand-alone JAVA application on the mobile device.
- To be successfully authenticated to the application, using the cryptographic credentials associated to the application.

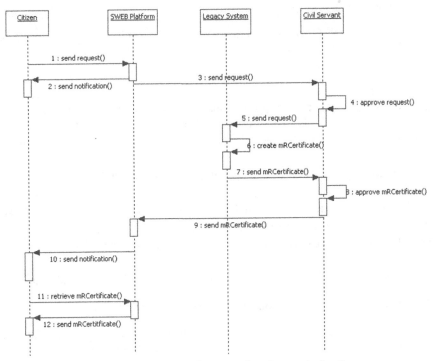

Figure 2: Local m-Residence certificate's scenario details

5 Secure JAVA Mobile Web Service Application

In this Chapter, we give a functional description of the secure JAVA mobile Web Service application for a purpose of secure communication with the described m-government SOA-based platform [MaDj10], [MaDj11].

The assumption is that the user already has the JAVA application on his mobile phone/terminal and thus a procedure of downloading and activating the application is beyond a scope of this paper.

This client application comprises of following functionalities objects:

- Graphical User Interface (GUI) for presenting business functionalities to the end user. The GUI object of the proposed JAVA mobile web service application is responsible to show user interface that enable calling of function for authentication of the end user and presenting the core functionalities to the end user.
- Business functionalities object is responsible for implementation of the core SWEB client-base functionalities:
  - Secure requesting and receiving the m-residence certificate from the corresponding municipality SOA-based platform, receiving a notification and delivering the obtained certificate to some interested party.
  - Secure sending of other kind of predefined message (for example m-invoice) to the corresponding municipality platform and receiving the notification from the platform.
- The Security object of the considered JAVA mobile application is responsible for overall application-level security functionalities.
- Communication object.

The Java mobile client used for communication with the platform is developed by using J2ME CDC1.1 platform. There are forms (screens) on mobile phone application used to perform communication with the platform.

The first form is ‚Logon form'. The user should enter its username and password after which verification will be passed to the next form. Also, the language that will be used in the whole application can be chosen on this form. After successful verification of username and password, ‚Functions form' will be passed to the user where a task that needs to be done can be chosen. The available tasks are:

1. Change Password - used for changing login password in order to access the mobile application.
2. mResidence Certificate Request - used for sending request for mResidence certificate to the municipality (to the Web service of the m-government platform).
3. Download mResidence Certificate - used for downloading prepared mResidence certificate from the municipality.
4. Send m-Invoice - used for preparing and sending m-invoices to the municipality.

The change of logon password can be done via ‚New Password' simple form.

By pressing button for sending of mResidence Certificate Request, user will jump to ‚Residence Cert' form where the receiving municipality should be chosen from the list that appears on the form.

The next step is entering PIN used for reading user private key that is stored in KeyStore on the file system on the user mobile device. This should be done on the ‚PIN' form. The result of request processing (error or success) is displayed on the ‚Final' form. All communications between client and servers are here synchronous. It means that each request produces response.

After successful processing of user's mResidence Certificate Request, the platform prepares the required mResidence Certificate and sends the SMS message to the user mobile device as an approval that the m-government document is ready for this user. This part of communication between user and the platform is asynchronous.

The received SMS message is a signal for the user to perform download of mResidence Certificate via option of Download certificate. On the ‚Doc ID' form, the Task ID should be chosen from the list. The Task ID uniquely identifies the mRCertificate that should be downloaded. The result of download will also be displayed on the ‚Final' form (see Fig 2).

In order to realize the abovementioned functionalities, the mobile JAVA application communicates with following external entities:

- STS server,
- XKMS server,
- TSA server,
- M-government platform – Web service exposed for the SOAP based m-government platform.

The communication between JAVA mobile application and STS server is realized by using WS-Secured SOAP communication. According to the scenarios, the JAVA mobile application sends the RST (Request for Security Token) to the STS server and, if everything is ok, receives back the RSTR (RST Response) which consists of URL of the municipality and the SAML token with the user's role on the m-governmental platform.

The communication between the JAVA mobile application and the Web service of the platform is realized as WS-Encrypted SOAP communication. According to the scenarios, the JAVA mobile application sends the signed mRCertificate request or m-invoice (signing is done by using XML signature mechanisms) to the Web service platform of the municipality. Before sending it to the municipality, signed mResidence Certificate request or m-invoice must be timestamped. In order to accomplish this, the JAVA mobile application communicates with TSA server via HTTP communication. In this sense, the JAVA mobile application sends a hash of the signature of the mResidence Certificate or m-invoice to the TSA server and receives back a timestamp (signed hash with added time information) which is signed by the private key of the TSA server.

Only in the mResidence Certificate scenario, when the mResidence Certificate is ready for delivery at the platform, the platform sends a SMS to the mobile user informing him that the mResidence Certificate with the given TaskID is ready for download. After that, the JAVA mobile application will send a request for mResidence Certificate download also as a signed and timestamped request in a body of the WS-Encrypted SOAP message to the platfom's Web service.

During the abovementioned communication, in order to verify signatures and validate different X.509v3 certificates, the JAVA mobile application needs to communicate with XKMS server which outsources a part of the time and resource consuming PKI functionalities from the JAVA mobile application. Namely, the JAVA mobile application could obtain a suitable digital certificate from the XKMS server (by using LocateRequest XKMS function) and, more importantly, could validate certificate of some party (by using ValidateRequest XKMS function). This way, the most time consuming PKI operations, like certificate validation, will be excluded from the mobile phone. The communication with the XKMS server is SOAP communication without applying security features. Only, the XKMS server's response is always digitally signed by using the XML signature mechanism.

6 SOA Based e/m-Government Platform

As an example of possible Web service endpoint implemented on the governmental side, we give brief description of Web Service Endpoint (WSE) of the m-governmental platform [MaDj10], [MaDj11], [PKPM08], [CGH+08]. The WSE module includes all the components that are directly used for accessing the considered m-governmental platform using mobile devices or software applications utilizing SOAP protocol as well as for implementation of all security features on the platform and for user authentication. These features are mainly based on SOA security principles [KaCh08].

The WSE module is a frontend e/m-governmental platform component which represents one of key components of the platform and which implements the following functionalities:
- Communication with end-users of the m-governmental platform:
  - Users with JAVA mobile or .NET application for sending mRCertificate requests as well as m-invoices.
  - Users with JAVA mobile or .NET application for sending mRCertificateDownload requests.
  - Users with desktop application for sending e-invoices (JAVA desktop allication).
- Communication with the TSA (Time Stamping Authority) server.
- Communication with the XKMS server.
- Communication with the Service Token Service (STS) server.
- Communication with the corresponding component of the platform's enterprise tier.
- Communication with the Civil Servant application.
- Implementation of all platform security functionalities.
- Communication with WSE module of the another platform.

In order to securely communicate with end-users, as well as with WSE module of the another platform, the WSE module implements functionalities comprised of the WS-Secured SOAP communication, as well as of signature verifications of the signed mRCertificate request/e-document or m-invoice, timestamp and SAML token [MaDj10], [MaDj11].

Regarding user authentication, the WSE module implements application functionalities which enable strong user authentication to the platform based on the certificate validation and data cross-check between the user's X.509v3 certificate and SAML token issued by STS.

In case the user authentication is positive, the WSE module processes a generated dynamic User-Profile as well as the signed and timestamped message body to the corresponding component of the platform's enterprise tier for further processing.

Implemented security functionalities inside the WSE module of the platform are following:
1. WS-Secured SOAP communication with end users.

2. Signature verification of signed and timestamped requests, SAML token and m-invoices as well as validations of certificates from all parties.

3. Create UserProfile from Civil Servant's X.509v3 certificate.

4. Timestamping documents signed by Civil Servants.

5. Signing and timestamping cross-border mRCertificate request that should be sent to the other municipality.

6. Requesting and receiving SAML token for Civil Servant and for the platform itself.

7. WS-Secured SOAP communication with the WSE module of another platform.

8. Locate and validate certificates by using corresponding functions of the XKMS protocol and communicates with the XKMS server using via SOAP protocol.

In order to implement the above mentioned functionalities, the WSE module communicates with following parties:

1. End users – WS-Secured SOAP communication.

2. WSE module of another platform – WS-Secured SOAP communication.

3. Platform's enterprise component – SOAP communication.

4. STS server – WS-Secured SOAP communication.

5. Time Stamping server – HTTP communication.

6. XKMS server – SOAP communication.

7. Civil Servant application – WS-Secured SOAP communication.

7 Conclusion

In this paper, we present a possible model of secure SOA-based e/m-government system based on JAVA mobile Web service application and SOA-based Web Service platform. In fact, this work is related to the consideration about secure mobile communication between citizens and companies with the small and medium governmental organizations, such as municipalities. We elaborated some possible m-government framework which is based on secure JAVA mobile application, PKI certificates, SOA-based platform, XML-security, WS-Security, SAML, Time Stamping and XKMS.

The work presented and examples described are included in the general framework of the EU IST FP6 SWEB project. Presented example could lead to conclusion that this m-government model could be a very efficient and very effective solution for secure interoperable governmental communication since it needs only a cross-certified PKI system and network of connected SWEB like SOA-based platforms. This is completely inline with many other pan-European electronic ID interoperability initiatives based on mutual acceptance of users X.509v3 electronic certificates.

Having in mind the above mentioned text, main contributions of the paper are:

- A proposal of the possible secure cross-border m-government model based on JAVA mobile application and SOA-based m-government platform, as well as secure communication between the two SOA-based platforms in the cross-border case.
- Usage of secure JAVA mobile application in which all modern security techniques are implemented (XML security, WS-Security, SAML, Time Stamping, PKI, XKMS)

- Usage of SOA-based request-response m-government platform (Web Services) which is more suitable for usage of secure mobile application compared to the session-based web application platform [LeLS07].
- Usage of XKMS service which is more suitable for mobile PKI system since it outsources complex operations such as PKI validation services to the external entity – the XKMS server, compared to usages of other techniques [LeLS07].

Future work could include implementation of SIM-based security solution into the proposed global m-governmental model and create a secure environment for additional m-governmental services, such as: sending electronic document with qualified signature through JAVA mobile application, etc.

References

[KoVi04]   Kolsi, O., Virtanen, T. (2004). MIDP 2.0 Security Enhancements, In Proceedings of the 37th Hawaii International Conference on System Sciences, Honolulu, Hawaii, USA, January 2004.

[MaDj10]   Marković, M., Đorđević, G. (2010). On Possible Model of Secure e/m-Government System, Information Systems Management, Taylor & Francis Group, LLC, 27:320-333, 2010.

[MaDj11]   Marković, M., Đorđević, G., On Secure SOA-Based e/m-Government Online Services, in Handbook "Service Delivery Platforms: Developing and Deploying Converged Multimedia Services", Taylor & Francis, 2011, p. 251 – 278, Chapter 11.

[PKPM08] Papastergiou, S., Karantjias, A., Polemi, D., Marković, M (2008). A Secure Mobile Framework for m-Services, In Proceedings of the Third International Conference on Internet and Web Applications and Services, ICIW 2008, Athens, Greece, June 2008.

[CGH+08] Cuno, S., Glickman, Y., Hoepner, P., Karantjias, T., Marković, M., Schmidt, M. (2008). The Architecture of an Interoperable and Secure eGovernment Platform Which Provides Mobile Services, Collaboration and the Knowledge Economy: Issues, Applications, Case Studies, Paul Cunningham and Miriam Cunningham (Eds), IOS Press, Amsterdam ISBN 978-1-58603-924-0, pp. 278-256.

[LeLS07]   Lee, Y., Lee, J., Song, J. (2007). Design and implementation of wireless PKI technology suitable for mobile phone in mobile-commerce. Computer Communication, 30 (4): 893-903.

[KaCh08] Kanneganti, R., Chodavarapu, P. (2008), SOA Security, Sound View Court 3B, Greenwich: Manning Publications Co.

PKI Implementation for Romanian Schengen Information System

Adrian Floarea · Constantin Burdun · Ionut Florea · Mihai Togan

certSIGN
107A, Oltenitei Rd., Building C1, ground floor, Bucharest, Romania
{adrian.floarea | costin.burdun | ionut.florea | mihai.togan}@certsign.ro

Abstract

Romania is preparing for the Schengen admission, the Romanian Ministry of Administration and Interior (MAI) being the institution coordinating this process.

Besides strengthening border control and surveillance, Schengen admission implies a close cooperation with the other Schengen member states and access to Schengen Information System (SIS). SIS will be upgraded soon to SIS II being a shared resource among Schengen member states. It helps the border control and law enforcement institutions to access the same information and share data about border crime. SIS is considered a key element powering the Schengen area. Once the new states are admitted, more than 500000 computers will have access to information from SIS. This requires a strong control of the identities of persons accessing information and their access rights.

Before uncontrolled access to SIS becoming an issue, the Romanian Ministry took a preventive action to avoid this. A grant from the European Union was awarded to build a security infrastructure to protect the national component of SIS and the user access to resources.

1 Schengen Admission of Romania

After becoming a member of NATO, in 2004, and a member of the European Union, in 2007, Romania's effort was focussed to be a signatory of the Schengen Agreement. This will allow Romanian citizens to move freely within the borders of Schengen member states.

At this moment, 25 European states are full members of the Schengen Agreement. These are, in alphabetic order: Austria, Belgium, Czech Republic, Denmark, Estonia, Finland, France, Germany, Greece, Hungary, Island, Italy, Latvia, Lithuania, Luxembourg, Malta, Nederland, Norway, Poland, Portugal, Slovakia, Slovenia, Spain, Sweden, and Switzerland (associated country).

There are signatories of the Schengen Agreement that are not members of the European Union: Island, Norway, and Switzerland. Meanwhile, there are 2 European Union member states, Ireland and United Kingdom, which decided not to apply in full the Schengen acquis, but co-operates with Schengen Member States in certain fields.

The following states are working to fulfil the Schengen aquis in order to become members of the Schengen Agreement: Bulgaria, Cyprus, Lichtenstein, and Romania.

N. Pohlmann, H. Reimer, W. Schneider (Editors): Securing Electronic Business Processes, Vieweg (2011), 317-329

Besides benefits, abolition of controls at internal borders within the Schengen area can have a negative impact for the internal security of Member States.

In order to prevent these disadvantages, Schengen States introduced a set of compensatory measures [MAIS11]. These include:
- movement of persons (visas and consular cooperation)
- police cooperation:
  - mutual support of police forces in the field of judicial assistance;
  - liaison officers exchange between police forces;
  - cross-border cooperation at internal borders, especially by setting up common services of police, customs and border police for all Contracting States;
  - police missions of cross-border surveillance and pursuit
- judicial cooperation of Schengen Member States

The most significant compensatory measure is setting up a common European system called the Schengen Information System. All Member States enter data in the system directly from the national databases.

Romania deployed the National Schengen Information System (NSIS). NSIS is connected to SIS allowing information exchange regarding the operative situation at Schengen borders and identification of alerts. The designated organisations from Romania use NSIS to perform searches and information update while performing specific activities regarding border control, issuance of visas and residence permits.

The security requirements to protect SIS are described in Volume 2 of Schengen Catalogue, Schengen Information System, SIRENE: Recommendations and Best Practices [SCHE02]. The requirements apply to NSIS as well and include:
- personnel security and users access control to resources
- protection of equipment storing SIS information to prevent unauthorized access, loss and accidental damage
- security of workstations and of remote access to resources
- network management, security of data in transit, protection of networks against unauthorized access
- users' access control providing unique and secure user identification elements, rapid management of users' credentials and access rights to information.

In order to fulfil the security requirements, as per Schengen recommendations and best practices, and to be prepared for the future security threats, MAI started to develop a dedicated infrastructure to provide SIS information protection, as well as information exchanged between national organisations involved in border related issues.

The project implementation had a very tight schedule. The time frame from the agreement conclusion until the deployment of the solution was of only 12 months. The scheduled Schengen audits added significant time pressure, also verifying the information security components.

2 Information Security Architecture

The information security architecture was designed to be deployed among 9 MAI organizations dealing with border surveillance, border control, immigration problems and law enforcement, which are among the topics relevant for Schengen admission. The Ministry has a decentralized structure, each of the organizations being independent, with its own management and following particular rules and regulations. Therefore, the security infrastructure had a distributed designed, with a central point to maintain a common framework and facilitate information exchange.

The following were involved within the project:
- 9 structures from the Ministry dealing with Schengen related topics
- The General Directorate for IT&C (GDITC), as central point to facilitate information exchange among the structures of the Ministry and information exchange with external organizations

To be able to follow the schedule of Schengen evaluation visits and to have a better management and control of the implementation of the project there was a single contractor responsible for the deployment. The design of the architecture was created by the Ministry in close collaboration with a consultant and the contract was awarded after an international tender.

The project was broad, laying on the implementation of a Public Key Infrastructure (PKI) within the Ministry to guarantee for the identity of the users. The access control solution, digital signature and encryption software, user training and new organizational policies were implemented on top of the PKI architecture. The entire IT infrastructure came together with the required hardware resources, data centre solutions for each of the institutions implementing PKI and disaster recovery location, facility security component and TEMPEST protection.

For the structures of MAI, the PKI infrastructure will ensure:
- the identity of the electronic users
- the authentication and authorization of access to the MAI information systems
- services of securing information exchange among the users and/or the information systems of MAI
- real-time validation services of the digital certificates
- key recovery services for private encryption keys
- timestamp services
- support for the interconnection with the PKI of external institutions, as the basic element for the secure information exchange between the external institutions and MAI structures
- scalability for subsequent development, which does not necessarily concern the accession to the Schengen area, taking into account the institutional attributions of MAI

The PKI architecture of MAI was designed taking into account the underlying principles applied when building the various models of public key infrastructures.

Within the PKI infrastructure of MAI, the users obtain the certificates from various Certification Authorities, depending on the structure to which they belong. This is a standard PKI architecture, comprising several independent CAs, which have to be connected among each other by trust paths. Such connection ensures interoperability among the users of the various MAI structures. Without the existence of the trust paths, a user of a MAI structure cannot validate the authenticity and integrity of a message received from a user member of another structure or external institution.

The PKI interconnection solution belonging to the MAI structures is the Bridge CA solution, which ensures a high level of flexibility and scalability. The Bridge CA solution will be also used to establish the trust relationships between PKI and the institutions outside MAI, as well as with the Transit Certification Authority (TCA) at the level of the System for Defence, Public Order and National Safety, managed by the Romanian Special Telecommunication Service. The TCA is practically another Bridge Certification Authority, the first one implemented in Romania. It provides interoperability for the PKIs implemented within the Ministry of Defence, Ministry of Administration and Interior and Special services.

For information exchange with external institutions, MAI Bridge CA provides two main interoperability mechanisms:
- Cross certification, the classic approach to establish a trust relationship between two PKI architectures
- Certificate trust lists (CTL)

Each PKI implementation has a full range of services:
- Registration Authority
- Certification Authority
- Certificate validation services using On-line Certificate Status Protocol (OCSP) [256099]
- Time stamp services [316101]
- Key recovery services for encryption certificates
- Smart Card Management System

Centrally, Bridge CA is provided together with:
- Proxy validation services using OCSP – each of the interconnected PKI which cannot provide certificate status information for a digital certificate forwards the validation request to the Bridge CA OCSP. This OCSP finds the validation service in charge to answer the request, forwards the request to it and then forwards the received answer to the OCSP service that initiated the validation process
- Central directory service
- Time source for the entire system

The architecture was built to provide, besides access to Schengen resources, the interoperability framework for Administration which shall provide services according to Services Directive from the European Union level. As this is considered a critical infrastructure for Romanian administration, the applications implemented were chosen to hold security certifications allowing them to protect classified information.

The other components of the IT solution for the 49000 users of the system are the following:
- User authentication and access management to resources based on digital certificates
- Digital signature and encryption applications for files, e-mails and disks together with file shredding application
- Secure e-mail services together with e-mail non repudiation component
- Document management system

Although not included in the solution required for the secure access to Schengen IT resources but very important for the deployment and management of the system, two other software applications are provided:

- E-learning application to support user training during the entire lifecycle of the system
- Faults management application, to keep trace of all hardware and software components deployed in 11 data centres

Information exchange between Bridge CA and PKI of MAI structures is realized using the Ministry's Integrated Data Voice Communication Network while within each structure the communication is realized using its own Intranet.

The disaster recovery site allows fast recovery of any of the PKI architecture in case of an incident.

The PKI Architecture is described in the following figure.

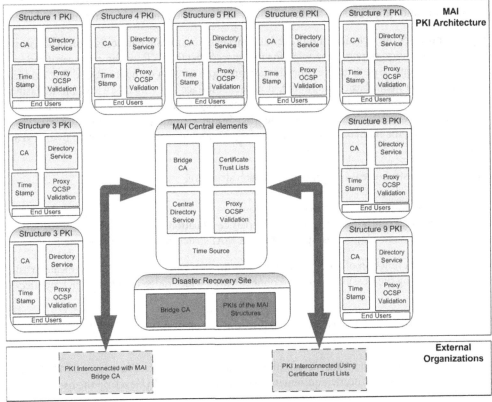

Fig. 1: MAI PKI Architecture

2.1 Security Requirements

When designing the PKI architecture, one of the key principles was to provide easy access of end users to PKI services, such as directory services, certificate validation and time stamp while keeping secure the CA elements dealing with issuance of digital certificates and CRL. Therefore, the services offered were divided in 2 categories:

1. Public services, accessible to all users: the Registration Authority, the LDAP directory service, the OCSP validation service, the proxy OCSP validation service and the Timestamp service. These services are available in a public area of the communication network of each of the MAI structure.

2. Internal CA services, which concern the PKI operation and management. These services are the Certification Authority and the key recovery service, the most important services for PKI, from the viewpoint of security. For this reason, the internal CA services will be physically separated from the public services.

2.1.1 Bridge CA

The central part of MAI PKI comprises the Bridge CA, at the GDITC level, whose role is to establish the trust relationships both inside the Ministry and with the external institutions.

Bridge CA provides the technical and procedural mechanisms for the harmonisation of security policies and realization of policy mapping for the interconnected PKIs, as the cross certification preserves the specific aspects of the procedures/regulations of each component CA. The Bridge CA represents the main, basic component; it is the "interface" by which MAI is able to easily establish trust relationships with other organizational PKIs, at national and international level. A trust relationship was established between the MAI Bridge CA and the Transit CA operated by STS, thus allowing the interconnection with the organizational PKIs interconnected by the STS Transit CA.

A three-level infrastructure is implemented for each structure:
- Root CA
- Sub CA subordinated to the Bridge CA Root;
- Policies. Both central policies, for which cross certification with Bridge CA is performed, and new framework policies, specific to each MAI structure can be implemented.

Another important function of the MAI Bridge CA is the implementation of the Certificate Trust Lists, thus providing the possibility to interconnect with a wider range of external PKI architectures.

The Certificate Trust Lists are used according to the specifications of ETSI 102231 standard [ETSI09].

By implementing the mechanisms which allow the use of Certificate Trust Lists, MAI PKI is prepared to respond to the future requirements which may occur at EU level, on the use of PKI.

To achieve a maximum level of trust in the certificates managed by this authority, Bridge CA architecture has two areas of security, which allow differentiated access of the operators.

Bridge CA uses hardware cryptographic devices (Hardware Security Modules – HSM), which meet the FIPS 140-2 level 3 standard for all the operations which involve the generation and use of private keys (certificate or CRL signing).

2.1.2   PKI of MAI Structures

A hierarchical PKI architecture was implemented at the level of each MAI structure and it was connected to MAI Bridge CA.

The implementation of PKI for a structure took into account the following requirements:
- Implementation of a certification authority
- The cryptographic material of the users is stored on an USB token (key generation and usage)
- Creation of a certification policy template and mapping with Bridge CA policies

For the Root CA of each structure an offline software-hardware system was used.

In order to ensure a maximum level of trust in the certificates managed by PKI of MAI Structures, it has to implement an architecture based on two areas of security, which are separated both logically and physically. The areas will clearly delimit the user registration from the management of certificates and keys.

In order to obtain a high level of security, it is necessary that the public and private area of the certification authority not be connected through the network equipment. Thus, the private area can be protected in case the public area is compromised. However, for the solution to function it is necessary to have data transfer between the two areas, for which non-Ethernet equipment of information transfer and filtering was used.

This equipment has to allow only the data transfer from one area to the other, not allowing the execution of commands or applications between the two areas. In addition, the devices have to block the communication in case the transferred data are not ASCII encoded. After an attempt to transfer unauthorized information, the device can be unlocked only manually.

The user keys and certificates (persons or devices) are manageable both in software format and on cryptographic devices such as USB tokens, FIPS 140-2 level 2 compliant.

The certification authority uses hardware cryptographic devices (Hardware Security Modules – HSM), which meet the FIPS 140-2 level 3 standard for all the operations which involve the generation and use of private keys (certificate or CRL signing, key recovery).

The security requirements of the MAI structures entail the existence of a procedure for encrypted documents, by which the respective documents can be retrieved in case the cryptographic device no longer exists or it can no longer be used (fault, loss etc.). In order to fulfil this condition, the certification authority has to implement a module dedicated to the recovery of private keys used for encryption.

The private encryption keys are stored in encrypted form, using encryption keys different from the signing keys of the certification authorities.

The recovery of these keys will require the presence of a minimum number of users, based on a threshold schema, where a minimum of k out of n administrators ($K \geq 2$) have to be present in order to retrieve the keys.

A high level of security is required for the operation of the certification authority, both for authentication and for protection of the information transmitted. Therefore, it was necessary to implement an authentication method which allows the encryption of the data transmitted and the secure identification of the two communicating entities. To this end, the SSL protocol was be used, on the basis of double authentication.

The certificates of the CA operators allowing the operation of the certification authority and the certificates of the user were not signed using the same cryptographic keys. In order to meet this requirement, it was necessary to implement a completely separated PKI infrastructure, for the management of certificates for the operators of the MAI Structure PKI infrastructure.

2.2 Unification of Repositories and Cross-border Certificate Validation

Being distributed, the MAI PKI architecture requires mechanisms to allow interoperability between users of MAI Structures as well as access to information regarding each digital certificate, no matter the PKI responsible for its management. Therefore, a central repository was created together with an on-line cross-border certificate validation system. These allow independent management of each PKI while aggregating public information, relevant to all the users.

2.2.1 Central Directory Service

Each PKI is providing to the users access to the CA certificates, to the certificate revocation lists and to the cross certification certificates it signed. For each structure this is realised using an LDAP v3/X.500 directory service [225197], accessible to the users without requiring their authentication.

In order to create a uniform security context for the applications and systems, a central directory service was required at the Bridge CA level. It has to comprise the following:
- the certificate and the CRL of the Bridge CA authority
- the certificates issued and received by the Bridge CA authority
- the certificates and CRLs of the structures' certification authorities
- the certificates issued by the structures' certification authorities

In order to meet these security requirements, the central directory service was integrated with each directory service in the structures' certification authorities. The integration involved synchronization of information in the directory services of the structures with the central directory service, so that a possible disturbance of communication between the structures and the central directory has a minimum impact on the functionalities of the systems and applications.

The synchronization of directory services is a complex operation, which has to be continuous. The temporal nature of the information which requires synchronization (validity period of certificates and CRLs) requires a synchronization of this information, as it is updated in the directories of the structures' authorities.

Since each PKI solution uses a LDAP as directory for digital certificate publication, the solution was developed using LDAP synchronization. OpenLDAP has its own, built-in replication mechanism using syncrepl. This mechanism allows having a mirror image of a LDAP, each update of master LDAP being propagated almost instantly on mirrored LDAP (replicated). The solution goes one step further and consolidates all LDAPs from MAI Structures to one central LDAP at Bridge CA level, allowing for instant update of central LDAP when the LDAP of the MAI structure is updated. Since each structure uses a different subtree there is no problem of conflict or concurrent update. Central LDAP acts only as a client, only the replication mechanism writes in it, and there is no update which is propagated to the LDAP of MAI Structures. At this moment, some 50.000 entries are stored in central repository, and a few hundred entries are updated daily (even several times a day – CRLs for example).

Instant update of central repository allows realtime access to latest information from each and every one of the MAI structures, and ensures a high level of security. Once access is revoked from one MAI Structure, no system from another structure or Ministry level is allowing user access.

2.2.2 Certificate status validation service

To verify the status of certificates, it was required to implement an online certificate validation service, using the OCSP protocol (Online Certificate Status Protocol), which is meeting the current RFC 2560 standard.

The digital certificate online validation service provides a real time response concerning the status of the certificates. The certificates of the authorities and the CRLs are retrieved using:

- LDAP v3 directory service of each PKI
- HTTP protocol (published on a web server);
- locally stored (on the hard drive of the server running the validation service) digital certificates and CRLs.

In addition, the OCSP solution allows the validation of digital certificates on the basis of the information extracted directly from the database of the certification authority.

In case the service receives a validation request for a certificate for which no information is available, the former is able to connect to a different OCSP service, which is able to respond to this request. This proxy functionality is able to accept configurable routes for the transmission of requests. Thus, depending on the information available about the other OCSP services and the information in the certificate which requires validation, the request is sent directly to the service that is able to respond for the status of the respective certificate. In addition, it is configured that the requests is sent to an implicit OCSP service, in case the service cannot respond to the request and it does not have information on the service able to provide validation.

The certificate validation service uses hardware cryptographic devices (Hardware Security Modules – HSM), which meet the FIPS 140-2 level 3 standard for all the operations which involve generation and storage of the keys and for signing the responses sent to the customer.

3 Support Infrastructure for MAI PKI

The PKI architecture is doubled by two other very important elements included in the implementation of the project:

1. Applications using digital certificates to protect information. These include user authentication application, digital signature and encryption applications and document management.

2. Hardware and software infrastructure to operate the PKI. These include the deployment of 11 data centres together with the entire hardware and communication equipment, resilient power generators and TEMPEST protection and implementation of Smart Card Management System, e-learning solution to train the 49.000 users and faults management application to keep trace of all hardware and software components deployed

3.1 Applications using digital certificates

Besides usage of the digital certificates to access NSIS MAI decided to use them in order to provide a better protection of the information its users store, process and transmit. Therefore, together with the PKI deployment were also delivered:

- Authentication and authorisation application, allowing user authentication and authorization based on digital certificates and certificate extensions, SSO and advanced security for WEB Services, Online Certificate Status Protocol (OCSP) integration for certificate validity and SSL acceleration for heavy loading conditions
- Digital signature and encryption security suite allowing: digital signature and encryption of files and e-mails, hard drive encryption and file shredding
- Document and Workflow Management solution providing collaborative environment for document handling and tracing within the Ministry
- Electronic Postal Authority transposing classical postal services into electronic environment (correspondence receipt acknowledgement). The application provides non-repudiation mechanisms for e-mail messages such as untampered and undisclosed message delivery and trustworthy receipt acknowledgements by using digital signature and encryption mechanisms.

3.2 Hardware and software infrastructure

For the deployment of the data centres all the required hardware and communication equipment was provided. The data rooms were prepared to host the data centre, TEMPEST protection was provided and the physical security mechanisms were put in place.

For 7 of the data centres the location was set within the buildings of the MAI structures while for 4 of them containers were used. The containers were provided with the same physical security mechanisms and TEMPEST protection, allowing the Ministry to rapidly deploy them, airborne or on road, to any place requiring fast intervention.

The hardware and communication provided allowed the deployment of the solution in high availability architecture. Uninterruptible power supply and redundant diesel generators were provided for all the data centres and for the disaster recovery site.

The physical security mechanisms included:
- Closed Circuit Television (CCTV) surveillance
- Access control including biometrics
- Physical intrusion detection
- Perimeter security system, including concertina wire fences for the containers
- Fire detection and prevention
- Flood detection
- TEMPEST Zone 0 protection

The software support infrastructure included:
- Smart card management application allowing management of USB tokens (PIN change, token unlocking, management of certificates on the token), management of javacard tokens (applet configuration) and integration with the cryptographic key retrieval module. The module is accessible to the users, on the Web, through SSL protocol, based on double authentication in order to execute the USB token management operations. For the cases in which the token is no longer accessible (lost PIN, lost or destroyed token), the module is accessible to the administrators who will adequately modify the status of the token in the system. In addition, a revocation request will be generated for the certificates on the respective token.
- E-learning application to support the training of PKI MAI users.
- Faults management application allowing planning and execution of maintenance activities, inventory of assets and real time monitoring of the status of equipment.

4 Project deployment and lessons learnt

Implementation of PKI for MAI to support the integration of Romania in Schengen area was a very challenging project. It required highly specialized technical abilities of the people involved and a tremendous logistic support. For a 12 month deployment period in 11 data centres there was no room for errors or mistakes.

The project had 3 important milestones, at the end of each being delivered complete PKI architectures for a group of MAI Structures. The deliveries followed the importance of each structure for the Schengen evaluation:
- 3 months – deployment of Bridge CA and GDITC and of PKI for 1 other structure
- 6 months – deployment of PKI for 4 structures, of document management and of e-learning application
- 9 months – deployment of PKI for 4 structures, of the disaster recovery site and of faults management application

Each delivery consisted of a fully functional data centre and of PKI architecture and applications configured, ready to issue digital certificates for the end users.

The main challenges were:
- Choosing the correct technical solution and performing fast configuration
- Creation and mapping of certificate policies to interconnect 9 Structures of the MAI with the Bridge CA
- Deployment of the solution to all the users involved

- Logistic challenges, from delayed deliveries due to eruption of Eyjafjallajökull volcano in Iceland to unexpected, last moment, issues inevitably occurring on the field.

It was important that the deployment of the security infrastructure was accomplished having as core services the PKI architecture, implemented at Governmental level in one of its most complex scenarios: hierarchic PKIs for decentralized organizations with a trust relationship established through a Bridge CA together with Certificate Trust Lists. It is the second Bridge CA implementation in Romania at Governmental level, proving that the technology is mature enough and can be deployed to secure large scale infrastructures. There are good reasons to assert that, having the right expertise and know how, the same approach can be replicated at international level to provide the backbone for secure information exchange among information systems running in Schengen and European Union member states.

A key element was the human factor that was able to overcome in due time the difficulties encountered, to find fast solutions for the technical issues encountered. A close collaboration between the Ministry and the supplier of the solution was also essential for the success of the project.

Several figures regarding the project are presented in the following table.

Table 1: Figures of the project

Key element	Value
Duration of the project (months)	12
MAI structures involved	9
Data centres deployed	11
Servers deployed	>200
Time to deliver the first data centre (months)	3
End users	49.000
People involved in the project (from the supplier)	>100

5 Conclusion

The project was a success as the supplier was able to deliver on time and on budged the Romanian information security infrastructure for Schengen admission. Its outcome was successfully verified during the evaluation visits.

This paper is created 8 months after the final deployment of the project at national level, allowing for a close observation of the results and the dynamics of the population of users. It is the largest deployment of a PKI in Romania as a single project, covering 9 Governmental organizations. All these MAI structures are interconnected from the beginning, through MAI Bridge CA and Transit CA from STS, with the other Romanian organizations that are part of the National Defence System.

The future development of the project involves establishment of new trust relationships between MAI Bridge CA and other external organizations, mainly at European level. This will allow the Ministry to securely exchange information with its peers, acting as a trustworthy partner, with a broad expertise in the field of information security.

References

[256099] RFC 2560, X.509 Internet Public Key Infrastructure Online Certificate Status Protocol – OCSP, Network Working Group, 1999

[316101] RFC 3161, Internet X.509 Public Key Infrastructure Time-Stamp Protocol (TSP), Network Working Group, 2001

[225197] RFC 2251, Lightweight Directory Access Protocol (v3), Network Working Group, 1997

[ETSI09] ETSI TS 102 231 V3.1.2 (2009-12), Electronic Signatures and Infrastructures (ESI); Provision of harmonized Trust-service status information, ETSI, 2009

[MAIS11] Schengen Romania, http://www.schengen.mai.gov.ro/English/index.htm, 2011

[SCHE02] EU Schengen Catalogue, Volume 2, Schengen Information System, SIRENE: Recommendations and Best Practices, Council of the European Union, 2002

The Electronic Visa – Solutions to Shift from Paper to Chip

Dan Butnaru

11-13, rue René Jacques 92131 Issy-Les-Moulineaux, FRANCE
Keynectis SA
dan.butnaru@keynectis.com

Abstract

The rapid growth of ICT and their successful penetration in everybody's daily life has amplified the need for security and privacy. Electronic and biometric passports as well as electronic Identification Cards initiatives are reflecting these changes.

This work summarizes the evolution of the passport from a paper based document to a full fledge biometric and electronic travel document and exposes how the integration of an electronic Visa into the chip could be implemented.

The so called Machine Readable Visa (MRV) follows in analogue manner the Machine Readable Travel Document and its electronic evolutions the e-MTRD (electronic passport) and e-MRV (electronic Visa).

Of utmost importance are in both cases the security aspects, with an obvious requirement of authenticity and privacy. The electronic documents must guarantee that they are unforgeable and unambiguously identify its holder as well divulge sensitive information only to trustworthy entities.

Public Key Infrastructure (PKI) based on cryptography is the backbone for implementing those security mechanisms.

This contribution outlines possible schemes of implementing chip based electronic Visa and its underlying security infrastructure, taking advantage of the already proven use case of the electronic and biometric passport.

1 Introduction

The development of terrorist threats and of identity fraud has led the international community to reinforce border security checks and therefore the reliability of travel documents. This endeavour can only be conducted within the framework of international standardization.

ICAO (International Civil Aviation Organization) is tasked with standardizing travel documents as well as the associated production and verification processes. ICAO's work has thus enabled the development of standardized specifications that are complied with by manufacturers to set up electronic passport systems.

A major advantage of the electronic passport lies in the fact that it improves significantly the protection against falsification. This level of security is based on Public Key Cryptography, which guarantees integrity, authenticity, and confidentiality of stored data.

N. Pohlmann, H. Reimer, W. Schneider (Editors): Securing Electronic Business Processes, Vieweg (2011), 330-337

Passport holder personal information, like name, gender, date of birth, etc. as well as photo are structured in data groups (16 in total) and stored and managed by the RF-chip on the travel document.

The two objectives of the passports are to guarantee the document's authenticity and to identify the individual possessing the passport.

In order to provide electronically an access control, different Authentication Protocols have been defined, depending on the sensitivity of related data, i.e. Basic Access Control (BAC) and Extended Access Control (EAC).

Therefore two distinct Information Systems have been designed, implying each a Public Key Infrastructure (PKI).

As a next step one can imagine similar approaches for the electronic Visa.

Today, ICAO specifies the Machine Readable Visa (MRV) and the e-MRV[Doc 9303 vol. II part 1]. Taking advantage of the possibilities of a smart card chip, we can securely write and erase data, replacing thus all paper based process of traditional Visa handling and increasing security and privacy protection.

Typical use cases like application forms are already available on-line in some countries. The next step would be a paperless Visa "token" stored onto the smart card chip.

This feature represents a particular interest for individuals who need to travel different sensitive countries. Today's practise to possess two passports would not be necessary anymore, since readable Visa information can be erased electronically if desired.

2 Evolution of the travel document

2.1 The electronic passport

Preventing fraud always has been a major challenge for document security. Since passports exist, they have been counterfeited and more and more security printing techniques were added in the past.

A major step has been the introduction of the so-called Machine Readable Travel Document (MRTD), indicating passport holder's data like name, gender, nationality in an encoded way printed on high security paper. These data are read out optically in order to enable methods of automatic border control.

In additional to these printing security features, a major change has been made by choosing smart card chip technology to securely store passport data into the e-MRTD or more commonly electronic passport.

The chip based solution brings in several new security concepts, which benefit from smart card's inherent security combined with cryptographic approaches. Smart cards, which dispose in the case of the electronic passport of a contactless communication interface, are tamper proof. Also, as a prerequisite, chip and embedded application must undergo a Common Criteria Evaluation.

Personal Data is structured in 16 data groups, like DG1 (MRZ), DG2 (picture), DG3 (finger-prints), DG15 (chip's public key), etc.

MRZ and picture are mandatory. Though optional, fingerprints are more and more considered to be included onto the RF-chip (Radio-Frequency chip) of the passport, but require more stringent protection, see §2.2.

When dealing with e-passports, two application fields must be separated, i.e. securing production on one hand and verification of document authenticity on the other.

2.1.1 Secure Production of the e-MRTD

In terms of production, the electronic passports stores in its memory the MRZ, electronically signed by a state authorized entity.

Since this process constitutes the foundation of document verification, only trusted entities are allowed to sign personal data, by using their private cryptographic key.

The Country Signing Certification Authority (CSCA) has the function of a national Root CA, which issues the Signing Certificates of the Document Signers Entities.

The Document Signer (DS) has the role to sign with its "State Authorized" private key the pass-port data, see figure 1.

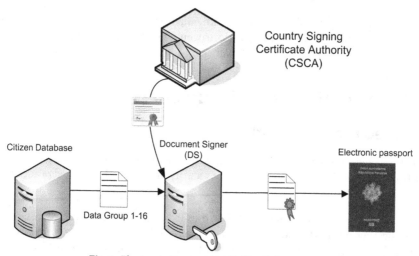

Fig. 1: Electronic Passport Public Key Infrastructure

The produced passport includes at least the signed data and the DS certificate.

At the moment of verification, the Border Control Point reads out the data groups and verifies cryptographically the signature by means of the DS public key contained in the DS Certificate.

The electronic passport contains by definition private data, like name, residence, birthday, gender and photo. This information shall be read out only at the Inspection System at Border Control Point.

2.1.2 Verification of Authenticity

At Border Control Checkpoints, one will need to verify that the electronic passport is a genuine one, which means that it is protected against forgery, skimming and eavesdropping.

Passive Authentication (PA) is used to verify authenticity by checking optically read out data and electronically signed.

Since this approach does not prevent skimming, Active Authentication (AA) is used. It is a challenge-response mechanism based on the fact that the e-passport private key signs a random, which is verified by the reader using the public key from DG15.

In order to access to chip resident data, the so-called Basic Access Control (BAC) is processed, which is a DES-like algorithm protecting read-out of data.

2.2 The biometric passport

The inclusion of biometric data, i.e. fingerprint stored in DG3, implies a more stringent mechanism of authentication, linked to the sensitivity of the data. To achieve this goal, a Mutual Authentication scheme is implemented, based on a defined PKI architecture.

In this protocol both entities, the e-Passport and the Inspection System (Reader), authenticate each other by using respective public keys and certificates.

In case of verification of biometric data, the Inspection System (IS) has to request the e-Passport read access to be granted. This is achieved by transmitting its certificate to the passport, which analyses it and then allows reading out the biometric data stored.

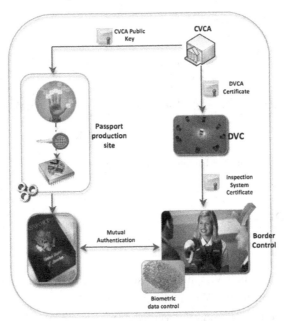

Fig. 2: Biometric Passport Public Key Infrastructure

The reader receives its certificate from a Document Verifying Certification Authority (DVCA). Figure 2 depicts the global PKI necessary for the biometric passport.

In order to provide to the biometric passport all relevant information to authenticate a reader, the Root CA is stored at production stage. The Country Verifying CA (CVCA) certificate is hence stored together with all chip specific information.

2.2.1 Verification of Identity

Scope of the biometric passport is the identification of the passport holder. This is achieved by reading out the stored fingerprints and compared to the one presented at check point. As biometrics is considered sensitive data, only an authenticated reader is granted access.

Authentication is achieved by presenting the IS certificate, delivered by the DVCA managing the IS and authorized by the CVCA of the country which allowed reading out biometrics of their citizens. This authentication scheme is defined as Extended Access Control (EAC), as specified in [BSI08] and described schematically in fig. 3 herunder.

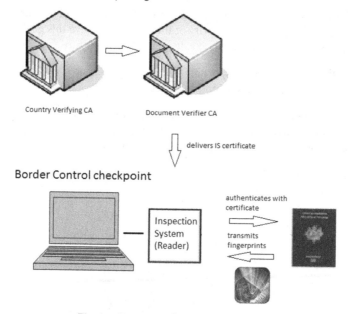

Fig. 3: e-Passport Public Key Infrastructure

3 The Visa document

3.1 Managing the Electronic Visa

Today one can split the electronic Visa into two distinct domains of intervention:

1. Paper-to-digital transition of Visa application forms
2. Machine readable and electronically secured document (MRV, e-MRV)

The traditional visa document can be obtained through embassies and presented at border entry. Several countries have implemented e-Visa web sites, facilitating the application process via non paper procedures. Australia has been the first country for this type of procedure, set up in 1996, see also [UNWT09].

The applicant is filling in on-line the form which is treated in a database.

Currently there is no standardized framework for e-Visa management, and thus countries tend to implement the IT Infrastructure according to national specification initiatives.

3.2 Chip based solution

In a nutshell, an e-passport chip is a RF-chip complying to ISO 14443 contactless communication protocol with classic building blocks like antenna, cpu and memory, as figure 4 shows hereunder.

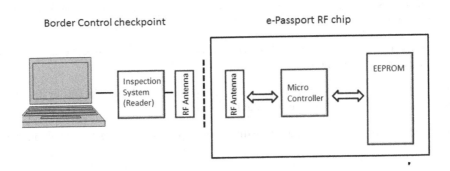

Fig. 4: High level structure of e-passport RF chip

Data is stored in the EEPROM (Electrically Erasable Programmable Memory) and read/write/erase transactions can be performed. The embedded OS manages objects/file structure and conditions access by means of rights management procedures.

In order to read and, in the particular case of the e-Visa, to write/erase information, access right management needs to be set up. The advantage of a microcontroller chip is the ability to store securely information and condition access to it.

We can adopt a similar approach than the biometric passport, where a PKI is managing read access rights. With the same system, an Inspection System (IS) would not only *authenticate* with its digital ID for reading biometric information, but could use a dedicated key (and thus a dedicated certificate) to *grant access for writing/erasing* e-Visa data on the passport chip.

Given the sensitivity of this information, a strict delimitation of write/erase objects is mandatory. Possible solution could be new data groups and special zones reserved in the chip's EEPROM.

If we review the whole lifecycle of the electronic Visa, we could now combine the paperless application form submitted on-line by the applicant and a token generated and stored onto the e-passport chip at border control check-point. A data base would provide the necessary information and the passport holder is identified beforehand through above mentioned mechanisms based on Extended Access Control.

The token can be for instance the hash code of the obtained visa document, allowing thus to track visitors when entering and leaving the country. Stored securely on the chip, state entities, like border control, immigration authorities, etc. would be able to verify the status.

Taking advantage of already proven methods, like active authentication, one can make sure that the e-Visa token is not skimmed, since signed by the chip's private key.

As we can write information into the chip, it is even possible to manage cases, where people could upon leaving the country ask for erasing Visa information.

All described actions on the e-Passport chip require sophisticated rights management, since not only sensitive data is written and read, but the access itself to the chip must be controlled rigorously. An efficient way to achieve this is combining chip intrinsic security features with Public Key Infrastructure:

For e-Visa application, the chip EEPROM can reserve a dedicated space, where special rights are controlling read/write transactions.

In analogy to the EAC, the IS (reader) would beforehand authenticate with its certificate, which must be different from the one used to read out biometrics.

With this approach countries would be able to differentiate clearly between e-Visa and biometrics data management.

4 Conclusion

The passport document has evolved dramatically in the last years.

Driven by ICAO initiatives, people dispose today of an electronically secured travel document, where even sensitive personal biometric data can be stored and read out securely.

These efforts have allowed decreasing substantially fraud and improving automated border control. Increased security and faster check-in procedures at border control check points are the major benefits of a successful implementation of the electronic passport scheme.

The Visa management is the next challenge to tackle on international level.

Profiting from all achievements in the past, we can imagine functional schemes where the traditional paper document will be replaced by fast, reliable and citizen friendly procedures and applications.

Based on the possibilities of the embedded RF-chip, one can handle Visa electronically by writing relevant information in the chip's memory and verify data in-the-field.

Public Key Infrastructure represents the backbone of necessary security layer for this field of application. Indeed, only by controlling rigorously access rights, one can prevent misuse and forgery. The electronic Visa can benefit largely from the established electronic and biometric passport infrastructures and set up a security framework on top of them.

Thus, by delivering dedicated write certificates to authorized readers, we can use an enhanced EAC scheme to secure and control access to the travel document.

Therefore, only little additional investments have to be made. Already existing IT systems would only need to be updated for additional certificate issuance and lifecycle management.

References

[ICAO06a] ICAO: Doc9303 –Machine Readable Travel Documents, Part 1, vol.1, ICAO Secretary General, 2006.

[ICAO06b] ICAO: Doc9303 –Machine Readable Travel Documents, Part 1, vol.2, ICAO Secretary General, 2006.

[ICAO05] ICAO: Doc9303 –Machine Readable Travel Documents, Part 2, ICAO Secretary General, 2005.

[ICAO08a] ICAO: Doc9303 –Machine Readable Travel Documents, Part 3, vol.1, ICAO Secretary General, 2008.

[ICAO08b] ICAO: Doc9303 –Machine Readable Travel Documents, Part 3, vol.1, ICAO Secretary General, 2008.

[UNWT09] UNTWO: eVISAS: A pressing need for global standards, specifications and interoperability, A37-WP/136, UNWTO, 2010

[BSI08] BSI, BSI-TR 3110 – Advanced Security Mechanisms for Machine Readable Travel Documents – Extended Access Control (EAC) v1.11, BSI, 2008

[MKV+08] Mevaa, Karppinen, Pepy, Plessis, Ventadour, Viljanen: Operating Software in Secure Electronic Documents, Gemalto Whitepaper, 2008

[Hage10] Claudia Hager: The Future of a Visa: Universal Doc9303 compliance and Beyond, ICAO MRTD Symposium, 2010

[Lyle10] Chris Lyle: eVisas: The time is Now. Conceptual Framework and a way forward, ICAO MRTD Symposium, 2010

[Slav10] Erik Slavenas: Visa and eVisa: rationale, specifications and reflections on future trends, ICAO Regional Seminar, 2010

[ANS10] Abuadhmah, Naser, Samsudin: E-Visas verification Schemes Based on Public-Key Infrastructure and Identity based Encryption, Journal of Computer Science 6, 2010, 723-727

Device &
Network Security

Objectives and Added Value of an Internet Key Figure System for Germany

Sebastian Feld · Tim Perrei · Norbert Pohlmann · Matthias Schupp

Institute for Internet Security
Gelsenkirchen University of Applied Sciences
{feld | perrei | pohlmann | schupp}@internet-sicherheit.de

Abstract

This work is motivated by the fact that the Internet can be seen as a critical infrastructure, whose on-going operation is particularly worth protecting. Problematic when considering the state of the Internet are two things: On the one hand, there are many dependencies in the context of the Internet, on the other hand there are only a few key figures that allow comprehensive statements. In the course of this work, a Key Figure System will be described in which the control object is the Internet by itself. The complex structure of the Internet is to be made more transparent and the condition, changes and future potential are to be expressed. In addition to the various objectives that are to be achieved during the design and implementation of such an Internet Key Figure System, this work describes the problems that have to be solved. These are less technical, but in fact organisational and legal nature. Each Key Figure System requires a control object, that is a clearly defined scope, which the data collection, data processing and data visualisation refer to. In the following the definition of an „Internet Germany" is given and the appropriate stakeholder and criteria are described. This work concludes with an explanation of the different added value of an Internet Key Figure System for the various addressees.

1 Motivation

Today's Internet consists of a variety of networks, called Autonomous Systems (AS), which are operated by Internet Service Providers (ISPs), large companies and universities. There are currently more than 37,000 AS[1], which build the Internet with more than 70,000 connections. For a more detailed consideration and a proper assessment of the significance of each AS, it is important to see what role each AS occupies in the interaction of the Internet. AS are acting completely independent, so the operators have different strategies on how to organise the communication of IP packets on their network with the help of routing protocols.

Not only within Germany, the Internet as a part of the information and telecommunications technology is reckoned to the critical infrastructures [BMI09]. The impairment or loss of parts of the Internet can have an enormous impact. For example, the disturbance of IP telephony as the Skype outage in 2007[2] can lead to sustainable economic damages if a company is no longer able to conduct telephone business.

---

1 See, amongst others, the routing table of the project "Route Views" under [Rout11].
2 See [Skyp07].

N. Pohlmann, H. Reimer, W. Schneider (Editors): Securing Electronic Business Processes, Vieweg (2011), 341-351

Currently, an on-going operation of the Internet is essential. To ensure the most trouble-free operation, it is necessary to be able to observe the current state and also to estimate the future development of the Internet. It is the only way to face novel events (both positive and negative) optimally.

Basically the motivation for an Internet Key Figure System can be divided in two aspects: First, it is about the many different dependencies in the context of the Internet and second, it is about the barely available, pre-existing key figures.

1.1 Dependencies in the context of the Internet

There are many different dependencies in the context of the Internet, and in some cases, a dependency on a country – often the United States of America – can be noted. The dependencies can occur at various levels, including:

- Technical dependencies, such as the combination of parts of the Internet by means of intercontinental-laid undersea cable
- Dependencies at the service level, for example the „web surfing" without the transparent use of the Domain Name System (DNS) is hardly feasible
- Administrative dependencies, for example the Internet Corporation for Assigned Names and Numbers (ICANN) coordinates, among other things, the management of top-level domains

In the following two examples of dependencies in the context of the Internet are highlighted.

There are few very large AS (so-called Tier 1 providers) that connect large parts of the Internet and thus achieve a connectivity of almost all end systems all over the Internet. These are enormously important for the stability of the Internet. Currently the largest and most important AS are American. The largest German AS, the one of Deutsche Telekom, can be found in the lower places of the TOP25 sorted by the number of connections[3].

Another example are Border Gateway Protocol (BGP) router, which are necessary for the smooth operation of the Internet. Under certain circumstances, the failure of particular BGP router can cause many user of the Internet to be unreachable. These may be customers of an ISP or an entire nation[4].

The idea of introducing an Internet Key Figure System is to make the complex architecture of the Internet more transparent and to express its condition, changes and future potential. The Internet economy receives a common Internet Key Figure System, with which the current state of the Internet can be represented with respect to different scales (see section „5.2 Stakeholder and criteria").

1.2 Barely statistical key figures

There are barely statistical key figures for the critical infrastructure Internet. Though there are local data silos, these are not in a broader context.

---

3 See, amongst others, the routing table of the project "Route Views" under [Rout11].
4 Libya can serve as an example, which was completely separated from the rest of the Internet for some time in the spring of 2011. See, amongst others, [Heis11].

For example, large website operator or services for web traffic analysis (such as „Alexa Internet" [Alex11]) can make statements about the distribution of the website visitors' used operation systems, web browsers, software and the like. E-mail provider or blacklist operators can provide statistics on the current amount of spam. Additionally, projects such as „Route Views" [Rout11], BGPmon [Bgpm11] or „RIPE Atlas" [Ripe11a] provide information regarding the connection of Autonomous Systems or the availability of Internet services.

The various information on aspects of the Internet offer, due to the lack of a global or comprehensive nature, only a limited statement. Many findings can only be generated when different data are linked. For example, a message about a serious vulnerability in a web browser is more relevant if the software is actually used by many users. If there would be this global or at least "higher" perspective, one could measure the current state of the Internet, assess the development of the Internet better and thus make better-informed decisions for the future.

2 Basic idea of an Internet Key Figure System

Key Figure Systems are used in the area of business administration for the quick receipt of concentrated information about a company's performance and efficiency. They can also assist in planning, monitoring and controlling of a company.

Such a **Key Figure System** describes an ordered set of interdependent business key figures. It aims to inform as fully as possible about a given situation. Thus a Key Figure System groups and processes logically related key figures. Thereby the information content of the Key Figure System is about to be higher than the sum of the information content of the individual key figures.

Basically a **key figure** describes an exact quantifiable measure, which results from a reproducible measurement of a parameter, state or process. In the context of a Key Figure System a comprehensible collection of the key figures is most important. Key figures can be divided into two areas: Absolute (atomic) key figures and relative key figures. Absolute key figures are those that are integrated from outside into the Key Figure System and can not be disaggregated further. Relative key figures, however, arise from the relationship of other key figures and are formed within the Key Figure System.

An **Internet Key Figure System** is in conclusion a Key Figure System in which the situation subject to investigation is not a company, but the Internet itself. It collects key figures that relate to the Internet or that are generated by the Internet.

The idea of introducing an Internet Key Figure System is to make the complex structure of the Internet more transparent and to express its condition, changes and future potential. The Internet economy receives a common Internet Key Figure System, with which both the current state of the Internet can be represented and a retrospective consideration with respect to the measured scales can be carried out. In the course of this work the objectives, problems and added value in the design, implementation and use of an Internet Key Figure System will be treated in detail.

3 Objectives in the design of an Internet Key Figure System

An Internet Key Figure System has to provide a view on the Internet as comprehensive as possible. This requires many different aspects of the Internet to be treated and also the individual findings to be linked.

There are a number of objectives that an Internet Key Figure System has to reach. They can be divided in the three following components: Data Collection, Data Processing and Data Visualisation.

3.1 Data Collection

An Internet Key Figure System should be able to read **various data sources** in the actual data collection component. It is also important in terms of the significance of the gathered data to collect data as general as possible. For example, active measurements must take geographical backgrounds and different technologies into account. Availability and quality measurements must take place from different locations in a wide-ranging way and at best via various access technologies as well.

The data sources also have different requirements regarding the **refresh period of the key figures** that must be met through the Internet Key Figure System. We divide the requirements in three different time periods. The shortest time range covers minutes and hours. Key figures with this requirement may already have a significant amount of impact on the Internet Key Figure System just with short-term changes. In particular, data on availability of services on the Internet are very important. The medium time range covers days and months. Key figures are sorted here, when changes show medium-term effects on the Internet Key Figure System. This can include routing data from the Boarder Gateway Protocol. For example, the degree of "intermeshing" of the various Autonomous Systems can thus be observed. The third time period is for long-term data, which change only rarely or over extended periods of time. A survey is meant to be in the area of quarters or years. Interesting data are those about the development of the Internet's infrastructure, such as the average end connection's bandwidth.

Based on the different refresh periods, **various measurement methods** arise. Short and medium-term data updates are of practical use only through automated procedures. Therefore, the Internet Key Figure System must be able to independently collect data using external sensors or systems. Datasets, that have to be collected over long periods, need generally to be applied to manually.

In order to compare different key figures and to interpret the collected information, there has to be defined a certain **scope**. This may be the global Internet or a subarea such as an "Internet Germany" (see section 5.1 "Definition Internet Germany").

In connection with the scope of the Internet Key Figure System is the definition of **criteria**. It is determined which realms or layers of the Internet will be measured and treated. Defined criteria roughly structure an Internet Key Figure System (see section 5.2 "Stakeholder and criteria").

3.2 Data Processing

An Internet Key Figure System requires an **analysis and evaluation module**, with which the information collected can be processed. Different algorithms for data analysis, especially those in the field of data mining, are needed. In addition, methods are required to describe the "normal state" of the measured part of the Internet. Building on this, techniques for anomaly detection are necessary in order to detect changes in the key figures automatically. Not only the current state, but also the development of the key figures should be estimated and evaluated.

Additionally, an Internet Key Figure System should be able to highlight **different relationships** between the key figures. This can be for example logical relationships ("threat potential = threat / utilisation ratio", "encrypted = total - unencrypted"), empirical relationships ("greater use of firefox browser causes more AES/SHA1 with SSL") or hierarchical relationships ("more botnet activity leads to more DDoS attacks leads to more SYN requests").

Finally, the information gathered need to be stored in the **backend** of the Internet Key Figure System properly. Under certain circumstances there can be accumulated very much information. This is why a mechanism is needed that stores alongside established key figures also significant detail data in a privacy-compliant and economical way. This allows a retrospective analysis for relationships that were not considered or known in advance – that means at the time of data collection.

3.3 Data Visualisation

An Internet Key Figure System must be in the position to represent the collected and consolidated data specifically. There are various tools needed to allow **different views** on the key figures. Expert tools for a detailed analysis allow the user to display certain key figures (for example as time series or pie chart) and to compare them. It must be easy to verify assumptions about relationships (see section 3.2 "Data Processing") between different key figures. An information portal provides a general overview, without going into the depths. Real-time relevant information can be reduced to the essentials and be made available for example as barometers. Finally, an Internet Key Figure System must provide reporting functions. A user should be able to generate comprehensive reports on arbitrary time periods and datasets, in order to perform a quick survey or recapitulation of past developments, for example. All options for visualising the information should be designed for different devices, including implementations as a web application or "app".

4 Problems with the development of an Internet Key Figure System

Creating a Key Figure System described above is extensive and comprises many tasks and problems to be solved. Most important are less the technical aspects, but the organisational and legal aspects.

Regarding the technology, the implementation of an Internet Key Figure System is indeed a challenging but very solvable problem. During data collection, interfaces are necessary for the integration of third party data as well as sensor technologies for the active measurement of certain values. Within data processing, various algorithm for data analysis, especially those in the field of data mining, are needed. Building on this, techniques for anomaly detection are required in order to detect changes in the key figures automatically. The data visualisation component can access many frameworks that can represent comprehensive information intelligently.

In the following four problem areas are presented, which has to be solved during the development and operation of an Internet Key Figure System.

4.1 Participating companies

One of the biggest problems is to identify and to integrate participating companies. Like any other key figure system an Internet Key Figure System also relies on a variety of data. Some information can usually be collected, processed and visualised with no effort by the operator of the system itself. There are also lots of data, which have a considerable explanatory power, but are not freely accessible. A combination of these data with existing information would possibly bring new findings and thereby constitute an added value (see chapter 6.1 "Identification of relationships").

Without corresponding agreements, it is hardly possible to incorporate non-public information in the Internet Key Figure System. This is particularly true if the company is not interested in the results of the Key Figure System or does not see any added value in the cooperation. Does the operator of an Internet Key Figure System fails to motivate relevant enterprises into a cooperation or to convince them of the added value, the development and operation of an Internet Key Figure System turns out to be difficult.

4.2 Privacy

Another focus is on the privacy. The required data must be collected and stored in a manner that meets two requirements.

On the one hand, the necessary privacy of each collected information must be met. There are data that are less critical – in the sense of privacy – than others. As an example, the number of DSL lines in Germany at a certain time shall be compared with the communication parameters measured at an Internet exchange point within a given period.

On the other hand, there has to be created a solid date base in spite of the privacy-compliance, which allows a later reinterpretation of the data. The retrospective interpretation of a dataset regarding criteria, that were not considered in a first analysis, must be feasible.

4.3 Scope

It is necessary to define a clear demarcation for the measured part of the Internet (a scope). This has the background that the key figures and the derived findings must be interpretable and comparable. For example, the demarcation of the Internet can be accomplished by a country (see section 5 "Internet Key Figures for Germany"). Due to the nature of the Internet, it is difficult to draw clear "boarders". The significance of some key figures is strongly influenced by the definition of the scope, for which reason a certain fuzziness of the used Internet Key Figure System remains.

4.4 Financing

Another problem is the financing of an Internet Key Figure System. A Key Figure System as such does not achieve any revenue from operating activities. It rather relies on the fact that interested groups and companies, that possibly are involved in data collection and data processing, involve in maintaining the Key Figure System. At this point it is again the task of the Key Figure System's operator to create incentives for using and supporting the system.

5 Internet Key Figures for Germany

The necessity for an Internet Key Figure System described in this work is also specifically given for the Federal Republic of Germany. A system is needed that allows to collect and process key figures for the Internet. Such information, made available and compressed, about a to be defined "Internet Germany" (see section 5.1 "Definition Internet Germany") can serve appropriate points as a basis for the creation of options for actions regarding the Internet. Targets of these recommendations may be different decision-maker: The politics, participating companies, or even citizens. Using an established Internet Key Figure System it is possible to evaluate, whether implemented actions achieved the desired effect.

5.1 Definition "Internet Germany"

One of the most important requirements for a Key Figure System for Germany is the definition of a scope. One way to define an "Internet Germany" refers to the Autonomous Systems (see figure 1): .

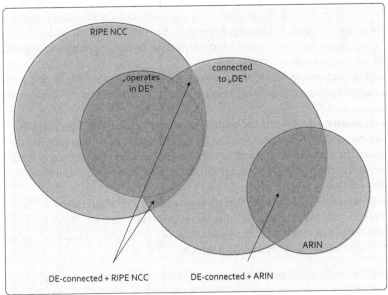

Fig. 1: Possible definition of an "Internet Germany" via Autonomous Systems.

From the approximately 37,000 currently active Autonomous Systems on the Internet only those are relevant, where the operator is active in Germany. This can be justified, for example, with the geographic use of the assigned IP addresses (for instance via a GeoIP database), or the country classification of the RIPE database [Ripe11b]. Beyond that, such Autonomous Systems are counted to the "Internet Germany", which are directly connected with the aforementioned AS and in addition are placed in Europe or North America. This corresponds to the registration at RIPE NCC or ARIN.

5.2 Stakeholder and criteria

The Internet in general – and thus the "Internet Germany" in particular – can be divided in different aspects or actors, which contain all the elements involved in the Internet. In business administration these views on a control object are also called perspectives [Kuet03].

The Internet's aspects are divided into four areas:

- **Participants**: All Internet-connected user end devices (PCs, laptops, smart phones, cars, refrigerators, …).
- **Infrastructure**: Equipment and structures, which allow participants to use the Internet's services (AS with BGP routers, connections, …).
- **Services**: Any provision of service that are made available to the Internet's users (e-mail, Web, VoIP, …).
- **Threats**: These are all dangers lurking on the Internet for other aspects of the Internet (malware, botnets, …).

From the four aspects those criteria are derived, about which the Internet Key Figure System has to provide information:

- **Capability**: Represents the infrastructure aspect of the Key Figure System and contains parameter that make statements about the capacity and dependencies of the Internet. Such parameters include the average hop count, bandwidth and packet loss rate. Furthermore, the information is relevant, what proportion of the Autonomous Systems can be reached without the use of transit.
- **Availability**: Represents the services aspect of the Key Figure System and covers statements regarding the availability of services on the Internet from the perspective of end users.
- **Usage estimation**: Represents the participants aspect of the Key Figure System and contains parameter that make statements about the utilisation of the Internet and the technologies used. These include, for example, the penetration rates of operating systems, browser software and access technologies such as DSL or UMTS, as well as the breakdown of the total data volume.
- **Threat potential**: Represents the threats aspect of the Key Figure System and covers parameter that make statements about the threat of the Internet. Examples for a threat indicator can be the number of new virus signatures per measured period, the total number of infected websites or the measured data rates of DDoS attacks.

Using an Internet Key Figure System various key figures with regard to different criteria of the "Internet Germany" are made available. Via these key figures, a comprehensive view on the German Internet in terms of different aspects are getting possible.

6 Added value through the use of an Internet Key Figure System

The objective of an Internet Key Figure System for Germany is to provide added value, which would not be possible without such a system. The first of the two most important added value is the possibility to detect relationships between different measurements. This is possible at all by the second added value, the comprehensive context of the key figures. Other added value are the possibility to provide the Internet Key Figure System as a data base to third parties, as well as the supply of a comprehensive data base for the generation of options for actions.

6.1 Identification of relationships

Probably the biggest added value of a Key Figure System for the Internet is the collection and consolidation of much information that promote the understanding of the critical infrastructure Internet. For example, availability key figures can be determined to give information about the accessibility of websites and services. Statistics on protocols and technologies of the Internet are possible if anonymous data of central Internet infrastructure points is collected and processed. Interesting aspects are, for example, the distribution of used web browsers, operating systems, or the ratio of IPv4 to IPv6. It can be given a view of the interdependence of the Internet, if (freely available) BGP routing data is retrieved and processed. In particular, the connections of the AS among each other are interesting. Different service provider on the Internet have massive data bases with respect to the Internet and make parts of it freely accessible for the retrieval via APIs. New findings by a combination and analysis of the key figures become possible. Infrastructure data, such as information on the spread of mobile devices, Internet access technologies and more, can be integrated by statistics or reports of various institutions. Publicly available vulnerability databases of security initiatives and security barometers can be used in order to collect the spread of security breaches, damage due to cyber crime or spam volumes and more.

6.2 Comprehensive Context

Through a comprehensive Key Figure System there is a data base available that not only exists locally, but has also a broader context. Knowledge can be generated, the current state of the Internet can be measured, the development of the Internet can better be assessed and thus better-informed decisions for the future can be made. In summary, possibly unknown relationships can be better established, forecasts using the newly acquired findings be created and developments be explained.

6.3 Data base for third parties

A recently described Internet Key Figure System will collect much information and perform a lot of analysis and interpretations, but also provides a good basis for further work and observations by third parties. On the one hand a collaboration is thus possible through participating companies together with their key figures provided. On the other hand, the system can be used by third parties and accordingly serve as a data base itself. Users can not only base on experience, but also refer to specific numbers and draw their own conclusions.

6.4 Generation of options for actions

An Internet Key Figure System provides plenty of processed and compressed information, which can be used as a base by competent authorities to create options for actions. Targets of these recommendations are different decision-maker: The politics, participating companies or citizens. In addition, an evaluation is possible whether the measures implemented have achieved the desired effect.

- **Politics**: Good information is the basis for effective management and proper decisions on regulatory and legal issues. Statements can be confirmed using the Internet Key Figure System where possible or arguments can be disproved.
- **Participating companies**: Good information can reveal trends and developments in the Internet market and thus improve the basis for strategic decisions. In addition, internal company data can be correlated with Internet Key Figures and thus be enriched or cross checked.
- **Citizens**: Appropriate represented information can promote the interest in sub topics of the Internet – for instance the aspect of security. Awareness raising can take place, for example, when a strong increase in phishing emails or infected websites are presented and appropriate warnings or behaviours are issued.

7 Summary

An Internet Key Figure System that meets the requirements described in this work is a powerful expert tool for performance control and trend detection on the Internet. In particular, a specialised focus on a certain part of the Internet, for example an "Internet Germany", allows findings that would not be that apparent within generalised (global) systems. Furthermore, the current state of the Internet can be measured, normal conditions can be defined and deviations or anomalies can rapidly be detected.

The collected data allow, by means of their quantification, to discover, substantiate and analyse possibly existent, but yet unknown relationships. The type of key figures, relationships and statements is not limited to one particular aspect – such as an exclusively economic or technical issue –, but depends largely on the rules that generated and analysed the key figures. The composition and analysis of the key figures provide a great potential for further research and work.

Far from that, the success of an Internet Key Figure System depends mainly on the participating companies. Like any Key Figure System an Internet Key Figure System is also only as good as the data entered. In addition to the freely available data, the on-going and voluntary contribution of so far unpublished data is absolutely desirable and necessary. This enhances the significance of the Internet Key Figure System.

Acknowledgment

This work is part of the project "Deutscher Internet-Index (DIX)"[5], which is funded by the Federal Ministry of Economics and Technology (BMWi). The contents of this publication is solely in charge of the authors and reflect in no way the BMWi's opinion.

5　German for „German Internet Index".

References

[Alex11]   Alexa Internet Inc.: Alexa the Web Information Company. http://www.alexa.com (Last Access: 01.08.11), 2011.

[Bgpm11]   BGPmon: BGPmon.net, a BGP monitoring and analyzer tool. http://bgpmon.net (Last Access: 01.08.11), 2011.

[BMI09]   Bundesministerium des Innern: Nationale Strategie zum Schutz Kritischer Infrastrukturen (KRITIS-Strategie). Berlin, 12. Juni 2009.

[Heis11]   heise Netze: Internet-Abschaltung: Libyen hat von Ägypten gelernt. http://www.heise.de/netze/ meldung/Internet-Abschaltung-Libyen-hat-von-Aegypten-gelernt-1206016.html (Last Access: 01.08.11), 2011.

[Kuet03]   Martin Kütz: Kennzahlen in der IT - Werkzeuge für das Controlling und Management. dpunkt Verlag, 2003.

[Ripe11a]   RIPE Network Coordination Centre: RIPE Atlas. http://atlas.ripe.net/ (Last Access: 01.08.11), 2011.

[Ripe11b]   RIPE Network Coordination Centre: Delegated RIPE NCC Latest. ftp://ftp.ripe.net/pub/stats/ ripencc/delegated-ripencc-latest (Last Access: 01.08.11), 2011.

[Rout11]   University of Oregon Route Views Project: Route Views Project Page. http://routeviews.org (Last Access: 01.08.11), 2011.

[Skyp07]   Skype Technologies SA: What happened on August 16. http://heartbeat.skype.com/2007/08/ (Last Access: 01.08.11), 2007.

Improved Feature Selection Method using SBS-IG-Plus

Maher Salem · Ulrich Bühler · Sven Reißmann

University of Applied Sciences Fulda
Faculty of Applied Sciences
Marquardstraße 35, 36039 Fulda, Germany
{maher.salem | u.buehler | sven.reissmann}@informatik.hs-fulda.de

Abstract

Any network can be represented by a set of attributes (features). There are several methods attempting to derive the best feature set at all. In our proposed method we exploited the anomaly detection rate and the false positive rate by using a Sequential Backward Search (SBS) method followed by Information Gain (IG) to get the best and valuable feature set properly. In SBS we used several classifiers to evaluate our results. These are Neural Network, Naïve Bayes, Decision Tree and Random Tree. Our method outperformed other approaches because of involving SBS method. We could reduce the huge data set to a more efficient and usable data set without any irrelevant features that defer the performance. Using these features we have enhanced the detection rate and reduced the alarm rate in the network. We have chosen the improved dataset from DARPA 98 Lincoln Lab evaluation Data set (NSL-KDD Set), because it is universally used for learning and testing in the IDS.

1 Introduction

In Network Intrusion Detection System (NIDS) the selected features have a dominant role of affecting the detection rate and the false positive rate. NIDS is being investigated in the last decade to detect and defend attacks and illegality on the network and to improve the performance of the network. There are two types of NIDS; that is, Misuse detection and anomaly detection system [JaVa91]. In Misuse detection we compare the traffic against known signatures and raise an alarm if the comparison finds a match, else the traffic will be normal. But the drawbacks here are that unknown attacks will not be classified and recognized and the value of the false positive will be increased rapidly. Therefore the second type of NIDS has solved this problem by detecting the unknown attacks and any abnormal event in the network. Anomaly detection is working by building a model and monitors any deviation of this model to classify it as normal or most possibly as anomaly.

Any network can be represented by a set of features with related instances. This can help understanding the network and detecting the malicious that are threatening it. These features and instances are called data set and they are collected or derived from several resources such as system logs and connection data. According to rapid network expansion, a data set is very large and has a high dimensionality. In our approach a filter and wrapper methods have been investigated into two steps to explore the best feature set. The first step is the Sequential Backward Search (SBS) method by which a general evaluation test for all features in NSL-KDD [NLSK99] has been done to measure the detection rate and the false positive rate. The used classifiers in the previous evaluation test are Naive Bayes, Decision Tree-J48, Random Tree and Neural Network – Multilayer Perceptron. The second step is to rank the selected features from step one using Information Gain (IG) method. Most of approaches have used the IG method to select the best features from NSL-KDD data set, either alone or with another method to define a threshold or selecting criteria. IG alone fails to identify discriminatory features [MWR+07]. Therefore, because it is suitable to reduce dimensionality and remove irrelevant features in a huge data set, we have proposed a floating search method SBS. In addition this method is capable of discovering out the features affect detection rate and the false positive rate.

The remainder of this paper is organized as follows. Section 2 will discuss some related work in this field whereas section 3 will clearly explain our proposed method. Section 4 will show and discuss our results, and finally section five will summarize our work by a conclusion and future works.

2 Related Work

In the past decades, a large number of feature selections in NIDS have been proposed. Some proposals have examined floating search methods. P.Pauli et al. [PFNK94] discussed forward search and backward search methods and compared them to the (l,r) search method, but they did not mentioned the best search method for a huge data set. Yao-Hung Chan et al. [CWYC10] studied only the searching methods sequential backward search and sequential forward search with the Localized Generalization Error (L-GEM) as threshold criteria and Radial Basis Function Neural Network (RBFNN) as classifier. The SBS showed better performance when the number of features is large enough. P. Somol et al. [SPNP99] modified the floating search to adaptive floating search and focused on forward search. The proposed method yielded with a better feature set. Due to the space limitation in the paper we could not discuss all papers here. For more details about floating search methods refer to [JaZo97], [HaHo03] and [YNW+07]. In order to prepare a statistical data set for IG, a Discretization method must be applied to the features with continuous value in NSL-KDD data set. In this respect, Chotirat "Ann" Ratanamahatana [Rata03] compared between Equal Width Discretizer (EWD), Proportional k-interval method (PKID), Entropy minimization heuristic and proposed method CloNI. As a result, the method CloNI is optimal for discretization in a large data set and outperforms other methods. Usama M. Fayyad and Keki B. Irani [FaIr93] used information entropy minimization heuristics with minimum description length principle as a criterion to decide the partitions of intervals. This approach pointed to better classification only with decision tree classifier. V. Bolon-Canedo et al. [BoSA09] combined several discretizers together. They found out that the detection rate and the false positive rate are dependable on classifier typ. It is worth mentioning that only 7 features from the KDD Data set can achieve good performance. Based on these discussions, our selected Discretization method is the Equal Frequency Discretizer (EFD) in [JLZW09], because of its simplicity and promising results in NSL-KDD data set. Moreover we can apply it directly in the simulation tool Weka 3.7 [MEG+09].

C.S. Dhir et al. [DhIL07] utilized information gain with independent component analysis to perform better detection rate especially in face recognition. Yang Li et al. [LFCG06] exploited Chi-Square with information gain. Chi-Square fulfills the requirements of the maximum entropy model for intrusion detection. We used IG just to rank the features after classification. These research investigated IG to build a classification model. Therefore, we are neither concerned with face recognition nor with building a model based IG.

3 Proposed Method

3.1 Sequential Backward Search

Recently, search methods are used in intrusion detection systems to improve selecting features. Sequential Backward Search (SFS) is one of floating search method. Other floating search methods are Sequential Forward Search (SBS) and Plus-L minus-R selection (LRS). SBS shows better feature selection with large data set. In contrast, the SFS deals with small data set or several small data sets. The following steps are explaining our proposed SBS method:

1. Initialize D as full data set with F features and I instances.
2. let F_{plus} for selected features and F_{minus} for removed features
3. Initialize $F_{plus} = \Phi$ and $F_{minus} = \Phi$
4. Choose different classifiers to evaluate the detection rate and the false positive rate
5. Loop
   a. Remove feature fi from D and its related instances as well
   b. If the detection rate and the false positive rate deviate from a certain threshold
      Then $F_{plus} \leftarrow \{fi\}$
      Else $F_{minus} \leftarrow \{fi\}$
   c. $i = i+1$
6. Repeat until D is empty
7. F_{plus} has the selected features that affect the detection rate and the false positive rate
8. F_{minus} has the features that not affect the detection rate and the false positive rate.

In SBS, the data set consists of 41 features (see table 1) and 126000 instances have been used. Using this method we could reduce the dimensionality of the data and remove the redundant features. The tool for classification is Weka 3.7.

Our selection criterion is the mean value and the standard deviation of both the detection rate and the false positive rate for each classifier. We have illustrated this in section 4.

3.2 Discretization

Discretization is concerned with converting a feature with continuous value into discrete value to be able to process. IG method in our approach handles only discrete values. Therefore, features with continuous value in NSL-KDD have been discretized. Equal Frequency Discretizer (EFD) divides the interval into k groups (Bins) with equal occurrences each. We have initialized the number of bins to 20. EFD is simple and easy to implement. Moreover, compared with EWD, the latter may produce bad results when most of occurrences fell into one group. The following figure shows an example of EFD.

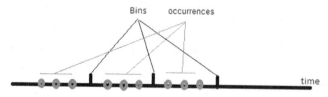

Fig. 1: Equal Frequency Discretization example

Figure 1 shows a data set grouped into 3 Bins and each group (Bin) has 3 occurrences.

3.3 Information Gain Method

Information Gain (IG) method has been used to rank the selected features. The most important quantity of information is entropy. Quantity of information or information gain uses the entropy to measure the uncertainty of attribute x associated with the value of the random variable X. Or it called Shannon entropy.

Let us suppose that X and Y are discrete random variables, $I(Y;X)$ is the information gain of a given attribute with respect to the class attribute .

When Y and X are discrete variables that take values in $\{y_1,...,y_k\}$ and $\{x,...,x_l\}$ with the probability distribution function $P(X)$, then the entropy of X is given by:

$$H(X) = -\sum_{i=1}^{l} P(X = x_i)\log_2\left(P(X = x_i)\right)$$

Information gain of feature F on the dataset D in our proposed method is defined as:

$$IG(D,F) = H(D) - \sum_{Attr \in Value(F)}\left[\frac{|D_{Attr}|}{|D|} \cdot H(D_{Attr})\right]$$

where $Value(F)$ is the set of possible value of F, D_{Attr} is the subset of D where F has value $Attr$, $H(D)$ = entropy of class attribute and |.| donates cardinality. For example, let be $F='protocol type'$, then $Value(F)=\{TCP,UDP,ICMP\}$ and $D\_Attr=\{D\_TCP,D\_UDP,D\_ICMP\}$, D_ICMP is the subset that contains only ICMP of feature $'protocol type'$

3.4 Model explanation

Figure 2 below explains our model and that joins all three steps, SBS, Discretization and IG together.

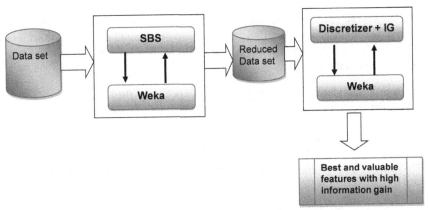

Fig. 2: Architecture of the proposed Model

The above diagram illustrates our proposed model and the flow of steps. NSL-KDD data set loaded into Weka by using SBS algorithm. Reduced data set should be generated and input to be discretized. Then IG will be calculated for all selected features and ranked in a descending order. All features with zero IG value or close to zero will be neglected. As a result, we have a set of the best valuable features.

4 Results and Discussion

The following table shows the NSL-KDD features used in our proposed method:

Table 1: All features listed in NSL-KDD Data set

1	duration	15	srv_count	29	Hot
2	protocol_type	16	srv_serror_rate	30	num_failed_logins
3	service	17	srv_rerror_rate	31	logged_in
4	flag	18	srv_diff_host_rate	32	num_compromised
5	src_bytes	19	dst_host_count	33	root_shell
6	dst_bytes	20	dst_host_serror_rate	34	su_attempted
7	land	21	dst_host_rerror_rate	35	num_root
8	wrong_fragment	22	dst_host_same_srv_rate	36	num_file_creations
9	urgent	23	dst_host_diff_srv_rate	37	num_shells
10	count	24	dst_host_srv_count	38	num_access_files
11	serror_rate	25	dst_host_srv_serror_rate	39	num_outbound_cmds
12	rerror_rate	26	dst_host_srv_rerror_rate	40	is_hot_login
13	same_srv_rate	27	dst_host_srv_diff_host_rate	41	is_guest_login
14	diff_srv_rate	28	dst_host_same_src_port_rate	42	Class

4.1 Results of SBS method

After loading the data set into Weka we removed one feature and recorded the detection rate and the false positive rate for each classifier. This process has to be repeated until the data set is empty. Finally, the mean value and standard deviation have been calculated. A certain deviation from the mean value is our selected criterion.

Suppose we have N samples and the samples set is $X=\{x_1,...,x_N\}$ then the Mean value and the Standard Deviation are defined as

$$\bar{x} = \frac{1}{N}\sum_{i=1}^{N} x_i \text{ and } \sigma = \sqrt{\frac{\sum_{i=1}^{N}(x_i - \bar{x})}{N-1}}.$$

We have evaluated the detection rate and the false positive rate, then calculated the mean value and standard deviation for the previous mentioned classifiers.

Due to large tables size and data calculation we presented a result for one classifier. The following table shows the detection rate, the false positive rate, and the mean and standard deviation of Neural Network-Multilayer Perceptron classifier.

Table 2: Detection rate using SBS method and neural network classifier

Removed feature	Detection rate	False Positive rate
Protocol_type	0.9720	0.029
Count	0.9750	0.026
Src_bytes	0.9750	0.026
.....	......	....
Service	0.9720	0.03
Mean value	0.9739	0.0271
Standard deviation	0.0013	0.0012

As shown in the table we label the first column by 'Removed feature'. That means we remove one feature out of the data set and classify the rest of the data set, then record the detection rate and the false positive rate. Next we returned the feature back into the data set and removed the next feature to record the detection rate and the false positive rate again. For example, when we remove the feature "count" from the data set, we get a detection rate of 0.9750 and a false positive rate of 0.026.

The figure 4 illustrates the selection criterion e.g. in Neural Network-Multilayer Perceptron.

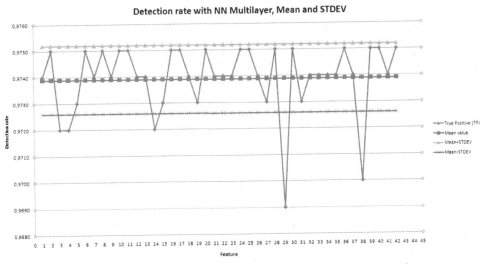

Fig. 3: Detection rate result using SBS method and neural network Classifier

Features on the figure are numbered from 1 to 42 (see table 1). We have calculated the maximum deviation and the minimum deviation from the mean value. These derivations are considered the margin of our selected criterion. If the detection rate of the removed feature fell outside the deviation margin, then it is an important feature. In this case we call it 'Most valuable feature'. In contrast, if the feature fell into the deviation margin then it is not an important feature and it will be removed. Finally, if the feature fell on the deviation margin (border) we call it 'Relevant feature'.

For example, the mean value of detection rate is 0.9739. Our criterion margin is the interval, which is the margin between 0.9726 and 0.9752. When we removed the feature "hot" (feature number 29) from the data set we got detection rate of value 0.969. This value is out of criterion margin, so removing it from the data set will decrease the detection rate. Therefore, it is our 'Most valuable feature'. On the other hand, feature "logged_in" (number 31) which fell into our criterion margin. Therefore, it is not an important feature and should be removed. Finally, the resulted feature sets for all 4 classifiers are:

Table 3: result feature sets of the detection rate and the false positive rate for all classifiers

Classifier	Features affect the detection rate	Features affect the false positive rate
Neural Networks (NN)	3, 4, 14, 29, 38	3, 4, 14, 15, 27, 29, 31, 38
Naïve Bayes (NB)	4, 9, 28	4, 9, 28
Decision Tree (J48)	11, 22, 30	21, 29
Random Tree (RT)	3, 6 ,8, 9, 10, 20, 21,26,29,34,39	3,6,8,9,10,12,13,20,21,26,29,34,39

Venn-Diagram shows the logical relation between all feature sets. The following Venn-Diagram for 4 sets shows the resulted features.

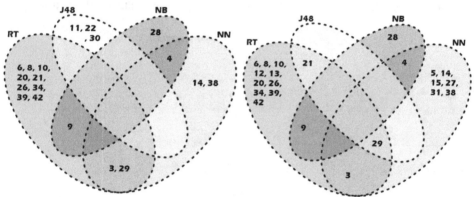

Figure 4: Venn-Diagram for all features affecting the detection rate (left) and the false positive rate (right)

As a result, the intersection shows the 'Most valuable features'. We generated two final feature sets: Most valuable feature set, Most valuable and Relevant feature set. The Most valuable feature set is the intersection from the 'Most valuable features' of the detection rate and the 'Most valuable features' of the false positive rate. The Most valuable and Relevant feature set is the intersection from the 'Most valuable and Relevant features' of the detection rate and the 'Most valuable and Relevant features' of the false positive rate. The following table shows our results of SBS method.

Table 4: result feature sets of SBS method

Feature set	Feature
Most valuable feature set	3, 4, 6, 9, 8, 10, 14, 20, 21, 26, 28, 29, 38, 39
Most valuable and Relevant feature set	3, 4, 6, 9, 8, 10, 14, 20, 21, 26, 28, 29, 38, 39, 11, 12, 13, 15, 22, 27, 30, 31, 34

4.2 Result of IG Method

The information gain method uses the result from SBS. So we have prepared two data sets for information gain, the 'Most valuable feature set' and the 'Most valuable and Relevant feature set'.

We have discretized both data sets before using IG. The following tables present the information gain values for the features in both data sets ranked in descending order.

Table 5: information gain for all features in Most valuable data set

Feature	Information Gain
Service	0.6715649
dst_bytes	0.58435007
Flag	0.51938822
diff_srv_rate	0.50089399
dst_host_serror_rate	0.39539431
Count	0.34681662
dst_host_same_src_port_rate	0.17893258
dst_host_srv_rerror_rate	0.08504881
dst_host_rerror_rate	0.05090946
Hot	0.01093148
wrong_fragment	0.00960996
num_access_files	0.00216444
Urgent	0.0000089
num_outbound_cmds	0

Table 6: information gain for all features in Most valuable and Relevant data set.

Features	Information Gain
Service	0.6715649
dst_bytes	0.58435007
Flag	0.51938822
diff_srv_rate	0.50089399
same_srv_rate	0.47857645
dst_host_same_srv_rate	0.41792864
logged_in	0.40475154
dst_host_serror_rate	0.39539431
serror_rate	0.37787435
Count	0.34681662
dst_host_srv_diff_host_rate	0.25915986
dst_host_same_src_port_rate	0.17893258

dst_host_srv_rerror_rate	0.08504881
rerror_rate	0.05451864
dst_host_rerror_rate	0.05090946
srv_count	0.04413898
Hot	0.01093148
wrong_fragment	0.00960996
num_access_files	0.00216444
su_attempted	0.00052957
num_failed_logins	0.00011326
Urgent	0.0000089
num_outbound_cmds	0

Our selected criterion in IG is removing the feature with zero value or close to zero. Feature is close to zero when its IG value is less than 10^{-4}. According to this criterion our resulted feature sets are:

Most valuable Feature set:
{Service, dst_bytes, flag, diff_srv_rate, dst_host_serror_rate, count, dst_host_same_src_port_rate, dst_host_srv_rerror_rate, dst_host_rerror_rate, hot, wrong_fragment, num_access_files}

Most valuable and Relevant Feature set:
{Service, dst_bytes, flag, diff_srv_rate, dst_host_serror_rate, count, dst_host_same_src_port_rate, dst_host_srv_rerror_rate, dst_host_rerror_rate, hot, wrong_fragment, num_access_files, same_save_rate, dst_host_same_srv_rate, logged_in, serror_rate, srv_count}

5 Conclusion and Future Work

Any network can be represented by several features, which can then represent a normal network behaviors and upon these features any deviation from the normal activities will be detected. In our proposed work we have used the sequential backward search method to reduce the data set dimensionality and remove the irrelevant features. We have generated two data sets, each has different features. We have ranked these features using the information gain.

Our proposed method has shown outperform results. We could reduce the huge data set to a more efficient and usable data set without any irrelevant features that defer the performance. Using these features we have enhanced the detection rate and reduced the alarm rate in the network.

Our future work will focus on building a Dependability Model, which derives correlated features that accelerate the performance of network and boost the classification by increasing the detection rate and decreasing the false positive rate in intrusion detection systems.

References

[MWR+07] Mukras, Rahman, Wiratunga, Nirmalie, Lothian, Robert, Chakraborti, Sutanu, Harper, David: Information Gain Feature Selection for Ordinal Text Classification using Probability Re-distribution. In Proc. of IJCAI Textlink Workshop. 2007.

[JaVa91] S. Javitz, Harold, Valdes, Alfonso: The SRI IDES Statistical Anomaly Detector. In Research in Security and Privacy. Proceedings. IEEE Computer Society Symposium. 1991, p. 316-326.

[PFNK94] P. Pudilr, F.J. Ferrii, J. Novovicova, J. Kittler: Floating search methods for feature selection with nonmonotonic criterion functions. In Pattern Recognition, Vol. 2 - Conference B: Computer Vision & Image Processing., Proceedings of the 12th IAPR International Conference. 1994, p. 279-283.

[CWYC10] Yao-Hong Chan, Wing W.Y.Ng, Daniel S. Yeung, Patrick P. K. Chan: Empirical Comparison Of Forward And Backward Search Strategies In L-GEM Based Feature Selection With RBFNN. In Proceedings of the Ninth International Conference on Machine Learning and Cybernetics, Qingdao, 2010.

[SPNP99] P. Somol, P. Pudil, J. Novovicova, P. Paclik: Adaptive Floating search methods in feature selection. In Pattern Recognition Letters 20, 1999, p. 1157-1163

[JaZo97] Jain, Anil, Zongker, Douglas: Feature Selection: Evaluation, Application, and Small Sample Performance. In IEEE Transactions on Pattern Analysis and Machine Intelligence - PAMI, 1997, vol. 19, no. 2, p. 153-158.

[HaHo03] Hall , Mark A., Holmes Geoffrey: Benchmarking Attribute Selection Techniques for Discrete Class Data Mining. In IEEE TRANSACTIONS ON KNOWLEDGE AND DATA ENGINEERING, VOL. 15, NO. 6, 2003, p. 1437 – 1447.

[YNW+07] Daniel S. Yeung, Wing W. Y. Ng, Defeng Wang, Eric C. C. Tsang, Xi-Zhao Wang: Localized Generalization Error Model and Its Application to Architecture Selection for Radial Basis Function Neural Network. In IEEE TRANSACTIONS ON NEURAL NETWORKS, VOL. 18, NO. 5, 2007, p. 1294 – 1305.

[Rata03] Ratanamahatana, Chotirat: CloNI: Clustering of sqrt(N)-Interval Discretization. In proceedings of the 4th International Conference on Data Mining Including Building Application for CRM & Competitive Intelligence, Rio de Janeiro, Brazil, December 2003.

[FaIr93] Fayyad, Usama M., Irani, Keki B.: Multi-Interval Discretization of Continuous-Valued Attributes for Classification Learning. In Proceedings of the 13th International Joint Conference on Artificial Intelligence, 1993.

[BoSA09] V. Bolon-Canedo, N. Sanchez-Marofio and A. Alonso-Betanzos: A Combination of Discretization and Filter Methods for Improving Classification Performance in KDD Cup 99 Dataset. In Proceedings of International Joint Conference on Neural Networks, Atlanta, Georgia, USA, June 14-19, 2009.

[JLZW09] Sheng-yi Jiang, Xia Li, Qi Zheng, Lian-xi Wang: Approximate Equal Frequency Discretization Method. In Intelligent Systems, GCIS ‹09. WRI Global Congress, 2009, p. 514 – 518.

[DhIL07] Dhir, C.S., Iqbal, N., Lee ,Soo-Young: Efficient feature selection based on information gain criterion for face recognition. In Information Acquisition, 2007. ICIA ‹07. International Conference, 2007, p. 523 – 527.

[LFCG06] Yang Li, Bin-Xing Fang, You Chen, Li Guo: A Lightweight Intrusion Detection Model Based on Feature Selection and Maximum Entropy Model. In Communication Technology, ICCT ‹06. International Conference, 2006, p. 1-4.

[NSLK99] http://iscx.ca/NSL-KDD/

[MEG+09] Mark Hall, Eibe Frank, Geoffrey Holmes, Bernhard Pfahringer, Peter Reutemann, Ian H. Witten (2009); The WEKA Data Mining Software: An Update; SIGKDD Explorations, Volume 11, Issue 1.

SCADA Security: A Risky Environment

Maarten B. Nieuwenhuis

KPMG IT Advisory
Amsterdam, The Netherlands
nieuwenhuis.maarten@kpmg.nl

Abstract

Process Control Domain systems, which are often referred to as SCADA, are crucial for our society. These systems can be found throughout – from power plants to water processing facilities to traffic light controlling systems, also referred to as critical national infrastructure. The state of security of these crucial systems is not well. This is caused by a lack of security focus for these systems which can be explained by assessing the topics people, process and technology: non-security aware people manage complex, real-time processes using technology which is used for purposes outside of original design scope.

1 Introduction: what is SCADA?

Supervisory Control And Data Acquisition (SCADA) systems provide monitoring and management of critical infrastructure such as transport and processing of water, electricity generation and transport, chemical production plants, pharmaceuticals production plants, food production environments, refineries for gas and oil and traffic control systems.

Process Control Networks (PCNs) take care of communications between SCADA networks and the systems these interact with.

In general, these systems are referred to as Process Control Domain (PCD), since these types of systems are often used in controlling very specific processes within a set domain: controlling the process of water cleaning, production of specific chemicals or controlling traffic lights.

1.1 Terminology

SCADA systems are the management and control systems within a specific PCD, where PCNs take care of the communication between systems involved. SCADA is a popular term which is often used to refer to what is in fact the PCD. Throughout this document will be referred to the described systems as PCD.

Figure 1 depicts a typical plant layout within the PCD with separate hierarchies of control exerted over the PCD, typically referred to as layers one through three, with one being the most detailed level of control (control and automation level):

N. Pohlmann, H. Reimer, W. Schneider (Editors): Securing Electronic Business Processes, Vieweg (2011), 362-370

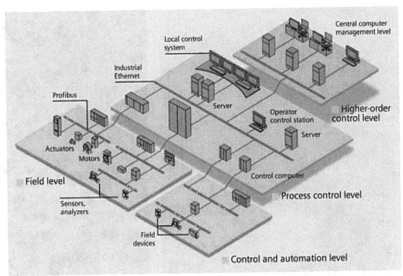

Fig. 1: Layout of a typical plant in the Process Control Domain. Source: [SIEM]

1.2 Relevance

Why is PCD relevant? The PCD is an environment which exerts control over the 'real' physical world, as opposed to office IT, which is concerned with manipulating data in various formats. Robots, pumps, valves, heaters and so on are all actuators controlled via the PCD. Problems with security in the PCD can have serious consequences in the 'real' world. Think of bridges which suddenly close, oil pipelines which rupture or nuclear power plants which start going out of control and the consequences this may have for the 'real' world.

1.2.1 Examples of PCD security gone wrong

To illustrate the impact PCD security can have: figure 2 shows clearly what the consequences can be in case of problems with PCD security. A combination of increasing pressure by pumping more and more fuel into an already damaged pipeline led to the rupture of the pipeline, the discharge of one million gallons of fuel that ignited in a big explosion, huge damage, the death of people and five days worth of putting out the resulting fires.

Fig. 2: Gasoline Pipeline Rupture and Explosion at Whatcom Creek [TCAB01].

2 How to assess PCD security?

2.2.1 Topics

There are multiple ways to go about analysing PCD security: three topics will be consistently used to analyse the problem surrounding PCD security: people, process and technology. This model has been used many times and seems appropriate to help analyse in assessing PCD security, because of the orthogonal nature of these topics.

- People will concern employees, organisational causes and those elements which can be ascribed to human behaviour and key stakeholders;
- Process will concern behaviours coming forward from priorities set within a business environment;
- Technology will concern those aspects which have to do with the level of development or implemented technology.

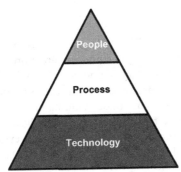

Fig. 3: The PPT pyramid used for structuring this proceeding on SCADA security.

2.2.2 Structure

Using these three topics, the following questions will be discussed:
- What is the reason that security problems exist in the PCD?
- How can PCD security problems be addressed?
- What do we expect for the future?

3 What is the reason that security problems exist in the PCD?

Within the PCD the topic of 'security' is a relatively hot topic which was not addressed as such before. Trying to grasp from experience in the field why PCD security issues exist leads to the following, an analysis of root causes for PCD insecurity. References for existing security problems in PCD can be found here: [CIIP, SCAD].

3.1 Currently observed security problems in PCD

Currently security risks exist within the PCD. These risks will be specified, based upon publicly available sources and practical experience from PCD security assessments as performed for companies by the author.

Current PCD security issues that have been observed are the following:
- A general lack of security awareness and criticality of PCD systems;
- Immature organisation managing the PCD;
- No strong network segregation between PCD and other networks;
- No network traffic plans for PCD communications;
- Old systems and software in use;
- System hardening non-existent;
- Poor user management;
- Logging and monitoring limitedly implemented;
- Anti-virus often lacking;
- Little PCD vendor support for security;
- Poor procedures in place for managing the PCD.

3.2 People

Historically people involved with the PCD were engineers, turning nuts and bolts when the PCD was still contained to the 'real' world, when engineers were more like mechanics. With the digitisation of process controlling systems from 'flipping relays' to modern operating systems based devices – PCD engineers more and more became IT managers (as opposed to mechanics). Theoretic knowledge on physical processes and understanding of how physical processes operate in the field needs to be complemented by IT knowledge on designing, operating and maintaining IT systems which control these processes. Now these engineers even need to be able to identify, assess and address IT security problems. Finding people with this valuable hybrid skill set is hard.

Varying levels of legislation exists for different countries. For some countries regulations exist for securing the PCD environment, such as in the US which introduced legislation in 1998 regarding national infrastructure protection, recently president Obama has proposed a far stretching legislative proposal wherein companies will be categorised in risk tiers and need to write a cyber security plan on how PCD systems will be secured. The EU followed in 2006 with a programme to protect critical infrastructure [DIGI, WIKI]. Nevertheless, in many countries, PCD security is left to the responsibility of companies themselves. The lack of legislation for securing the PCD may have the effect that business interests take precedence over security.

Problems which come forward from the topic 'people' are:
- Lack of security skills;
- Lack of security awareness, PCD criticality;
- Lack of 'outside' pressure to secure.

3.3 Process

Availability is paramount for PCD systems. Simply put: these systems need to operate. Whether to open bridges, produce oil or cool nuclear power plants; when systems are down consequences range from adverse, a direct loss in production to disastrous. This makes it undesirable to bring these systems down to maintain them for security purposes. When systems cannot be maintained this leads to an adverse effect on systems' security such as installing a new virus scanner or more secure software. This is simply hard to do during 24/7 operation.

In addition, people working with the PCD need the ability to access these systems to make sure 24/7 operation is maintained and, in case of looming incidents, need to be able to intervene. For historic reasons there was never a necessity to restrict logical access to isolated systems, with the introduction of a more networked environment, this has also introduced problems regarding user management and logging & monitoring: who are allowed to access what systems? What activities should we log?

Business reasons are driving factors to introduce more and more interfaces with the PCD. If money can be made, for example, by reacting in real time to market circumstances when electricity prices rise by switching on remote power plants or to have the ability to assess in real time what is in stock to run the business more efficiently. Both can be business drivers for interfacing with the PCD.

PCD vendors have gone through the same evolution as PCD companies have. What is observed in practise is a lack of security mindset with PCD vendors as well. Some improvements regarding security awareness can be seen, however, security has not become a discriminating factor as of yet.

Little maturity exists within PCD management processes. As such, associated procedures (design) on how a secure PCD environment should be managed can be considered poor. The result is that companies cannot mature to a 'measured and monitored' status, from which can be learned and can prevent recurring (security) issues.

Problems which come forward from the topic 'process' are:
- Availability more important than security;
- Poor user management;
- Logging and monitoring limitedly implemented;
- Remote control takes precedence over security;
- Little PCD vendor support for security;
- Poor procedures in place for managing the PCD.

3.4 Technology

PCD systems are designed to run for many years: a power plant is built to last for decades as are water treatment plants, bridges, nuclear plants and so on. Not only the plants, also the PCD systems controlling the plant need to last a long time. In the world of IT the winds of change blows often and strong: technology develops with a pace as in no other field. Decades old IT systems are riddled with security problems.

Old PCD systems were designed to run in isolation and were not designed for security. Increased interconnectivity enabled by new technology interfacing with old technology introduces security risks. As a consequence, these systems need to be adapted to operate within a connected environment, which is not easy to do. Traffic plans and network segregation of PCD with neighbouring systems are often lacking as is the implementation of antivirus software.

In addition, running single control systems to control production plants is observed in practice, although one would expect that all measures to support maximum availability would have been taken.

Problems which come forward from the topic 'technology' are:
- Old and insecure system technology in use;
- Old systems run in an interconnected environment, for which these were not designed;
- Lack of network traffic plan and network segregation;
- Lack of anti-virus software;
- Vulnerable and unfit PCD design to start off with, including single points of failure.

4 How can PCD security problems be addressed?

4.1 People

Problems which came forward from the topic 'people' are:
- Lack of security skills;
- Lack of security awareness, PCD criticality;
- Lack of 'outside' pressure to secure.

Addressing these can be done in many ways. More attention towards this field of technology would be the main driver. It would be great if attention to this field would start with the involvement of the following relevant stakeholders:
- Companies, becoming more risk aware and wanting to secure their PCD systems;
- PCD product vendors, promoting security to distinguish from competitors;
- Governments, with stricter legislation for PCD security to protect their countries, or;
- Security experts, helping companies becoming more risk aware and secure.

As opposed to attention for PCD coming forward from:
- Hackers or terrorists, breaking into systems and wreaking havoc in the 'real' world or;
- Foreign governments, trying to gain a competitive edge or causing conscious damage by sabotaging other countries' critical infrastructure.

This would be the undesirable way of demonstrating a lack of security within PCD environments. Company employees should be taught awareness of present risks and should require of PCD product vendors to deliver secure products. PCD Governments can introduce legislation which would enforce companies to secure PCD by some standard (which are already available from the IT office environment). Security consultants can help all three with checking PCD environments and providing advice on how to secure.

4.2 Process

Problems which came forward from the topic 'process' are:
- Availability more important than security
- Poor user management
- Logging and monitoring limitedly implemented
- Remote control takes precedence over security
- Little PCD vendor support for security;
- Poor procedures in place for managing the PCD.

Companies need to re-prioritise or be made aware of what risks are associated with the PCD. Security experts should be able to explain what poor user management and associated logging and monitoring may lead to. Awareness of risks for making external connections to the PCD should be part of the above. Restricting access to the PCD based on 'need to have' would be a good starting point. Though this is not always easy to explain as it is hard to predict what may be the consequences of making new interfaces with the PCD.

It needs to be made clear that growing maturity for PCD security mindedness is the only route for both PCD vendor's and companies alike to be able to increase security support and implement security procedures.

4.3 Technology

Problems which came forward from the topic 'technology' are:
- Old and insecure system technology in use;
- Old systems run in an interconnected environment, for which these were not designed;
- Lack of network traffic plan and network segregation;
- Lack of anti-virus software;
- Vulnerable and unfit PCD design to start off with, including single points of failure.

It is hard to secure old and insecure technologies, especially when these need to be remotely available. What can be done is to isolate these systems wherever possible to minimise contact with external factors. This could be accomplished by the following measures:
- filtering traffic;
- removing old systems from networks, or;
- physically isolating systems.

These measures could be applied to systems that simply cannot be turned off to minimise risk in existing environments. Wherever possible secondary (back-up) devices should be introduced to make systems 'maintainable' and less vulnerable (by removing single points of failure). As such, primary systems can be taken offline and updated, configured to be more secure with secondary systems taking over.

Network traffic plans and network segregation can be implemented by introducing firewalls to record ongoing traffic, contacting vendors to help and let them explain, to understand how systems interact. This is not easy to do, because availability of systems may not be interrupted. Nevertheless, systems which should never interact can be segregated quite easily.

For new PCD systems, maintainability and security should be incorporated within systems' design (before operation).

5 Conclusion: What can we expect for the future?

PCD security will get more focus over the coming years, through more awareness and potential security incidents.

It is hard to tell what will happen, but we can assume with those who want to break into PCD systems and those who want to secure these systems more, PCD security will get more focus and security will actually increase in the future. Perhaps as a result of business maturity or more strict government legislation. It can be expected that PCD systems will be targeted to achieve maximum impact by those who want to cause harm.

5.1 People

On the topic of people we expect the following for key stakeholders:
- Terrorists or foreign countries: may specifically target PCD systems to harm critical national infrastructure;
- Support staff of PCD systems: will be better educated to secure these systems;
- Vendors: will be asked to provide / can distinguish products by delivering more secure systems;
- Governments: will adopt tougher legislation and enforce periodic independent security checks.

5.2 Process

More security awareness due to more incidents/increased maturity will have a positive effect on security governance – which needs steering information and sufficient data to demonstrate security accountability or measures in place. As a result, security awareness will be more embedded within business processes, because PCD systems may no longer be able to operate in the future if not secure, having a direct impact on availability and direct business needs.

The maturity of processes related to PCD will grow to the level of 'measured and measurable' therewith illustrating measures to comply with security requirements and preventing risks.

5.3 Technology

More secure PCD technology will be introduced, although old systems will be running for the next few decades as a 'heritage' from times when these systems were first setup.

References

[SIEM]   Siemens website http://www.siemens.com/innovation/en/publikationen/publications_pof/pof_spring_2005/history_of_industrial_automation.htm

[TCAB01]   Thor Cutler and Anthony Barber, U.S. Environmental Protection Agency, January 2001 http://www.iosc.org/papers/00888.pdf

[CIIP]   WordPress website http://ciip.wordpress.com/2009/06/21/a-list-of-reported-scada-incidents

[SCAD]   Open Scada Security Project website http://www.scadasecurity.org/index.php/Incidents

[DIGI]   Digital Bond website http://www.digitalbond.com/2011/05/17/white-house-proposed-legislation-would-regulate-ics

[WIKI]   Wikipedia website http://en.wikipedia.org/wiki/Critical_infrastructure_protection

From the same author

Thesis of the postgraduate study program on EDP auditing at VU University Amsterdam, winning the Dutch national Joop Bautz Information Security Award in 2010. http://www.jbisa.nl/download/?id=16249370

ESUKOM: Smartphone Security for Enterprise Networks

Ingo Bente[1] · Josef von Helden[1] · Bastian Hellmann[1] ·
Joerg Vieweg[1] · Kai-Oliver Detken[2]

[1]Trust@FHH Research Group – Fachhochschule Hannover
Ricklinger Stadtweg 120, D-30459 Hannover
{ingo.bente | josef.vonhelden | bastian.hellmann | joerg.vieweg}@fh-hannover.de

[2]DECOIT GmbH
Fahrenheitstraße 9, D-28359 Bremen
detken@decoit.de

Abstract

The ESUKOM project aims to develop a real-time security solution for enterprise networks that works based upon the correlation of metadata. The ESUKOM approach focuses on the integration of available and widely deployed security tools (both commercial and open source like Nagios, iptables or Snort) by leveraging the Trusted Computing Group's IF-MAP protocol. A key challenge for ESUKOM is to adequately address the emerging use of smartphones in business environments. The ESUKOM approach aims to correlate metadata in order to increase the security of smartphone supporting IT environments.

1 Introduction

The ESUKOM project aims to develop a real-time security solution for enterprise networks that works based upon the correlation of metadata. A key challenge for ESUKOM is the steadily increasing adoption of mobile consumer electronic devices (smartphones) for business purposes that generates new threats for enterprise networks. The ESUKOM approach focuses on the integration of available and widely deployed security measures (both commercial and open source) based upon the Trusted Computing Group's IF-MAP (Interface to Metadata Access Point) specification. IF-MAP is part of a suite of protocols for network security developed by the Trusted Network Connect (TNC) Working Group. The IF-MAP standard enables heterogeneous systems to share arbitrary information in real time.

The idea of ESUKOM is to integrate services that are available in typical enterprise environments in order to share security relevant information via a single metadata pool. A metadata object reflects some information of the enterprise environment (such as authenticated users or currently connected devices). The notion of what a metadata object actually represents is not restricted by the ESUKOM approach. All metadata objects are constructed according to a well-defined, extensible metadata model. By establishing a common metadata pool, already deployed security measures can easily share their knowledge with other services. We envision that this will provide benefits for both the security and the manageability of enterprise networks.

Nowadays, a reliably working IT infrastructure is essential for any enterprise. IT services are inherently necessary in order to support employees by their daily work. Those IT services get even more important when they are also exposed to external customers. Thus, they have also become a worthwhile target of attack. The current threat level is known to anybody who follows the well-known websites that post IT-Security related news. Especially industrial espionage is a major subject for concerns.

One of the key challenges that modern enterprise environments have to face is the steadily increasing adoption of smartphones. Smartphones emerge to small mobile computers with lots of processing power and storage capabilities. Enterprises can benefit from their versatility, using services that allow them to communicate with their employees immediately ant any given time. For the ESUKOM project, smartphones play a key role when current threats for IT infrastructures are considered. Threats that are known from commodity devices like laptops and desktop PCs are now also present on modern smartphones. In order to provide appropriate countermeasures, the special characteristics of smartphones must be taken into account:

1. **Mobility:** Ultra-portable smartphones are used in different environments with different security levels. Physical access to those devices eases to mount a successful attack.

2. **Dynamic networking:** Smartphones are dynamically connected to arbitrary networks. This includes unsecure networks like the Internet as well as more secure networks like a company's LAN. Furthermore, smartphones are able to establish ad hoc mesh networks by leveraging various communication techniques like Bluetooth.

3. **Application-based architecture:** Modern smartphone platforms enable the users to customize their phones by installing additional, third party applications. Dedicated online stores normally provide these applications. The details of the application provisioning process are platform specific. Applications can leverage the phone's resources in order to provide their functionality (such as using GPS for location-based services).

Smartphones are widely used across companies in order to manage appointments and contacts and to communicate via email. However, security policies specifically addressing smartphones can hardly be enforced by technical measures in practice. In order to mitigate the threats that are imposed by smartphones, companies need to adapt their currently deployed security measures.

1.1 Contributions

This paper presents the first results of the ESUKOM project. The contribution is twofold: (1) we provide a threat analysis that addresses the use of smartphones in enterprise environments. Based on this analysis, key features are derived that mitigate the identified threats. (2) In order to realize the proposed key features, we suggest the ESUKOM approach. It features a centralized metadata pool that reflects the current status of the network. We provide a metadata model that encapsulates the special characteristics of modern smartphones, thus enabling smartphone specific security decisions. By correlating the gathered metadata objects, sophisticated security measures can be provided.

1.2 Outline

The remainder of this paper is organized as follows: information on the technical background and the ESUKOM project itself is given in section 2. The threat analysis of smartphones and the derived key features that aim to mitigate them is given in section 3. The current status of the trustworthy metadata correlation approach is presented in section 4. We discuss related work in section 5. Finally, we conclude and highlight areas of future work in section 6

2 Background

2.1 Trusted Computing Group

Modern IT-networks have changed during the last years, from static and homogenous to dynamic and heterogeneous. The amount of mobile devices like Smartphones and notebooks that join and leave a network at any time has increased. As these mobile devices are sometimes not under control by the administrators of the network, the security state of a single device is crucial to the security of the whole network. The Trusted Computing Group (TCG) [Trus07], which is a non-profit organization, has defined an approach to this situation. They specify an open, vendor-neutral framework for trustworthy hardware and software. The term of Trust in the means of the TCG is, that a component that is called trustworthy has to behave as it can be expected, regardless if the behavior itself is good or bad. That is, a trustworthy malware program can be trusted to always behave badly. The decision, if a system is trustworthy or not, relies on securely obtaining the status of a platform with all installed components.

2.2 Trusted Network Connect

Trusted Network Connect (TNC) is a Network Access Control approach by the TCG. The main purpose is to control the access of an endpoint to a network, based on the integrity state of that specific endpoint. The measured state is compared to a policy, which was defined by the network operator of a TNC protected network. For example, an enterprise could enforce that any endpoint must have Antivirus software running and that its virus signatures are up-to-date. To securely gather the required information on an endpoint, special software components [Trus09] are used, which also communicate this information to the TNC protected network. In the context of TNC this is called assessment. In case the integrity check fails, several network access restrictions are possible, like a port-based control in 802.1x based networks or restricting access by a firewall filter when using VPNs. Together with its open architecture, TNC distinguishes from other Network Access Control solutions by using the capabilities of Trusted Platforms as proposed by the TCG. By using the TPM of a Trusted Platform, the TNC handshake can be seen as the Remote Attestation of an endpoint, thus showing that TNC is by design capable of doing such a Remote Attestation.

A TNC extended network consists of three different components, namely the Access Requestor (AR), the Policy Decision Point (PDP) and the Policy Enforcement Point (PEP). The Access Requestor is the client that wants to access the network and thus has to authenticate itself to the PDP. During this authentication the client has to proof its integrity state. The PDP then decides if the AR is allowed access to the network, based on the identity and integrity state of the client and by comparing this information with its policies. Afterwards it communicates its recommendation to the PEP, which then enforces it by granting or denying network access. In a 802.1x based network, the PDP could be a server inside the TNC enabled network, the PEP a 802.1x capable switch, and the network access would be controlled by opening or closing ports on the PEP.

2.3 IF-MAP

The IF-MAP specification by the Trusted Network Connect subgroup of the Trusted Computing Group describes a protocol for exchanging metadata in a client-server based environment. Its main purpose is to interoperable exchange security related data between components in a network. So-called MAP clients can publish new metadata to a MAP server and also search for metadata. They also can subscribe to specific metadata and will get informed, when new metadata is published.

The specification in its actual version 2.0 is separated into several documents. The basic communication protocol based on SOAP is specified in [Trus10a] and metadata definitions for network security are defined in [Trus10b]. Thus, new metadata definitions for non-security environment can be specified without changing the specification for the underlying protocol.

2.4 Smartphone Security

2.4.1 Android

Android is both an operating system and application framework designed for mobile devices like smartphones and tablets. Google develops it under an open-source license. An Android system offers possibilities to extend it with third party applications, called apps. Apps can be downloaded from the so-called Android market and are installed by the user. The Android SDK provided by Google allows anyone to develop own applications. The bottom layer of Android is based on the Linux kernel in version 2.6, which handles the hardware resources. In the layer above lies the Android runtime as well as some native C and C++ libraries like SSL or WebKit. The runtime environment consists of Java libraries and a virtual machine called DalvikVM. It launches and runs the Android apps, each one in an own instance. A layer called Application framework resides above the runtime layer and provides high-level services in the Java programming language. These services allow easy handling of windows in the GUI, access to the file system or exchanging data between applications. The top layer is the application layer that holds functions like phone, contacts or applications that use the build-in sensors like GPS or motion-sensors. These applications use the underlying libraries and services. Apps developed by third parties also reside in this layer.

2.4.2 Android Security Model

Android's security model consists of two main concepts. In the first place, every application gets a unique process ID and an own user at installation time, as well as an own directory. At runtime, every app runs in a sandbox so it cannot act malicious to other apps. All communication between apps uses specific services of the Android SDK.

Secondly, the access of applications to vital parts of the system like sending SMS or starting a phone call is controlled via permissions. If an application wants to use such services, it has to define the necessary permissions in its Manifest file. At installation time, the user has to grant or deny the use of the permissions to the application. When the app is running, every access to services that are not registered by their permissions in the Manifest file or that were declined by the user during the installation will throw an exception.

2.5 The ESUKOM Project

ESUKOM is a research project funded by the German Federal Ministry of Education and Research. It was launched in October 2010. The overall goal of the ESUKOM project is the prototypical development of a security solution with open source software (OSS) that works based upon the Trusted Computing Group's IF-MAP specification. In order to achieve this goal, the following tasks will be accomplished:

1. **Implementation of IF-MAP software components** A MAP server and a set of MAP clients will be developed. The MAP server as well as most of the MAP clients will be published under an open source license in order to ease their dissemination. Currently, at least the well-known open source tools Nagios, iptables and Snort will be extended with IF-MAP client functionality, in addition to commercial products that are provided by the ESUKOM consortium members.

2. **Development of an advanced metadata model** The IF-MAP specification currently defines a model for metadata that specifically targets use cases in the area of network security. This metadata model will be extended and refined within the ESUKOM project. We aim to add new types of metadata as well as to improve drawbacks of the current metadata model.

3. **Development of correlation algorithms** The analysis and correlation of metadata graphs that are managed by a MAP server is a challenging task. The available specifications give only rough indications how a user might benefit from such a common data pool. We aim to develop algorithms and approaches in order to ease the analysis of large metadata graphs.

4. **Integration of deployed security tools** Another important goal is the conceptual integration of security tools that are already deployed. It must be clarified which sort information should be shared across which existing tools.

To address the threats imposed by modern smartphones that are used in enterprise environments is the mandatory objective. Further information can be found on www.esukom.de.

3 Smartphone Threat Analysis

The following section analyses threats that arise when using Smartphones in a business environment. This emphasizes the influence of the features modern Smartphones possess on to the overall security of business networks. Only by identifying these specific threats, appropriate countermeasures may be developed.

So-called malware poses an essential problem within this context. According to current predictions, there will be a soaring spread of such malware in the following years. For example, 10% more malware was discovered in the first half of 2010 than in the second half of 2009. Furthermore, the malware discovered in the first half of 2010 is more than what has been discovered in whole 2008 [BeBe10].

Being more and more used and due to their increasing capabilities, Smartphones and other mobile devices (e.g. Tablet computers) become preferred targets of such malware [Wals09]. The number of shipped Smartphones increased to more than 54 million devices, which is a growth of about 57% compared against the previous year. Although the number of known malware is rather low compared against PC platforms (about 40 million malware programs for PC platforms versus about 600 for Smartphones), forecasts assume, that his number will increase dramatically within the next 12 months [Culv10].

Due to these threats and the increased usage of such devices within business networks, a lot of additional attack vectors, which need to be taken into account by network administrators, arise. The German Federal Office for Information Security (BSI) issued a recommendation to no longer use Smartphones (especially iPhones and BlackBerrys) within business networks. Exceptions from this recommendation should only be made if the devices support Simko-2-encryption. [Spie10]

3.1 Threat Analysis

The relevant threats for ESUKOM are located within the field of Smartphone (resp. mobile consumer electronic devices) usage in business networks. The following features are therefore defined for Smartphones within this context.

- Inherent sensors: Modern Smartphones possess a high number of sensors, thus allowing to easily gain audio, video and location based information.
- High connectivity: Smartphones are able to communicate through a variety of channels, e.g. Wireless LAN, 3G network connectivity, Infrared (IrDA) protocols or Bluetooth.
- Internet connected: A mobile utilization of the Internet is nowadays possible with a Smartphone. Due to appropriate pricing schemes, services that require a high amount of data transfer volumes may also be used.
- Resource Paradox: Smartphones provide more and more capable hardware components. While there are currently devices with gigahertz processors and more than 256 MB of RAM available, this provided computing power is limited due to the rather small battery capacity.
- App-based architecture: Applications to be used by Smartphones are normally published within special online platforms (commonly called App-Stores). Derived by this development, malicious applications for Smartphones are often called MalApps.
- Platform-variety: There are open-source and closed-source Smartphone platforms by now. The most important platform developers are Apple with their iOS based iPhones, Google with their Android platform as well as Research in Motion (RIM) with their Blackberry devices.

This feature list allows the definition of so called target of attacks (ToA). A ToA may be either the target of a passive or active attack mounted within the context of the business network. A successful attack results in a threat. The following ToA are considered in the context of ESUKOM.

1. Physical environment: The physical environment where the Smartphone is located within is being attacked.

2. Smartphone: The Smartphone itself or data stored on the Smartphone is the target of the attack.

3. It-infrastructure: Smartphones act as man-in-the-middle, thus allowing attacks which target the infrastructure where the Smartphone is connected to.

By using this scheme it is possible to categorize appropriate threats and attack scenarios. The following section provides a short non-complete ToA-categorized summary of threats.

3.1.1 ToA Physical Environment

This type of attack aims on sniffing data from the physical environment by using the Smartphone. This data may be potentially critical and classified. Considering which data is being collected, different threats arise:
- Violation of privacy, for example eavesdropping of personal calls.
- Industrial espionage, e.g. taking photos of critical business processes.
- Creation of movement profiles.

Example attacks within this category are so called sensory malware attacks, where a MalApp uses the appropriate sensor of the Smartphone, or insider sniffing attacks.

3.1.2 ToA Smartphone

There are several threats that arise if an attack targets the Smartphone itself. There may be for example the threat of:
- Stealing data directly from the Smartphone, for example sensitive information.
- Exhausting the resources of the Smartphone. This could be achieved by simply mounting a denial of service attack or by using the accounting information of the Smartphone.
- Placing MalApps on the Smartphone.

Attacks in this category are for example a distributed denial of service attack mounted by Smartphones where a Botnet MalApp has been placed on. Furthermore a simple loss of the physical Smartphone device is also handled by this category.

3.1.3 ToA IT-infrastructure

Attacks within this category use the Smartphone as a man-in-the-middle to attack the network itself. These attacks are in general similar to commonly known types of network attacks as the Smartphone only acts as attacker. Example attacks could be a so-called Smartphone mounted data theft or some kind of network profiling. An overview of exemplary attacks according to their ToA is given in figure 1.

Target of Attack	Physical Environment	Smartphone	IT-Infrastructure
Examples	Sensory Malapps Insider Sensor Sniffing	Resource Exhaustion Malapps Trojan Premium SMS Local Data Sniffing Malapps Botnet Malapps Physical Loss/Theft	Smartphone Mounted Data Theft Smartphone Mounted Profiling

Fig. 1: Exemplary Attacks grouped by Targets of Attack

3.2 Key Features

Based upon the threat analysis the following set of desirable key features for the ESUKOM solution were identified:
- Anomaly Detection: Consolidation of metadata that was created by different components in order to detect outliers, indicating potential fraud activities. Furthermore, smartphone driven attack patterns (like sensory malware approaches) will be analyzed.

- Smartphone Awareness: Identification of smartphones within the business environment, enabling to provision services that are specifically tailored towards them or to make policy decisions based upon the type of smartphone.
- Single Sign Off: Immediate and global de-provisioning of user accounts, ensuring that revoked credentials cannot be used anymore within the respective environment, no matter which service or device is used.
- Secure Evidence: Generation and integration of evidence records that proof the integrity of metadata objects within the MAP server, thus increasing the trustworthiness of the IF-MAP data set itself.
- Identity Awareness: Making the user's authenticated identity available within a business environment beyond the scope of the authenticating entity, thus enabling use cases like automated, identity based configuration of low level security tools (for example packet filters).
- MalApp Detection: To defend against the spread of potentially malicious applications and to limit the amount of damage they can cause to the respective business environment. This also implies to develop new means in order to assess the security state of a smartphone including its installed applications and their respective privileges that go beyond well-known approaches like Trusted Computing or application certification.
- Location-based Services: To provision services based upon the smartphone's location as well as to support detection capabilities (like the Anomaly and MalApp detection components) by providing location information on users and devices.
- Real-time Enforcement: To enable immediate reaction on identified anomalies by any component that can help to mitigate the potential damage (like flow controllers and network enforcement points).

By implementing this set of key features through open standards, the ESUKOM approach will enable existing business environments to successfully face the challenges that are introduced by the increasing number of smartphones in use. Furthermore, we aim to push the research on mobile phone security in general by developing new security metrics for the most prominent platforms as well as to prove the feasibility of a network oriented approach for smartphone security by implementing a prototype IF-MAP infrastructure.

4 Trustworthy Metadata Correlation

In order to realize the key features mentioned above, the ESUKOM approach relies on the concept of trustworthy metadata correlation based upon the IF-MAP protocol. This section introduces the current status of this approach. Any security relevant data, whether it stems from a smartphone or a service that is provided by the IT infrastructure (such as an IDS, a Firewall or an AAA service), is expressed according to a well-defined metadata model. In addition, a trust model is defined that enables to reason about the trustworthiness of the metadata instances. Both the metadata model and the trust model are based on the IF-MAP protocol. An open question is still to evaluate the correlation approaches that perform best in order to realize the desired key features.

4.1 Metadata Model

The metadata model is the fundamental basis for any further analysis and correlation approaches that are performed. The challenge is to encapsulate both smartphone specific features as well as other metadata of interest that might be generated by arbitrary services in the network in a common model. In addition to only name the relevant metadata concepts, it is also necessary to model the relationships between them.

The current version of the metadata model developed within ESUKOM is based upon the IF-MAP metadata model. That is, the basic components are identifiers, metadata objects and links. However, smartphone specific features are currently not part of the IF-MAP protocol. In order to realize the described key features, it is necessary to (1) name smartphone features of interest and to (2) integrate those features into the IF-MAP protocol.

To decide whether a certain smartphone feature might be of interested for further processing or not is hard. Within the Andromaly project [SKE+11], 88 different features were taken into account in order to detect malicious applications. Each feature even might perform differently, depending on the correlation method that is used.

At this stage, the ESUKOM approach suggest a set of few smartphone features that should be taken into account for further correlation tasks. However, since the metadata model itself is extensible, arbitrary features can be added later on. The current set focuses on Android specific features and the phone's built-in sensors (features of other systems are omitted for brevity). It is depicted in figure 2. Features (white boxes) are hierarchically grouped in categories (grey boxes) and can have alphanumerical values. All features can be easily obtained via standard Android API calls, thus avoiding the burden to extend the Android middleware itself.

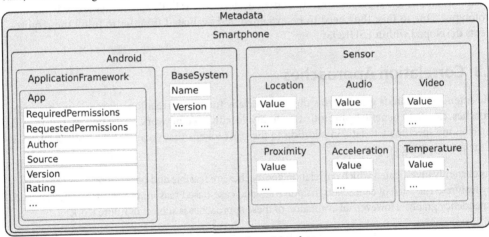

Fig. 2: Smartphone Metadata

In order to integrate these new features to the IF-MAP protocol, two requirements must be fulfilled: (1) the features need to be expressed by means of an XML schema that complies to other standard IF-MAP metadata types (which is trivial) and (2) it must be defined how these new metadata types can be used within IF-MAP. That is, how they fit into the IF-MAP metadata graph. In the current model, the new metadata types are attached to a device identifier that represents the corresponding smartphone.

4.2 Trust Model

A Trust Model is required in order to use data for any further correlation approaches. That is, the Trust Model ensures the integrity of the data that is used as input for the correlation. Without ensuring this integrity, due to potential wrong data, the results of the correlation may be useless.

The Trust Model is currently under development within ESUKOM and is not yet fully defined. However, there is a first approach that allows to reason about the integrity of the data. This approach adds the concept of a so-called Trust Level (TL) to the metadata graph. The TL expresses the trustworthiness of a certain data set. That is for IF-MAP, the TL expresses the integrity of the data that has been published into the metadata graph. Besides the concept of adding a Trust Level, there is also a process model, which defines how the Trust relation evolves. The model is divided into three core phases: initialization, reasoning and update. The initialization phase establishes the TL value. The reasoning phase allows us to issue about the TL, for example within a correlation process. Finally, the update phase recalculates the TL according to events that may have happened.

In addition to the concept of the TL and the appropriate process model, there is a first implementation approach for IF-MAP. The TL is expressed as a so-called Trust Token (TT), which is published into the metadata graph. In particular, published into means that the TT is attached to an IF-MAP client. Using this mechanism, all data published by this IF-MAP client is connected to the TT, thus allowing to reason about the integrity of this data.

As already stated, this topic is currently under development as both approaches are only the first prototypes. Due to this, they need to be extended and evaluated in order to fulfill the requirements developed within ESUKOM.

4.3 Correlation Approaches

The extended metadata graph forms the basis for any further correlation approaches. Those approaches can now benefit from both the ability to consider network generated metadata and smartphone specific metadata, in addition to the trust tokens that vouch for the trustworthiness of the participating entities.

It is currently investigated which correlation approaches are feasible and perform best for the desired key features. The current candidates include rule- and case-based reasoning, neuronal networks and dependency graphs. However, an evaluation of these approaches is subject of future work.

5 Related Work

The field of smartphone security is still gaining momentum. Kirin proposed by Enck et al. [EnOM09] is a security service for the Android platform. Kirin aims to mitigate malware at install time by checking the respective application's security configuration against a predefined policy. Kirin is a host-based security extension. In contrast to that, ESUKOM aims to realize a network-based approach in order to mitigate malware threats.

Ongtang et al. [OMEM09] propose the Saint framework. As Kirin, it is a security extension for the Android framework. Saint addresses the issue that the Android platform does not provide sophisticated means in order to enforce policies on the inter application communication on a single phone. The only way to regulate this type of communication is by using the Android permissions labels. Saint introduces are more sophisticated approach. It supports two types of policies: (1) install-time and (2) run-time policies. The install-time policy allows the user to define under which conditions a permission label P defined by an application A is granted to another application B at install-time. Run-time policies on the other hand allow that the IPC that takes place at run-time is regulated according to the respective policy. A remarkable feature of these run-time policies is that it is possible to include conditions based on context information like location, time or the status of communication interfaces like Bluetooth. Furthermore, conditions can cover requirements related to the application developer's signature key.

Porscha [OnBD10] is a Digital Rights Management (DRM) extension for Android. They address the drawback that today's smartphones, including Android based phones, provide almost no means to enforce DRM policies on content that is delivered to the phone. Porscha supports to enforce policies within two separate phases: (1) when the content is in transit, which means when it is delivered to the respective phone and (2) when the content is located on the platform. Porscha allows that content is bound both to a particular phone as well as to a set of endorsed applications on the phone. Furthermore, the use of delivered content can be constrained (for example allowing to play a video within 48h of the purchase date). Such a DRM mechanism could be leveraged in an enterprise environment in order to protect sensitive data.

Portokalidis et al. [PHAB10] propose the Paranoid Android system. Similar to our approach, they follow a network-based paradigm. Remote servers host exact replicas of the smartphones. Based on these virtual replicas, various security checks are performed. In order to establish security measures that are independent of the smartphones resource constraints, the authors suggest that security services in terms of attack detection is provided as a cloud service. A monitoring component on the smartphone, called tracer, gathers execution traces. These traces are then send to a component located on the remote server, called replayer. The execution trace covers all necessary information to replay the execution that has taken place on the smartphone within its virtual replica (such as system calls that pass data from kernel to user space or operating system signals). The ESUKOM approach aims to abstract the smartphone status, thus avoiding the overhead of running N replicas for N smartphones. Furthermore, ESUKOM does not restrict its analysis components to solely work on smartphone metadata but supports to correlate smartphone specific aspects with other aspects of the network infrastructure.

6 Conclusions and Future Work

Smartphones that are used in business environments introduce new threats that have to be addressed by appropriate security measures. Recent work in the field of smartphone security has shown that their special capabilities can be abused to mount successful attacks. Approaches to mitigate some of these threats exist, but often require special extensions for the smartphone platform in use.

The ESUKOM approach aims to address smartphone threats by introducing a network based correlation mechanism based on the TCGs' IF-MAP protocol. By integrating metadata from arbitrary security services as well as from the smartphones themselves, analysis techniques will be employed in order to detect security issues like the presence of malicious applications.

The current status of the ESUKOM approach enables to gather a set of relevant metadata from existing security services (such as VPNs, Firewalls and IDS tools) as well as from Android based smartphones. However, the implementation and evaluation of concrete correlation approaches is a subject of future work.

Acknowledgements

We would like to thank the ESUKOM partners for their valuable feedback and comments on this paper. This work was funded by the Federal Ministry of Education and Research under grant number 01BY1050.

References

[EnOM09] Enck, William and Ongtang, Machigar and McDaniel, Patrick: On lightweight mobile phone application certification. In Proceedings of the 16th ACM conference on Computer and communications security (CCS '09). 2009, p. 235-245.

[OMEM09] Ongtang, Machigar and McLaughlin, Stephen and Enck, William and McDaniel, Patrick: Semantically Rich Application-Centric Security in Android. In Proceedings of the 25th Annual Computer Security Applications Conference (ACSAC'09). 2009, p. 340-349.

[OnBD10] Ongtang, Machigar, Butler, Kevin and McDaniel, Patrick: Porscha: policy oriented secure content handling in Android. In Proceedings of the 26th Annual Computer Security Applications Conference (ACSAC '10). 2010, p. 221-230.

[PHAB10] Portokalidis, Georgios, Homburg, Philip, Anagnostakis, Kostas and Bos, Herbert: Paranoid Android: versatile protection for smartphones. In Proceedings of the 26th Annual Computer Security Applications Conference (ACSAC '10). 2010, p. 347-356.

[SKE+11] Shabtai, Asaf and Kanonov, Uri and Elovici, Yuval and Glezer, Chanan and Weiss, Yael: "Andromaly": a behavioral malware detection framework for android devices. In Journal of Intelligent Information Systems. Springer Netherlands. 2011, p. 1-30.

[Trus10a] Trusted Computing Group: TNC IF MAP Binding for SOAP Version 2.0 Revision 36. 2010.

[Trus10b] Trusted Computing Group: TNC IF-MAP Metadata for Network Security Version 1 Revision 25. 2010.

[BeBe10] Benzmüller, Ralf and Berkenkopf, Sabrina: GData Malware Report Halbjahresbericht Januar-Juni 2010. Retrieved on 08.11.2010 http://www.gdata.de/uploads/media/GData_MalwareReport_2010_1_6_DE_mail2.pdf

[Wals09] Walsh, Lawrence: More Virulent Smartphone Malware on the Horizon, 2009. Retrieved on 05.11.2010. http://www.channelinsider.com/c/a/Security/More-Virulent-Smartphone-Malware-on-the-Horizon-365284/

[Culv10] Culver, Denise: Smartphones: The New Hacker Frontier, 2010. Retrieved on 10.11.2010 http://www.lightreading.com/document.asp?doc_id=196519

[Spie10] Spiegel Online: Sicherheitsbedenken – Regierung verbietet Mitarbeitern Blackberry und iPhone. 2010. Retrieved on 05.08.2010 http://www.spiegel.de/netzwelt/netzpolitik/0,1518,710227,00.html.

Index

A

B

C

R

S

Printed in the United States
By Bookmasters